THE SHORES OF AMERICA

University of Illinois Press   *Urbana*   *Chicago*   *London*

The Shores of America

THOREAU'S INWARD EXPLORATION

by Sherman Paul

Illini Book edition, 1972
Originally published in a clothbound edition, 1958

© 1958 by The Board of Trustees of the University of Illinois
Manufactured in the United States of America
Library of Congress Catalog Card No. 58-6998

ISBN 0-252-00281-4

FOR JIM

I am reminded by my journey how exceedingly new this country still is. You have only to travel for a few days into the interior . . . to come to that very America which the Northman and Cabot, and Gosnold, and Smith, and Raleigh visited. If Columbus was the first to discover the islands, Americus Vespucius and Cabot, and the Puritans, and we their descendants, have discovered only the shores of America. While the republic has already acquired a history world-wide, America is still unsettled and unexplored.

—Thoreau, *The Maine Woods*

It is notorious how metaphysical was the passion that drove the Puritans to those shores; they went there in the hope of living more perfectly in the spirit. And their pilgrim's progress was not finished when they had founded their churches in the wilderness; an endless migration of the mind was still before them, a flight from those new idols and servitudes which prosperity involves, and the eternal lure of spiritual freedom and truth. The moral world always contains undiscovered or thinly peopled continents open to those who are more attached to what might or should be than to what already is.

—Santayana, *Character and Opinion
in the United States*

PREFACE

For ten years now I have been compelled by Thoreau—compelled, of course, by this singularly integral man, by the authenticity of his life, and by the ideas that he enacted. What has made Thoreau so interesting to me has been the fact that, accepting the ideas of Transcendentalism, he tested them by living them out in their practical issue. Thus, it seems to me that he can tell us better than any of his contemporaries what it meant to live a transcendental life. Such a life, however, is an inner one, for Transcendentalism, and the Romanticism with which it was allied, made the self the center of existence and all beyond it its horizon. The self was called into the world to realize itself—that was its vocation, its destiny. "Every man is tasked to make his life, even in its details," Thoreau said, "worthy of the contemplation of his most elevated and critical hour." And the drama of this engagement with one's "life," the experience, tensions, and meaning, were played on an inner stage. Accordingly, I have tried to get inside, and perhaps what I have written might be called a spiritual biography or a biography of vocation.

A study of the inner life must take for its primary data the thoughts of the man and trace their genesis and growth; it must rely heavily on what the man said and wrote and confessed, as well as on what he did; and it must search out the crises the man may have buried deep in the ambiguities of expression, whether in deed or word. There are, of course, many pitfalls here; much depends on the validity of one's reading. Because much that Thoreau wrote has not been closely read—or because such readings have not been made public—I have found it necessary, not only in trying to unfold the direction transcendental ideas took in Thoreau's life but in establishing a fund of evidence for others, to provide for almost everything he published, and for much that he did not, the close reading by which I myself proceeded and came to my conclusions. In spite of the necessity of treating each work separately, these readings have the progressive development of Thoreau's life. And though I cannot say, as Thoreau did of his criticism of Carlyle, that "we have not attempted to discriminate between his works," I can say that I have "regarded them all as one work, as is the man himself."

Of course, there are many things—Thoreau's relations with Emerson, his "tragedy," and the socializing of transcendental ideas in his mature works—that may seem to some to be merely flying in the face of the wind. I can only say that I have let the evidence speak, that, in Champlain's words, "It seems to me that I have done my duty as far as I could, if I have not forgotten to put in my said chart whatever I saw, and give a particular knowledge to the public of what had never been described nor discovered so particularly as I have done it, although some other may have heretofore written of it. . . ." As a scholar I can also subscribe to Thoreau's remark that "it will be found that he who speaks with most authority on a given subject is not ignorant of what has been said by his predecessors. He will take his place in a regular order, and substantially add his own knowledge to the knowledge of previous generations." And as one inquirer in this succession, I have acted with an ever-deepening awareness of this human wisdom: "A gentleman," Mencius wrote, " 'when he makes the framework, leaves a loose thread hanging'; for he thinks of those who are to continue his task."

The debts of a scholar increase rather than diminish over the years, for given time and humility he discovers the root and branch of all he has done. I must at last—and with gratitude— acknowledge my debt to Professor Austin Warren, from whose example I first learned that the study of literature was, in the proper but old-fashioned word, a vocation, a moral enterprise. That stain, I now see, is ineradicable; and I am pleased to recall that my teachers at Harvard, especially Professors Kenneth Murdock and Perry Miller, who did most to guide me, rather than removing it, only made it deeper. My debt to them is also substantial, for they gave me substance; and for a long time and over great distances, with Austin Warren, their friendship has kept me at my work. Scholarship is a lonely labor, and more immediately I have enjoyed the community—simply by their presence in my study—of Professors Arthur Sherbo and Royal Gettmann; they have always been willing to talk out my spontaneous ideas or hear my written words. I am especially grateful to my colleague, Professor Edward Davidson, and to Professor Alexander Kern for their careful reading of the manuscript. In Professor Milton Stern I have had a co-worker in American literature whose hostility to Transcendentalism has been challenging and who, unknowingly, has driven me hard, but whose enthusiasm for my work has at times been greater than my own.

Unlike other debts, scholarly ones are pleasant to pay. I owe many to those students, both at Harvard and Illinois, who heard portions of this work in its many stages of growth; in fact, the ideas which prompted this book grew out of lectures intended only for them. To editors I am equally indebted for preliminary hearings: to *The New England Quarterly* for publishing my first essay on Thoreau, "The Wise Silence"; to *Accent* for publishing my lecture on *Walden;* to the *Journal of English and Germanic Philology* for publishing the portion of this book on "The Landlord." Some of my ideas on the *Week* were presented to the Mississippi Valley Historical Association, and parts of the final chapter were delivered as a lecture at The Ohio State University; and my summary views on Thoreau as well as some of my analysis—and inevitably even some of my words—found their way to the Riverside edition of *Walden,* which was a by-product of this work.

I owe a great debt, of course, to the many people and institutions who made all this possible: to the Research Board of the University of Illinois for the funds to procure the microfilms of the manuscript holdings and for financial assistance in preparing this book, and to the following librarians and libraries for generously providing these manuscripts and the permission to quote from them: Mr. William A. Jackson of The Houghton Library of Harvard University, Mr. A. P. DeWeese of The New York Public Library for materials in the Henry W. and Albert A. Berg Collection, Mr. George K. Boyce of The Pierpont Morgan Library, and Mr. Leslie E. Bliss of The Huntington Library. I am also indebted for the firsthand use of the manuscripts in both the Widener and Houghton collections of Harvard University, and to Miss Isabelle Grant of the Rare Book Room of the University of Illinois Library for the use of rare and first editions. Miss Eva Faye Benton of the English Library of the University of Illinois has—as always—been unfailingly helpful, and Mrs. Arthur Pennell has devotedly readied the dog-eared and often illegible manuscript of this book for the press. And by her care in criticizing other of my writings, Mrs. Lovell Thompson has contributed to the clarity and readability of this book.

Finally I gratefully acknowledge permissions from the following authors and publishers to quote from their works: to The Houghton Mifflin Company for *The Writings of Henry David Thoreau, The Complete Works of Ralph Waldo Emerson,* the *Journals of Ralph Waldo Emerson,* F. B. Sanborn's *The Life of Henry David Thoreau,* and Anna and Walton Ricketson's *Daniel Ricketson and His Friends* (from which I have also been granted permission to use the frontispiece); to Odell Shepard and Little, Brown and Company for *The Journals of Bronson Alcott;* to Kenneth W. Cameron and the Thistle Press for *Emerson The Essayist;* to Ralph L. Rusk, the Ralph Waldo Emerson Memorial Association, and the Columbia University Press for *The Letters of Ralph Waldo Emerson;* and to Carl Bode and Packard and Company for *Collected Poems of Henry Thoreau.* Of unpublished studies I would like to acknowledge and cite the excellence of Edwin I. Moser's *Henry David Thoreau: The College Essays Edited, With an Introduction* (Master's thesis, New York University, 1951); William Drake's *A Formal Study of H. D. Thoreau* (Master's thesis, University of Iowa, 1948); Christian P. Gruber's *The Education of Henry Thoreau, Harvard, 1833-1837* (Doctoral dissertation, Princeton University, 1953); and Lawrence S. Willson's *The Influence of*

Early North American History and Legend on the Writings of Henry David Thoreau (Doctoral dissertation, Yale University, 1944). I would also like to call attention to David Donald's study of the Abolitionists as a displaced social elite in *Lincoln Reconsidered*, for it helps to explain Thoreau's own peculiar quest for significant public influence.

S. P.

Urbana, Illinois
August, 1957

FOR CONVENIENCE, THE TITLES OF THE FOLLOWING
STANDARD WORKS HAVE BEEN ABBREVIATED:

W *The Writings of Henry David Thoreau*, 20 vols.,
Walden edition, Boston and New York, 1906. W
is used here, however, to designate only the first
six volumes, which include the published writings, letters, and poems.

J *The Journal*, vols. VII-XX of the above edition,
edited by Bradford Torrey and Francis H. Allen.
Since *The Journal* is also numbered from I-XIV,
I have adopted this numbering.

C *The Complete Works of Ralph Waldo Emerson*,
12 vols., Centenary edition, Boston and New
York, 1903.

Emerson, J *Journals of Ralph Waldo Emerson*, edited by
Edward Waldo Emerson and Waldo Emerson
Forbes, 10 vols., Boston and New York, 1909-14.

MANUSCRIPT HOLDINGS, UNLESS SPECIFIED, ARE
IDENTIFIED AS FOLLOWS:

MA The Pierpont Morgan Library

HM The Huntington Library

CONTENTS

Chapter I

A TERRIBLE PAUCITY OF ALTERNATIVES

> In our lonely chambers at night we are thrilled by
> some far-off serenade within the mind, and seem to
> hear the clarion sound and clang of corselet and
> buckler from many a silent hamlet of the soul,
> though actually it may be but the rattling of some
> farmer's waggon rolling to market against the mor-
> row.
>
> —Thoreau, (Conclusion to)
> *Sir Walter Raleigh*

I

Born, as he said, in the nick of time, Thoreau
was fortunate to find in an emerging Transcendentalism a program for his life. He did not
have to formulate a "first philosophy" as Emerson
had; he found one ready to hand. He had read
Emerson's *Nature* (1836) and Carlyle's *Sartor
Resartus* while at Harvard College,[1] and had
leaped to liberation over that great distance
from Locke to Coleridge that had caused his
elders, Emerson, Alcott, Ripley, and Parker, so
much anguish and doubt.[2] Leaving college, he
had undoubtedly heard among other commence-

---

[1] Kenneth W. Cameron, "Thoreau Discovers Emerson:
A College Reading Record," *Bulletin of The New York
Public Library,* LVII (July, 1953), 319-34.

[2] See W, VI, 25-26.

ment week addresses Emerson's Phi Beta Kappa oration, "The American Scholar," and had been challenged as no one else in the Class of '37 to enact Emerson's heroic proposals for the American intellectual. Written in part to announce his determination to serve the truth in his own way, this oration set the seal on Emerson's long struggle to find a vocation outside of the church. More than Edward Everett's Phi Beta Kappa oration thirteen years earlier, which had awakened Emerson's generation to the glories of literature and scholarship, Emerson's "The American Scholar," made glamorous by his own example of rebelliousness, placed a heavy burden of responsibility on the expectancies of the younger generation.

But even before this genuine commencement Thoreau had had personal contact with the transcendentalists. In an interval of schoolteaching at Canton, Massachusetts, during his junior year, he had lived for six weeks with Orestes Brownson, who was then at work on his *New Views of Christianity, Society, and The Church* (1836). Brownson helped Thoreau with German, the passport to transcendental domains—though Thoreau seems never to have used it; but he also provided the young scholar with some spirited intellectual conversation and a living example of the independent thinker, one, incidentally, who, like Thoreau, did not belong to the acknowledged higher classes. How much Thoreau was in Brownson's debt is difficult to assess; one notices, however, the transcendental direction of Thoreau's college essays after his return to Harvard. In a senior essay, "Whether Moral Excellence tend directly to increase Intellectual Power," he levied on Brownson's study of Benjamin Constant, citing Byron, as mentioned in Constant's *De la religion, considérée dans sa source, ses formes et ses developpements,* to support his claim that one must reject religion as the first step toward moral excellence. And it is quite probable, too, that Brownson's personal protestantism and his disdain for religious institutions prompted Thoreau's first transcendental gesture, his "signing off" from the church. In any case, Thoreau knew a transcendentalist well enough by 1837 to write Brownson in the new vocabulary of the Reason and the Over-Soul.[3]

Thoreau had also been fortunate at Harvard in having Jones Very for his tutor in Greek. Very, who was already one of the most accomplished transcendental poets, was soon to take flight into

[3] See Henry F. Brownson, *Orestes A. Brownson's Early Life: From 1803 to 1844,* Detroit, 1898, pp. 204-6.

religious mysticism and so lose the chance to become a permanent influence. For Thoreau, however, Very was the first practicing poet whom he knew personally; and the pupil's admiration took the New Englander's form of tribute, that of copying out Very's poems as they appeared. Emerson's early poems were also as patiently hived, and both Very's and Emerson's poems were neatly copied into a college notebook that contained as well Thoreau's favorites among the metaphysical poets.[4] In these years at college Thoreau had also found his way to *The Western Messenger,* that harbinger of the "newness" in the West. Here, as another college essay of Thoreau's shows, he had encountered Margaret Fuller writing on her favorite hero, Philip van Artevelde.[5]

As a student, then, Thoreau had already felt the stirring beginnings of Transcendentalism. His later college essays and the exhibitions of his classmates show that the Harvard curriculum of Locke and Stewart could not prevent the contagion. When he left college in August, 1837, he had been prepared to respond to Emerson's manifesto. The heyday of Transcendentalism was just beginning, and with it Thoreau's uncertainty over how to realize the prospects that its vistas opened to the imagination.

The Transcendentalism that shaped and sustained Thoreau's youthful aspirations was a revolt of such depth and magnitude that its force is still alive today. Rejecting most of the philosophical assumptions of the eighteenth century, it attempted to reorient the possibilities of life, to give the individual new powers and a new stage for action; and its urgency was felt especially in America where its desire to make all things new promised so much for the new democracy. Emerson had made the issues of Transcendentalism American in his first book, *Nature,* where, boldly discarding "the dry bones of the past," he turned America away from European tradition and demanded of us a society founded freshly on our own firsthand experience with the American environment. "The sun shines to-day also," he told his retrospective age; "There is more wool and flax in the fields. There are new lands, new men, new thoughts. Let us demand our own works and laws and worship." Emerson's appeal to the rising nationalist sentiment, however, was grounded on something deeper than literary patriotism; it was

[4] MA 594.
[5] *The Western Messenger,* I (Dec., 1835), 398-408.

prompted by his own desire—which was the essential need of Transcendentalism—to "enjoy an original relation to the universe." He had written his book to affirm the possibility of that relationship; in it he traced his own way to that assurance, a return to the springs of Idealism that was representative of other attempts to overcome the spiritual doubts of the time.

These doubts were the legacy of his training, of the whole push of the previous century of enlightenment in the liberalization and rationalization of religion. Although the focus of contention was religion, what was really at stake were the philosophy and psychology—the entire structure of thought about man's nature and his relation to the universe—that underlay the faith. A Unitarian, like Brownson, Ripley, and Parker, Emerson had been educated—as was Thoreau at Harvard—in the philosophical and scientific views that supported this liberal religion. But being essentially a religious seeker, he required a more certain conviction of God than the "pale negations" of Unitarianism provided. For Unitarianism had not only lost a vigorous emotional piety in its passage from Calvinism, it had found itself defending the sovereignty of reason and free will at the same time that it strengthened itself on the determinism of Lockean psychology and the mechanism of Newtonian physics; and while claiming to be a rational faith, with nothing but natural law for its guide, it had irrationally insisted on the historicity of miracles. A faith at second hand, building on the testimony of other men, Unitarianism did not answer the needs of the seeker who wanted to know the living God, who demanded in his experience the presence and agency of Spirit. Nor, with its adherence to the phenomenal world and the absentee God to which the Lockean-Newtonian world-views limited it, could it satisfy Emerson's desire to penetrate appearances to the reality of things-in-themselves. The quest for an original relation to the universe, therefore, was one and the same as seeking a direct communion with God; the transcendentalists' hunger for Reality was a hunger for God. And having had the ecstatic liberating experience of this communion, as Emerson testified in the transparent-eyeball passage of *Nature*, the grounds of faith had to be reformulated, a more adequate philosophy and psychology had to be found to replace those of Unitarianism. What had begun as a crisis of faith, therefore, in the next two decades ended in something more than a familial squabble within the church; it ended in what Emerson called "a silent revolution in opinion," a revolution that made it possible for Thoreau to approach nature in a new and intimate way.

As every reader of Emerson knows, *Nature* was his attempt to account for the new miracle—"the miracle of being"—in terms of the contemporary *Naturphilosophie* that Coleridge and Carlyle had imported from Germany. Nature had become the battle cry because with the new conception of an organic universe—evolutionary, vitalistic, immanent with spirit—there was a way to revitalize the root of religious experience—the act of perception. The universe was no longer a mechanism set in motion by the Great Watchmaker, it was a growing universe, alive with the presence and purpose of deity; and man could know that spirit. For having found Lockean sensationalism with its conception of a passive mind too narrow a description of the powers of mind, Emerson repossessed the conception of an active mind that had been given new life by Kant and his followers. Coleridge's famous distinction between the Reason and the Understanding was, Emerson said when he first discovered it, a philosophy in itself. For this distinction did not so much divide the mind into intuitive and discursive faculties of thought as add a mode of knowing scanted by the sensationalism of Locke. Intuitive apprehension (the capitalized Reason of the nineteenth century as opposed to the reason of the eighteenth) was man's creative power, the warrant of his freedom, and his key to the universe. Not only did its synthesizing powers account for the way in which experience becomes meaningful, but being an imaginative faculty as well, it could directly seize reality. And this apprehension of reality, though mystical in the epistemological sense of making the knower one with the thing known, was not the vaporous emotional state usually ascribed to mysticism; it was a cognitive experience, the liberating power of which came from possessing Ideas—not the mere Lockean representative idea, but the Idea in the mind of God, the Idea in the Platonic sense of being the correlative of Reality itself. The tradition of Lockean idealism in which Emerson had been thoroughly trained had its use, of course, in establishing the primacy of mind and idea: the ideas in the mind were the only reality one could know; the world outside the mind was phenomenal. Such an idealism, however, did not permit the sovereignty of ideas, because the idea was the product of circumstance, merely residual sensation, and because, knowing only the ideas in one's mind, one never knew the reality outside of one's self.

Here, indeed, was the egocentric predicament Emerson despaired of in *Nature:* "It leaves me in the splendid labyrinth of my perceptions, to wander without end." A captive idealism, it provided no means for conquering matter. But if the Coleridgean Idea was the correlative of Reality, one could know something outside of one's self—the Godhead itself was open to the advancing mind, and the Ideas one now had were not shadowy reflexes of an unknown world but the very instruments by which that world was made. As Emerson proclaimed in *Nature:* "We learn that the highest is present to the soul of man . . . that spirit creates; that behind nature, throughout nature, spirit is present . . . it does not act upon us from without, that is, in space and time, but spiritually, or through ourselves: therefore, that spirit, that is, the Supreme Being, does not build up nature around us, but puts it forth through us, as the life of the tree puts forth new branches and leaves through the pores of the old. As a plant upon the earth, so a man rests upon the bosom of God; he is nourished by unfailing fountains, and draws at his need inexhaustible power."

The transformation brought about by these new conceptions of organic nature and active mind was therefore tremendous. Man's intimacy with the external world was restored. No longer estranged from God, no longer passive and determined, he was free to fashion his fate. "Who can set bounds to the possibilities of man?" Emerson concluded. "Once inhale the upper air, being admitted to behold the absolute natures of justice and truth, and we learn that man has access to the entire mind of the Creator, is himself the creator in the finite." Armed with such perception, matter lost its power to tyrannize; before the Idea its fixity and bruteness disappeared; it became fluid, awaiting the impress of man's mind. As Thoreau was to reaffirm later in *Walden,* not only nature, "but the institutions upon it, are plastic like clay in the hands of the potter." [6]

Nature was written to celebrate this rediscovery—that with Ideas man can remake the world, can "deal sovereignly with matter." The world that lay before him was not alien to him (for that is what external means), but in every way serviceable and beneficent, an accessory of his being.[7] Where Puritan nature had been a barrier between man and God, and the Deists' nature a field for scientific

[6] W, II, 341.

[7] As Thoreau was to say later in a letter to William E. Sheldon, "The farthest and largest star is but a lamp to light the way for man."

inquiry into the handiwork of God, transcendental nature was "a remote and inferior incarnation of God, a projection of God in the unconscious." "We are as much strangers in nature," Emerson said, "as we are aliens from God." For nature is "the present expositor of the divine mind"—a forest of symbols, spirit objectified. Man had only to come into sympathy with it and make it conscious in order to possess both the Ideas of God and his own spiritual being. Going to nature, then, was not an idle pastime; in "The American Scholar" Emerson told the student that nature was the proper field of intellectual activity. It was a new field of exploration and discovery. Interpreting nature, turning it into consciousness, this was genius, here was a new frontier for originality.

The major shift that *Nature* described was from outer to inner dominion, from sensation to experience—a process of taking up the Not-me by the Me. Mind, ideas, consciousness were primary, and the external world existed to be assimilated as the stuff of thought. The cognitive act was not a knowing of things, but a having, an inner possession of them. As much of the external world as man transformed into himself and radiated with meaning, so much did he truly possess: and again, this was not knowledge, but an acquisition of being, an enlargement of self. Cognition, therefore, became an activity, a nurture by absorption somewhat like the protoplasm's encirclement of food. It was knowledge by contact, intimacy, sympathy. If the Deists had also said that "God is the creation," their mode of knowing the creation was scientific rather than sympathetic. It ended in fact, not truth; and fact was still unrelated to man. This difference Thoreau made clear in his first study of nature for *The Dial,* "Natural History of Massachusetts."

Let us not underrate the value of a fact; it will one day flower in a truth. . . . Wisdom does not inspect, but behold. We must look a long time before we can see. . . . The true man of science will know nature better by his finer organization; he will smell, taste, see, hear, feel better than other men. His will be a deeper and finer experience. We do not learn by inference and deduction, and the application of mathematics to philosophy, but by direct intercourse and sympathy. It is with science as with ethics, we cannot know truth by contrivance and method; the Baconian is as false as any other, and with all the helps of machinery and the arts, the most scientific will still be the healthiest and friendliest man, and possess a more perfect Indian wisdom.[8]

Known in this way, by finer organization or sensibility, nature was

---

[8] *The Dial,* III (July, 1842), 39-40.

truly the servant of man. "Nature is thoroughly mediate," Emerson told his generation; "It is made to serve." From necessary physical satisfactions its uses mounted to those of the spirit. Not only did it provide the commodities of life, the "mercenary benefit," but it was so perfectly adapted to the constitution of man that in his interaction with it his being was unfolded. In its natural forms and organic integrations he learned the lessons of beauty; [9] and because the laws of nature and the laws of mind had a common source in God, he found in natural things and phenomena the language of his thought. As a field of experience and action it was a school of discipline, teaching him to interpret the physical laws of life as the moral laws of human conduct. Nature, therefore, was another self, an adjunct of man. Above all it was a moral realm, and the patient teacher of his character. Whitman, indebted to Emerson, expressed a similar view: "The whole theory of the universe is directed unerringly to one single individual—namely to You." [10] The end of nature was man's spiritual aggrandizement. Because nature only served by being assimilated into consciousness, man was the center around which the universe revolved; the whole passing show existed for his self-culture.

Emerson's theory of nature, therefore, terminated in the moral regeneration of man. "The problem of restoring to the world original and eternal beauty," he said, "is solved by the redemption of the soul." This was not a theory to be taken over passively, but to be lived out—it was a new way of seeing and acting. Like "Song of Myself" and *Moby-Dick*, *Nature* was a call to experience. Trying to explain why his generation did not find in nature all his treatise promised, Emerson said that "man is a god in ruins. . . . Once," he continued, "he was permeated and dissolved by spirit. He filled nature with his overflowing currents. Out from him sprang the sun and moon. . . . The laws of his mind, the periods of his actions externized themselves into day and night, into the year and the seasons." But living now on the prudential level of life, applying the penny wisdom of the understanding to his affairs, he had lost his power over matter; he had become a slave. The fault was not in nature, but in man: "The reason why the world lacks unity, and lies broken and in heaps, is because man is disunited with himself." The problem, then, that Emerson set before his genera-

---

[9] Thoreau always used Κόσμος [Cosmos], signifying both beauty and order.
[10] Section 15, "By Blue Ontario's Shore," *Leaves of Grass*.

tion was that of adjusting Reason and Understanding, Idea and Sensation—that of harmonizing the spiritual self and the actual self, the living of an organic life, that is, a life of principle and self-direction. The summons of *Nature* was clear: "Build therefore your own world. As fast as you conform your life to the pure idea in your mind, that will unfold its great proportion." There was only one solution, as Thoreau was to say later: living deliberately, agreeably with one's imagination.

Nothing could have been more liberating than Emerson's affirmation of the continuity of man and nature, with all it implied of the naturalization of the powers of spirit, and with this, of a new universe of novelty and adventure and resplendent individualism. Whitman, paying his debt to Emerson's inspiration, said that the Master had discovered "that new moral American continent without which . . . the physical continent remained incomplete. . . . Those shores you found." "It is yours," he told Emerson, "to have been the original true Captain who put to sea, intuitive, positive, rendering the first report. . . ." [11] Emerson had discovered the continent of being.

Nothing was more liberating and challenging—and more difficult. Emerson's moral fervor had the familiar New England ring; his moral individualism, however, did not. He had made nature a moral teacher and the supreme educative means—or "nurture"; he had insisted that the end of man's intercourse with nature was character, that character and being were one, that man was divine. But he had taken the culture of man away from social institutions, and instead of adhering to the traditional Christian notion of character as a withholding of the self—a part of Puritanism that had been transformed into the social virtue of the eighteenth century— he had spoken daringly of the expression and expansion of self. Though he used the term character, he meant by it what we now mean by personality. Not uniformity, but individuality; not education by imposition from without, but by an unfolding from within —these he demanded, glorifying individual uniqueness and the duty of developing it. All this he proclaimed in accents of joy and ecstasy that undoubtedly reminded the orthodox of the "enthusiasm" their ancestors abhorred. He intended only spiritual freedom, however, an obedience to the impulses of the self that was not

---

[11] Letter to Emerson, August, 1856. Appendix to 1856 edition of *Leaves of Grass*.

wayward because its monitor was the spirit within. What he meant when he preached on the present need of forming "entire men" was spiritual wholeness. Aware of what Whitman called the "ossification of the spirit," [12] of the dangerous externality of man in American life, he wanted especially to restore man's spiritual birthright: the reign of principle within man. To this end he had made nature a living revelation and created the possibilities of a democratic religion. But he did not go so far as Whitman (or even Thoreau) in developing the implications of the natural; he did not explore the natural life, nor envisage a natural man. He created the essential stance of man-seeing, but he did not live out its actual requirements and provide an example.

He had done enough, nevertheless, by indicating the new source of power and truth available in man's relation to nature. One might rest on the bosom of nature, but if he had known the currents of being and had beheld Ideas, he had also the duty to proclaim them. If the new religion of man and nature was a personal ecstasy, its social responsibility lay in making known the Truth which had guaranteed that unity. For Emerson, therefore, it was a religion of Ideas and Truth; Self-reliance was a dedication to Truth, and that is why its fitting priest was the scholar, and the place of the scholar was no longer among his books or in the church but in the active warfare of life. "Religion," he said in "The Present Age," "does not seem now to tend to a *cultus,* but to a heroic life. He who would undertake it is to front a corrupt society and speak rude truth. . . ."[13] Thus "The American Scholar," which defined a new vocation for the newly enfranchised intelligence of the age, in effect brought all the issues of *Nature* to the point of action.

Emerson's scholar was an intellectual without a school, church, or political party. He was a partisan only of Truth. Having neither the patronage nor fulcrum of institutions, he belonged to the new brand of nineteenth-century intellectual that the destruction of traditional authorities and the rise of a powerful and literate bourgeoisie had furthered. Like the American man of letters who had also purchased his freedom by leaving the pulpit and assembly, his patronage was uncertain; his audience had to be gathered by the demand that he himself created. His commodity was "genius." The new intellectual, being a product of the age, was therefore as

---

[12] Clifton J. Furness, *Walt Whitman's Workshop,* Cambridge, 1928, p. 81.

[13] C, II, 421n.

much a necessity as the lyceums and magazines that arose to give him voice. Both were representative of a desire to find unrestricted channels for ideas and to give opinion and intellect a democratic basis. It was for these reasons that Emerson himself had resigned his pulpit; he thought of the scholar as the great man, the appointed spiritual leader of society, the hero of democracy. Uncommitted, serving only the Truth he knew, like Whitman's wander-speaker and Melville's look-out, his mission was to descry the signs of the times. He was to announce new symbols (new values) and galvanize public opinion, thereby saving society from the rot of materialism. By opening to society the resources of spirit, he was to renew it and harmonize it with absolute moral law. Emerson's scholar, then, was a reformer, even if his only instrument was Truth; the test of his worth was his ability to stand for Truth and, by bringing it to bear on actual events, make it prevail. "We want men and women," he said, "who shall renovate life and our social state. . . ." [14]

Emerson, however, was only a reformer by example; his personality and character were perhaps as influential in his time as his ideas. He placed the utmost reliance on personal force, on eloquence —on the act of utterance as a direct sally of the spirit. And he had tried by these means to be an active reformer, to fill his own specifications for the scholar. Early in his career, therefore, he assailed those institutions with which he was familiar and which he felt could do most to reform the times because they had always claimed leadership—the college and the ministry. "The American Scholar" and *The Divinity School Address* were his genuine attempts to further the renovation of society by applying the principles of *Nature*. But the bitter controversy over *The Divinity School Address* taught him that ideas did not necessarily prevail by themselves and that truth did not have the force to compel immediately. Stamped too strongly perhaps in the mold of the Puritan minister, but without his institutional strength, Emerson worked always from above. His faith in ideas was so great that he readily assumed that matter would dissolve before them—that provided the idea, society would reorganize itself around it. Not willing to "descend to meet" and personally incapable of the strenuous life of the reformer, he never attempted the programmatic reforms of other transcendentalists. And after *The Divinity School Address* he used the lecture as

---

[14] C, II, 75.

he suggested one might use literature, "to afford us a platform whence we may command a view of our present life, a purchase by which we may move it." [15] This is not to say, however, that he expected less of the scholar. The problem of vocation—of greatness and heroism—was his lifelong preoccupation. How to make character felt, how to serve, were the fundamental problems of a self-reliance that did not end in itself. Action, he felt, was essential to it, and if he failed himself here it was a measure by which he judged others.[16] Where he could not, others were to engineer for America.

In fact, Transcendentalism had more active reformers than sayers and poets; and, especially after the depression of 1837, the transcendentalists tried to transform a materialistic society into an idealistic one. George Ripley of Brook Farm, Theodore Parker at the Melodeon, Orestes Brownson in *The Boston Quarterly Review,* Margaret Fuller in the columns of Greeley's *Tribune,* Bronson Alcott at Temple School and Fruitlands—all were protesting against the rapacious commercialism of State Street, a commercialism allied to a now conservative and decorous Unitarianism and guided by the rule of expediency. Their hue and cry might have been Whitman's

> *fiercely* and with screaming energy
> This great earth that rolls in the air, and the sun
> and moon, and men and women—do you think nothing
> more is to be made of them than storekeeping and
> books and produce and drygoods and something to
> pay taxes on? [17]

"Talk of a divinity in man!" Thoreau was to exclaim in *Walden.* "Look at the teamster. . . . does any divinity stir within him? . . . What is his destiny to him compared with the shipping interests?" [18] All were trying to create a society in which the transcendental goal of individual self-realization could be fulfilled, in which a man could complete himself by living intellectually and spiritually as well as materialistically. The transcendentalists denounced the sway of commodity, the devotion to "trifles," and the perversion of the rights of personality by the rights of property. They were among

---

[15] C, II, 312.

[16] See *The Journals of Bronson Alcott,* ed. by Odell Shepard, Boston, 1938, pp. 128, 134.

[17] Furness, *Walt Whitman's Workshop,* p. 46.

[18] W, II, 8.

the first to protest against a society that made it difficult to live a
moral life—a society that instead of serving man enslaved him. With
the startling headway of industrialism, urbanism, and immigration,
the dehumanization of man seemed imminent to them; they saw
the individual lost and dwarfed, his personality truncated by the
burdens of labor which destroyed the leisure he needed to "loafe
and invite my soul." And so they appealed to absolute principle,
and demanded that America build itself on nature: the moral truths
we needed were available here and now; all previous human experience was merely tradition, the grip of the dead past. And the
past could be discarded, because the mission of America was not
to follow, but to build anew.[19] From the standpoint of ultimate
principles, they saw that the expediency of a business civilization
was not a sound basis for America—it would not produce men;
and their faith in the progress of civilization made it necessary for
them to extend our already won religious and political liberties into
the spheres of social life. Nothing would vindicate the American
experiment but the complete liberation of all men. They were
active, therefore, in all the humanitarian reforms of the time—public
education, popular culture, feminism, penal reform, lien laws, and
abolition. And what they opened up for America was a democratic
vista. In a period of westward expansion and enterprise they gave
American society its rationale, its ends; they crystallized the human
hopes and ideal assumptions of our civilization.

Transcendentalism did produce men who tried to enact ideas.
"The American Scholar" had called for men whose work would be
"the study and communication of principles . . . the conversion of
the world." [20] But in creating the vocation of scholar Emerson also
had in mind a more retired and less active vocation, that of the
man of letters. Ideally, for him, the man of letters would have been
the active reformer; failing in this, however, he could become the
writer who, at one level, perhaps, would influence the world. Loyal
to his own gifts, he let others carry on the work of reform; and for
himself he stuck to the primary duty to which he felt he had been
called—the duty of perceiving and reporting truth. Early in his
relations with Emerson, Thoreau recognized that Emerson was "a
critic, poet, philosopher," that he lived "the life of an Artist," and

---

[19] "The perpetual admonition of nature to us, is, 'The world is new, untried.
Do not believe the past. I give you the universe a virgin to-day' " (C, I, 167).
[20] C, I, 115.

that the task he set himself—"to realize a divine life"—was a higher and more arduous one than that of reform. Indeed, it was the supreme reform, the reform of man and not his exterior life. "In his world," Thoreau went on, "every man would be a poet, Love would reign, Beauty would take place, Man and Nature would harmonize." And he added: "His personal influence upon young persons [is] greater than any man's." [21] If "The American Scholar" defined the responsibility of the intellectual, like the whole thrust of Emerson's thought, it also defined—and this is the influence Thoreau had in mind—the idea of success. Emerson created a new calling with its own rewards: the poet who, in harmonizing with nature, realized a divine life. Success was therefore identical with self-realization, with the "more intense life." [22] It was tantamount to inspiration. "He shall see," Emerson said of the budding scholar, "that nature is the opposite of the soul, answering to it part for part. . . . Its beauty is the beauty of his own mind. Its laws are the laws of his own mind. Nature then becomes to him the measure of his attainments. So much of nature as he is ignorant of, so much of his own mind does he not yet possess." [23]

Communion with nature, therefore, was not only the school of the scholar but his primary vocation. Nothing could gainsay this experience; without it the scholar was shorn of his power. For he was to speak from behind the veil as a partaker of truth. Now it was of this aspect of the scholar's life that Emerson spoke most convincingly. The quest for spirit is the content of his essays. He knew its denials and ardors and rewards; it called for a life of poverty and solitude, perhaps even of misunderstanding and scorn, but it had its consolations: to experience, to be, to live—to exercise "the highest functions of human nature." [24] Although he provided the young men of his time with a new prospect of social fame, his descriptions of the rewards of the scholar's life in "The American Scholar" and "Literary Ethics" were almost wholly personal and qualitative. He offered them a new kind of life, one, unlike most of those open to them, that demanded resolution and heroism, that called from them those gifts that they felt were uniquely theirs. He

[21] J, I, 431-33.
[22] J, I, 432.
[23] C, I, 86-87.
[24] C, I, 101.

proposed to them that they make their individuality count. "That which I call right or goodness," he said, "is the choice of my constitution; and that which I call heaven, and inwardly aspire after, is the state or circumstance desirable to my constitution; and the action which I in all my years tend to, is the work for my faculties." From this perspective, therefore, a man was responsible for his choice of calling; "it is not an excuse any longer for his deeds that they are the custom of his trade." "Has he not a *calling*," he asked, "in his character?" [25]

"Emerson's belief that the individual must in reason be adequate to the vocation for which the Spirit of the world has called him into being, is the source of those sublime pages, hearteners and sustainers of our youth, in which he urges his hearers to be incorruptibly true to their own private conscience." [26] So spoke William James, paying his own debt to the "beloved Master" in his address at the Emerson Centenary in Concord. "Each man," Emerson had said, "has his own vocation." Indeed, as he was to say later, "Your condition, your employment, is the fable of *you*." [27] All this, of course, required self-reliance and a nonconformity that placed the scholar in opposition to society. If his ultimate goal was the renovation of society, his solitary and individual way of life was a repudiation of society. "Why," Emerson asked, "should you renounce your right to traverse the star-lit deserts of truth, for the premature comforts of an acre, house, and barn?" [28] Thus, showing them the difference between prudence and spirit, he gave a generation of young men another alternative. No one had made the life of intellect so adventurous, daring, and heroic—even in its renunciations and austerities he had assured the young men that the "scholar is the favorite of Heaven." [29] No one had shown them how responsible they were for the vocations that became their lives. "The hour of that choice is the crisis of your history," he told the graduating class at Dartmouth, "and see that you hold yourself fast by the intellect." [30]

---

[25] C, II, 140.

[26] William James, "Address at the Emerson Centenary in Concord," in *The James Family,* ed. by F. O. Matthiessen, New York, 1947, p. 456.

[27] C, II, 140; C, VIII, 23.

[28] C, I, 186.

[29] C, I, 155.

[30] C, I, 186.

II

If Thoreau did not have to break the way from Locke to Coleridge, his problem was no less difficult. For his problem was to apply transcendental ideas, to bring them to the test of living— to embody them, to enact them, to realize them vocationally. Of all the young men who found a patron in Emerson—William Ellery Channing the younger, Charles King Newcomb, Charles Stearns Wheeler—Thoreau alone was acknowledged the fittest to make an organic life. John Albee was to remark, later on, that all Emerson's young men had trouble in choosing careers; [31] indeed, in looking back over that generation one finds in the wake of Transcendental-ism a series of personal failures. As we shall see with Thoreau, one can legitimately speak of these failures as romantic tragedies. Only Stearns Wheeler, Thoreau's classmate at the Concord Academy and Harvard College, found a way to success. But he took the tried path of the New England literary "vocation": a model student, second in the Class of '37, he turned to scholarship and editing, became an instructor at Harvard College and a student at the Divinity School, was licensed to preach, and capped his education by going to Heidelberg to study, where his promising career was closed by an untimely death.[32] Both Emerson, who was in his debt for his editorial help with Carlyle's *Sartor Resartus* and *Miscellaneous Essays* and for his letters to *The Dial,* and Thoreau, who shared with Wheeler the denials and bravery of scholarship, felt that a beacon of New England letters had been put out. Rev-erence for scholarship, however, had much to do with this appraisal of Wheeler's worth, for the landmarks of his career point only to a literary respectability.[33] This sterling classical scholar from a Lincoln farm would have become, one suspects, a worthy Brahmin, a proper confrere of Lowell, with whom he had associated in a secret literary society at Harvard. For he found his way too easily. That he had found a vocation and achieved something had, of course, singled him out of the younger generation; but in spite of a dedication to truth he had none of the force needed for a tran-

[31] *Remembrances of Emerson,* New York, 1901, pp. 73-74.

[32] See John Olin Eidson, *Charles Stearns Wheeler: Friend of Emerson,* Athens, Ga., 1951.

[33] Thoreau said of Wheeler that "he was made to work very well in this world" (W, VI, 91). Wheeler reminds one of Moncure Conway in the next generation.

scendental success, and he did not understand its terms. If he flirted with Transcendentalism, he remained a conservative at heart; a joiner, a conformist, a giver of "aesthetic teas," a devotee of theology—and all of this must be balanced against the impression one has been given of a daring spirit who lived in a shanty on Flint's Pond presumably to save money for books. His success must also be measured by an emotionally starved nature closed to the riches of sense experience: however much one respects the type, Stearns Wheeler belongs to the legions of Reverend Babcocks who find life in books and "truth" and turn in horror from experience. He was one of the first priests of culture who would in time make Transcendentalism genteel and acceptable.

By comparison, Thoreau was perhaps as troublesome to Emerson as the ne'er-do-well poet William Ellery Channing or as great a failure in his way as Charles King Newcomb. Emerson, ever loyal to his "men," served Thoreau in many ways and tried not only to nurture his genius but to guide it to literary recognition. Abstractly, no doubt, he could applaud a truculence buttressed by the claim that "I'll not think that society has any bribe which will tempt me." [34] He had approved of the self-reliant Thoreau, "My brave Henry here who is content to live now, and feels no shame in not studying any profession, for he does not postpone his life, but lives already. . . ." [35] He incorporated these words in "Self-Reliance," but by 1844 he speaks of Thoreau as one more of "the other grand promisers" who had failed him, and might even have sympathized with Henry's Aunt Maria who said, "I wish he could find something better to do than walking off every now and then." [36] Hawthorne recorded in 1842 that "for two or three years back, he has repudiated all regular modes of getting a living, and seems inclined to lead a sort of Indian life among civilized man—an Indian life . . . as respects the absence of any systematic effort for a livelihood." [37] For the Emerson, then, who thought of Thoreau as Napoleon, as

[34] Houghton. MS AM 278.5.

[35] Emerson, J, V, 208 (May, 1839).

[36] C, II, 76. Here Emerson first associated Thoreau with Stoicism (Emerson, J, VI, 515). Cited in Henry Seidel Canby, *Thoreau*, Boston, 1939, p. 22. In 1850 Emerson proposed a new profession of practical naturalist in order that Thoreau's "employment" might become legitimate (Emerson, J, VIII, 131).

[37] *The American Notebooks by Nathaniel Hawthorne*, ed. by Randall Stewart, New Haven, 1932, p. 166.

an executive genius, the Thoreau who had postponed all vocations, who was staying at home and going about surveying and seemed in no hurry to publish *Walden,* was indeed wanting "a little ambition in his mixture." [38] As early as 1851 he passed this final judgment on Thoreau, and that which adds the sting to his Funeral Speech, that "instead of being the head of the American engineers, he is captain of [a] huckleberry party." It was unfortunate that Emerson never read Thoreau's notes on the meaning of huckleberrying—he would have understood, then, that Thoreau's life was not without ambition or perversely unsocial, that in his way his brave Henry was engineering for America. But Emerson was too close to Thoreau to fully measure his achievement, just as he was too much concerned with his investment in Thoreau as an idea (it was Emerson who was responsible in the Funeral Speech and the editing of *Letters to Various Persons* for the portrait of Thoreau as a stoic) [39] to recognize in this quiet, unremarkable Concord life the fullest enactment and vindication of his own early proclamations. He wanted Thoreau to be a success, and from the standpoint of Concord, Boston, or New York he had not been one. He passed his life pretty much as he began it in his first few years out of college, never having been more than a village teacher, a surveyor, a seldom-wanted lecturer, and a small manufacturer of pencils and graphite. As a writer he had hardly troubled the literary currents of his time.

Thoreau, of course, had a decent share of ambition: his *Journals* are full of passages on the desire to serve. He wanted to be a writer—the one transcendental vocation that had already been given specific shape by Emerson. He wrote his sister Helen in 1840 that "an honest book's the noblest work of man." [40] But the reception of *A Week on the Concord and Merrimack Rivers,* upon which it seems Thoreau staked so much, taught him that even in this line success was dispensable. Carrying the unsold copies of his first book to his attic room, Thoreau was indeed Emerson's admirable stoic. But the issue of success really lay deeper; it was not a matter of writing "companionable" articles or of reaching the audiences

[38] Emerson, J, VIII, 228.

[39] See the correspondence of Daniel Ricketson and Sophia Thoreau, *Daniel Ricketson and His Friends,* ed. by Anna and Walton Ricketson, Boston and New York, 1902, pp. 153, 155, 165-66.

[40] W, VI, 31.

that did not want to hear any prophets, but of learning how to live without such tangible success. Living itself was the end, not writing; had it been otherwise Thoreau might well have managed to be successful, for he had all the qualifications of a Stearns Wheeler, except the willingness to be intimidated by the necessity for success. To write in order to harvest one's thoughts was a transcendental necessity.[41] It was not necessary, however, to write for bread, although earning one's way by selling one's thoughts was, as Emerson had pointed out in "Literary Ethics," the most agreeable solution for a transcendentalist. Thoreau had tried this vocation: if anything he was a writer, and one can see in his *Excursions* that he was finding a form for his thought that was popular. But if how to become a writer was the vocational dilemma of his early years, how to get inspiration—the process itself of transcendental living—was the greater dilemma of his later years. He was always to think of himself as Apollo enslaved by Admetus, but he had also learned from Menu that mean occupations do not matter, that "although Bráhmens employ themselves in all sorts of mean occupations, they must invariably be honored; for they are something transcendently divine." [42] The truculence and stubbornness that Thoreau's contemporaries recognized in him were there; they were the outward sign of his resistance to fame. He had a greater success to win than literary eminence: he had to achieve his own self-fulfillment, to keep the bloom of life and ripen in his own way.

It is understandable that his more successful elders, Margaret Fuller, George Ripley, and even Emerson, from their better-established position in the intellectual world, should have been unprepared to see in his dogged intercourse with nature and his village life a determination to find an organic way of life that beggared their own. But it is here, certainly, that Thoreau continues to represent a kind of success that appeals to our imaginations. For the very failure to succeed in an approved way adds force to the question no American life was more given to answering: How to live? Considering the vocational hazards of our own time and the lurking failures of a success-ridden culture (one of the dominant strains of our literature from Franklin to Willy Loman has been success), Thoreau's "life-style," even when the specific content of his life is overlooked or misunderstood, has a portentous urgency.

[41] C, II, 142.
[42] MA 594.

It is a life that harbors the seeds of a great repudiation—so close to that of Melville's wanderer and Whitman's man on the open road, so close in its self-sufficiency to that of Natty Bumppo, in its moral integrity to Huck Finn's, and in its resisting of pressures to Augie March's. Here is a life given to adventure, to joy, to experience and being—to the quality of life. Here is a success not of prudence but of spirit, an inner success of consciousness and personality, a success of self. A later generation, sick of the business ideal of success, would find it properly life-enhancing and would give it social dimensions, but it would be the same essential creative life, what T. K. Whipple called the way of the "poetic temper."

Of the elders, however, only Alcott seems to have understood Thoreau's purposes; and if he did not subscribe to Thoreau's views of nature he was himself sufficiently vocationless and experimental to sympathize with a way of life as unpretentious, unsettled, and aspiring as his own. And William Ellery Channing, foot-loose poet, dilettante, and irresponsible husband though he was, could become Thoreau's constant companion because he, unlike others to whom Thoreau showed nature, belonged to the same generation and shared the disruption Transcendentalism had created in the lives of the seeking few.

For by rediscovering and affirming a spiritual life, by demanding something more than the prose existence of a materialistic life, Emerson had rejected the acknowledged vocations of his time. He had made them suspect, but he had also, by leaving the new vocations free and undetermined, created difficulties for those who wished to follow him. In "The American Scholar" he had expressed the younger generation's disgust with business, and in a letter to Carlyle had written that the boys "do not wish to go into trade. . . . they reject all the ways of living of other men, but have none to offer in their stead." [43] Having been the spokesman of this discontent, he, of course, had in part created it; he had preached the need for nonconformity and self-reliance and had reclaimed the values of solitude. It is common to interpret the problem of solitude and society that came of this as a renunciation of society for an individual life—as basically uncivil and irresponsible as when Diderot branded Rousseau's solitude as the most heinous crime—but solitude was the initial condition of a vocational re-

---

[43] C, I, 114; *The Correspondence of Thomas Carlyle and Ralph Waldo Emerson, 1834-1872*, ed. by C. E. Norton, Boston, 1888, II, 15.

orientation that, for all its protective defensiveness, had as its goal the transformation of an entire society. Like Brook Farm, which tried on a larger scale to reorganize society, it ran against society, it had to operate within society, creating the very tensions and dimensions of spirit and prudence that Transcendentalism had to accommodate. The test of Transcendentalism was its ethics; unlike so many philosophies it had its issue in a conduct of life. As Thoreau said in *Walden,* "To be a philosopher is not merely to have subtle thoughts, nor even to found a school, but so to love wisdom as to live, according to its dictates, a life of simplicity, independence, magnanimity, and trust. It is to solve some of the problems of life, not only theoretically, but practically." The true philosophers do not "live merely by conformity" but are "the progenitors of a nobler race of men. . . . The philosopher is in advance of his age even in the outward form of his life." [44] For the transcendentalist, therefore, the test of Transcendentalism was a vocation consonant with its ends and aims; and the value of Thoreau's life, like that of Randolph Bourne's in a later generation, was not so much the vocation he found but the very battle itself for vocational self-determination and fitness. The point at which a society bears down on the individual is in the choice of vocation: here is the battlefield of values and the gamble for rewards. Thoreau's lifelong postponing of a recognized vocation was his choice. He learned the lesson Bourne later preached, that where one cannot accept his society he must dodge its pressures. As Emerson quoted from Landor, "keep them off civilly, but keep them off." [45] Thus he became, as he humorously said—for he knew that his "fellow-citizens were not likely to offer me any room in the court house, or any curacy or living anywhere else" —a "self-appointed inspector of snow storms and rain storms. . . ." But the moral of his example was explicitly stated: "The life which men praise and regard as successful is but one kind. Why should we exaggerate any one kind at the expense of the others?" [46] In a letter to Isaiah T. Williams in 1842 he wrote:

I must confess I am apt to consider the trades and professions so many traps which the Devil sets to catch men in—and good luck he has, too, if one may judge. But did it ever occur that a man came to want, or the

44 W, II, 16.
45 C, II, 389.
46 W, II, 19-21.

almshouse from consulting his higher instincts? All great good is very present and urgent, and need not be postponed. What did Homer—and Socrates—and Christ and Shakespeare & Fox? Did they have to compound for their leisure, or steal their hours? What a curse would civilization be if it thus ate into the substance of the soul—Who would choose rather the simple grandeur of savage life for the solid leisure it affords? But need we sell our birthright for a mess of pottage? Let us trust that we shall be fed as the sparrows are.[47]

The challenge of Transcendentalism for Thoreau, therefore, was in its demands on his moral bravery; it called for "a trade of heroism." "I doubt if men ever made a trade of heroism," he wrote in *The Maine Woods.* "In the days of Achilles, even, they delighted in big barns, and perchance in pressed hay, and he who possessed the most valuable team was the best fellow." [48] Instead, shunning a life measured by commodity, Transcendentalism had proposed a purposeful, developing life, one of self-aggrandizement, of spiritual culture, in which man would overcome his dross and, by living in communion with the Law or Spirit of life, grow to perfection. Indeed, the goal of Transcendentalism was human perfection, that perfect oneness or relatedness to the universe that comes from the assimilation of the world by the mind: it was a conquest by consciousness. Within himself, in the essential centrality of the soul, man was to become the link between the actual and the ideal. This is what Emerson meant when he spoke of the whole man; this is what he meant by self-culture—to shape one's actual life by the idea in his mind, to make an organic life as one would make a poem, the materials being the self and the world. To control circumstance and to become one's destiny involved, however, the ceaseless discovery of principle; except for a dedication to this search it was necessarily an uncommitted, open life, the images for which, properly, Thoreau took from the fields of warfare and exploration because they were the symbolic equivalents of his determination to adventure spiritually. One did not retreat to the past or to society, one pushed forward into nature to find the absolute law. Here the battle was epistemological, for the victory was insight; but the drill and discipline that led to it was the kind of life that enabled one to have insight. The life and the insight, as Thoreau found, were ultimately one; the organic life was achieved by living it. The immediate and perma-

---

[47] Berg Collection.
[48] W, III, 142.

nent need, therefore, was a sympathetic correspondence with nature, a relationship that provided inspiration. The perfection he sought was the state of communion, those moments of intense life that rewarded his faithfulness; and communion was itself both means and end. Such an experience and a devotion to its behests was the only valuable kind of regeneration; the primary duty of man, his spiritual vocation, was self-culture. Aware that other means would not produce this end, Thoreau found the problem of getting a living to be a major obstacle because it had to serve both prudential and spiritual ends. That is to say, how one made his living had to offer a way to self-development; it had to fit one's bias and not cut across his temperament. As Thoreau wrote Williams: "That you may find in Law the profession you love, and the means of spiritual culture, is the wish of your friend. . . ." [49] Failing to find such a vocation only because writing and lecturing did not get him even the small living he needed, Thoreau did not sacrifice the spiritual for the prudential goal. Instead, with fine Yankee common sense, he learned to minimize his needs and so reduce the extent of his bondage to labor: he tried as far as possible to eliminate the need for a mere vocation; for him it was only an instrument, not an end, not a form of distinction or status. "His aim," as one reviewer scornfully wrote, "was the very remarkable one of trying to be something, while he lived upon nothing. . . ." [50] First things first, values, goals, principles—this is the central doctrine of the transcendental ethic, and the tenor of Thoreau's example is still one of its major applicable doctrines.

III

Emerson made Thoreau's determination to "reconcile his practice with his own belief" too easy; he explained it by saying that Thoreau "was a born protestant." Admirable though this life was, Emerson insisted on giving it a negative cast. "Few lives," he said, "contain so many renunciations"—as if the renunciations of wife, taxes, church, vote, meat, wine, and tobacco were losses compared to what Thoreau gained. They cost him something because he had to learn not to set his heart on them; but they were not the result

---

[49] Berg Collection.

[50] Charles F. Briggs, "A Yankee Diogenes," *Putnam's Monthly Magazine*, IV (Oct., 1854), 443-48. Reprinted in *Pertaining to Thoreau*, ed. by Samuel A. Jones, Detroit, 1901, pp. 35-48.

of the perversity Emerson attributed to this "hermit and stoic":
"It cost him nothing to say No; indeed he found it much easier
than to say Yes." [51] Emerson's impression of Thoreau's life had
much in common with those of the contemporary reviewers who,
if they praised Thoreau, made a point of his unsociability. His
was a cranky, uncivil life, hardly worth fussing over because it
was unsuitable to the rest of mankind. As Oliver Wendell Holmes
wrote within the safety of his life of Emerson, "Thoreau [was]
the nullifier of civilization, who insisted on nibbling his asparagus
at the wrong end. . . ." [52] Views such as this show the stake that
even Emerson had in society, and how difficult it was for Thoreau
to turn aside from the path he was expected to follow. "It required
rare decision," Emerson admitted, "to refuse all the accustomed
paths and keep his solitary freedom at the cost of disappointing
the natural expectations of his family and friends. . . ." [53]

Because Thoreau was the son of a family in middling straits,
for whom his education had meant sacrifices on all sides—a family,
too, with intellectual aspirations—going to Harvard College inevitably raised for Thoreau the question of vocation. It was a
question that required of him a considerable humor all his life;
indeed, much of the humor in Thoreau's writing came from his
awareness of the figure he cut—more often than one realizes his
humor was directed at himself. It is most obvious in his replies
to class and alumni letters, where one was supposed to be able to
report a standing equal to that of his contemporaries—contemporaries who, minding the main chance, were, as Emerson knew,
"choosing their profession, or eager to begin some lucrative employment." [54] By going to college, of course, Thoreau was supposed
to be preparing himself for a profession, and perhaps his later
remarks on the inadequacies of his Harvard education were due to
the fact that he did not follow it through to its proper goals: the
clergy, the law, business, and, at last resort, teaching. College
introduced him to these alternatives, none of which fitted his character (at least if we see the case with hindsight), and limited him

[51] C, X, 452-56.

[52] Oliver Wendell Holmes, *Ralph Waldo Emerson*, Boston, 1885, p. 86.

[53] C, X, 452. Hawthorne, having himself strayed from the main path, was
more sympathetic with Thoreau.

[54] C, X, 452. For Thoreau's reply to an alumni inquiry of 1847, see Henry
S. Salt, *Life of Henry David Thoreau*, London, 1896, pp. 88-89.

to them. As the younger Henry James said, in looking over the
New England of Emerson and Thoreau, "we get an impression of
a terrible paucity of alternatives. . . . [New England] was not
fertile in variations"; and as John Jay Chapman said, its spiritual
life was "one-sided, sad, and inexpressive in many ways." [55] Still,
as James went on to say, Emerson's conception of the moral life—
and it seems to me to be as true of Thoreau's—was the result and
had the strength of "the limited way in which he saw our capacity
for living illustrated." [56] Emerson's "The American Scholar," which
revitalized New England's spiritual heroism, added another and
more acceptable choice, but it still cut the coat to fit the minister.
It was his personal solution, his way of finding a vocation that fitted
his gifts and that did not compromise his desire for greatness; as
a specific calling it was not Thoreau's solution. Considering this
lack of alternatives, one no longer wonders why Thoreau found
it so hard to find a calling and contented himself with leading
huckleberry parties. Was there anything more for him to do? Or
considering what it meant to him, was there anything better for
him to do? Was it possible for him to realize his early heroic ideals
—to be as completely fulfilled in statecraft, discovery, war, and
art as Sir Walter Raleigh; to lead a crusade, like Godfrey of
Bouillon in the age of Daniel Webster? One feels in Emerson's
early journal entries as well as in Thoreau's an insistent desire to
be used greatly, to serve the rising glory of America. James is
right when he looks back to their New England and "its queer
search for something to expend itself upon." [57]

In the preparation for the competitive life that Harvard provided
with its rank system and commencement honors, Thoreau did not
prove himself an exceptional student. Unlike the Emersons (Ralph,
Charles, and Edward) he did not expend himself on or find any
relish in prizes. Sixth in his class at the end of the first term of
his sophomore year, he dropped to twenty-third in his junior year
and graduated nineteenth in a class of forty-five.[58] This was not
because he was a poor student but rather because of a long illness,
an inability to satisfy the composition requirements of Professor

---

[55] "Emerson," in Matthiessen, ed., *The James Family*, p. 441; *Emerson and
Other Essays*, New York, 1898, Preface to 1909 edition, pp. vii-viii.

[56] James, "Emerson," p. 441.

[57] James, "Emerson," p. 444.

[58] See Eidson, *Charles Stearns Wheeler*, p. 8.

Edward Tyrrel Channing (and composition was rated higher than any other subject), and a preference for the modern languages, which were voluntary and rated lower than the classical languages. There seems also to have been a real determination to use the college's facilities in his own way—to read widely, for example, in early English literature—and, as President Josiah Quincy's letter to Emerson shows, to decline the lures of rank. "He had," Quincy wrote, "imbibed some notions concerning emulation and college rank, which had a natural tendency to diminish his zeal, if not his exertions." [59] By this time, however, Thoreau had met Orestes Brownson, and it is quite likely that during his illness, from the spring to the fall of 1836, he had read Emerson's *Nature*, which appeared in September. If he had turned his back on the prescribed path to success even at college, he had not lost sight of a higher goal. As his college essays bear out, he had from the beginning a desire for superiority and a need to extend himself in order to be worthy of it. Whatever their faults as exercises, these college essays reveal a morally intense young man in search of a hero. They are important because, as Emerson said in "Literary Ethics," "The youth, intoxicated with his admiration of a hero, fails to see that it is only a projection of his own soul which he admires." [60]

It is impossible to date with any accuracy the college essays, and thereby plot the stages of Thoreau's early development. Nevertheless, they show better than anything else we have from these early years the impact on Thoreau of his Harvard training. These fortnightly themes were the core of the liberal discipline, forcing the student not only to master the forensic skills upon which so much store was laid, but to ransack his reading and crystallize his opinions. To those concerned with Thoreau's later high performance as a writer they might appear, as they do to Professor Canby, to be "as empty of first-hand human contact as a stale sermon." [61] But the contact here, as one expects in a collegian, was still vital even if it was only with books. Others, investing too much attention in these college exercises, find in their

---

[59] Cited by F. B. Sanborn, *The Life of Henry David Thoreau,* Boston and New York, 1917, p. 58.

[60] C, I, 162.

[61] Canby, *Thoreau,* p. 50.

required argumentative logic the origin of the organization and tone of his mature writing; or, looking backward for his ideas, find all of them here in the germ.[62] While none of these estimates is false, they assert too much: the essays, though certainly better than those of a contemporary undergraduate (and for all the weaknesses in the Harvard curriculum, they are evidence of high standards of intellectual and verbal skill), have some of the woodenness of writing to an assignment. The topics, of course, were handed out by Professor Channing; we may find them texts for moralism and didacticism, but they were designed to draw out the undergraduate on those literary and ethical issues which were significant to him. The topics covered ranged wide: the imagination, the sublime, style, storytelling, the keeping of journals, the literary life, national literature, conformity, the varieties of energy in men, the delights of a discoverer, vocations. They were exercises toward the formation of taste and character, and they had the virtue of relating literature and life. One can argue for and against their literary influence on Thoreau, depending on whether one sees Channing as the guardian of neoclassical taste or as the apostle of an "intuitional individualism" preparing the way for Romanticism.[63] In any case, one can trace in them Thoreau's passage from the Scottish Common-Sense philosophy of Harvard to Transcendentalism,[64] and, more important, his determination to be, within the terms of Transcendentalism, the superior man.

The essays show a desire for wholeness and independence, for a thorough self-reliance. They are not so much concerned with the metaphysics of the change from the Scottish moral sense to transcendental Reason as they are, like Emerson's Bowdoin essay on Socrates, with finding the stance of a fully liberated man.

---

[62] See Edwin I. Moser, *Henry David Thoreau: The College Essays Edited, With an Introduction,* unpublished Master's thesis, New York University, 1951; Christian P. Gruber, *The Education of Henry Thoreau, Harvard, 1833-1837,* unpublished Doctoral dissertation, Princeton University, 1953.

[63] M. F. Heiser, "The Decline of Neoclassicism, 1801-1848," in *Transitions in American Literary History,* ed. by Harry Hayden Clark, Durham, N.C., 1953, p. 148.

[64] See E. W. Todd, "Philosophical Ideas in Harvard College," *The New England Quarterly,* XVI (March, 1943), 63-90; Joseph J. Kwiat, "Thoreau's Philosophical Apprenticeship," *The New England Quarterly,* XVIII (March, 1945), 51-69; Merrill R. Davis, "Emerson's 'Reason' and the Scottish Philosophers," *The New England Quarterly,* XVII (June, 1944), 209-28.

Emerson, having traveled that philosophical road earlier, had arrived at a rough statement of self-reliance that, in its intensity and challenge, could stand for what Thoreau was striving for here: ". . . what you can get of moral or intellectual excellence out of this little plot of ground you call *yourself*, by the sweat of your brow—is your portion." [65] Thoreau was chiefly interested in self-cultivation; he wanted the warrant to stand outside of anyone's world, and thereby make his own—he wanted to try the universe on his pulses, to live only on that which he had certified by his sovereign reason to be true. Such a moral life was to his mind a life of daring; its superiority over the conformities of the lives of the majority of men was in its necessity for the bravery of self-determination. In what is supposed to be his first sophomore essay, on the text, "We are apt to become what others think us to be . . ." (Sanborn entitles it "Following the Fashion"), he is already what we would call today an inner-directed man. "The majority of mankind," he wrote, "are too easily induced to follow any course which accords with the opinion of the world. Nine out of ten will tell you, in answer to the question, 'How shall you act with regard to this matter?' 'I haven't concluded; what do *you* think best?' or something similar." A life of drift and chance, its terrors were described by Thoreau in the imagery of shipwreck; it was a life of "surrender," an abdication of one's "strength and powers." And the principal cause of this conformity to forces outside of one's self, he wrote, was "a false shame which many feel, lest they be considered singular or eccentric. . . ." [66]

Conformity, of course, was commonly accepted as a social virtue, as one sees in the text of another essay taken from Mrs. Montagu's *Letters*: ". . . I have ever held conformity one of the arts of life; and though I might choose my own hours, I think it proper to follow theirs." Against this Thoreau wrote a severe argument, beginning with two forthright paragraphs on the absolute natures of vice and virtue. Religion, he stated, is not con-

[65] Cited from a manuscript sermon by Ralph L. Rusk, *The Life of Ralph Waldo Emerson*, New York, 1949, p. 158.

[66] Where possible, the citations from the college essays will be taken from F. B. Sanborn, *The Life of Henry David Thoreau*, Boston and New York, 1917. The references here are to pp. 66-67. All the essays, however, were checked against Edwin Moser's edition, which was freshly prepared from the manuscript sources. This edition, in turn, was checked against the manuscript sources.

cerned with "the comparative enormity of different vices. . . . vice,
under whatever form, is condemned in positive and unqualified
terms." The apparent conflict of duties in life came from the "prevalent" notion that duty is an outward act instead of an act "in
conformity to the dictates of an inward arbiter, *in a measure independent of Matter, and its relations, Time and Space.*" Thoreau
defended *this* duty unequivocally: "Duty is one and invariable; it
requires no impossibilities, nor can it ever be disregarded with
impunity. So far as it exists, it is binding. . . ." Duty, for Thoreau,
became a capitalized Duty which had nothing to do with "mere
conformity to another's habits or customs . . ."; it was not determined by "the general practice of mankind. . . ." And therefore—and this was the essential proposition of his argument—
"the fear of displeasing the world [society] ought not in the least
to influence my actions." [67] He had raised duty from the prudential to the spiritual level, and in practice this meant an opposition to society. In his concluding sentence, that without his conception of duty "the principal avenue to Reform would be closed,"
one sees already an individualist who hoped for little from society
and everything from his own regeneration and who had, by his
very distinction of levels, placed himself against society. This is
the tenor of most of his college essays; the basic tension that first
created his notion of heroism was the opposition of the spiritual
individual and a worldly society.

Here was a young man, then, who already felt no need for the
good opinion of society. In an essay, "On what grounds may the
forms, ceremonies, and restraints of polite society be objected to?"
he spoke of compliance as "a very silly thing," and found the
forms of society useless, a sacrifice to politeness of "truth, sincerity
and candor. . . ." [68] The fundamentals of his later social intercourse and his ideas on friendship were thus made clear, and
though they have been criticized for being unaccommodating, one
should see in them not puerile defiance but a dedication to truth.
In "The Superior and The Common Man" Thoreau admitted that
"Man does not wantonly rend the meanest tie that binds him to

[67] Sanborn, *Life,* pp. 150-52. The italicized portion was crossed out in the
manuscript, but not in Moser's edition. In a letter (October 13, 1837) to
Henry Vose, Thoreau mockingly cited the text of this essay (MS, Berg
Collection).

[68] Sanborn, *Life,* pp. 166-67. The quotation, however, was omitted by Sanborn; see Moser, *College Essays,* p. 171.

his fellows; he would not stand aloof even in his prejudices, did not the stern demands of Truth, backed by conviction, require it." He knew that the superior man—the man who is not content with the common reasons for things—has "not only the burden of the proof, but that of reproof to support." His only armor was sincerity—perhaps the highest value for Thoreau, who added, "Where there is sincerity is truth also." [69] This superior man, moreover, was Thoreau's attempt to sketch an ideal man (before he had heard "The American Scholar") to fit the philosophy of Emerson's *Nature*. Sanborn dates the essay May 5, 1837, and with his last essay of June 22, 1837, on "Barbarism and Civilization," it shows how fully Transcendentalism had entered his thought. For the superior man has had the transcendental experience; he has felt the doubt of the existence of matter, and his world has dissolved into "Mystery." He has questioned "the reality of outward existence"; he has laughed "through his tears at the very mention of a mathematical demonstration." He recognizes only "Nature and Spirit." As a result of his "original views of things," the recommendations of common reason are "now a positive objection." His world has become fluid, and "he feels that he is not secure till he has gone back to their most primitive elements, and taken a fresh and unprejudiced view of things." And, with the Emerson of "Prospects," out of this dynamic experience "He builds for himself, in fact, a new world." [70] The superior man is a truth seeker, Melville's deep-diver.

And being so, he relies wholly on his Reason, which, by the time of a senior essay on "Whether Moral Excellence tend directly to increase Intellectual Power," has superseded the moral sense of Scottish philosophy. "What is moral excellence?" he asked, only to clear the field of accepted notions: "Not, surely, the acknowledgement of the divine origin of the Scriptures, and obedience to their dictates as such; nor yet an implicit compliance with the requisitions of what may be termed popular morality. It consists rather in allowing the religious sentiment to exercise a natural and proper influence over our lives and conduct—in acting from a sense of duty, or, as we say, from principle." That is, moral excellence is not the accepting of an expedient morality, but a search for a universal morality: the morality of truth itself, which is "the

[69] Sanborn, *Life,* pp. 137-40.
[70] Sanborn, *Life,* pp. 137-40.

only real and universal right. . . ." No one who has read "Civil
Disobedience" or "Life Without Principle" would deny Thoreau's
moral intransigence; what one often fails to see, however, is that
for him it was the insignia of superiority and heroism. For "none,"
he wrote, "but the highest minds, can attain to moral excellence."
And it was, furthermore, an excellence which was proven by
opposition to "worldly and temporal" morality. "With by far the
greater part of mankind," he wrote with hard honesty, "religion
is a habit, or rather, habit is religion, their views of things are
illiberal and contracted, for the very reason that they possess not
intellectual powers sufficient to attain moral excellence." This
being the case, it led Thoreau to conclude that "to reject RE-
LIGION is the first step towards moral excellence; at least, no
man ever attained to the highest degree of the latter by any other
road." [71] Already on that road, Thoreau made good his intention
of becoming the superior man: his first act on coming home was
to leave the church.

By the autumn of 1836 Thoreau had also begun to appreciate
the Coleridgean distinction between the Fancy and the Imagination. In a review of Henry Nelson Coleridge's *Introductions to the
Study of the Greek Classic Poets*, dated October 1, 1836, he
quoted the poet's nephew on the difference between these faculties.
"Fancy," H. N. Coleridge wrote, "collects materials from the visible
world, and arranges them for exhibition; Imagination takes and
moulds the objects of nature at the same moment. . . ." [72] In an
essay, probably of September, 1836, Thoreau wrote on the text,
"Whether the Cultivation of the Imagination conduces to the
Happiness of the Individual?" And here he included the cultivation of the imagination as an essential faculty of the mind. The
cultivation of the mind, of course, was the necessary work of the
superior man; now Thoreau gave it a philosophical basis, one that
seems to have been taken from Emerson's *Nature*. The growth of
the faculties is his central concern; he wants the education of all
of man's faculties—indeed, in a fumbling way he has got to the
root of the problem of self-culture. His argument, carefully couched

[71] MS, Abernathy Library. Printed in Reginald Cook, *The Concord Saunterer*,
Middlebury, Vt., 1940, pp. 60-61. In an essay on sublimity (Sanborn, *Life*,
pp. 142-48) Thoreau wrote: "We reverence greatness, moral and intellectual. . . . " "Truth shall be policy enough for him," Emerson reminded the
scholar when he enjoined him to "Explore, and explore" (C, I, 183, 186).

[72] Carl Bode, "A New College Manuscript of Thoreau's," *American Literature*, XXI (Nov., 1949), 311-20.

in the acceptable language of the Common-Sense philosophy, is an
argument from the design of the creation; but the pivotal idea,
that the universe is made for man, has the Emersonian transvalua-
tion. Endowed by the Creator with the intellectual faculties and,
because of them, a "free agent," man has a duty to cultivate them;
but the universe itself, as Emerson claimed, was fitted to their
nurture. "The wisdom of the Creator has ever been the theme of
the Christian's admiration and praise," Thoreau wrote; "shall then
wisdom for a man's self be rejected?" His answer was Emersonian:
"In supplying his physical wants Man but obeys the dictates of
Nature's law; shall the intellect be neglected? If Reason was given
us for any one purpose more than another, it was that we might
so regulate our conduct as to insure our eternal happiness." The
faculty he is most interested in is that of Imagination—an intellectual faculty "almost coeval with Reason itself. . . ." Although he
cites Dugald Stewart on its importance to the artist, he leaves
unspecified the author of his quotation on its general powers of
fusing conceptions; but this mastery of sensation by the mind is
the important thing for Thoreau—this, and its freedom from all
circumstances. "Its province is unbounded," he wrote, "its flights
are not confined to space; the past and the future, time and eternity
all come within the sphere of its range." [73] In another essay of
the same year on "The Love of Stories . . . ," this restless faculty
is associated with man's insatiable curiosity and love of novelty. In
one's youth it leads from the familiar to the mysterious, but in
one's maturity it leads back to "the more serious, though scarcely
less wonderful annals of the world"—to nature and history. For
both the young and the old, as he said in this and the previous
essay, it is a "divine faculty," offering in its "cob-houses and air-
castles" pleasures more permanent than those of sense. The love of
stories, moreover, is for Thoreau merely an occasion for developing his views on the uses of the imagination: the love of stories is
really a love of the imagination which can transform the stuff of
life and help one to "a proper regard *for* and independence *of* the
petty trials of life. . . ." [74]

---

[73] Sanborn, *Life,* pp. 114-17. The unspecified quotation is: its "province" is
" 'to select the parts of different conceptions, or objects of memory, to form
a whole more pleasing, more terrible, or more awful than has ever been presented in the ordinary course of nature.' " In another theme on the love of
stories, the same idea is given in his own language (Sanborn, *Life,* p. 118).

[74] Sanborn, *Life,* pp. 117-20.

Both Reason and Imagination were liberating faculties for a Thoreau in search of self-reliance. They armed that "somewhat military in his nature" that Emerson properly noted. "Not to be subdued, always manly and able," Emerson wrote of Henry, "he did not feel himself except in opposition." [75] Where a principle, and thus a social question, was at stake, Thoreau's tone was always to be uncompromising and sharp; and since this Thoreau has been fixed in our minds by critics like Lowell and Emerson (who had personally felt his steel), we have overlooked his tender and reverential side. This side was also strengthened by the faculties of Reason and Imagination, but it was the side of Thoreau that was turned to nature rather than to society. It is best seen in his essay on the sublime, which was written in the spring of 1837, and seems to be of a piece with his transcendental essays on "Barbarism and Civilization" and "The Superior Man." It is a well-argued essay against Burke's idea that terror and fear of death are the ruling principles of the sublime. For Thoreau, however, fear is unmanly and cannot be associated with an emotion as grand as the sublime; not death and pain but "inherent respect or reverence" is its master emotion. Here, then, is his newly acquired transcendental attitude toward the universe, the ground of his own faith in the sustaining presence of nature. He is describing his own emotional experience in nature, and developing a natural basis for religion; for the sublime is really the sentiment of the Reason and the Imagination, the pleasure they give the explorer of Mystery. "The philosopher [his superior man] sees cause for wonder and astonishment in everything," he wrote, "in himself and in all around him; he has only to reflect that he may admire." Terror, of course, is not consonant with this transcendental reflection and acceptance of creation: "The Deity," he asserted, "would be reverenced, not feared." And the attributes of Divinity are those of the sublime, "Mystery, Power, Silence," all tokens of the Infinity that is its essence. This, if you will, is the romantic universe: "What is more grand," Thoreau wrote, "than mystery?" And the experience it occasions "is pleasure mingled with reverence, and tempered with humility." Reason and Imagination may fortify the ego, but in the presence of sublimity one feels "a consciousness of our littleness . . . ," one measures himself against

---

[75] C, X, 455-56.

an incomparable grandeur. This "reverence for the grand," further-more, is not a reflex of fear but an "original principle of our nature"; "the most unearthly and godlike" emotion, it is "the very basis of our religion." This is a description of the kind and quality of experience that inspiration or the intense moment of ecstasy came to mean for Thoreau; its religious significance for him should be remembered—it is a naturalized grace. But since this response to the sublime is "implanted in us by our Maker,—a part of our very selves," it will, for the Thoreau who no longer had this response, have its burdens of guilt and responsibility. Failing this godlike emotion, he will become a desperate searcher for it. All the more, as he so confidently affirmed in this essay, because "We cannot eradicate it, we cannot resist it; fear may be overcome, death may be despised; but the Infinite, the Sublime, seize upon the soul and disarm it. We may overlook them, or rather fall short of them; we may pass them by,—but so sure as we meet them face to face, we yield." [76]

If the college essays forced Thoreau to consider the moral and intellectual sources of greatness, they also forced him to canvass the vocations in which greatness might have a place. In a jocular essay on "The Methods of gaining or exercising Public Influence" he dismissed the high office of minister because of its limited in-fluence and because, while this influence was assured by the calling itself, the duty to heed the minister reduced his authority. Sanborn

[76] Sanborn, *Life*, pp. 142-48. Like Whitman, Thoreau was interested in "himself," in the miracles of the body. In his essay on storytelling he wrote: "*We* are curiously and wonderfully made,—yet how few, comparatively, see anything to admire in the structure of their own bodies!" (Sanborn, *Life*, p. 117). That one need only reflect that he may admire reminds one of Whit-man's central act in "Song of Myself" and Emerson's reflections on the black-berry (*Young Emerson Speaks*, ed. by Arthur C. McGiffert, Jr., Boston, 1938, pp. 207-8). This essay also first employed the "Silence" so important to Tho-reau's later thought, first suggested the romantic landscape, and first evoked the imagery of battle Thoreau developed in *The Service*. "To the coward the cannon's peal, the din and confusion of the fight, are not sublime, but rather terrible; the calm and self-collected alone are conscious of their sublimity. Hence, indeed, they are supplied with courage to sustain the conflict" (San-born, *Life*, p. 145). Finally, unknowingly, Thoreau anticipated the direction of his life, that movement from the quest of the larger mystery of nature to the mystery of the minute, the common, and the familiar. His life might be described as a quest for the "face to face" that took him from atmosphere to law and, as he said in the essay on storytelling, to the "annals of the world"—to nature and history (Sanborn, *Life*, p. 119).

suggests that Thoreau was sketching the Rev. Ezra Ripley, the "aged Shepard" he memorialized in the *Week;* the essay, however, is irreverent, leaving the impression of the minister's ineffectuality, and is more likely drawn from Thoreau's immediate experience of the Rev. Henry Ware, Sr., professor of divinity at Harvard College. As for the press (a medium which was to provide the new intellectual with a democratic form of patronage), its influence was diminished by its very scope and impersonality. Even though Thoreau was later befriended by Horace Greeley, his scorn of newspapers and imbecile editors was unremitting, a scorn apparently that dates from this essay. Authorship, too, fell before his humor. The traveling author (the European in America) and the native author were not literary men; they were popular writers who had their eye on sales, not truth—writers of the type he criticized again in the *Week.* In an essay on this topic one would have expected that the minister would have taken the highest place; he does manage to get the least of Thoreau's disrespect. But Thoreau cannot take any of these callings seriously, and even the ministry shares the weakness of the others. Though all have an influence that Thoreau seems to have forgotten as he developed his paper, they are ridiculed for their common want of truth: the minister is not to be criticized, the editor is an abominable logician, and the writer a caterer of opinion—all "at the expense of truth." [77]

Influence perhaps is not a just word for what Thoreau expected of a vocation; even then it suggested the connotations of our current self-help books. He did not want to influence but to serve. In writing on "The Varying Pursuits of Men" he accorded true greatness only to the few "who labor for the public good"; both the pursuit of money and of power were base.[78] And in a theme, "Explain the phrases, a Man of Business, a Man of Pleasure, a Man of the World," he could not, in spite of his Yankee approval of the businessman's "despatch," accept the motive of self-interest which all had in common. Of the three, the Man of the World, the professed gentleman, was Thoreau's target, for he is the "viper" who regulates "his honor and morality . . . by the fashions of the times"—he is the artfully prudent and conforming man, at the other pole from Thoreau's own ideal.[79]

[77] Sanborn, *Life,* pp. 159-62.

[78] Sanborn, *Life,* pp. 76-78.

[79] Sanborn, *Life,* pp. 164-66. Thoreau also mocked the gentleman in an essay on social forms and restraints. See Sanborn, *Life,* p. 167.

Thoreau's ideal character was not taken from his age; nowhere did he mention Daniel Webster, Emerson's great man, or any other of the acknowledged leaders of the time. Instead he turned to an earlier age. His heroes were aristocrats, men who had fulfilled the demands of personality, leadership, and individuality; and his turning to them, like his own problem of a heroic vocation, was not so much an individual matter as a characteristic of the age. It may seem odd that in the age of the common man, the great man was so much insisted on; but he represented an imaginative protest against the mediocrity and uniformity of bourgeois society, a desire, as one sees in Emerson's naked essay on "Heroism," for unimpeded personal development. Even Whitman, the democrat par excellence, admired the ideal personality of the aristocrat of feudal society. Indeed, the great man was a preoccupation of the nineteenth century, and his delineations were everywhere: in border romances,[80] in Mill's defense of paganism in *On Liberty*, in Carlyle's *Heroes, Hero-Worship, and the Heroic in History* and his *Oliver Cromwell*, in Emerson's *Representative Men*, in the genteel conception of the gentleman, Nietzsche's superman, and Stendhal's happy few. Byron was the hero of the age because he dared to live above the commonplace conventions of bourgeois life; he expressed a widespread yearning for a lost individuality, just as much of romantic literature expressed the loss of color, variety, and wonder in life. One might even say that Thoreau's arduous reading of the literature of the Renaissance (which he discovered in his sophomore year) and his insatiable delight in travel literature and the narratives of discovery and exploration (freshman reading) were, like the more general enthusiasm for biography in this period, prompted by a profound distaste for the common life and a desire for the heroic.

Thoreau's first sketch of the hero appeared in an essay on "Energetic Character." Limited by the text, what he wanted in the hero was constant energy, a force subdued by calm and deliberation, and he found it not in the impetuous Francis I or the dogged Charles V, but in Philip van Artevelde, the Flemish leader of the fourteenth century.[81] There is no record that he withdrew Sir

[80] In a review of May 3, 1836, of two biographies of Sir Walter Scott, Thoreau mentioned these romances and also used the phrase "pilgrimage à la Terre Sainte" that he later transformed into saunterer and defended as his vocation in "Walking." See Wendell Glick, "Three New Early Manuscripts by Thoreau," *Huntington Library Quarterly*, XV (Nov., 1951), 70.

[81] Sanborn, *Life*, pp. 70-73.

Henry Taylor's closet drama, *Philip van Artevelde* (1834), from the college library; but he might have seen the enthusiastic review by Margaret Fuller in the December, 1835, issue of *The Western Messenger*. Margaret Fuller, whose taste in great men was unimpeachable, had found one of her lifelong heroes, a man who could forsake the contemplative life for that of action, who could take a public role. In *Summer on the Lakes* (1844) she wrote again of Philip van Artevelde, this time using him as a standard to measure her Concord friend, Waldo Emerson: "When will this country have such a man? It is what she needs; no thin Idealist, no coarse Realist, but a man whose eye reads the heavens while his feet step firmly on the ground and his hands are strong and dexterous for the use of human implements. A man religious, virtuous, and sagacious; a man of universal sympathies, but self-possessed; a man who knows the region of emotion, though he is not its slave. . . ." [82] Emerson did not measure up: if he had the spirit, he did not have the muscle of the hero; he did not enter public life. Margaret Fuller's ideal was Emerson's (and she tried him sorely by reminding him of it), and it was also Thoreau's.

The man of action who seemed to capture Thoreau's imagination most was Godfrey of Bouillon. He had read Tasso's *Jerusalem Delivered* in Chalmers' *Works of the English Poets*, the major find of his college reading; and the imagery of the crusade was henceforth to give his work a militancy and by the time of "Walking" to become the symbol of his own heroic vocation.[83] It is fairly well established that his ballad, "Godfrey of Boulonge," is a college piece, written after his reading of Tasso during the autumn of 1836 and the winter of 1837.[84] As poetry there is nothing especially noteworthy in the poem, which relates Godfrey's march from Provence to Byzantium; but there is in the first three stanzas a

[82] *The Writings of Margaret Fuller*, ed. by Mason Wade, New York, 1941, pp. 50-51.

[83] He also read in 1834 Charles Mills, *The History of The Crusades for the Recovery and Possession of the Holy Land*, London, 1822. See Kenneth W. Cameron, *Emerson The Essayist*, Raleigh, N.C., 1945, II, 192. In a portion of "Walking" read in April, 1851, but omitted in the final version, he defended walking as his work, as the exercise of the soul, and to his detractors he said, "I am not ashamed to say that they might as well preach in this strain to Don Quixote and Sancho Panza, aye even to Godfrey of Boulonge & Richard Coeur de Leon as to me" (Houghton. MS AM 278.5).

[84] Kenneth W. Cameron, "Thoreau, 'Sic vita,' and *Harvardiana*," *The Thoreau Society Bulletin*, XLIX (Fall, 1954), 1.

contrast of peace and war, of passivity and action, that magnifies the resolution of Godfrey and turns the warrior into a hero who would save the spirit for a sleeping Europe.[85] Godfrey is marching to his own music.

Such large action for Thoreau was a requisite of heroism, and it had for him the connotation of marching against the battlements of conformity. This was the ardor of the campaign. In one of his last college essays, on Titus Pomponius Atticus, he praises the dedication to truth, but deprecates the policy and inaction of the man who tries to pursue it and still avoid the turmoil. "It is not a characteristic of Truth to use men tenderly," he wrote, "nor is she over-anxious about appearances." And he cited approvingly George Herbert's lines on the man "Who rides his sure and even trot, /While the World now rides by, now lags behind." Nowhere in his essays was the truth, here coupled with action, so ardently and yet so aggressively hymned. The hero prized the truth; there was no heroism without it. But he had also to make it prevail; and if he could not deliver Jerusalem he could deliver himself. "Character," Thoreau concluded, "shapes his lot for each of us." [86]

The bold outlines of the hero were fixed by the time Thoreau left Harvard College. *The Service* and "Sir Walter Raleigh" were the personal and public descriptions of what Thoreau had already, with less stylistic daring and felicity, touched on. Other themes that would later become more fully fused with the heroic, however, appear in his college essays, especially those on native literature, solitude, and nature. In keeping with the criticism of the time, Thoreau wrote (in March, 1836) on the "Advantages and Disadvantages of Foreign Influence on American Literature." He made the usual statements, that each nation has its peculiar literature (an idea appropriated from Herder) and that New England

---

[85] In July, 1840, Thoreau entered in his *Journal* a passage he later used in *The Service:* "What are Godfrey and Gonsalvo unless we breathe a life into them, and reënact their exploits as a prelude to our own? The past is only so heroic as we see it; it is the canvas on which our conception of heroism is painted, the dim prospectus of our future field. We are dreaming of what we are to do" (J, I, 158).

[86] Sanborn, *Life*, pp. 183-85. The essay was probably written after June 26, 1837, when Thoreau withdrew Nepos, *Vitae Excellentium Imperatorum*. See Moser, *College Essays*, p. 137. See also a passage Sanborn attributes to Thoreau's college years, where Thoreau elaborates the idea, "Truth leads directly to action; she calls for a practical application" (Sanborn, *Life*, pp. 195-96).

—not America!—must have its own. Our literature, unfortunately, was "still in the gristle," and still being molded by English models. This did not disturb Thoreau, who had been schooling himself in English literature and who praised it for helping to establish "a pure and nervous language." The enemy was not so much foreign food for the mind, not even the scurrilous criticism of the English and Scottish reviewers, but the utilitarianism (as W. E. Channing had already said) of the native mind. "Utility is the rallying word with us," Thoreau wrote; "we are a nation of speculators, stock-holders and money-changers. We do everything by steam, because it is most expeditious, and cheapest in the long run; we are continually racking our brains to invent a quicker way or cheaper method of doing this or that." The consequence in literature was the saleable book, and authors who were "too fashionable to write for posterity." The independence and maturity of our native literature, therefore, had to be achieved *against* the popular taste: here was a field for the hero. "Its future eminence must depend . . . upon the impressions it now receives, and the principles it imbibes: how important, then, that these impressions be of a manly and independent character!" "Manly and robust"—such was the character our literature would take from the "cuffs and hard knocks" of foreign critics. Thoreau, like Whitman, wanted a "this-side book," and he knew that it took courage to give up the popularity that came from conforming to English popular literature. In part, it was to be his fate to write of "the homely robin-red-breast, and the straggling rail-fence" of his native land when others found a readier audience for "skylarks and nightingales, perched on hedges. . . ." No American author—unless it was Whitman—turned so heartily from Europe as Thoreau; for him it became a matter of principle, a proud determination to claim his own place.[87]

It also rested on his belief that human nature is universally the same, and that it may be studied as readily in America as in Europe, and that history, too, can be unlocked by a knowledge of man. Thoreau was already aware of the fact that national and individual genius color one's perception, and that Goldsmith, Dante, and Shakespeare, for example, took their materials from the life they knew. But this did not destroy the universality of what they wrote. The subject of the poet was Man, and even though it was necessary for him to view his subject through him-

[87] Sanborn, *Life,* pp. 130-34.

self, this was, as he might have learned from Cousin,[88] the only way of understanding: "Is human nature our study,—the humanity of the Romans, for instance,—we ourselves, our friends, the community, are our best textbooks." Thus it was that Dante found the hell of his *Inferno* in the world he inhabited, and Shakespeare adapted his genius "to the reality of things. . . ." Although Thoreau never explicitly stated the principle that underlies his argument, both found the universal in the particular. The poet's method must be inductive: "he has only to learn particulars. . . . the phenomena he observes are to be referred to a general law." Thoreau was here working toward the transcendental doctrine of expression, toward the imaginative rendering of fact as symbol, and the native as universal. But he knew already that the imagination provided the way: Shakespeare's power of portraying the universal, the "humanly true," was not, as Pope said, the result of "Invention"; one cannot, Thoreau argued, separate "Invention from Imagination," and he quoted Pope's "What can we reason but from what we know?" to make his point. Where there is imagination—and the word "reason" in Pope's line begins to suggest a higher "Reason"—where there is an original seeing of things, Concord can become the world, and all the world Concord.[89] Thus this explorer found his new world at home.

In spite of the desire for action that seems in these college years the dominant characteristic of the hero, Thoreau also wrote approvingly of solitude. It was, of course, one of the popular ideas of the day, having been introduced by the romantic poets and by Johann Zimmermann's treatise on solitude. When Thoreau first wrote about it, probably in September, 1835, he made it the chief pleasure of the literary life. His text (oddly anticipating the tenor of *Walden*) was: "I live like a Prince: not, indeed, in pomp of greatness, but in pride of liberty; master of my Books, master of my time. *Speak of the Pleasures and Privileges of a Literary Man.*" At this time, although he was enjoying the rural opportunities

[88] Victor Cousin was especially popular after the translations of his *History of Philosophy* (1832) and *Elements of Psychology* (1834). In September, 1836, Brownson published a long article extolling Cousin's eclecticism in *The Christian Examiner*, XXI, 33-64. Thoreau, not long from Brownson, might have discovered Cousin here, though, as Perry Miller points out (*The Transcendentalists*, Cambridge, 1950, p. 107), this article has some of the motifs of Emerson's *Nature*.

[89] Sanborn, *Life*, pp. 106-13.

of Cambridge and, as he remarked later, was homesick for the woods of Concord, he did not associate solitude with nature; nor was it explicitly the polar term for "society." He did not even find his example in Wordsworth, but in Horace, whose *Epistles* he had read in his sophomore year. Solitude was merely one of the needs of the literary man, a necessity of "those minds most devoted to study and elevated by genius." It was the condition of meditation, or withdrawing from the world in order " 'to view the world moving within ourselves. . . .' " The requisite of this "pure enjoyment," however, was an "enlightened and cultivated mind": "it is folly for him, whose intellect has not been trained to study and meditation, to look for pleasure here: to him the path is dark and dreary, barren and desolate." For Thoreau, then, the enjoyment of solitude was a sign of intellectual distinction more than an opportunity for communion with nature. Knowledge, he wrote, "creates the difference between man and man . . ."—and it was this superiority of the richly stored mind that made solitude pleasurable, and made it a life of independence. "He who is dependent upon himself alone for his enjoyments,—who finds all he wants within himself," Thoreau wrote self-approvingly, "is really independent; for to look to others for that which is the object of every man's pursuit, is to live in a state of perpetual trust and reliance." Solitude, however, would signify a more stalwart independence and a hardier genius when nature became the field of transcendental exploration; for the student, more absorbed in books than in nature, it set a value on scholarship that Thoreau never outlived. The Walden solitary who wrote in "Reading" of heroic studies might, if not so platitudinously, have written: "Happy is the man who is furnished with all the advantages to relish solitude! he is never alone . . . he holds sweet converse with the sages of antiquity, and gathers wisdom from their discourse; he enjoys the fruits of their labors,—their knowledge is his knowledge, their wisdom his inheritance." [90] Professor Canby said that Harvard College made Thoreau a scholar, but that is to construe "scholar" too meanly and narrowly.[91] Thoreau was indeed a user of books, but his debt to Harvard, which he never acknowledged, was a historical imagi-

---

[90] Sanborn, *Life*, pp. 85-87. Later, when writing of the imagination, he said of Shakespeare, "He was . . . never less alone than when alone" (Sanborn, *Life*, p. 113).

[91] Canby, *Thoreau*, p. 50.

nation, a remarkable sense of the past, a liberation into antiquity which for him was almost as vital as the liberation of nature—or, perhaps, became vital because of the liberation of nature.

At the end of this essay on the literary life, Thoreau used a commonplace sentiment of the eighteenth-century religion of nature: man (through reflection, not inspiration) " 'is led through nature up to nature's God.' " By March, 1836, however, the "rich store-house" of the mind was not only filled with learning but with the imagery of nature; and the love of nature, and " 'sweet converse' " with her were associated with the pleasures of solitude. This change was not as yet thoroughly absorbed; it was the result of his reading, although what he read indicated the direction he was taking. He had come upon William Howitt's *The Book of the Seasons; or The Calendar of Nature* [92] and had written a review of it, probably intended for *Harvardiana*. The essay, which was not meant for Professor Channing, exhibited a youthful levity not to be contained by the required seriousness and formal manner of his themes. It was not forensic, although it began with a parade of learning symptomatic of his personal but as yet unassimilated reading. Moreover, certain moral maxims on the love of nature were taken directly from Howitt's introduction and did not tally with the youthful experience he worked into Howitt's calendar.[93] "There are certain pure and substantial pleasures," he began, "pleasures springing from a never failing source, which are absolutely denied those who are destitute of pure and elevated principle, whose sordid views extend no further than the profitable, who cannot contemplate the meandering brook, without, in imagination, polluting its waters with a mill-wheel." Meandering or not, the imagery was his own, to become in the *Week* an ominous portent for America; and the idea, too, would soon appear with more conviction in his senior essay on "Barbarism and Civilization" and his commencement address on "The Commercial Spirit." The Indian, too, already served as his example of this pure and richer happiness. But with the necessity of proof in mind—here, perhaps, only a sign of his classroom training, but later a characteristic of his use of history—he cited a wider geographical range

[92] London, 1831. Published in Philadelphia in 1831. The review is printed in Glick, "Three New Early Manuscripts by Thoreau."

[93] He mentioned the Greenlander and Symme's hole, the African—he confounded him with the American Negro (" 'de dear native land' ")—and Irving, whose *Columbus, Alhambra,* and *Sketch Book* he already knew.

of examples of the universal love of nature. Nature, in every instance, however, translated into "home"; and Thoreau ended this passage on the attachment to nature with a disguised description of Concord: "his [he is speaking of a mariner] thoughts revert to the well-known steeple, the most conspicuous object in a country village, the slowly winding stream which flows at the foot of the hill where he netted in Autumn and coasted in Winter, the cart path that leads down to the great meadows where the grapes were as thick as blackberries. . . ." This "love of natural scenery . . . so interwoven with the best feelings of our nature" was hardly more than nostalgic. If it called to mind his reading in the English poets it was because Howitt, like many who wrote popularly "in the fields of nature and of literature," referred constantly to the poets; and perhaps it made poignant the fact of Milton's blindness, which could easily stand for Thoreau's own sense of absence. In any case it made possible the transition from the love of home to that special relation of the poet to nature at the very heart of Transcendentalism.

Thoreau did not describe the transcendental communion with nature; he had not experienced it, even though the feeling for nature-as-home, with its vague sense of oneness, was essential to it. He cited instead Howitt's quotation from Schlegel whose *Lectures on the History of Literature, Ancient and Modern* he later withdrew from the college library in the fall of 1836.[94] Schlegel wrote:

Between the poet and nature, no less than between the poet and the man, there is a sympathy of feeling. Not only in the song of the Nightingale, or in the melodies to which all men listen, but even in the roar of the stream, and the rushing of the forest, the poet thinks that he hears a kindred voice of sorrow or of gladness; as if spirits and feelings like our own were calling to us from afar, or seeking to sympathize and communicate with us from the utmost nearness to which their natures will allow them to approach us. It is for the purpose of listening to these tones, and of holding mysterious converse with the soul of nature, that every great poet is a lover of solitude.[95]

There is no evidence here that Thoreau had more than nodded his approval of a fine, if vague, moral sentiment; the Thoreau of March, 1836, was hardly aware of the importance of this relation of sympa-

---

[94] Cameron, *Emerson The Essayist*, II, 193.

[95] The Indian in Thoreau's "Barbarism and Civilization" will have this experience.

thy, nor is there in this and a passage where he quotes Howitt's "Nothing can perhaps illustrate so livingly our idea of a spirit as a mighty wind" any indication of his later mystical ecstasy with sounds. In fact, even by October, 1836, when he had read *Nature* and had withdrawn the first volume of Schlegel's *Lectures* from the college library, he seemed to prefer the "recourse to symbolical images" and the "appetite for visible images" of the southern to the "mystical conceptions" of the northern literature. This famous distinction between classic and romantic, of course, was Schlegel's, but the preference for seeing, for the material image, was Thoreau's. "We *see* with Dante," he wrote in the review of H. N. Coleridge, "but we *feell* [sic] with Milton." The northern "fondness for the dark and mysterious" was explained environmentally, by the sublime scenery;[96] similarly, in his review of Howitt, the mysterious converse with nature was domesticated in America by referring to a scenery still more sublime than Germany's. "America," Thoreau quoted from some "Novelist," "with her beautiful and stupendous scenes of nature; her immense lakes; her broad and sweeping rivers; her clime melting into all the varieties of the globe; her cataracts shaking the earth; her mountains kissing the heavens; her solitudes and forests, yet hushed in primeval silence"—certainly, if a sympathetic relation to nature was to be prized, America was the place for it.[97] But Thoreau was unable at this time to see how sympathy became seeing; his feeling for nature and his delight in imagery (and mythology) were still to be reconciled by the power of imaginative intuition. Nature was a "soul," not yet the expositor of the divine Mind.

All this is clear in the remainder of the review. There is nothing mystical in his account of the pleasures of nature; those pleasures that he knew and described month by month following Howitt's calendar are entirely boyish. For May, for example, he wrote at length and spiritedly of hunting in a style unlike that of the rest of the paper. Speaking of ramrods and musketry, he showed his bent for puns: ". . . what a scatteration takes place. . . ." The "thousand ripening berries [that] invite the wanderer to prolong his walks" is his own addition to July, and so is the tribute to the

<hr>

[96] Bode, "A New College Manuscript of Thoreau's," pp. 315-16.

[97] Thoreau thought in terms of "climate" for the rest of his life. See "Barbarism and Civilization" (Sanborn, *Life,* p. 181) for his remarks on the moral influence of scenery; and see especially "Walking" (W, V, 222-23).

"stately oak" that suggests independence in his account of September. The month of November, often considered desolate, called forth a vigorous defense of the statement that " 'There is nothing melancholy in Nature.' " "To the eye of the dyspeptic," Thoreau wrote, "all is stamped with melancholy." "Behold dame Partlet sailing up the avenue with feathers all erect," he said, "urged by rude Boreas to an unwonted pace; or see how familiarly that Northwestern plays with the coat-flaps of the traveller, or sends him over stone walls and rail fences to fish his beaver out of a pond-hole. This is indeed melancholy." If nothing else, Thoreau's relish for the seasons is apparent, and with it a scorn for those who do not share it. "The so-called rich may *enjoy* all the honors that titled rank can confer," he concludes, having found his theme,

they may revel in luxury and disipation [sic], and count their wealth by thousands and tens of thousands,—but if they reject or are denied those gifts which Nature alone can bestow,—they are poor indeed. Is it poverty to breath [sic] the free air of heaven, to satisfy the cravings of hunger with the simple fruits of the soil, to quench the natural thirst from the running water of the brook, or to seek refreshment for the wearied limbs on the lap of our common mother Earth? Is it wealth to monopolise the confined air of a pleasure carriage, to wage continual war with Nature, to pore over the hues of a few homesick and stinted exotics to gratify the least intellectual of the 5 senses? Does it consist in the possession of one half this sunny little farm the Earth without enjoying a foot, or in the putting in jeopardy the health and spirits by swallowing the earliest green cucumber?

Thoreau's experience with nature has obviously been limited, and the language he often uses is as obviously platitudinous—Howitt being an excellent source book—but his feeling of opposition to those who gladly relinquished nature to the uncivilized man and the poor is strong and clear.[98]

Near the end of his college career, on June 22, 1837, in a theme on "The Mark or Standard by which a Nation is judged to be

[98] Howitt's influence on Thoreau may have been greater than one would willingly like to attribute to a writer of sentimental literary nature studies. Even this blend of poetry and natural description may have been a model for Thoreau. Probably he got the calendar idea for his later nature studies from Howitt, and Howitt's charts of flowers are similar to those that fill many pages of Thoreau's unpublished factbooks of natural phenomena. Thoreau continued to read Howitt, not for natural facts but for his account of the Australian gold diggings (J, VII, 491). His friend of his last years, Daniel Ricketson, was a correspondent of Howitt's, indeed a sentimental nature lover himself; and though he could interest Thoreau in Bewick's engravings of birds and in Gilpin, he could not renew his interest in Howitt.

Barbarous or Civilized. Barbarities of Civilized States," Thoreau, having mastered the ideas and language of Emerson's *Nature,* firmly renounced civilization and defended the Indian. The distinction between civilization and barbarism was now that of art and nature: "Civilization is the influence of Art, and not Nature, on Man." Art was artifice, the mingling of man's will with "the unchanged essences around him," and it made man "the creature of his own creations." Although he once said that man in primitive society is "buried in ignorance" and at the same time mocked the conformities of polite civilized society,[99] he was now able to reconcile his views, and place then on solid ground. For he had discovered the central idea of Emerson's theory of the progressive uses of nature. "The end of life," he said, "was education." The education that he now positively affirmed was not that of books, but of "Life"—the leading out of the powers of man which was the heart of Emerson's faculty theory and belief in the necessity of action. Education, Thoreau wrote, was "the bringing out or development of that which is in man, by contact with the Not-me,— that is by Life. . . ." Its end was not prudential, but spiritual: "to cherish and develop the religious sentiment,—continuously to remind man of his mysterious relation to God and Nature,—and to exalt him above the toil and drudgery of this matter-of-fact world. . . ." Such an education was best left to nature rather than art; civilization, he said, "is directly adverse to it." Indeed, the civilized man was immured in the city, debarred from natural influences. The "slave of Matter," he was less of a man than the Indian; his education was "learning," not "wisdom." "Learning is Art's creature," he wrote, "but it is not essential to the perfect man. . . ." He had in mind the scientist whose microscopic, atomistic studies he compared with the Indian's "liberal and enlarged views of things," that mountain prospect that embraced the whole landscape. For all his learning the scientist was not a man; he did not advance "the great objects for which life was given him. . . ." The Indian, however, "lives as a man . . . thinks as a man . . . dies as a man." This larger view of things was associated with the original view of the superior man. Following Emerson's doctrine of the moral influence of nature—"she accommodates herself to the soul of man"—Thoreau linked the enlarged view with the mountain prospect, which was to become so frequent and important in his

[99] Sanborn, *Life,* p. 166.

experience; and the mountain as an influence was, by association with Scotland, Switzerland, and Wales, linked with "Liberty." What he claimed for the Indian—the "practical poetry," the "perfect epic" of the natural harmony and fullness of his life—was also associated with the poet, and translated into spiritual seeing and communion. The Indian, he said, "looks far into futurity, wandering . . . familiarly through the Land of Spirits. . . ." And when he hears the thunder, "he is reminded of the Great Spirit,—it is *his* voice."[100] He experiences the sublime, not with dread but reverence. All those transcendental values that Thoreau had in piecemeal fashion already written about were incorporated in the Indian.[101] His prose was as certain as his definitions;[102] he had embraced and embodied the transcendental point of view. And he had already defined the "Indian wisdom" with which he permanently identified it in the "Natural History of Massachusetts."

On commencement day, August 16, 1837, Thoreau took part in a conference on "The Commercial Spirit," and all the transcendental values that he had acquired were directed against the "unmanly love of wealth" that sustained the commercial spirit. He recognized in the commercial spirit the signs of the times, even heralding it as an indication of freedom. "Man thinks faster and freer than ever before. He is more restless, because he is more independent than ever." But this freedom was corrupted by expediency; it served use, not enjoyment. As yet unable to make the same point from the vantage of his own experience, as in the *Week* or in *Walden,* he defined the difference by describing the universe from "an observatory among the stars. . . ." From this height, the "hammering and chipping in one quarter; baking and brewing, buying and selling,

---

[100] Sanborn, *Life,* pp. 180-83.

[101] He also spoke of the Indian as "our rude forefathers," suggesting a historical dimension especially significant in his writing from the time of the *Week.* The American past and nature were associated in this way.

[102] Where Thoreau was positive he was often ironic. Here he wrote: "The savage dies and is buried; he sleeps with his forefathers, and before many winters his dust returns to dust again, and his body is mingled with the elements. The civilized man can scarce sleep in his grave. Not even there are the weary at rest, nor do the wicked cease from troubling. What with the hammering of stone, and the grating of bolts, the worms themselves are well nigh deceived. Art rears his monument, Learning contributes his epitaph, and Interest adds the 'Carey fecit' as a salutary check upon the unearthly emotions which a perusal might otherwise excite." In the *Week* Thoreau wrote in a similar vein about tombstones. Appropriately his own gravestone is as unobtrusive as possible.

money-changing and speechmaking in another" would appear to be "abusing" the world. How trivial it would seem compared with "the profuse beauty of our orb. . . ." And where the observer "found one man to admire with him his fair dwelling-place, the ninety and nine would be scraping together a little of the gilded dust upon its surface. . . ." Instead of this enslavement to matter, Thoreau proposed the "manly and independent" life that permitted the cultivation of the moral affections, and that forsook work to the end of acquisition for leisure to the end of joy. He proposed a reversal of the reigning values: he asked that the bases of life be changed so that man might have the leisure to loaf and invite his soul. "This curious world which we inhabit," he said, "is more wonderful than it is convenient, more beautiful than it is useful; it is more to be admired and enjoyed than used." This being the case, "the order of things should be somewhat reversed; the seventh day should be man's day of toil, wherein to earn his living by the sweat of his brow; and the other six his Sabbath of the affections and the soul,—in which to range this widespread garden, and drink in the soft influences and sublime revelations of Nature. . . ." [103]

Here, indeed, was a general proposal for his own life, one that he fulfilled almost to the letter in the *Week* and in *Walden*. It was a proposal, too, requiring the hero's ardor and courage, for the hero was Whitman's "heroic person," one who "walks at his ease through and out of that custom or precedent or authority that suits him not. . . ." [104] If he was not in name the geographical discoverer he praised in a sophomore theme, the anxieties and delights were to be his own. "He has the prejudices of the whole world to combat," he wrote; trials, ridicule, and contempt await him. But, as he said of Columbus, "What must have been his reflections on finding himself the discoverer of a New World! Did he ever regret his perseverance? . . . Nay,—did not rather a sense of what he had endured serve to heighten the enjoyment of his success?" [105]

---

[103] W, VI, 8-10. Thoreau used the same phrase, "slave of matter," in "Barbarism and Civilization" (Sanborn, *Life*, p. 180). His polar phrase, "Lord of Creation," with which he closed his commencement piece, had been used before in his review of Howitt. See Glick, "Three New Early Manuscripts by Thoreau," p. 66.

[104] Preface to 1855 edition of *Leaves of Grass*.

[105] "The Anxieties and Delights of a Discoverer," Sanborn, *Life*, pp. 68-69. His example was Columbus because he had been reading Irving's histories. See Cameron, *Emerson The Essayist*, II, 192. By 1834 he had begun his lifelong reading in the narratives of discovery.

Chapter II

THE BEGINNING OF VICTORY

Ἀρχὴ γὰρ ὄντως τοῦ νικᾶν τὸ θαρρεῖν.
(Verily, to be brave is the beginning of victory.)

—Thoreau, *Journal*, 1839

Men claim for the ideal an actual existence also, but do not often expand the actual into the ideal.

—Thoreau, *Journal*, 1837

I

When Thoreau wrote Henry Vose, his "fellow soldier [in the] campaign of 37," on October 13, 1837, he was back in Concord "vegetating." He told Vose that he had been idle since commencement. Vose, however, had found a teaching position in Butternuts, New York, where Thoreau hoped that the natives were "less absorbed in the pursuit of gain than the good clever homespun and respectable people of New England." Other members of his class had begun the study of law and divinity, and for all the banter of his letter Thoreau was as eager to get in the "swim." [1] Though he did not tell Vose, he had taught in the town school for two weeks in September, and had resigned because of his refusal to flog the students. Schoolteacher, how-

[1] Berg Collection.

ever, he would become, like his sister Helen and his brother John; and from June, 1838, to March, 1841, he carried on the Academy in Concord with his brother. It was his first and last regular employment, giving Thoreau an interval of assurance in which to muster his forces and chart his course. He had, of course, a desire for independence; teaching school was never a vocation for him, only a stopgap, a job. But the decision for independence, and the vocation that would embody it, came gradually and hard. Not only had he returned home in a year of depression, but there were the sacrifices of his family to be repaid—repaid momentarily, perhaps, by the intellectual respectability of keeping school, for his mother undoubtedly had high aspirations for her college-educated son. And there was the pencil business, far from well established, which remained in its way a lifelong employment, something of a moral duty to a deeply affectionate son whose offices to the family would have satisfied every precept for that relation that he would soon read in the stern lawgivers of the East. The family business, which Thoreau compared with the worldly enslavement of Apollo by King Admetus,[2] was at least something to which Apollo could always return, and which for the last decade of his life was his economic mainstay.

If his family had heard his commencement piece with those brave words about the Sabbath of the soul, they had still to be educated to recognize and respect Thoreau's determination for independence. Little did they know that they harbored a poet, or that their Henry had resolved to be a twice-born man, or that, as he confided to Mrs. Lucy Brown, he was unfit for "the world's ends"—that serve Admetus as he would, "I shall hold the nobler part at least out of service." [3] High-principled as Thoreau's family was, they were no less good New Englanders than Hawthorne's or Longfellow's family, and writing, as Hawthorne once said, was not generally considered an American vocation. Schoolteaching, therefore, put a buffer between Thoreau and the expectations of his family; his three years at the Academy allowed him the leisure to find himself and to continue his literary apprenticeship: to find a teacher in Emerson, to hear Alcott converse, to see his "first printed paper of consequence" in the first issue of *The Dial*, to

---

[2] W, VI, 39.

[3] W, VI, 39.

appropriate at last the label "transcendental." [4] Busy as he was with the routine of the school, pleasantly boyish and healthily joyous, visited by his college friends, helpful in the village, and already a lecturer at the Lyceum—and as in his earliest letters, without the weight of spiritual burdens—how was his family to know he felt that "the life of every man is a profound secret" and that from his attic room, from his "perspective window," his "upper empire," Thoreau was intent on seeing all things "in their true relations?" [5] There was probably some tension. On October 27, 1837, Thoreau had written his sister Helen, whose teaching had helped finance him at Harvard, "You know we have hardly done our own deeds, thought our own thoughts, or lived our own lives hitherto. For a man to act himself, he must be perfectly free. . . ." [6] One understands, then, why Thoreau preferred a school in the West, why he journeyed to Maine to find one in the spring of 1838, why, when he left the Academy in 1841, he was looking for a farm, and why, on the most expedient level, he went to Walden. And one can see, perhaps, the reason for the sudden concern with solitude that begins his *Journals*.

When he wrote Vose he did not have a vocation. On October 22, 1837, he did. The *Journals* began; their first entry: " 'What are you doing now?' he asked. 'Do you keep a journal?' " The questioner, presumably, was Emerson, and the question—could Emerson have asked a better one? Journal keeping, of course, was an inveterate New England habit, almost its genre, and Thoreau had already begun to store his reading by 1836. He had even written a theme on "Shall We Keep Journals?" in which he described journal keeping as a kind of moral and intellectual banking of one's spontaneous thoughts. [7] But coming from Emerson, the idea of a journal had an added appeal: the "American scholar" had proffered it, and with it invited Thoreau to a new life. "So I make my first entry today," Thoreau wrote, signing the bond of his apprenticeship. His new vocation was self-culture, "to yield that peculiar fruit which each man was created to bear. . . ." [8]

By June, 1838, when he began teaching school, Thoreau's ex-

---

[4] J, VIII, 66; W, VI, 32.

[5] J, I, 36, 80.

[6] W, VI, 12.

[7] Sanborn, *Life*, pp. 73-74.

[8] J, I, 3; C, I, 115.

ternal relationships seemed to be established. Actually, however, he was slowly discovering the extent of his relations. What he later wrote in *Walden* described the inner experience of these early years of bouyancy and confidence: "not till we have lost the world, do we begin to find ourselves, and realize where we are and the infinite extent of our relations." [9] The *Journals* of this period reveal the ecstatic pains of that discovery. For when he returned to Concord from Cambridge, he became aware of more than the need for a vocation. Even nature was not yet his primary concern: instead, the self and the infinite were. His problem, as he called it in 1840, was the "social condition of genius"—to establish those relationships that would make possible and bearable one's "reverence for the mystery of the universe." [10] His early *Journals,* therefore, though rather literary (and the writing often a continuation of his college exercises), are almost exclusively devoted to themes that he felt were peculiarly his own: the bravery of virtue, solitude, society, friendship, and sound and silence [11]—themes that he attempted to bring together in his first extended compositions, the essay on "Society" and *The Service.*

That Thoreau meant what he said in his commencement piece and had no intention of compromising was apparent in the *Journals* and the miscellaneous writing of these early years. His militancy was spiritual; one feels his attempt to rally his forces for the service of some high end, to surmount difficulties, to measure his faith by the ardor of striving—he sought the infinite. Not yet the devoted student of nature, he was the seeker of another world. Saunterer ("*Sainte-Terrer,* a Holy-Lander") already described him, though he was hardly as defensive as he would be in "Walking" and could now speak of himself as "an open sole." [12] The otherworldly strain was prominent, always thereafter to give his utterance on actual life its unrelenting edge; for his universe, which soon took shape in terms of sound and silence and light and dark, had the absolute polarity of Hawthorne's temporal and spiritual or Melville's Chronometricals and Horologicals—and the youthful Thoreau was as much an artist of the beautiful as he was a Pierre. In Henry James's words, he was seeking something upon which to expend

---

[9] W, II, 190.

[10] J, I, 117.

[11] Thoreau listed the titles of the essays he wrote in these *Journals* in the *Index Rerum.* See Sanborn, *Life,* p. 519.

[12] J, I, 60.

himself; the dominant quality of his work, as of his life, is already
that of being on the spiritual stretch.

The infinite he sought, however, he found within himself, in his
own ecstatic experiences and radiant aspirations, in the dilation of
physical health as well as in the intimation of his genius. He felt
within himself something to be preserved from the world, that
genius, he said, by which "he is," rather than the talent, the instru-
mentality by which "he lives." [13] These different selves, this genius
and talent, this head and feet, this soul and body, had to be har-
monized; the tension of his life was in their resolution. "The perfect
man," he wrote, "has both genius and talent. . . . The body is the
first proselyte the Soul makes. Our life is but the Soul made known
by its fruits, the body. The whole duty of man may be expressed
in one line,—Make to yourself a perfect body." [14] Make to yourself, he might have said, a perfect life. For, written large, the
resolution of the selves was achieved by finding a way—a vocation—that would accommodate the self and society. The real self
and the actual self were externalized by the individual and society,
by being and doing—as Whitman would do, for example, in section
4 of "Song of Myself." There his social or actual self was distinguished from the "Me myself," the real self that "idle, unitary,
/Looks down" on "the pulling and hauling," "Both in and out of
the game and watching and wondering at it." For Thoreau, too,
there was this division, and a battle for unity that was the chronicle
of his spiritual life.

From the very beginning of his *Journals,* Thoreau's thought took
on the division of self and society, of other world and actual world.
In 1838, for example, he wrote an essay on sound and silence and
delivered a lecture on society. One side of his work—the most
prominent, at the start at least—was devoted to his personal aspirations, to virtue, bravery, purity, those qualities by which he measured his superiority and which he blazoned in *The Service.* The
other was devoted to society. Between them he began to work out
the relationships that were the test of his life: friendship, nature,
vocation. His immediate practical concern, however, was writing,
for by it he thought he could resolve the polarities that Transcendentalism had given him. He began as a poet, not so much because
his genius ran that way but because his private reading had given

---

[13] J, I, 119. Unlike Emerson, Thoreau was not seeking power, but joy.
[14] J, I, 119, 147.

him a start, and mostly because the calling of the poet was worthy
of his aspirations. From Goethe, with whom he began his tutelage
in the *Journal*, he copied the description of Tasso:

> His eye hardly rests upon the earth;
> His ear hears the one-clang of nature;
> What history records,—what life gives,—
> Directly and gladly his genius takes it up:
> His mind collects the widely dispersed,
> And his feeling animates the inanimate.
> Often he ennobles what appeared to us common,
> And the prized is as nothing to him.
> In his own magic circle wanders
> The wonderful man, and draws us
> With him to wander, and take part in it:
> He seems to draw near to us, and remains afar from us:
> He seems to be looking at us, and spirits, forsooth,
> Appear to him strangely in our places.[15]

The poet here is inviolable, the wonderful man living in his own
magic circle; and yet he is the servant of men, doing for them the
highest work, that of genius. The attraction of the vocation of poet
was in the fact that his self-culture, like the "American scholar's"
dedication to truth, was a public good. There was, nevertheless,
enough distance from society to provoke its misunderstanding—
the self-determined utility of the poet had to be proven useful,
and though the poet was sure of his vocation he was never sure
that society was. Thus, Emerson had written in "The Apology":

> Think me not unkind and rude
> That I walk alone in grove and glen;
> I go to the god of the wood
> To fetch his word to men.

And Thoreau, too, interrupting his notes on writing, confessed his
awareness of his neighbors' eyes, that questioning of what he was
about that forced him to shape an image of himself and that, as
time moved on and the demonstrable vocation was postponed, gave
him a sense of personal crisis. He not only felt those inspirational
crises that are the abysmal darkness of the poet's calling—the
personal failure that he lamented as early as 1840 in "The Poet's
Delay"—he felt the public judgment on his "loitering." In 1842,
when as handy man at Emerson's he began to see the end of his
apprenticeship, he wrote: "I must confess I have felt mean enough

---

[15] J, I, 4-5.

when asked how I was to act on society, what errand I had to mankind. Undoubtedly I did not feel mean without a reason, and yet my loitering is not without defense." But still he did not propose going back to schoolteaching, nor did any other "vocation" come to mind as a solution. Instead he wrote out a declaration of faith: "I would fain communicate the wealth of my life to men, would really give them what is most precious in my gift. I would secrete pearls with the shellfish and lay up honey with the bees for them. I will sift the sunbeams for the public good. I know no riches I would keep back. I have no private good, unless it be my peculiar ability to serve the public. . . . I inclose and foster the pearl till it is grown. I wish to communicate those parts of my life which I would gladly live again myself." He would give "the only individual property," the self; he would bestow all. But he would not choose a lesser vocation. He wanted to be "a good citizen of the world" in the greatest sense, and if his gift was not used by society he preferred to keep it unimpaired.[16]

Cherishing the ideal of the poet then, the problem of his relations became especially important to him. Everything he had gleaned in his college reading had resolved fate into character, and from Emerson he had sensed the adventure of making a new world through himself. If, as Emerson proclaimed, we could conform things to the ideas in our minds, then man could make his own relations. Beginning with this faith in subjective idealism, Thoreau could write in "The Inward Morning,"

> Packed in my mind lie all the clothes
> Which outward nature wears. . . .

The corollary of this faith, however, like that of inspiration which made it possible, was that one was responsible for his relations, that not an opaque or adamant world, but the very self itself was the cause of failure.[17] And if, as Thoreau had been reading in Sir Thomas Browne, man is a microcosm and the self is a world, then a man's world (as Whitman, too, declared) *is* his relations.

Typical of aspiring youth, Thoreau began with the self, and unconditionally wrote out the absolute laws of his relations to friends, society, and employment. These prescriptions remained fixed; they were the infinite he sought—the imaginings to which he would

---

[16] J, I, 350-51.

[17] See Thoreau's college essay on "Fate," Sanborn, *Life*, pp. 175-77; J, I, 25.

conform his life, the promptings of his real self to which he submitted his actual self. His lofty goal was represented by his favorite
lines of Samuel Daniel—"Unless above himself he can/Erect
himself, how poor a thing is man!"—lines which set the nature of
his striving and which have their echo in his

> Great God, I ask thee for no meaner pelf
> Than that I may not disappoint myself,
> That in my action I may soar as high,
> As I can now discern with this clear eye.
> . . . .
> That my weak hand may equal my firm faith
> And my life practice more than my tongue saith;
> . . . .[18]

This self-transcendence, this perfectionism, brought with it the
many laments, the brooding over failure and unworthiness, with
which the *Journals,* if not his published writing, were stored.
Melancholy is but the reflex and index of aspiration; ecstasy, of
necessity, is followed by loss. And this is the rhythm of the *Journals.*
Thoreau is the "parcel of vain strivings tied/By a chance bond
together." [19] But if his melancholy was there, it was deeper and
more infrequent than in most romantics; he took no joy in it, it was
not a romantic indulgence, but a disease, and it drove the spiritual
soldier to his post. This was the sign of that firmness of character
which permitted Paul Elmer More to approve of Thoreau. "To
regret deeply," Thoreau wrote in 1839, "is to live afresh." [20] In a
letter to Isaiah T. Williams in 1842 Thoreau cited Byron's "No
more, no more! Oh never more on me/The freshness of the heart
can fall like dew" as an example of the universal elegy, "the effect
of time on our youthful feelings." But here, and in the whole effort
of his life, he repudiated the necessity of that lapse. "It would be
well if we could add new years to our lives as innocently as the
fish adds new layers to its shell—no less beautiful than the old,"
he wrote in the preaching strain that he began to use in speaking
of his personal condition and which became more intense as his
battle wore on and as his disciples increased. "And I believe we
may if we will replace the vigor and elasticity of youth [he was
only twenty-four!] with faithfulness in later years." [21]

[18] *The Dial,* III (July, 1842), 79-80.
[19] *The Dial,* II (July, 1841), 81.
[20] J, I, 95. See also J, I, 146.
[21] Berg Collection.

Thoreau never lived so harmoniously with himself or with nature as in the few years after leaving college and in the interval at Walden Pond. The remainder of his life had its own quiet desperation; he never solved the equation of his life in the terms in which he cast it in these apprentice years. He did not bring the world to heel, nor get it, in the violent image of his later years, "by the nape of the neck, and [hold] it under in the tide of its own events, till it was drowned, and then . . . let it go down-stream like a dead dog." [22] The polarities of his thought did not narrow but widened, and the precarious harmony of his communion with nature was never restored. But his faithfulness remained constant; indeed, faithfulness became the final assurance of an aspiration he could never achieve, ultimately becoming an end in itself, and that in which he invested the health and ardor of more than a decade of his life. His faithfulness to the transcendental conception of nature and man, his determination to see it proved by his own increasingly detailed investigations, explain, perhaps, why he never went the way of Melville.[23] The measure of his faithfulness is in the discrepancy of his *Journals* and his published work. For while the bulk of his later *Journals* records a terrible spiritual struggle, the published work of the same period affirms his faith, and more indomitably as he moved from *Walden* to "Walking." Where Melville turned on the universe Thoreau turned on himself, demanding anew the purity of his youth and those qualities of the recruit he had postulated for his life.

II

Unemployed in October, 1837, Thoreau nevertheless was seriously reading in Anglo-Saxon and sixteenth- and seventeenth-century English poetry, having taken up again those private studies he had begun in college and which now had the more immediate use of training the poet.[24] Shortly he was reading the *Religio Medici* of Sir Thomas Browne, perhaps for the style which seems to have prompted the conceits of *The Service* but certainly, as his copious extracts indicate, for the light it shed on his own essential

---

[22] W, VI, 231.

[23] Apocryphal as it may be, one can see why on his deathbed Thoreau answered the question, "Henry, have you made your peace with God?" with "I've never quarreled with Him."

[24] MA 594.

problems. How was this twenty-year-old aspirant to face the universe? What were his infinite relations? Nature, at this time, was only a general conception filled with an emotional feeling of tender sustenance.[25] Thoreau practiced writing by describing natural facts, but his treatment was generally literary. Although John, Sophia, and Henry began a notebook on nature lore and birds in 1837, it was mostly the work of his brother and sister. Henry seemed more intent on his reading and writing, and on collecting thoughts for his private use. His walks had not yet become the ritual of his life, his tryst with nature. From poems like George Herbert's "Man," from Cudworth and others of the Cambridge Platonist persuasion, he fortified the lesson of *Nature*, learning the transcendental view of providence, that nature is the benevolent servant of man. From Sir Thomas Browne he copied out: "The world was made to be inhabited by beasts, but studied and contemplated by man . . . those highly magnify him [God], whose judicious inquiry into his acts, and deliberate research into his creatures, return the duty of a devout and learned admiration." [26] This was not yet Thoreau's practice, only his attitude toward nature; he did not see the need, apparently, to copy out passages that were more specifically useful, those on the symbolic (hieroglyphical) character of nature, but perhaps the chapter on "Language" in *Nature* had already been assimilated by him. He preferred the general sentiment that the study of nature is truly devotional: at this time he was interested in perspectives.

And what was apparently more exciting to him was the transference of the study of nature to man. He was fascinated in Browne and Cudworth and Raleigh with the conception of the microcosm. "There is no man alone," Browne wrote, "because every man is a Microcosm, and carries the whole World about him. . . . whilst I study to find how I am a Microcosm, or little World, I find myself something more than the great. There is surely a piece of Divinity in us. . . . Nature tells me I am the Image of God, as well as Scripture: he that understands not thus much,

---

[25] This passage from the *Veeshnoo Sarma* (*The Dial*, III [July, 1842], 85) expressed the general transcendental faith: "Man should not be over-anxious for a subsistence, for it is provided by the Creator. The infant no sooner droppeth from the womb, than the breasts of the mother begin to stream." In a letter of the same year Thoreau defended his own vocation of leisure: "Let us trust that we shall be fed as the sparrows are" (Berg Collection).

[26] All quotations from Sir Thomas Browne, unless specified, are from MA 594.

hath not his introduction or first lesson, and is yet to begin the Alphabet of man." [27] Thoreau was interested in nature only as it was the alphabet of man. He was never to forget the lines on "the cosmography of myself" that he appropriated from Browne; the conclusion of *Walden,* indeed his whole work, is an elaborate conceit on the exploration of the self, and one sees already that Thoreau's entire effort in studying nature was, like the correspondential method he employed, to be to the end of translating nature into human terms, to make fact flower into truth. "We carry with us," Thoreau noted in Browne, "the wonders we seek without us. There is all Africa and her prodigies in us. We are that bold and adventurous piece of nature, which he that studies wisely learns in a compendium, what others labor at in a divided piece and endless volume." Thoreau's relation to nature, therefore, was to be self-reflexive; he never studied nature apart from the self. This he could have learned as well from Emerson—and did; but the language of Sir Thomas Browne had the added attraction of putting this quest in the more inspiriting images of exploration and discovery to which Thoreau was personally more responsive. "What does Africa,—what does the West stand for?" he asked in *Walden.* "Is not our own interior white on the chart?" And in the *Week* he concluded a passage on the spiritual symbolism of nature: "It is easier to discover another such a new world as Columbus did, than to go within one fold of this which we appear to know so well. . . ." [28] The exploration of the self was the substantial lesson he learned from Browne, an exploration he almost took literally, living outwardly as well as inwardly the brave and energetic life of the discoverer. "Let us," he wrote in 1840, "migrate interiorly without intermission, and pitch our tent each day nearer the western horizon." [29]

Thoreau also selected from the *Religio Medici* those passages which appealed to his high demands for the other fundamental relationship of his life: friendship. Or perhaps one should say that in Browne he found a conception of friendship lofty enough to be worthy of him. It is significant that the "wonders in true affection" that Browne extolled in behalf of friendship should be followed in Thoreau's notebook by Browne's equally vigorous comments on

[27] *Religio Medici,* Everyman's Library, pp. 82-83.

[28] W, II, 353; W, I, 409.

[29] J, I, 131.

physical marriage. "I could be content," Browne said, "that we might procreate like trees, without conjunction, or that there were any way to perpetuate the world without this trivial and vulgar way of coition. It is the foolishest act a wise man commits in all his life. . . ." Though much has been made of Thoreau's love affair with Ellen Sewall—even that because of its failure he took nature for his bride—one suspects that his attitude toward marriage was similar to Browne's. His letters, chiefly to older married women like Mrs. Lucy Jackson Brown and Lidian Emerson, are more than conventionally spiritual, and one gathers from Lidian's letters on Thoreau's chivalry that the spirit of the Middle Ages did more than fire his desire for crusades. Love, for Thoreau, was always contrasted with or subsumed in friendship, as, for example, in the essay he sent to Harrison Blake which ended with those high sentiments on chastity and sensuality and in which Thoreau wrote that "the intercourse of the sexes, I have dreamed, is incredibly beautiful, too fair to be remembered." The marriage he had in mind, however, was likened to an "illumination." "In all perception of the truth there is a divine ecstasy," he wrote, "an inexpressible delirium of joy, as when a youth embraces his betrothed virgin. The ultimate delights of a true marriage are one with this." [30] Perhaps it is not fair to say of Thoreau, in Henry Adams' words, that he used love for sentiment and not for force. His attitude toward women is too much like that of Melville, Hawthorne, and Twain to gainsay Adams' profound distinction; he idealized purity, and though in everything else he demanded the participation of the senses and early wrote that "I never feel that I am inspired unless my body is also," [31] he conceived of love without this physical agency. "Friendship is more in the breast," he wrote in a manuscript draft of his essay; "Love descends to the organs of generation." [32] Friendship was a relation of sympathy for him, more supersubtle than that of contact or intimacy, and it is interesting that he chose the images of sight rather than of sound to describe it. His earliest imagery of the relationship in the poem on "Friendship" is similar in meaning:

> Two sturdy oaks I mean, which side by side
> Withstand the winter's storm,

---

[30] W, VI, 198, 209, 208.

[31] J, I, 147.

[32] HM 13196.

> And, spite of wind and tide,
>   Grow up the meadow's pride,
>   For both are strong.
>
> Above they barely touch, but, undermined
>   Down to their deepest source,
>   Admiring you shall find
>   Their roots are intertwined
>   Insep'rably.[33]

Friendship, here, is a radical identity in God; like man and nature at the base of the transcendental triangle, the apex of the relation is God. Thoreau conveys this meaning not only with "deepest source" and "roots," and the polarity of above and below, but with the best word in the poem, the pun, "undermined." The relation is not of the mind, is not conscious act, nor in need of verbal professions and bonds. It is unconscious or "under mind" in the sense that Thoreau employed when he wrote that "the unconsciousness of man is the consciousness of God, the end of the world." [34] As he told Blake, "In this relation we deal with one whom we respect more religiously even than we respect our better selves, and we shall necessarily conduct as in the presence of God." [35] In the manuscript he wrote: "Lovers are the children of Nature; Friends the children of God." [36] Though in no need of, indeed destroyed by, those civilities that Emerson called "the prostitution of the name of friendship," [37] the relationship was still one of service; to the end of force, forwarding the soul, it had nothing in it of idolatry or sentiment. Unrealizable as this relationship proved to be and therefore darkening Thoreau's life with the oppression of loss, this vision of the harmony of aspiring spirits and kindred in destiny, this selfless furtherance of one by another, was perhaps the summit of transcendental thought on the possibilities of man. Emerson spoke of it as "an absolute running of two souls into one"; [38] Thoreau, fresh from his reading of the metaphysical poets, wrote,

> While one and one make two,
>   And two are one;

---

[33] J, I, 42-43.
[34] J, I, 119.
[35] W, VI, 205.
[36] HM 13196.
[37] C, II, 205.
[38] C, II, 207.

and in the poem on "Love" in 1839, adding the meanings of the
music of the spheres he had found in Sir Thomas Browne, he
wrote:

> We two that planets erst had been
> Are now a double star,
> And in the heavens may be seen,
> Where that we fixèd are.
>
> Yet, whirled with subtle power along,
> Into new space we enter,
> And evermore with spheral song
> Revolve about one center.[39]

Friendship was important because it not only served the aspiring
soul but also tended to socialize the moral individualism of the
transcendentalist. One sees this best perhaps in Whitman. But the
inordinate demands made on friendship by Melville as well as by
Emerson, Margaret Fuller, and Thoreau show that the need for
this relationship was not merely an individual one. As de Tocqueville knew, it was a sign of the times, of the fact that democratic
individualism had broken the chain of humanity. Friendship, therefore, like "adhesiveness" but without the special connotations Whitman gave this phrenological word, was for Thoreau a way of
distinguishing sexual and social love. It was an attempt to recon-
struct society, to form new bonds of brotherhood, not in terms of
property or class but in terms of virtue and personality—"a relation
of perfect equality." [40] "Love is complementary, or for completeness," Thoreau wrote, "Friendship is equal and additive, or for
society. . . ." [41] One finds this new relationship more dramatically
expressed, perhaps, in Natty Bumppo's philosophy of "gifts" and
in the handclasp that binds Natty and Chingachgook at the end
of *The Last of The Mohicans* (1826); and the same brotherhood,
intensified again by the difference in colors, is also found in Ishmael
and Queequeg and in Huck Finn and Nigger Jim. Thoreau gave
us an example equally powerful—and it is the only example in
his long discourse on friendship in the *Week*—that of Wawatam
and the fur trader Alexander Henry, a relation of loyalties above
those of conventional society that pointed to a higher society and

[39] J, I, 72. See also J, I, 39. In the *Week* he wrote: "Friends do not live
in harmony merely . . . but in melody" (W, I, 283).

[40] W, I, 287.

[41] HM 13196.

that, like the others, seems to have flourished best in the "wilderness." [42] All these examples bespeak a new relationship consonant with democracy and nature, and are part of a submerged theme which runs its course in American life, occasionally appearing at the surface in Brook Farms and Fruitlands and in versions of the creative or personal society of thinkers like the early Van Wyck Brooks.

Emerson as well as Thoreau spoke of friendship as society, as the basis of the social organization. "Society," Emerson wrote, "is the finding of this soul [Over-Soul] by individuals in each other." [43] And Thoreau, in notes specifically written on society and reform, interjected: "Even friendship—the society of two, which is but laying the corner-stone of the State, and where the rudiments of the nation may be seen & its laws prophesied, is not yet in the experience of men." [44] Though he always tended to think of friendship as a society of two, Thoreau said that it was not exclusive, that "though its foundations are private, it is in effect, a public affair and a public advantage, and the Friend, more than the father of a family, deserves well of the State." [45] What Thoreau had in mind was the fact that friendship is usually dictated to by established class and social relations; that society itself determines it, not, as he would have it, friendship following laws of its own, spiritual ones, and thereby providing a leaven for existing social practice.

Social considerations aside, Thoreau personally needed a relation of sympathy, needed to share the life of striving. As a relation of souls, a loyalty to virtue, such a friendship was above compromise. It was this purer relation, the miseries of whose spiritual affections Sir Thomas Browne described, that appealed to him. For such a relation demanded a brave life and nurtured the seeds of virtue; it could only exist when the true object was the soul, that self which friendship, like nature, could reveal. If such a relationship appealed to Thoreau because of an ingrained horror of impurity and contamination, it also appealed to him because it was rare. The passages that Thoreau chose to copy out emphasized the necessity

---

[42] W, I, 291-92. *Alexander Henry's Travels and Adventures in the Years 1760-1776*, ed. by Milo M. Quaife, Chicago, 1921, pp. 154-55.

[43] C, II, 380n.

[44] Houghton. MS AM 278.5.

[45] W, I, 294.

of virtue, the rarity, and the superiority of friendship. "This noble affection," Browne wrote, "falls not on vulgar and common constitutions, but on such as are marked for virtue." His "Heroick examples," were Damon and Pythias, Achilles and Patroclus; [46] and Thoreau recalled the former when he wrote, "why should we not put to shame those old reserved worthies by a community of such?" and the latter when he read to Alek Therien, the woodchopper, Achilles' reproof of Patroclus on his sad countenance.[47]

Thoreau's introduction to the metaphysics of sound, which as early as 1838 had provided the language of his universe and his deepest experiences, also came from the *Religio Medici*. Here he copied out the passage on the relation of music and beauty—the Platonic notion that music is harmony which he later found applied to the education of the soul in Plutarch's *Morals*.[48]

For there is [a] music wherever there is a harmony, order, or proportion; and thus far we may maintain the music of the spheres; for those well-ordered motions, and regular paces, though they give no sound unto the ear, yet to the understanding they strike a note most full of harmony. . . .

All this, and more, Thoreau wrote out here, and again in 1843, when he added De Quincey's remarks: "I do not recollect more than one thing said adequately on the subject of music in all literature: it is a passage in the Religio Medici of Sir T. Browne, and, though chiefly remarkable for its sublimity, has also a philosophic value, inasmuch as it points to the true theory of musical effects." [49] This famous passage from Browne continued:

Whosoever is harmonically composed delights in harmony; which makes me much distrust the symmetry of those heads which declaim against all Church-Musick. For my self, not only from my obedience, but my particular Genius, I do embrace it: for even that vulgar and Tavern-Musick, which makes one man merry, another mad, strikes in me a deep fit of devotion, and a profound contemplation of the First Composer. [In the notes on sound in the Houghton manuscripts, Thoreau wrote that he wanted to hear "the Great Composer."] There is something in it of Divinity more than the ear discovers; it is an Hieroglyphical and shadowed lesson of the whole World, and creatures of God; such a melody to the ear, as the whole World, well understood, would afford the understanding. In brief, it is a sensible fit of that harmony which

[46] *Religio Medici*, p. 73.

[47] J, I, 113, 366.

[48] J, I, 105.

[49] Houghton. MS AM 278.5.

intellectually sounds in the ears of God. I will not say, with Plato, the soul is an harmony, but harmonical, and hath its nearest sympathy with Musick: thus, some, whose temper of body agrees, and humours the constitution of their souls, are born Poets. . . .[50]

Thoreau's copy of this passage also included the following, usually omitted, lines: "It unties the ligaments of my frame, takes me to pieces, dilates me out of myself, and by degrees resolves me into heaven"—lines that prefigure Thoreau's own ecstasy, and recall Whitman's response to sound, beautifully rendered in Browne's imagery in section 26 of "Song of Myself." This passage was undoubtedly of great significance to Thoreau, and he later thought it among the best on music, equaled only by a line of Richter, and the following from Jamblichus' account of Pythagoras: "Pythagoras did not procure for himself a thing of this kind through instruments or the voice, but employing a certain ineffable divinity, and which it is difficult to apprehend, he extended his ears and fixed his intellect on the sublime symphonies of the world, he alone hearing and understanding, as it appears, the universal harmony and consonance of the spheres, and the stars that are moved through them, and which produce a fuller and more intense melody than anything effected by mortal sound."[51] This intellectual music of the spheres, the soundless sound of divinity, became "Silence" for Thoreau, the word he used instead of the Over-Soul and which also described his mystical union with it.

Almost with the inception of his *Journals,* Thoreau began to explore the nature of sound. "Nature makes no noise," he wrote in the autumn of 1837; "The howling storm, the rustling leaf, the pattering rain are no disturbance, there is an essential and unexplored harmony in them. Why is it that thought flows with so deep and sparkling a current when the sound of music stikes the ear? When I would muse I complain not of a rattling tune on the piano —a Battle of Prague even—if it be harmony, but an irregular, discordant drumming is intolerable."[52] His earliest distinction was between harmony and discord, the joy of the universe and the wailings of man. "Some sounds," he noted in 1838, "seem to reverberate along the plain, and then settle to earth again like dust;

---

[50] *Religio Medici,* pp. 79-80.

[51] Houghton. MS AM 278.5. Pythagoras was said to have been fathered by Apollo, with whom Thoreau also identified himself.

[52] J, I, 12.

such are Noise, Discord, Jargon. But such only as spring heaven-ward, and I may catch from steeples and hilltops in their upward course, which are the more refined parts of the former, are the true sphere music,—pure, unmixed music,—in which no wail mingles." [53] Already, in the plain and the hilltop, in the dust and the "refined," he had begun to give the dimensions of his universe; and already responsive to the cricket (which he first appreciated in Goethe's *Italiänische Reise*), to Sabbath bells and evening sounds, he felt that "we tread on Olympus and participate in the councils of the gods." [54] Even his imagery for "grace" was appropriately musical: "The human soul is a silent harp in God's quire, whose strings need only to be swept by the divine breath to chime in with the harmonies of creation." [55] All of these meanings, and the first of many on spring-in-winter, were a part of his thought by April, 1838, when in a poem, "The Bluebirds," he used the return of the birds to symbolize his mystical experience. Similar to Emerson's passage on the transparent eyeball is

> I dreamed that I was a waking thought,
> A something I hardly knew,
> Not a solid piece, nor an empty nought,
> But a drop of morning dew.

The experience, however, was one of sound, not light, and of hill and plain:

> I felt that the heavens were all around,
> And the earth was all below,
> As when in the ears there rushes a sound
> Which thrills you from top to toe.[56]

In another poem of the same time, "The Cliffs & Springs," he recorded the experience of the veery's song:

> Fondly to nestle me in that sweet melody,
> And own a kindred soul, speaking to me
> From out the depths of universal being.

How

> No longer time or place, nor faintest trace
> Of earth, the landscape's shimmer is my only space,
> Sole remnant of a world.

---

[53] J, I, 53.

[54] J, I, 9-10, 54, 55, 57.

[55] J, I, 53.

[56] J, I, 43-46.

And how, the song done,

> . . . I walk once more confounded a denizen of earth.[57]

In their dimensions and content, in the sense of ascent and
ecstasy and descent and loss, these early poems reveal the fundamental pattern of Thoreau's experience. They omit one meaning,
however, that was always implied in the imagery of sound—bravery
or moral heroism. Sound, as Thoreau developed its significance
in *The Service*, inevitably became the herald of virtue. "Some
times," he wrote in 1838, "I hear the veery's silver clarion, or the
brazen note of the impatient jay, or in secluded woods the chickadee
doles out her scanty notes, which sing the praise of heroes, and
set forth the loveliness of virtue evermore." [58] Within the whole
complex of meanings that sound afforded him, Thoreau found a
place for the kind of heroism to which he now aspired. "What a
hero one can be without moving a finger!" he wrote. "The world
is not a field worthy of us, nor can we be satisfied with the plains
of Troy. A glorious strife seems waging within us, yet so noiselessly
that we but just catch the sound of the clarion ringing of victory,
borne to us on the breeze. There are in each the seeds of a heroic
ardor, which need only to be stirred in with the *soil where they
lie,* by an inspired voice or pen, to bear fruit of a divine flavor." [59]
Here, and in "The Peal of the Bells," there was the essential conceit
of *The Service:*

> When the echo has reached me in this lone vale,
> I am straightway a hero in coat of mail,
> I tug at my belt and I march at my post,
> And feel myself more than a match for a host.[60]

For the possibilities of using the imagery of sound as a spiritual
language Thoreau was probably most indebted to Sir Thomas
Browne. It is an ancient language, to be sure, and one that fills
the corpus of Cambridge Platonism, and Thoreau undoubtedly
came across it in his reading of Cudworth and the metaphysical
poets.[61] But to Browne, if the labor of copying is proof, he owed

---

[57] *Collected Poems of Henry Thoreau,* ed. by Carl Bode, Chicago, 1943,
p. 92.

[58] J, I, 70.

[59] J, I, 52.

[60] J, I, 73-74.

[61] Margaret Fuller, in her essay on "The Two Herberts" (1846), has George
Herbert say that music is "the necessity of my life . . . an elixir that fills the

his greatest debt. Browne also seems to have provided three mottoes with which Thoreau concluded his transcriptions. To the first—"For the world, I count it not an inn, but an hospital, and a place, not to live in but to die in"—Thoreau added a blunt "I hold the reverse." The other two apparently won his assent. "Let me be nothing," Browne wrote, "if within the compass of myself, I do not find the battle of Lepanto, passion against reason, reason against faith, faith against the devil, and my conscience against all." This, perhaps, defined Thoreau's resolution for self-reliance. The third defined the kind of armor needed to preserve it. "There are," the physician wrote, "in the most depraved and venomous dispositions, certain pieces that remain untouched, which, by an anti-peristasis, become more excellent, or by the excellence of their antipathies are able to preserve themselves from the contagion of their enemy vices, and persist entire beyond the general corruption."

The self, friendship, and sound were Thoreau's first probings into the relationships of man, society, and the universe. They were the dimensions of human conduct—of being—that raised the question of how to live, the problem that, from the start, compelled his experimental life and search for an authentic way. "My desire is to know *what* I have lived," Thoreau wrote long before *Walden* in the opening pages of his *Journal,* "that I may know *how* to live henceforth." [62] He was not content with things as they were, with the village life to which he had perforce related himself; the Sabbath bell did not always awaken pleasant associations, but made him "sick at heart of this pagoda worship," and his female-dominated home, where sanctimonious recreations had to be endured on a Sunday afternoon, prompted him to write: "Thus much *let* a man do: confidently and heartily live up to his thought; for its error, if there be any, will soonest appear in practice, and if there be none, so much he may reckon as actual progress in the way of living." [63]

---

dullest fiber with ethereal energy. . . . It answers to the soul's presage, and in its fluent life embodies all I yet know how to desire. . . . All that has budded in me, bursts into bloom under this influence." And Lord Herbert cites Pythagoras and the ancient belief that "the spheres made music to those who had risen into a state which enabled them to hear it." Margaret Fuller, of course, is speaking for her own experience. Of all of Thoreau's contemporaries she should have appreciated his ecstasy over sound; and yet she was blind to *The Service*: Wade, ed., *The Writings of Margaret Fuller,* pp. 287-88.

[62] J, I, 9.

[63] J, I, 54-55, 31-33.

At this time his reading was directed to the art of living as well as writing. Not only was Thoreau reading Goethe as the model of the poet and hard at work at his Greek studies by 1838, he was reading other "good sermon book[s]" than those that occupied the household.[64] We know from his college essays and notebook and the first *Journal* that Thoreau had discovered the literature and scriptures of the East before he went to live with the Emersons in 1841. Indeed, that Emerson—who is usually thought to have introduced Thoreau to the Oriental writings—should have had these scriptures in his library was due to the rather wide and general interest in the East that had begun nearly a half century before when the sailing ships of the East India trade began to tie up at India Wharf.[65] Exhibitions, poems, commencement pieces had dealt with Oriental themes even in Emerson's college years, and one can assume that an exploring reader like Thoreau would have sampled more than such exotic fare as Al-Asma'i's *Antar: A Bedoueen Romance,* which caught his eye in his freshman year.[66] He wrote familiarly in a college essay, for example, of the writings of the Persians, most notably of *The Gulistan* of Saadi, and if he read Tasso in Chalmers' *English Poets* he must have looked into, if not read, Mickle's "Inquiry into the religious Tenets and Philosophy of the Bramins" in volume twenty-one, which he withdrew, perhaps for a closer reading, in 1841.[67] In any case, he read Confucius and Zoroaster at the same time that he was reading the seventeenth-century English poets, for they are all entered together in the "Miscellaneous Extracts"; and Thoreau mentioned Confucius and the Zend-Avesta in his *Journal* in 1838, which would be about the time of this reading.[68] It is probable, therefore, that the "Sayings of Confucius" he selected for *The Dial* of April, 1843, were already in his notebook by 1838—for the selections are the same, concerned chiefly with friendship and virtue and the eloquent silence

---

[64] J, I, 32.

[65] See *Indian Superstition,* by Ralph Waldo Emerson, ed. by Kenneth W. Cameron, Hanover, N.H., 1954.

[66] Cameron, *Emerson The Essayist,* II, 199. Thoreau also read Southey, perhaps his *The Curse of Kehama.*

[67] Sanborn, *Life,* p. 127. Probably he had read "On the Poetry of the Eastern Nations" in Chalmers' *English Poets* (see MA 594) (Cameron, *Emerson The Essayist,* II, 194). Mickle, like most early commentators, had a Christian point of view, and disparaged the "superstition" of the Indians.

[68] MA 594; J, I, 55.

of the "sovereign principle" of the universe. Indeed, it was probably in Confucius that he found this central term. "Heaven speaks,"
Confucius said, "but what language does it use to preach to men,
that there is a sovereign principle from which all things depend;
a sovereign principle which makes them to act and move? Its
motion is its language; it reduces the seasons to their times; it agi-
tates nature; it makes it produce. This silence is eloquent." [69] The
music of the spheres was here treated as spiritual agency, as
agitator and producer, and was given a place in visible nature,
enabling Thoreau to actually see and hear—in the bending, sough-
ing trees of Concord, for example—that celestial music which for
Pythagoras was only intellectually intelligible. These selections
from Confucius were followed by a few more from Zoroaster on
the theme of virtue, especially that heroic virtue of marching to
one's own music, admonitions against directing the mind to the
measures of the earth—"The oracles often give victory to our own
choices, and not to the order alone of the *mundane* periods"—
with which Thoreau was strengthening his self-reliance.[70]

The most important Oriental scripture that Thoreau read before
the *Bhagavad-Gita,* however, was *The Laws of Menu,* which, like
all Oriental philosophy, answered the question of how to live by
explicitly showing the way, the conduct of life. Thoreau's reading
of *Menu* is not easily dated.[71] The selections were numerous;
Thoreau had taken elaborate notes on his reading, and they were
to appear almost as fully in *The Dial.* But one suspects that the
length of his offerings was determined by what he had already
put away for his personal use, for the excerpts from Confucius,
which were printed later, were needlessly brief—as brief as the
supply in his notebook. Thoreau may have got up the later pieces
on Mencius and Buddha, but it seems likely that the Confucius
and Menu were ready to hand. The selections from Menu followed
reading in Cudworth's *Intellectual System,* Sir Walter Raleigh's
History of the World (he withdrew Raleigh's *Works* from the

[69] *The Dial,* III (April, 1843), 494. See also J, I, 120-21, where this sovereign
principle is spoken of in terms of the harmony of friendship.

[70] MA 594.

[71] He may have first come across Menu in the notes to Southey's *The Curse
of Kehama* and in Stewart's *Philosophy.* Emerson rediscovered the *Gita* in the
spring of 1845 with the help of James Elliot Cabot (*The Letters of Ralph
Waldo Emerson,* ed. by Ralph L. Rusk, New York, 1939, III, 288). Thoreau
benefited by this enthusiasm as can be seen in the *Week.*

Harvard College Library in 1841, but was familiar with him from his college days [72]), and Aulus Persius Flaccus (of whom he was sufficiently the master to criticize in his first piece for *The Dial* in 1840). He was reading Cudworth in June, 1840, according to the *Journal*, but his reading notes from Plutarch, which were entered later, after a first installment of Menu, seem to have been at the same time that he mentioned him in the *Journal*—in December, 1839. This year, or early 1840, seems to be the probable one, for the extracts are divided by copies of Emerson's poems from *The Western Messenger* of 1839; and when Thoreau interpreted Emerson's "The Sphinx" in 1841 he was already able to use Menu in his gloss [73]—all this before the more literary treatment of Menu which he wrote later in March, 1841, and used in the *Week*.

The dating of Thoreau's reading of Menu is important only insofar as it helps confirm a major influence on the direction of Thoreau's life. It was an early influence, and 1839 or 1841 is of little significance, for by the later date, at least, Menu was in his possession and his conception of spiritual heroism was fixed. Emerson's renewed interest in the Oriental scriptures, which occurred at the same time, was undoubtedly stimulating (as Thoreau's interest was undoubtedly stimulating to Emerson), and judging by the use that was made of Oriental literature Thoreau was probably more indebted to it than Emerson. For although Emerson found the Hindu doctrines of the soul and karma congenial to his thought, Thoreau captured their spirit, their insistence on behavior and the way of life.

The selections Thoreau printed in *The Dial* were not quite so extensive as those in his notebook, nor did they have Thoreau's own comments. What these comments show is that Thoreau found in "this divinely inspired law giver" a pattern for the conduct of life, an elaborate codification of the behavior (the relationships) of the Brahmin—the superior man with whom he identified himself. The Brahmin, merging with his notion of the poet-as-seer, became Thoreau's spiritual hero. *The Laws of Menu*, of course, was directed to the education and discipline of the Brahmins or students and teachers of the Veda, the sacred law, and of all the books of the Orient that Thoreau might have read at this period of apprenticeship, this spoke most to his condition. The Brahmins

---

[72] Cameron, *Emerson The Essayist,* II, 195.

[73] J, I, 150, 229.

were not only the highest caste but their spiritual studies were the most important vocation. "When a Brahmin springs to light," Menu said, "he is born above the world, the chief of all creatures, assigned to guard the treasury of duties religious and civil." [74] "No where else," Thoreau wrote after the section on the education of priests, "is the dignity of the teacher's office so strenuously insisted on. . . . Divine knowledge was the most respectable thing." As early as 1837, commenting on the Druids, Thoreau had written: "In all ages and nations we observe a leaning towards a right state of things. This may especially be seen in the history of the priest, whose life approaches most nearly to that of the ideal man." [75] Kindled by "The American Scholar" and "Literary Ethics," Thoreau saw in Menu specific directions for the pursuit of this calling. "We seem to be dabbling in the very elements of our present conventional or actual and visible life," he wrote. "Here is a *history* of the *forms* which humanity has in all ages assumed. We forget that our whole outward life is but convention, and it is salutary to be reminded of it. The old law giver seems to have foreseen all the possible relations of men, and provided that they be maintained with adequate dignity and sincerity. This book would afford a maxim applicable to any condition in which a man may be found."

The maxims Thoreau selected were not only the ethical heart of the laws—as the reader of the long sections on ritual appreciates— but those that most urgently appealed to him. He was especially interested in the first two stages of the Brahmin's life, that of the student—through which he had just passed, and in which he perhaps felt he was still continuing—and that of the householder, the stage of life that followed the student's return home and upon which the support of all the others rested. The householder, of course, was still a student, his vocation was always the sacred law. But he was the student with the responsibilities of man, compassed round by innumerable relations and duties, not simply those of student and teacher which dominated the first stage and which, incidentally, seem the model of Thoreau's relation with Emerson in the earlier period of their friendship and of Thoreau's residence

---

[74] All quotations from Menu are from MA 594. Where they were used in *The Dial* this source is cited. *The Dial*, III (Jan., 1843), 335. "The very birth of a Brâhmaṇa is an eternal incarnation of the sacred law; for he is born to [fulfill] the sacred law, and becomes one with Brahman" (*The Laws of Manu*, Sacred Books of the East, XXV, 26).

[75] J, I, 18.

with the Emersons.[76] Thoreau reduced the long section "On Eco-nomick; and Private Morals" dealing with the householder's mode of life to the terse "He must avoid service for hire." "Let him live by the conduct of a priest," Menu said, "neither crooked, nor artful, nor blended *with the manners of the mercantile class.*" How much this injunction meant to Thoreau and how difficult it made his life can be seen perhaps in a still earlier passage in the *Journals* where he identified himself with Zeno.

Zeno stood in precisely the same relation to the world that I do now. He is, forsooth, bred a merchant. . . . He strolls into a shop and is charmed by a book by Xenophon—and straightway he becomes a philosopher. The sun of a new life's day rises to him. . . . And still the fleshly Zeno sails on, shipwrecked, buffeted, tempest-tossed; but the true Zeno sails ever a placid sea. . . . When evening comes he sits down unwearied to the review of his day,—what's done that's to be undone, —what not done at all still to be done. Himself Truth's unconcerned helpmate. Another system of bookkeeping this than that the Cyprian trader to Phoenicia practiced! [77]

The proof of a Brahmin was his way of life, the test of conduct and character; and this reliance on virtue alone to win spiritual wealth and fame and to get free of the world was what most at-tracted Thoreau in Menu as well as Confucius. "A man's life," Con-fucius said, "is properly connected with virtue." [78] From Menu Thoreau copied: "For, in his passage to the next world, neither his father, nor his mother, nor his wife, nor his son, nor his kinsmen, will remain in his company: his virtue alone will adhere to him." [79] There was a further attraction: that the Brahmin who was properly bent on the study of the sacred law—a study that was advised as the best way to control the senses—needed no other ritual observ-ances. "Their *idea* of sacrifice is great," Thoreau commented, "their tenderness toward all living creatures is true and noble. While tedious ceremonies of purification were required of others, kings and students in theology . . . were 'always equally pure with the celestial spirit.'" [80]

---

[76] The laws applied especially to the relation of the student to the teacher's wife.

[77] J, I, 26-27.

[78] *The Dial*, III (April, 1843), 493. Thoreau could hardly have subscribed to the Confucian views of tradition and the state.

[79] *The Dial*, III (Jan., 1843), 336.

[80] Thoreau also recorded that the Brahmin used meat only for sacrifice. And he also recognized that in the householder stage a Brahmin could choose a wife. From the many injunctions on this relationship, mostly dealing with the

The third and fourth orders, those of the hermit and the ascetic, were apparently not as pertinent to Thoreau's immediate needs; they were concerned with the later stages of life, when the householder had provided for his family and had fulfilled all his social duties. Then, an old man, the "grandfather" left behind his house and fields and retired to the forest, practicing ritual sacrifices and vigorous austerities in order to "dry up his bodily frame." Finally, as an ascetic he sought the final liberation.[81] All this, of course, was not yet for the Thoreau who had not yet begun to live; but the end of uniting the soul with the divine spirit was, and Thoreau, as if claiming his own, picked out the injunctions to solitude and devotion. "Alone let him constantly dwell," he recorded, "observing the happiness of a solitary man. . . ." And advising the efficient cause of devotion, Menu had said: "Whatever is hard to be traversed, whatever is hard to be acquired, whatever is hard to be performed, all this may be accomplished by true devotion; for the difficulty of devotion is the greatest of all." [82]

The Laws of Menu touched Thoreau's life at many points. As a guide for students it served one of the purposes for which Thoreau intended *Walden,* and though not a literal model it seems, even more than in the desire to be twice born, a suggestive paradigm of Thoreau's account of his relations. Most important, perhaps, was its devotional attitude, the insistence on a life of devotion and the need for virtuous conduct. Like Cambridge Platonism, which had something of the same spirit, it was more concerned with practice than with dogma, and it centered religion in experience and inner disposition rather than in external observances. The Oriental scriptures were wholly concerned with the way—the way of piety, the activity of contemplation that directed one to a union with the spirit.[83] They put foremost the participation in spirit, the bending of the mind to the spirit in all things, high or low, a kind of life hallowed in New England by lip service but not by practice.[84]

times of intercourse, Thoreau selected the most pleasant—that the wife's name should be agreeable (why Emerson called Lydia Lidian) and that she should be flawless "like a young elephant" and of "exquisite softness."

[81] *The Laws of Manu,* pp. 203, 212.

[82] *The Dial,* III (Jan., 1843), 340.

[83] One wonders what Thoreau would have done with Lao-tzu's *Tao Tê Ching.*

[84] "Let every Bráhmen with fixed attention consider all nature, both visible and invisible, as existing in the divine spirit; for, when he contemplates the boundless universe existing in the divine spirit, he cannot give his heart to iniquity" (MA 594).

And they proposed a rule of life that would have offended New England as much as the extended Sabbath of the *Week* or the even more strenuous spiritual pursuit of *Walden*. The Brahmin way of life described in Menu's *Laws* was not what New Englanders meant when they spoke of their own Brahmin class. For the New England Brahmin was sustained by that very commercial class that the Indian lawgiver disdained. The New England Brahmin, the cultural spokesman of the dominant conservative class, would never have read through the section of Menu on public law and forcefully written, as did Thoreau, that "a Bráhmen could not be taxed"; [85] he would not have copied out of the section on justice that anticipation of "Civil Disobedience"—"The soul is its own witness; the soul itself is its own refuge: offend not thy conscious soul, the supreme internal witness of men." [86]

III

One of the most persistent errors concerning Thoreau that has never been sufficiently dispelled is that Thoreau was an anarchical individualist. Truculence and principle breed such labels, and going off to the woods seems proof enough that Thoreau was a hermit. Thoreau himself denied the latter. "I think that I love society as much as most," he began the chapter on "Visitors" in *Walden*—a chapter entitled "Society" in the manuscript version and thus more closely connected with the preceding chapter on "Solitude" of which his protestation had originally been a part. "I am naturally no hermit," he continued, "but might possibly sit out the sturdiest frequenter of the bar-room, if my business called me thither." The reviewers and readers, however, did not take this seriously, nor Thoreau's statement that "to act collectively is according to the spirit of our institutions." [87] Hermit he was, because he had turned his back on society, refused to pay his tax, and lived a solitary life beside a pond: such is the penalty for rejecting those things of which society approves. Thoreau had warned against a literal reading of his book, but this label was a gross misconstruction.[88] Perhaps because of this, Thoreau told his publishers to call the book

---

[85] Thoreau also wrote in 1837: "The Druids paid no taxes, and 'were allowed exemption from warfare and all other things' " (J, I, 18).

[86] *The Dial*, III (Jan., 1843), 334.

[87] W, II, 155, 122.

[88] His friend Daniel Ricketson was attracted by the rustic aspect of *Walden*. Emerson called him a hermit in his eulogy.

simply *Walden* in its next edition, to leave off the subtitle, *or, Life in the Woods.*[89] Like Melville in *Mardi,* Thoreau made fun of misleading titles.[90] He would lead no one astray.

It is true that Thoreau was an individual, and that as Randolph Bourne probably wrote in *The Seven Arts,* "he marks better than any other figure in our social history the distance we have travelled from the unity of the one to the unity of the many." [91] If by individual one means, with Bourne, "self-coherent," or wholly occupied with the self as the center of life, then he was indeed individual. But one of the problems of the self is society, and one of the reasons for turning in on the self is to find within the self the ways of renovating society. When, as in transcendental thought, the self is both ideal and actual, the problem of society is inescapable: the actual self is social, and the renovation of society can take place, as Thoreau said of heroism, "without moving a finger!" [92] Still, this interpretation of social does not cover what is commonly meant in the disapproval of Thoreau. Thoreau was antisocial, uncivil in his behavior—personally perhaps he needed to distinguish himself in this way. But he was antisocial only in the sense that he wanted to change society. He chose an individual field and an individual way of doing this, but his thought was eminently social, as much a gospel as Alcott's or Whitman's. He said "simplify, simplify"—he should also have said as memorably that which is as central to his thought: find your relations, or better still, purify them.

Intent on erecting a "higher society," Thoreau did not go to the woods for himself alone, but to serve mankind. This selflessness and the misinterpretation of it provided one of the most haunting strains in his thought. His society did not welcome "what is most precious in my gift." [93] His own high vocation was mistaken for loitering. To the end of his life he felt the smart of disapproval, turning it back on his neighbors at least in the humor of his address before the Middlesex Agricultural Society in 1860.[94] Then he could say, "Every man is entitled to come to Cattleshow, even a transcendentalist . . . ," and could identify himself with the farmers who

---

[89] Letter to Ticknor & Fields, March 4, 1862. The Huntington Library.

[90] See his college essay on the titles of books, Sanborn, *Life,* pp. 123-28.

[91] *The Seven Arts,* II (July, 1917), 383.

[92] J, I, 52.

[93] J, I, 350.

[94] "The Succession of Forest Trees," W, V, 184-204.

"come as near being indigenous to the soil as a white man can. . . ." He could point to the oddities in the audience and ask, "Why choose a man to do plain work who is distinguished for his oddity?" —adding, "However, I do not know but you will think that they have committed this mistake who invited me to speak to you to-day." He referred to his habit of going across lots, and used it as the "title" of his special claim to knowledge about the mysteries of the succession of trees: what had been the sign of his oddity became instead—as he always hoped it would—the sign of his usefulness, and with considerable point he began the scientific portion of his address with, "Let me lead you back into your wood-lots again." This triumph, however, was momentary and belated; he had a more precious gift to communicate than his observations of oak and pine, gifts he spelled out with his last energy in "Wild Apples" and "Walking." But this did not temper the pain of being misused. His constant plea was: "Use me, then, for I am useful in my way, and stand as one of many petitioners, from toadstool and henbane up to dahlia and violet, supplicating to be put to my use, if by any means ye may find me serviceable; whether for a medicated drink or bath, as balm and lavender; or for fragrance, as verbena and geranium; or for sight, as cactus; or for thoughts, as pansy. These humbler, at least, if not those higher uses." [95]

If the first thing Thoreau did on returning to Concord was to sign off from the church, the second was to lecture on "Society" at the Lyceum. He replaced the pagoda worship with the service of truth. He had no idea of fleeing society: if he had followed Emerson's career, he knew instead that he must act on society. Where Thoreau approved, he was always socially helpful; indeed, his life was more social than most, noteworthy for his gifts to scientists and his activity in the cause of abolition. There was, as we shall see, a definite attempt in his later work to socialize his vision. But from the beginning he thought in social terms; that is, he did not use society for his personal ends, making it pay off in the way of merchants—society as a field for ambition—he hoped instead that society could be used to create individuals, to forward the general welfare. This was the standard by which he measured public influence. In a college essay he said that "the community ought to do what is for its own good," and he took a stand we little

[95] W, I, 304-5.

expect from an individualist, that "the Government ought to provide for the education of all children who would otherwise be brought up . . . in ignorance." [96]

His own initiation into the possibilities of public influence probably came from the Lyceum, which he attended almost from its beginnings in Concord in 1829, and which all his life represented the kind of "compulsory" education he felt the community needed.[97] When he returned to Concord he took an active part in its proceedings, not only lecturing some twenty times from 1838 to 1860, but organizing the lecture series as its curator from 1838 to 1840 and again in 1842, 1843, and 1845.[98] Here was the kind of collective action that he felt was in the spirit of our institutions, and he participated in it fully. It was, perhaps, the only platform to which he could aspire, and in 1838 it gave him the opportunity to prepare himself for a vocation other than teaching, a vocation that Emerson had pioneered and that seemed worthy of the poet.

"Society," delivered on April 11, 1838, was a lecture that in one form or another Thoreau never ceased giving. In it he struck his theme: that life should be infinitely richer than it is, that human relations should be so ordered, purified, and real that what is commonly taken for society would be transformed into a higher society better fitted to the nature of man. We do not have the lecture as it was given, only the few notes in the *Journal;* [99] but from them we can catch a glimpse of the twenty-year-old seer baring his heart and the heart of his vision to his neighbors. His sincerity was naked, his sense of disappointment with society poignant, his desire for the ideal, for a society to the end of friendship, intense. He did not preach, as his audience probably expected, on actual social ills and reforms; he spoke instead of the social self and the real self, of his hunger for a kindred soul. What he had in mind were the prescriptions on friendship with which he filled his *Journal,* sentiments like the one he recorded in June, 1838:

> In the busy streets, domains of trade,
> Man is a surly porter, or a vain and hectoring bully,

[96] Sanborn, *Life,* pp. 178-79.

[97] See W, II, 120-22.

[98] Hubert H. Hoeltje, "Thoreau as Lecturer," *The New England Quarterly,* XIX (Dec., 1946), 491; Walter Harding, "Thoreau and the Concord Lyceum," *The Thoreau Society Bulletin,* XXX (Jan., 1950), 2-3.

[99] J, I, 36-40.

> Who can claim no nearer kindredship with me
> Than brotherhood by law.[100]

Thoreau seemed most to lament the lack of the brotherhood of spirit. For the "mechanical contact" of society he would substitute "the influence of a subtle attraction," and for those societies that were only assemblies or conventions of men, true associations. In the former man was made for society; in the latter society was made for man. And in such a society he would not be leveled down to the mob, he would not "lose his own identity in the nonentities around him," he would not find a "meeting of heels" but of "heads," he would not "throw off his strait-jacket of a godship, and play the one-eared, two-mouthed mortal"—nor would he, as he always refused to do, have to prepare a face to meet the faces that you meet. He proposed, then, a society of real, not of actual, selves, one in which he would not be disappointed. "With a beating heart he fares him forth, by the light of the stars," Thoreau said apparently from his experience, "to this meeting of gods. But the illusion speedily vanishes; what at first seemed to him nectar and ambrosia, is discovered to be plain bohea and short gingerbread." He expressed this disappointment many times—this, and the fact that in the society of bohea and gingerbread he was not free to impart the "profound secret" of his being. He said that he preferred the battlefield to the drawing room—what he was preparing to write in *The Service* was already in his thoughts on society—that in warfare at least there was "no room for pretension or excessive ceremony. . . ." The society he wanted was above these insipidities. "Let not society be the element in which you swim, or rather are tossed about at the mercy of the waves, but be rather a strip of firm land running out into the sea, whose base is daily washed by the tide, but whose summit only the spring tide can reach." In a college essay he had compared conformity to shipwreck; so with society here. The metaphor conveyed as well as any Thoreau's position in society: he would stand fast (and "firm"), fixed where all was chaos, principled where all was expediency. But though the imagery suggests that he would be in society, the tides would wash only his "base"; far above it, in an image of isolation and loneliness, would be his summit, awaiting the higher tides of "spring"—of spirit. The imagery, indeed the lecture, anticipates *Walden* and the rising waters that may one day "flood the parched uplands. . . ." [101]

[100] J, I, 51.

[101] W, II, 366.

It was perhaps well for his neighbors who heard this manifesto[102] that Thoreau set fire to the woods and so gave their disapproval something demonstrable to fix on. Thoreau was never a successful lecturer, not so much because he talked into his manuscript but because of his subject matter and the already perceptible satire. Who wanted to hear the gospel of a twenty-year-old? No more did Bourne's generation want to listen to the demands of youth; "Youth grasps at happiness," Thoreau had written, "as an inalienable right." [103] Not until almost a decade had passed did Thoreau speak again so directly to his townsmen of his private vision, more perhaps to explain himself, and then in the sharp humor of the beginning of *Walden*. When he lectured next at the Lyceum in 1843 he read his paper on Sir Walter Raleigh; he did not, as he might have in the intervening years, read *The Service*. And he continued with literary subjects or travels: "The Ancient Poets," "Concord River," "The Writings and Style of Thomas Carlyle." [104] Most of his lectures were those of the naturalist and excursionist, incorporating the same lesson Thoreau learned again with the failure of the *Week* and applied in his essays on Cape Cod, Canada, and Maine. Perhaps, with the advent of *The Dial*, he was able to make the distinction one finds in his work between diffused and focused vision, between, say, the excursion to Canada and "Walking," between the solid travel report with its symbolic auras and those writings in which the symbol itself leads, directs, and radiates the thought. For *The Dial* gave him the chance to be a writer as well as a lecturer, and gave him a sympathetic editor and audience. It was to *The Dial*, therefore, that he offered his poems, which in these years were most crystalline with his aspiration and thought, and gave *The Service*, his most extravagant experiment in prose.

The Service was ready for *The Dial* in late July, 1840, completed almost with the last entry Thoreau had put in his *Journal*. Most of it was taken directly from the passages on bravery that Thoreau began writing out in December, 1839. This accounts, perhaps, for its failure to impress one as sustained prose. The passages in the *Journal*, each elaborating an image or an idea, seem richer and more forceful than the composite Thoreau made of them; read

---

[102] J, I, 27-28.

[103] J, I, 59.

[104] Hoeltje, "Thoreau as Lecturer," p. 491.

separately, they remind one of Bronson Alcott's "Orphic Sayings," which appeared in time to influence him.[105] Thoreau, as we shall see, did try to bind his sayings together, but the result has the effect of a rhapsody, perhaps of a litany, and in the bulk they seem weak, indeed a little precious. This was also due to the lack of concrete imagery, which one feels more in the whole than in the parts—to the high abstract level of discourse, with its literary allusions and book-derived imagery. The imagery of crusades and warfare, astronomy and music, had been personally felt by Thoreau, but for the reader they are intellectual rather than sensual and do not evoke the response that the pervading tone of the work demands. Though the prose is not overly ornate, *The Service* was apparently for Thoreau an exercise in metaphysical prose. The failure of this piece of *juvenilia*, however, was characteristic of Thoreau's lifelong difficulty at organization: without the factual foundation of his excursions or his nature studies, *The Service* only made the failing more obvious. There was, of course, a unity in everything Thoreau wrote, even *The Service*, but it was a hidden unity, one of underlying meaning. In *The Service* this unity can be made out, which is not to say that it was effective but rather that it was locked within the symbols. Nevertheless *The Service*, forgotten because it was never published in Thoreau's lifetime, has some interest. It was Thoreau's first attempt to bring some of his major themes together. Working toward the delineation of the superior man since his college days, he now had from his reading the imagery of that spiritual bravery to which he had dedicated himself.

Emerson sent *The Service* to Margaret Fuller with this explanation: "He is trying to give you a piece of prose out of his 'Brave Man,' an Essay which he read to Caroline [Sturgis]."[106] He had also sent along Thoreau's "Nature doth have her dawn each day," over which Margaret haggled but which, apparently under pressure, she printed.[107] "Our tough Yankee," as Emerson called Thoreau when he begged Margaret to let "his tough verse" stand, had won the first battle; Margaret, however, won the second. She re-

---

[105] *The Dial*, I (July, 1840), 85-98. Alcott held a "conversation" at Mrs. Thoreau's as early as May 3, 1839 (Shepard, ed., *The Journals of Bronson Alcott*, p. 127).

[106] Rusk, ed., *The Letters of Ralph Waldo Emerson*, II, 315.

[107] Rusk, ed., *The Letters of Ralph Waldo Emerson*, II, 322.

jected *The Service* for its want of order and its assuming tone. "Yours," she told Thoreau—and justly, "is so rugged that it ought to be commanding." [108] This criticism not only got at Thoreau's literary failure, it got at the stance Thoreau had taken in the lecture on "Society" and, though tempered by an ache and openness of feeling, had developed in his *Journals*. Sanborn, commenting on Thoreau's scorn of the conventional and customary, remarked that *The Service* was "a singular blending of the aristocratic and the democratic in its tone towards other men. . . ."

Thoreau's growing intimacy with Emerson's Concord Circle, indicated by his reading to Caroline Sturgis, accounted in part at least for his concern with friendship, which Emerson and his friends were personally exploring that summer. It might also have accounted in part for *The Service* which, though in no way derivative, was a personal version of the themes of "Self-Reliance" and "Heroism" that Emerson was preparing for his *Essays*. And if Thoreau had not yet fully entered into that exchange of private journals which was the bond of transcendental association, perhaps he intended *The Service* as a proclamation of his faith and worth: it described the "qualities of the recruit." Sanborn believed that Thoreau wrote *The Service* as a reaction to the numerous discourses on peace and nonresistance in 1840. Thoreau did indeed mention them, but as a sign of the lack of valor, which for him was equivalent to Emerson's or Parker's or Alcott's use of expediency or utilitarianism—for drift and apathy and refusal to fight falsehood. Thoreau did not demand war where the peace societies demanded peace; he demanded the moral equivalent of war, that spiritual crusading for truth, that "testy spirit of knight errantry" that would galvanize the feebler virtues of his age. "I have a deep sympathy with war," he wrote, "it so apes the gait and bearing of the Soul." [109] War was opposed to peace, as flashing steel to rust, or purpose and activity to insincerity and sloth. "What were Godfrey and Gonsalvo unless we breathed a life into them," he wrote, "and enacted their exploits as a prelude to our own?" The crusade he had in mind marched to the Eternal City, and its aim was nothing less than God, to replace being for seeming. To the sleeping herdsmen of New England this new Godfrey proposed a new bravery—"the life of a

---

[108] *The Service,* ed. by F. B. Sanborn, Boston, 1902, p. x. All quotations are from this text.

[109] J, I, 156.

great man," "a human life," that "restored original of which she [Nature] is the reflection."

The dominant images of *The Service* have to do with the restoration of the individual, with completeness or integrity—with what today we might call authenticity. "The exploit of a brave life," Thoreau wrote, "consists in its momentary completeness." The imagery of warfare was only a way of representing the life of this endeavor (as opposed to "livelihood"). "Effort," he wrote, "is the prerogative of virtue"—"It is not enough that our life is an easy one; we must live on the stretch. . . ." And again: "It concerns us, rather, to be somewhat here present, than to leave something behind us. . . ." The bravery he defines is that of being, that of the perfectly related but integral self. "For an impenetrable shield," he wrote, "stand inside yourself." One of his finest images, albeit borrowed, was *"mea virtute me involvo* (I wrap myself in my virtue)"; it explained his saying that "nor can we be cheated of our earnings unless by not earning them," and that "the brave man is a perfect sphere. . . ." Emerson also spoke of the spheral man, probably adapting this epithet for character from Thoreau's conceit:

We say justly that a weak person is flat; for, like all flat substances, he does not stand in the direction of his strength, that is on his edge, but affords a convenient surface to put upon. He slides all the way through life. Most things are strong in one direction,—a straw longitudinally, a board in the direction of its edge, a knee transversely to its grain,— but the brave man is a perfect sphere, which cannot fall on its flat side, and is equally strong every way. The coward is wretchedly spheroidal at best, too much educated or drawn out on one side commonly and depressed on the other; or he may be likened to a hollow sphere, whose disposition of matter is best when the greatest bulk is intended.

This sphericity was attained, as Emerson and Whitman also pointed out, by finding one's relation to the universe. Society did not figure in its achievement, for society was the sum of things base, the base itself, which the hero had to surmount—it was the friction that produced a din when the hero would have a harmony. Society entered only because it represented resistance; without it there would have been no need for militant imagery. It was the house Whitman left behind for the open field, and the attachments from which Emerson found release on the bare common. When one declares war, even for virtue's sake, all becomes terribly either/or. The stakes were that high for Thoreau (who was fighting, whether he knew it or not, the losing battle of the individual in the nine-teenth century), and the enemy was society, that *convention* of the hollow and flat. Nothing less than a crusade could represent it for him. Just as both Thoreau and Emerson treated the higher society in terms of friendship, and Whitman treated democracy in terms of adhesiveness, so Thoreau treated society as a moral conspiracy. He did not think of it institutionally, but humanly, and therefore as personally reprehensible: its failure was wholly moral. Accord-ingly he felt that he was justified in seeking his salvation outside society and in acting on it from above. What society needed most, to his way of thinking, was a MAN, a "stock-personality." This had prompted Thoreau's search for the superior man and for the friend, and it gave his highly individual works their claim to social use-fulness.[110]

Man became flat because he did not tend the "vestal fire" of divinity within him—the vestal fire, or vital heat, that Thoreau went to Walden to preserve. There was no other duty; not to develop the divine material of manhood was the greatest failure in a uni-verse designed for the furtherance of man, and this notion of "sin" accounted in part for the sense of guilt Thoreau had in his later years and which even his strenuous faithfulness could not alleviate. In *The Service*, as in Emerson's *Nature*, there was no portent of what the test of transcendental thought would inevitably bring. There was instead a sense of elation, an unbounded joy in the possibilities of an unbounded universe, one in which "*Spes sibi quisque*" ("Each one his own hope")—Thoreau's epigraph from Virgil—seemed certain of realization. "The brave man is the elder son of creation," Thoreau began his essay, "who has stept buoyantly into his inheritance. . . ." The brave man was now "The Lord of Creation" of Thoreau's commencement speech, stepping into nature like Emerson's scholar, claiming the universe as his own. Except for the intensification of the need for bravery, which was due to Thoreau's awareness of society rather than to the nature of the universe, *The Service* for the most part translated Emerson's *Nature* into Thoreau's idiom.

Emerson's treatise had explained the possibilities of the shift from outer to inner, and had placed man at the center of the universe. So Thoreau claimed that greatness came from building

[110] The mission of friendship was "to commend virtue to mankind" (J, I, 107).

inward, not outward, and that the inward was the "shorter way" to heaven. He also appropriated Emerson's image of man as an angle of vision: "His eye is the focus in which all the rays, from whatever side, are collected; for, itself being within and central, the entire circumference is revealed to it." And by using Emerson's "the axis of vision is not coincident with the axis of things" [111] he was able to develop the image of the sphere into an astronomical conceit. "Only by resigning ourselves implicitly to the law of gravity in us," Thoreau wrote, "shall we find our axis coincident with the celestial axis, and by revolving incessantly through all circles, acquire a perfect sphericity." The spheral man was, therefore, properly a part of the celestial system. The "ligature" that tied him to God was his own "muscle and sinew," the virtue or fortitude that for Emerson had turned an opaque into a transparent universe, and had restored its unity. Where all of nature was moral, to have its benefit man too must be moral; the astronomical figure was Thoreau's way of expressing Emerson's idea that the good prevails and the universe sustains it. "Always," Thoreau wrote, "the System shines with uninterrupted light. . . . We may bask always in the light of the System." The imagery he employed to demonstrate this idea was his most complex and "metaphysical":

If you will let a single ray of light through the shutter, it will go on diffusing itself without limit till it enlighten [112] the world, but the shadow that was never so wide at first as rapidly contracts till it comes to naught. The shadow of the moon when it passes nearest the sun is lost in space ere it can reach our earth to eclipse it. Always the System shines with uninterrupted light, for, as the sun is so much larger than any planet, no shadow can travel far into space. We may bask always in the light of the System, always may step back out of the shade. No man's shadow is as large as his body, if the rays make a right angle with the reflecting surface. Let our lives be passed under the equator, with the sun in the meridian.

As one sees in the last lines, Thoreau, like so many of his contemporaries, could not let the image stand without drawing its moral:

There is no ill which may not be dissipated like the dark, if you let in a stronger light upon it. [113] Overcome evil with good. Practice no such narrow economy as they whose bravery amounts to no more light than

---

[111] C, I, 73. See also J, I, 166.

[112] "Enlighten" gives this passage its moral cast.

[113] "There is no object so foul," Emerson wrote, "that intense light will not make beautiful" (C, I, 15).

a farthing candle, before which most objects cast a shadow wider than themselves.[114]

This, in effect, was the transcendental doctrine of good and evil in terms of light and dark. Thoreau had merely spelled out a note in his *Journal:* "Bravery and Cowardice are kindred correlatives with Knowledge and Ignorance, Light and Darkness, Good and Evil." [115]

This astronomy of virtue also supported Thoreau's belief in the transcendental doctrines of nature's beneficence and joy and of necessity or "inflexibility of good." Necessity, in fact, was so closely related in his mind with the good and the divine that he spoke of this attribute of divinity as divinity itself. It was "my elder brother" —reminding one of Whitman's lines of assurance, "And I know that the hand of God is the elderhand of my own,/And I know that the spirit of God is the eldest brother of my own." [116] "Then is holiday," Thoreau wrote, "when naught intervenes betwixt me and thee. . . . I ask no more but to be left alone with it." He said that the stars were the interpreters of this necessity—as Emerson had said they were the last outposts of God; and therefore he accepted what Emerson called the beautiful necessity with joy, because it guaranteed the ecstatic reward of the virtuous soul. "Necessity," he wrote, "is my eastern cushion on which I recline"; and in imagery equally soft and enclosing, "It is the bosom of time and the lap of eternity." In his first descriptions of ecstasy, Thoreau used the images of floating and drifting: "A boatman stretched on the deck of his craft and dallying with the noon," he said of his own experience at Walden Pond, "would be as apt an emblem of eternity for me as the serpent with his tail in his mouth." And again when he lost himself in the sea of consciousness, he said that he felt "eternity and space gambolling familiarly through my depths," and that "I am a restful kernel in the magazine of the universe." [117] Thus, his universe was good, and the all-disposing gods were kind, and Thoreau finely rendered this sense of assurance by elaborating, as he often did later, some lore of the past. "It was a conceit of Plutarch," he wrote, "accounting for the preferences given to signs observed on the left hand, that men may have thought 'things ter-

---

[114] Christian Gruber suggests that the source of this imagery was Thoreau's scientific training at Harvard (*The Education of Henry Thoreau,* pp. 173ff.).

[115] J, I, 99.

[116] Section 5, "Song of Myself."

[117] J, I, 53-54, 75.

restial and mortal directly over against heavenly and divine things, and do conjecture that the things which to us are on the left hand, the gods send down from their right hand.' If we are not blind, we shall see how a right hand is stretched over all, as well the unlucky as lucky, and that the ordering soul is only righthanded, distributing with one palm all our fates." This acceptance of necessity was undoubtedly furthered by Thoreau's current study of the Greeks, notably the works of Homer and Aeschylus. "What first suggested that necessity was grim," he asked, "and made fate so fatal?" Certainly not the Greeks, as Thoreau understood them.[118] He concluded the first section of *The Service* with one of his finest memorials to Greece: "Over Greece hangs the divine necessity, ever a mellower heaven of itself, whose light too gilds the Acropolis and a thousand fanes and groves."

The astronomical imagery was carried over to the second section of *The Service*, "What Music Shall We Have?" where it provided the basis of Thoreau's use of sound and the music of the spheres. "The universe needed only to hear a divine melody," Thoreau wrote, "that every star might fall into its proper place, and assume its true sphericity." The brave man, the spheral man coincident with the universe, was accordingly "the sole patron of music." "His language," Thoreau wrote, "must have the same majestic movement and cadence that philosophy assigns to the heavenly bodies. The steady flux of his thought constitutes time in music. The universe falls in and keeps pace with it. . . . Hence are poetry and song." [119] The poet, therefore, was the brave man. Music for Thoreau was "God's voice," the echo of the soul; and thus, as the sound of necessity, allied him with the universe and the cause of right. Not only was it the means of union—"He is no longer insulated, but infinitely related and familiar"—but the binding force of friendship and the "herald of virtue." Hereafter he always responded to sound as the indication of the "sound" state of the universe: "There is as much music in the world as virtue." And his own response to sound, which, he wrote, "brings out what of heroic lurks anywhere," became the sign of his own spiritual health, the sign of that harmony within the self that Plato had used music

---

[118] See his college essay on fate, Sanborn, *Life*, pp. 175-77.

[119] "The highest morality in books," he wrote at this time, "is rhymed or measured . . ." (J, I, 151).

to achieve. The coward, of course, was all ajar and "would reduce this thrilling sphere music to a universal wail, this melodious chant to a nasal cant"—he was obviously the humanitarian reformer of *Walden* who would "conciliate all hostile influences by compelling his neighborhood into a partial concord with himself. . . ." Not so the hero: "To the sensitive soul the Universe has her own fixed measure, which is its measure also, and as this, expressed in the regularity of its pulse, is inseparable from a healthy body, so is its healthiness dependent on the regularity of its rhythm. In all sounds the soul recognizes its own rhythm, and seeks to express its sympathy by a correspondent movement of the limbs. When the body marches to the measure of the soul [when the two selves are in harmony], then is true courage and invincible strength." The hero, according to Emerson, followed a law higher than that of prudence. As Thoreau said of the soldier, "He is the one only man. He recognizes no time-honored casts and conventions, no fixtures but transfixtures, no governments at length settled on a permanent basis. One tap of the drum sets the political and moral harmonies all ajar." This higher law was the "unheard music" to which Thoreau dedicated himself in *The Service*. "A man's life should be a stately march to an unheard music," he wrote, "and when to his fellows it may seem irregular and inharmonious, he will be stepping to a livelier measure, which only his nicer ear can detect. There will be no halt, ever, but at most a marching on his post, or such a pause as is richer than any sound, when the deeper melody is no longer heard, but implicitly consented to with the whole life and being. He will take a false step never, even in the most arduous circumstances; for then the music will not fail to swell into greater volume, and rule the movement it inspired."

Where the first two sections of *The Service* were well within the astronomical figure, wholly celestial as it were, the concluding section was more mundane. Here Thoreau was not depicting his "system" but proposing to live it, and the shift in perspective from heaven to earth was appropriate. The celestial phenomenon he used, therefore, was the day—the dawn, noon, evening cycle that, appearing for the first time in *The Service*, was more and more to be filled with the content of his spiritual experience—to become, indeed, a fundamental pattern of his work. In the final section, the sun and cloud challenge him to greatness and show him "the meanness of my employments." Like the Greeks at Troy, each day is for him a chance for valor, and he feels that he should "take up the gauntlet which the heavens throw down." For in his astronomy, the day and night are not of the almanac but are the very pulse of virtue and bravery. The mist of daybreak beckons to the battle-fields of life beyond, where the soldier is not to be defeated by his opportunities. "We will have," Thoreau wrote in the *Journal,* "a dawn, and noon, and serene sunset in ourselves." [120] Developing the metaphor, he wrote:

Shall man wear out sooner than the sun? and not rather dawn as freshly, and with such native dignity stalk down the hills of the East into the bustling vale of life, with as lofty and serene a countenance to roll on-ward through midday, to a yet fairer and more promising setting? In the crimson colors of the west I discover the budding hues of dawn. To my western brother it is rising pure and bright as it did to me; but only the evening exhibits in the still rear of day, the beauty which through morning and noon escaped me. Is not that which we call the gross atmosphere of evening the accumulated deed of the day, which absorbs the rays of beauty, and shows more richly than the naked promise of the dawn? Let us look to it that by earnest toil in the heat of the noon, we get ready a rich western blaze against the evening.

It was in this way that Thoreau conceived of a "Bravery so wide that nothing can meet to befall it," whose "silent sentries by night" were the stars, "and the sun its pioneer by day." [121]

---

[120] J, I, 159.
[121] J, I, 172.

Chapter III

THE CAPTIVE KNIGHT

It [the word] must have taken the place of a deed
by an urgent necessity, even by some misfortune, so
that the truest writer will be some captive knight
after all.

—*Sir Walter Raleigh*

I

The Service was a protestation of Thoreau's
relation to the universe, of his determination to
be authentic and to serve only the gods. It was
the sum of his aspiration and became his articles
of war. As a program for his life, however, it was
as vague as his own sense of destiny, and it laid
a heavy burden on the young schoolteacher. "I
am startled," Thoreau had written in 1840, "when
I consider how little I am *actually* concerned
about the things I write in my journal. . . . What
a tame life we are living! How little heroic it
is!" [1] His own aspirations were at once the measure of his failure; and the years that followed
The Service and that eventually brought him to
Walden Pond were troubled by the uncertainty
that he might not be marching to his own music
and advancing his destiny. He had written in

[1] J, I, 143, 115.

The Service that "he is the true artist whose life is his material . . ." and in the couplet

> My life hath been the poem I would have writ,
> But I could not both live and live to utter it [2]

he recorded the essential disharmony he felt in his life. "Even the wisest and the best are apt to use their lives as the occasion to do something else than live greatly," he wrote. "But we should hang as fondly over the work as the finishing and embellishment of a poem." [3] To live greatly, to fashion the self, was now his work. The spiritual restlessness and pain and self-assessment of the *Journals* of these years were not the record of a lack of communion and inspiration but only the record of his sense of delay.

He attributed the delay in part to society. Already chafed by his routine, he asked in 1840, "How shall I help myself?" He had given the answer in "Society" and would offer a similar one in *The Service:* "By withdrawing . . . determining to meet myself face to face sooner or later." Except for friendship he wanted no society; his relations were elsewhere. He wanted to unfold himself in "that public ground between God and conscience." "The most positive life that history notices has been a constant retiring out of life"— here was the first sign of his need for Walden—"a wiping one's hands of it, seeing how mean it is, and having nothing to do with it." [4] There was a real bitterness toward the society that clipped his wings. At this time Thoreau felt that his refusal to give a woman his seat was justifiable stuff for the spiritual vault of his *Journal;* and Emerson caught the temper of Thoreau during this period when he wrote of his "perennial threatening attitude. . . ." [5] The dominant strain of the *Journals* expressed this repudiation of the way of the world: it was otherworldly. "Their meanness," Thoreau wrote of his neighbors, "would drag down your deed to be a compromise with conscience, and not leave it to be done on the high table-land of the benevolent soul. They would have you doff your bright and knightly armor and drudge for them,—serve *them* and not God." [6] If society was servitude, his service lay elsewhere: "A greater baldness my life seeks," he wrote in the spring of 1841, "as

[2] *The Service,* p. 24; J, I, 275.

[3] J, I, 240.

[4] J, I, 132-33, 211. See W, II, 101.

[5] J, I, 133, 193-94; Rusk, ed., *The Letters of Ralph Waldo Emerson,* III, 75.

[6] J, I, 212.

the crest of some bare hill, which towns and cities do not afford. I want a directer relation with the sun." [7]

The sun and the heavens now became prominent images in his thought—as did nature which for the first time moved into the foreground. Time and eternity divided his thought, society and the soul. "We go about mending the times," he wrote, "when we should be building the eternity." [8] He had the feeling that time was not the measure of the progress of the soul, that his destiny was advancing in spite of what seemed a temporal delay. In April, 1841, he wrote of the sun:

> Methinks all things have travelled since you shined,
> But only Time, and clouds, Time's team, have moved;
> Again foul weather shall not change my mind,
> But In the shade I will believe what in the sun I loved. [9]

And he wrote of his destiny:

> My ground is high,
> But 'tis not dry,
> What you call dew
> Comes filtering through;
> Though in the sky,
> It still is nigh;
> Its soil is blue
> And virgin too.

The heavens became his farm; here he would gladly serve,

> And sow my seed broadcast in air
> Certain to reap my harvest there. [10]

"Let us know and conform," he wrote with Menu once more at hand, "only to the fashions of eternity." [11]

The assurance of his destiny that Thoreau felt in his pure moments of ecstasy, the sense that he was living on the level of eternity, made all vocations, except that of the self, indifferent, and robbed postponement of its sting. This was not the guilt he acknowledged. "Sin, I am sure," he wrote, "is not in overt acts or, indeed, in acts of any kind, but is in the proportion to the time which has come behind us and displaced eternity,—that degree [and here eternity was translated into purity] to which our elements are

---

[7] J, I, 248.

[8] J, I, 212.

[9] Bode, ed., *Collected Poems of Henry Thoreau*, p. 126.

[10] J, I, 245-46.

[11] J, I, 278.

mixed with the elements of the world. The whole duty of life is contained in the question how to respire and aspire both at once." [12] Trying to answer that question was Thoreau's most arduous task. In the spring of 1841, already looking to the end of his school-keeping, he began to look about for a farm, and he had proposed to himself the remedy of Walden. "My life will wait for nobody," he wrote in April, 1841, "but is being matured irresistibly while I go about the streets and chaffer with this man and that to secure it a living." [13] Farming, however, was not, as it might have been later, a satisfactory solution. "What have I to do with plows?" he asked himself, thinking of the cerulean fields. "I cut another furrow than you see." [14] He was not content with farming because he was startled to find "the old system of things so grim and assured" on the farms of his neighbors. "The youth," he complained, "must buy old land and bring it to"—which was not for the proprietor of the virgin heavens. What he wanted was a "clean seat." "I will build my lodge on the southern slope of some hill, and take there the life the gods send me"—thus he envisioned Walden. "Will it not be employment enough to accept gratefully all that is yielded me between sun and sun?" [15]

As it began to stir in his thought, Walden was associated with the splendid moments of drifting and floating that he had known on its water and with the freedom that would make them possible. Manifestly a Yankee even in matters of spirit, Thoreau had, as well, by temperament and inclination, the profound Oriental desire for serenity. When he assayed his life in 1840, he wrote that "there are two ways to victory,—to strive bravely or to yield." [16] And in the years that followed, the test of his bravery was his ability to yield to his destiny, to be, as he told Isaiah Williams, content with God's success.[17] He would let the world wag its tail and consult only his higher instincts. What had he to do with the world? He wrote in "Independence,"

> My life more civil is and free
> Than any civil polity.

. . . .

[12] J, I, 300.

[13] J, I, 244.

[14] J, I, 245.

[15] J, I, 249-50, 244.

[16] J, I, 147. This anticipates his dream of the rough and smooth.

[17] Berg Collection.

> The life that I aspire to live
> No man proposeth me—
> No trade upon the street
> Wears its emblazonry.[18]

Poverty did not disturb him, for wealth, he said, "cannot purchase any great private solace or convenience." [19] Citing the Hindu scripture, he wrote Williams the lesson of the life he was living: " 'Grass and earth to sit on, water to wash the feet, and fourthly, affectionate speech are at no times deficient in the mansions of the good.' " [20]

By this time, however, he had won his first battle with vocation and was living in the mansions of the good; he began to live with the Emersons by the end of April, 1841. For Thoreau, and for Emerson, this was an admirable solution, one that Thoreau would not have accepted if his willingness to yield to his destiny had not been great. On his part this new position offered him all he desired. "I would have men," Thoreau wrote of his longing for friendship, "make a *greater* use of me." [21] This, he felt, Emerson would do; and he entered Emerson's service as a spiritual equal, demanding of the arrangement all that he hoped of friendship. "A great person, though unconsciously, will constantly give you great opportunities to serve him," he wrote, "but a mean one will quite preclude all active benevolence." [22] Perhaps the most inspiriting thing his new adventure offered was such a friendship. But it offered as well a life free of routine and a life in which study and the unpredictable ways of genius were understood. When Emerson wrote his brother William, arranging for Thoreau's tutorship at Staten Island, he stipulated what he himself had undoubtedly provided: ". . . the evening is the best part of the day for the study, a matter of vital importance to all book reading & book writing men, to be at night the autocrat of a chamber be it never so small—6 feet by 6,—wherein to dream, write, & declaim alone. Henry has always had it, & always must. . . . You can take the library in the evening, & give him the basement, or give him the library when you wish the basement." [23] If Emerson was not fully aware of what he would

---

[18] Bode, ed., *Collected Poems of Henry Thoreau*, pp. 132-33.

[19] J, I, 309. See section 2, "Song of Myself."

[20] Berg Collection.

[21] J, I, 205.

[22] J, I, 211.

[23] Rusk, ed., *The Letters of Ralph Waldo Emerson*, III, 162-63.

have to provide in the matter of friendship, he knew he had a writing man on his hands—indeed, he engaged Thoreau in part to further his career, and he offered him the best possible graduate study.

Had Thoreau, however, gone to Emerson a few years earlier, the relation between them might have been a more satisfactory one —though given a Thoreau and an Emerson no equation seems solvable. In 1838 Thoreau was the "brave fine youth" who seemed about to fulfill Emerson's proposals for self-reliance.[24] He seemed to Emerson to be the very person to whom he addressed "The American Scholar" and "Literary Ethics." By 1841, however, there were other stars in Emerson's firmament: Charles Stearns Wheeler, Ellery Channing, and Charles King Newcomb. Emerson had had solid services from Wheeler; he had heralded Channing's poetry in *The Dial;* and what seems even more unaccountable today, had seen in Newcomb's "Dolon" the work of a genius of the first magnitude. He accorded Thoreau no comparable praise. Although he considered him one of his "men," Thoreau, perhaps because of his propinquity, had something of the status of a poor relation.[25] In fact, he came to Emerson as a "hired hand."

Discontented with his domestic arrangements by the advent of Brook Farm, Emerson had proposed in the spring of 1841 that the Alcotts come to live with him. If the Alcotts came, he wrote his brother William, then he would release young Alexander Mc-Caffery, who was living with him and working for his room and board. ". . . his work," Emerson wrote, "is very little valuable in the house. I had hoped he would be able to saw & split my wood, but he has done very little of it. In the summer he can be very useful to me." Alexander was let go to accept an apprenticeship, and Mrs. Alcott wisely refused the offer that her husband would have accepted. By April 21, 1841, however, Emerson reported to William that the double gap had been filled: "Henry Thoreau will come & live with me & work with me." To Margaret Fuller he announced that Thoreau would work with him in the garden "& teach me to graft apples." And in June he wrote again to William: "Henry Thoreau . . . may stay with me a year. . . . he is to have his board &c for what labor he chooses to do: and he is thus far a great

[24] Rusk, ed., *The Letters of Ralph Waldo Emerson,* II, 154.
[25] Sanborn said that Thoreau performed the office of "a younger brother or a grown-up son" (W, VI, 35).

benefactor & physician to me for he is an indefatigable & a very skilful laborer & I work with him as I should not without him and expect now to be suddenly well & strong. . . ." Then, he added: "Thoreau is a scholar & a poet & as full of buds of promise as a young apple tree." [26]

This was the beginning of that "very dangerous prosperity" that Thoreau wrote of to Isaiah Williams.[27] He did not know that he remained Henry Thoreau in Emerson's letters for nearly a year, nor that his Yankee skills and granite character were more appealing than his poetry. Even Margaret Fuller, who made Thoreau earn everything that came to print, approved of him as a teacher for her brother Richard.[28] The relationship had its undercurrent of antagonism, if only because of Thoreau's high expectancies and Emerson's benevolent but patronizing attitude. Thoreau was not much a part of Emerson's letters during his stay; he was, it appears, taken for granted, superserviceable, the perfect transcendental handy man, combining manual and intellectual skills. He was everyone's helper: Emerson's nature tutor and Cato, Lidian's squire, the children's friend—in time, as Emerson lectured away from home, not only the man of the house, but secretary and managing editor of *The Dial*.

This is not to say that Thoreau got the worst of the bargain. The interlude at Emerson's was his best and most primary experience in transcendental human relationships. He was never able to settle his mind about his relation to Emerson—the debate fills his *Journal* —but, as the New Englanders say, he got some good of it. Even before he went to Emerson he knew what he wanted. ". . . when the master meets his pupil as a man," he wrote in January, 1841, "then first do we stand under the same heavens, and master and pupil alike go down the resistless ocean stream together." He wanted some "unforeseen accident" to throw Emerson into a new perspective, for he had already discovered, in the lecturer's imposing voice, a "new side," and expected others.[29] That unforeseen accident would put their lives on the same platform; then the world would learn, he wrote, "what men can build each other up to be,

---

[26] Rusk, ed., *The Letters of Ralph Waldo Emerson*, II, 382, 393-94, 402. See Stewart, ed., *The American Notebooks by Nathaniel Hawthorne*, p. 166.

[27] Berg Collection.

[28] Rusk, ed., *The Letters of Ralph Waldo Emerson*, II, 449.

[29] J, I, 182, 194-95, 198.

when both master and pupil work in love." [30] Thoreau knew the conditions of friendship—the infrequent communions, the naked sincerity, the inexpressible worthiness ("You shall come to a palace, not to an almshouse") [31]—and he kept them in his intercourse with Emerson. "It may be a deference which he will not understand," but he trusted that "the nature which underlies him will understand it. . . . By such politeness we may educate one another to some purpose." [32] We can only gather in the frequent disclosures of sadness, in the pleas for criticism, and in the new insight into friendship ("Let Such Pure Hate Still Underprop"), that Emerson did not understand, or that, if he did, he was as incapable of meeting Thoreau on his high ground as he was of meeting Margaret Fuller's more elemental demands. Certainly there was no want of kindness; perhaps, as Thoreau's letter of gratitude implied, too much. [33] It was not within his conditions of friendship to be grateful. "If any man assist me in the way of the world," he wrote in August, 1841, "let him derive satisfaction from the deed itself, for I think I never shall have dissolved my prior relations to God. . . . The truly beneficent never relapses into a creditor. . . . If any have been kind to me, what more do they want? . . . My obligations will be my lightest load. . . ." [34] Although the deaths of John Thoreau and Waldo brought Emerson and Thoreau together in grief, and the growth of Thoreau's love explained his protracted residence, the running together of souls did not occur. "We do [not] wish friends to feed and clothe our bodies," he wrote in the spring of 1842, "—neighbors are kind enough for that,—but to do the like offices to ourselves. We wish to spread and publish ourselves, as the sun spreads its rays. . . ." But Emerson was not that friend—the friend who "is like wax in the rays that fall from our own hearts." Knowingly or not, Thoreau described Emerson in the very image that Emerson used to explain his temperamental fault: "My friend is cold and reserved. . . . These are the early processes; the particles are just beginning to shoot in crystals." [35] Even Thoreau's letter explaining the nature of friendship did not anneal the relation. Probably the

---

[30] J, I, 204, 206.

[31] J, I, 223.

[32] J, I, 255.

[33] W, VI, 53.

[34] J, I, 279-80.

[35] J, I, 339-40.

highest tribute Emerson ever got from Thoreau, this exposure of Henry's heart's desire was also the severest reproach.[36]

Where Emerson failed Lidian succeeded. When Thoreau went to Staten Island he thanked her, not for her gifts but for "your influence for two years." Everything he asked of friendship she provided. "I felt taxed not," he told her, "to disappoint your expectation. . . . You have helped to keep my life 'on loft,' as Chaucer says of Griselda, and in a better sense." Lidian was his "elder sister," his "lunar influence"—"You must know," he said, "that you represent to me woman. . . ."[37] When he wrote again in answer to her reply to this confession, he was ecstatic, having found at last a person who could share his destiny by overseeing it. "I see," he told Lidian of his response to her truthful answer, "that it will make my life very steep, but it may lead to fairer prospects. . . ." He protested, knight that he was, his unworthiness, and, lest his love be misinterpreted, he invoked the fates as the guarantors of its spirituality: ". . . they will not permit it wrongfully." Lidian undoubtedly felt that the relation had gone as far as it could go, that she had been partly responsible for it, for the letters made her aware of Thoreau's partisanship in the subtle antagonisms of her life. His greetings at the close of the letter "to my other friend and brother, whose nobleness I slowly recognize," made her position clear enough. And even Thoreau's reference in his next letter to "the great questions of 'Fate, Freewill, Foreknowledge absolute,'" which she had had to defend in that transcendental household, did not restore their correspondence to its former height. Nevertheless, for Thoreau the relation with Lidian was a permanent if unilateral one. "The thought of you will constantly elevate my life," he said; "it will be something always above the horizon to behold, as when I look up at the evening star."[38]

The Emerson household was not unsocial, as one might expect from the common notions of the "cold" Emerson. It was another Mrs. Thoreau's boardinghouse, only its guests were transcendentalists. The stream of visitors was full and continuous, filling the house with all the spiritually hungry, those who read and wrote for *The Dial* and those whom Emerson was gathering together for his personal community. It was social after the fashion of the Went-

---

[36] W, VI, 56-58.

[37] W, VI, 76.

[38] W, VI, 87-89, 112-13.

worths in James's *The Europeans.* Emerson was a gentleman; the
Concord Circle was high-toned; and the talk, which was the sacred
goal, was transcendental.[39] One did not meet to shake hands but to
exchange ideas. Alcott said that conversation was his idea of heaven,
and Emerson considered it the highest fulfillment of human communion. But there is no indication in Thoreau's *Journals*—only in
his businesslike reports to the lecturing Emerson—that Thoreau
was living at the intellectual center of Transcendentalism, that
social reform had so engaged Emerson and Alcott that they were
experimenting with their households, that Alcott had gone to
England and returned with Charles Lane, that Emerson had published his *Essays,* or that Hawthorne had taken the Old Manse.
There were no personalities in Thoreau's record of those years.
There was, however, from the beginning of his residence a sign
of discontent. He wrote in May, 1841, that "life in gardens and
parlors is unpalatable to me. It wants rudeness and necessity to
give it relish." [40] And he confided to Lidian's sister, Mrs. Lucy
Jackson Brown, who was his confidante (and lesser lunar influence)
that he was beginning to prefer nature to man. "I grow savager and
savager every day . . . and my tameness is only the repose of untamableness." Telling her of his wish "to be nature looking into
nature," he said that "from some such recess I would put forth
sublime thoughts daily, as the plant puts forth leaves." [41]

He was nevertheless putting forth thoughts daily at Emerson's.
It was his most productive period as a poet. And balancing his
sense of misgivings at his "strangely mixed life"—his Valhalla with
its kitchen, its "brooms, and scouring, and taxes, and housekeeping"
—was his sense of freedom. "We are all of us Apollos serving some
Admetus," he told Mrs. Brown.[42] And yet his servitude was not
galling. He may have looked again for a farm in 1842, but the tenor
of these years was an exhilarating freedom. "I have been your
pensioner for nearly two years," he wrote Emerson, "and still left
free as under the sky." [43] He had at last been permitted to meet his
fate head on, and, as he told Isaiah Williams, "My destiny is now

[39] See W, VI, 64-65, where Mrs. Emerson reported an Alcott "conversation"
in which Thoreau defended the love of nature.

[40] J, I, 256.

[41] W, VI, 36-37.

[42] W, VI, 44.

[43] W, VI, 53.

arrived—it is now arriving." [44] The letter to Williams, with its fierce joy in independence and trust in the universe, was the best proof of what Emerson had provided him. He had told Mrs. Brown that "I love my fate to the very core and rind, and could swallow it without paring it"; and at the time he had written Williams, he had given her in brief the same account of his life. "When I realize what has transpired, and the greatness of the part I am unconsciously acting," he wrote, "I am thrilled, and it seems as if there were none in history to match it." [45] His "estate," he told her a year later, included a happiness for which he could not account. "One while I am vexed by a sense of meanness; one while I simply wonder at the mystery of life; and at another, and at another, seem to rest on my oars, as if propelled by propitious breezes from I know not what quarter." [46]

II

Emerson, that nurturer of genius, had in mind another destiny for Thoreau; he was impatient for the fruit of his Apollo's solid seasons. Thus, though Thoreau had found a life in which vocation might be forgotten, there were also stirring around him the constant arrivals of genius, Emerson's own growing success, and the talk of *The Dial* to remind him of it. Yield as he might, Thoreau was not to remain at Emerson's forever. Like young McCaffery, who had worked for his board that he might get a schooling, Thoreau was expected to get *his* work done as well as the chores, to leave the household prepared to augment the thin ranks of transcendentalists. If Emerson was to learn gardening from his junior, Thoreau was to learn the transcendental craft from Emerson. And if the relation between them was not so warm as Thoreau desired, there was every evidence that where the practical matters of genius were concerned, Emerson was an insistent teacher. Not only did he prune the budding poet's work, he gave Thoreau almost free rein with *The Dial* when he assumed the editorship. His relation to Thoreau was undoubtedly literary and professional, and this perhaps accounted for the sudden increase of passages on the art and aim of writing that filled the *Journals* in these years. It

---

[44] Berg Collection.
[45] W, VI, 39, 41.
[46] W, VI, 47.

accounted certainly for Thoreau's considerable output in 1842-43, and for the fact that by the spring of 1843 Emerson felt that Thoreau was ready to storm the publishing citadels of New York. Emerson supplied a subtle push, and this, as much as anything, destroyed Thoreau's felicity. "I care not for the man or his designs," Thoreau wrote in 1842, "who would make the highest use of me short of an all-adventuring friendship." [47] He did not want to go to New York; he was overcome there by an unaccountable sleepiness, and almost from the beginning by a nostalgia for home. He probably went only to pay his debt to Emerson. And even writing, which Emerson expected of his protégés (Alcott complained that Emerson, "faithful to his own Genius, asserts the supremacy of the scholar's pen"),[48] was, under the pressure of vocation, contaminated by prudence. "I feel as if my life had grown more outward," Thoreau lamented, "since I could express it." He wrote that he had gained a talent but lost a character, that he was being judged for his skill, not for himself. "Society affects to estimate men by their talents," he explained, "but really feels and knows them by their characters. What a man does, compared with what he is, is but a small part. To require that our friend possess a certain skill is not to be satisfied till he is something less than our friend." [49] Thoreau's gains as a writer, therefore, were paid by a loss of friendship; and his failure to take his place with Wheeler, Channing, and Newcomb—with Emerson's proven pupils—probably put the remainder of his life under a misunderstanding that even in the funeral tribute Emerson never corrected.

When Emerson took over *The Dial* in April, 1842, he renewed his hope in Thoreau. "Henry is quite unable to labor lately since his sickness, & so must resign the garden into other hands," he wrote Margaret Fuller, "but as private secretary to the President of the Dial, his works & fame may go out into all lands, and, as happen to great Premiers, quite extinguish the titular Master." Emerson would forward Thoreau, where Margaret Fuller had only done so under protest. And that very day, he said, he had "set Henry Thoreau on the good track of giving an account of them [the Scientific Surveys of Massachusetts] in the Dial, explaining to him the felicity of the subject for him as it admits of the narrative

[47] J, I, 348.

[48] Shepard, ed., *The Journals of Bronson Alcott*, p. 134.

[49] J, I, 349, 352.

of all his woodcraft boatcraft & fishcraft." [50] Up to this time Thoreau had published only some poems and the minor piece of criticism on Aulus Persius Flaccus; now, because of Emerson, he was to publish the substantial essay on the "Natural History of Massachusetts." Had it not been for Emerson's prompting and awareness of materials, Thoreau might have continued writing literary criticism and abstract essays on high moral and transcendental themes. Emerson apprised him of the literary value of natural facts and introduced him to the hidden ore of his own *Journals*. What Emerson expected of Thoreau he announced in the "Preliminary Note" to Thoreau's essay: ". . . we found a near neighbor and friends of ours, dear also to the Muses, a native and an inhabitant of the town of Concord, who readily undertook to give us such comments as he had made on these books, and, better still, notes of his own conversation with nature in the woods and waters of this town. With all thankfulness we begged our friend to lay down the oar and fishing line, which none can handle better, and assume the pen, that Isaak Walton and White of Selborne might not want a successor, nor the fair meadows, to which we also have owed a home and the happiness of many years, their poet." [51] Emerson introduced Thoreau-the-naturalist.

Thoreau's essay supported the claim that here was the poet of Concord; but it did not follow in the tradition of Walton and White, nor did it, except for the texture of poetry and natural lore, owe anything to Howitt. Instead it was a treatise on the personal uses of nature, built almost entirely, and without great revision, out of the rather meager nature observations of his *Journals*. Fortunately the books he had to review, surveys of the insects, fishes, reptiles, birds, plants, and animals of Massachusetts, offered an easy organization of his own materials: in fact, this was the only use he made of them; they provided a structure, as did his walks and excursions, for his thoughts. The essay, therefore, not only introduces us to Thoreau's basic method of composition, but also shows us, since it brings together everything he had thought about nature, what his relation to nature was in 1842. For he had come a long way from his college review of Howitt, not so much in his interest in nature, which his essay shows was more intense than one would expect from the *Journals*, but in his deepening response

---

[50] Rusk, ed., *The Letters of Ralph Waldo Emerson*, III, 47. Thoreau had been ill, having undergone sympathetically John's agonies with lockjaw.

[51] *The Dial*, III (July, 1842), 19.

to and need for nature. As his hopes for a higher society darkened, nature rather than friendship became the polar term for society. "If any scorn your love," he wrote to steel himself, "let them see plainly that you serve not them but another. If these bars are up, go your way to other of God's pastures, and browse there the while. When your host shuts his door on you he incloses you in the dwelling of nature. He thrusts you over the threshold of the world. My foes restore me to my friends." [52] Later in the same year, 1841, he recorded his "inexpressible happiness" in nature, and pondered his "peculiarly wild nature, which so yearns toward all wilderness." "I know of no redeeming qualities in me but a sincere love for some things, and when I am reproved I have to fall back to this ground. This is my argument in reserve for all cases. . . . When I am condemned, and condemn myself utterly, I think straightway, 'But I rely on my love for some things.' Therein I am whole and entire. Therein I am God-propped." [53] His need for nature also grew with his desperation over his vocation, and even at Emerson's it became the refuge for his discontent. Before a year had passed he wrote: "I want to go soon and live away by the pond, where I shall hear only the wind whispering among the reeds. It will be success if I shall have left myself behind. But my friends ask what I will do when I get there. Will it not be employment enough to watch the progress of the seasons?" "I don't want to feel," he added the next day, "as if my life were a sojourn any longer. That philosophy cannot be true which so paints it. It is time now that I begin to live." [54]

Finally, when John died in 1842 and Thoreau was bereaved by the loss of his best friend, he turned to nature for his solace. As Emerson had done in "Threnody," so Thoreau: his own grief and disharmony were overcome by being allied with the larger purposes and order of nature. "What right have I to grieve," he wrote Mrs. Brown, "who have not ceased to wonder? We feel at first as if some opportunities of kindness and sympathy were lost, but learn afterward that any *pure grief* is ample recompense for all. That is, if we are faithful; for a great grief is but sympathy with the soul that disposes events, and is as natural as the resin on Arabian trees. Only Nature has a right to grieve perpetually, for she only is inno-

[52] J, I, 210.

[53] J, I, 295-96.

[54] J, I, 299.

cent. Soon the ice will melt, and the blackbirds sing along the river which he frequented, as pleasantly as ever. The same everlasting serenity will appear in this face of God, and we will not be sorrowful if he is not." [55] This faith, as one sees in "Threnody," was not an easy one; it was the greatest test of the spiritual resources of Transcendentalism.

The depths of Thoreau's faith are not recorded in his letter, but in "Great Friend" and "Brother Where Dost Thou Dwell?" In the first poem, Thoreau's "cosmos" has become a "chaos":

> I walk in nature still alone
> . . . .
> I still must seek the friend
> Who does with nature blend,
> Who is the person in her mask,
> He is the man I ask.

Having lost "an intelligent and kindred face," he must, as he later set out to do, make himself another universe:

> The center of this world,
>
> The face of nature
> The site of human life,
> Some sure foundation
> And nucleus of a nation—
> At least a private station.[56]

"Brother Where Dost Thou Dwell?" an elegy in the tradition of "Lycidas" which Thoreau admired, records a grief so great that nature herself is barren and silent. In both poems, John is the meaning of nature for Thoreau: he is the "presence" who has animated it and given it its significance—its tutelary deity, and for Thoreau the prism of his own subjective idealism. Though Thoreau is always thought of as a solitary walker, most of his excursions and many of his walks were made in the company of others—and Channing, it seems, replaced John. John, he said, was

---

[55] W, VI, 41. See also the letter of March 14, 1842, to Isaiah Williams, Berg Collection. In the "Natural History of Massachusetts" he wrote: "To him who contemplates a trait of natural beauty no harm nor disappointment can come" (W, V, 105). In a letter to Emerson on Waldo's death, March 11, 1842, he stressed the constancy of nature and the renewal of life out of death (Berg Collection). This was implicit in his earliest *Journal* entry: "Every part of nature teaches that the passing away of one life is the making room for another" (J, I, 3).

[56] J, I, 472-73.

his eyes and ears, and, in respect to nature, the leader. Thoreau
acknowledged that

> I was the strongest here,
> Of sturdiest pace

but that

> For then, as now, I trust,
> I always lagg'd behind. . . .[57]

John was the nature lover, and Thoreau's most famous natural
settings, the river and the pond, were associated with him. Indeed,
the *Week* was Thoreau's memorial to his brother and the wonderful
harmonies of friendship and nature that they enjoyed together in
their youth. And the "Natural History of Massachusetts," reminding
him of his debt to John, was not only an attempt to "waive disease
& pain/And resume new life again,"[58] as he wrote of the hawk,
it was his attempt to state his faith in the "health" of nature, and
in the face of all his discontent—the mounting crises of vocation
and friendship—to establish his relation to nature. Though he did
not immediately act on it, this essay announced the settled way
of his life.

Thoreau's "conversation with nature" was framed by an opening
section on the health in nature and a closing section on her proper
study. Instead of laboring for the facts, he proposed "enthusiasm";
instead of scientific method, he advised "direct intercourse and
sympathy"; and instead of apparatus and measurement, the senses
—"a deeper and finer experience."[59] The Scientific Surveys lacked
this "Indian wisdom," and the purpose of his essay was to show in
his own approach to nature how much of the human value of
nature had thereby been lost. The transcendental method he
sketched at the end of the essay was also the way of finding the
health he affirmed at the beginning: the common theme was joy.
"Surely," he proclaimed, "joy is the condition of life." Enthusiasm,
the play of the senses, joy—all that he meant by health—were
articles of that philosophy he would no longer postpone, and as
he entered on his life they became the insistent theme of his major
work. Indeed, it was here that Thoreau broke most completely from
the New England past—from that enmity with joy of which

---

[57] Bode, ed., *Collected Poems of Henry Thoreau*, p. 314.

[58] J, I, 471-72.

[59] All citations, unless otherwise noted, are from "Natural History of Massachusetts," W, V, 103-31.

Santayana spoke. "They are sick and diseased imaginations," Thoreau said, "who would toll the world's knell so soon"; he had in mind, among others, the Millerites. He did not want "the preacher's consolation," adding in the *Journal* original, "This is the creed of the hypochondriac." And he wrote: "The doctrines of despair, of spiritual or political tyranny or servitude [he omitted "priestcraft"], were never taught by such as shared the serenity ["harmony"] of nature." He also omitted an entire paragraph on the Sabbath, on the church as a "hospital for men's souls"—themes he used in the *Week*.[60] For he had known "moments of an azure hue." In the poem that initiates this theme of nature-as-ecstasy, of nature as a release from "this plodding life" and of spring as the breaking up of the winter of man's discontent, he wrote that the "moment" makes

> The best of philosophy untrue that aims
> But to console man for his grievances.

His key word is "health," and it always is synonymous with ecstasy. "You must converse much with the field and woods," he omitted from the original passage, as if this explicit statement were not needed, "if you would imbibe such health into your mind and spirit as you covet for your body." [61]

Such was his thesis: the re-creation of man in nature. He introduced it pleasantly enough by telling of his "accession of health" on reading natural history in the winter—the spring-in-winter metaphor which does the work of the essay was thus introduced, adumbrating the structure of his account of various natural phenomena which he always takes through the seasons, beginning with winter and moving into spring and summer and occasionally fall. His wariness in leading up to his theme was as purposive as his many and telling omissions from the original passages in the *Journal*. "Much more is adoing," he easily remarked of the life in nature, "than Congress wots of." Then, a little more sharply, "The merely political aspect of the land is never very cheering; men are degraded when considered as the members of a political organization." (He omitted: "As a nation the people never utter one great and healthy word.")[62] And finally, after commenting on the

---

[60] J, I, 307, 309.

[61] J, I, 306.

[62] J, I, 306.

"paltriness" of Bunker Hill and other landmarks of man when the wind blows over them, he affirmed: "In society you will not find health, but in nature." Nature and health were thus opposed to society and decay, and the individual to the mob. "Society is always diseased, and the best is most so," he claimed. "There is no scent in it so wholesome as that of the pines, nor any fragrance so penetrating as the life-everlasting in high pastures."

Put in this way, so aggressively and so positively, Thoreau's thesis even disturbed his transcendental friends. Emerson may have written his "Preliminary Note" to soften the shock; Alcott, however, with his doctrine of nature as lapsed spirit, was as deeply distressed as the majority of Thoreau's readers, who enjoyed his picturesque qualities when they read the *Week*, but who refused his philosophy and called it pantheism. Lidian reported in a letter to her husband that Alcott had held a "conversation" on "The Love of Nature" and that he had said that "this love was the most subtle and dangerous of sins; a refined idolatry. . . ." Thoreau, who attended, took the opposing view, telling Alcott that he was "deficient in the faculty in question. . . ." [63] Alcott, of course, was a social man, the philosopher of family life, and though he approved of the spiritual uses of nature and had the greatest admiration for Thoreau, he could not accept the social renunciation of Thoreau's preference for nature. Nor could New England.

For what Thoreau said he heard in the pulpits, lyceums, and parlors was a "din of religion, literature, and philosophy. . . ." All this he repudiated (using the imagery of *The Service*) for the silence of nature: indeed, he repudiated Emerson, Alcott, and *The Dial*. "When I detect a beauty in any of the recesses of nature," he wrote, "I am reminded, by the serene and retired spirit in which it requires to be contemplated, of the inexpressible privacy of a life,—how silent and unambitious it is." He had confessed himself. But he went on to assert the bravery of science—of nature study— finding here incidentally a place for the passages he could not use in *The Service*. He, too, would serve by discovering the truth, by "breaking ground like a pioneer for the array of arts that follow in her train." He did not want his going to nature to be interpreted as a retreat from the social claims that had been made on his life. "What an admirable training is science," he said, "for the more active warfare of life." He was not a deserter, nor coward; Lin-

---

[63] W, VI, 64-65.

naeus, he wrote, setting out for Lapland, "to take in fish, flower, and bird, quadruped and biped," was as admirable in his "quiet bravery" as Napoleon. Though he never knew it, his identification with Linnaeus rather than with Napoleon was one of the reasons for Emerson's disapproval. For in Emerson's private list of representative men Thoreau was Napoleon, the executive genius. And Napoleon would have engineered for America rather than waste his ambition and genius on huckleberry parties. Thoreau's argument with Alcott revealed that even for the transcendentalists, to take nature for one's bride (as Emerson said of solitude) was only a metaphor. The Concord Circle wanted no Indians: to go to nature with the ardor of Thoreau was as dangerous as the abandonment to primitivism that Melville saw in the South Seas.

What was acceptable, and grudgingly admired since it was consonant with the cherished spiritual rigor of the Puritan, was Thoreau's brave determination for character. The image that Thoreau perhaps unwittingly used in the "Natural History" to suggest the health of nature was the "life-everlasting in high pasture." Though he never made it explicit, the pursuit of the flower was the metaphor of his life, and Emerson, preparing his funeral oration fresh from Thoreau's manuscripts, found it. In 1840 Thoreau noted in the *Journal* that "if my path run on before me level and smooth, it is all a mirage; in reality it is steep and arduous as a chamois pass." [64] The imagery of mountains and ascent are among the dominant images of Thoreau's spiritual language; they are the symbols of his recurrent dream.[65] As in the lecture on "Society," the mountain is the individual prospect, from which the spiritual seeker overlooks the plain. So here, the life everlasting is put against society, its penetrating scent contrasting with the scent of social decay. Like the mountain, where it grows, it is an image of purity. "Though the pleasure of ascending the mountain is largely mixed with awe," Thoreau said of his dream, "my thoughts are purified and sublimed by it, as if I had been translated." Written in 1857, this is nevertheless a constant in Thoreau's thought, and the life everlasting, used only as a detail in his discussion of "health," reveals the real intent of his first espousal of nature: a quest for purity that became more intense as time went on and more pronounced in his writing. "The dry, pearly, and almost incorruptible

---

[64] J, I, 152.
[65] See J, X, 141-44.

heads of the Life Everlasting," Thoreau copied into his *Journal,* commenting, "Ah! this is a truly elysian flower now, beyond change and decay, not lusty but immortal,—pure ascetics, suggesting a widowed virginity." [66] Emerson's closing paragraph, therefore, reached to the heart of Thoreau's life. "There is a flower known to botanists," he said, "one of the same genus with our summer plant called 'Life-Everlasting' . . . which grows on the most inaccessible cliffs of the Tyrolese mountains, where the chamois dare hardly venture, and which the hunter, tempted by its beauty, and by his love (for it is immensely valued by the Swiss maids), climbs the cliffs to gather, and is sometimes found dead at the foot, with the flower in his hands. It is called by botanists the *Gnaphalium leontopodium,* but by the Swiss *Edelweisse,* which signifies *Noble Purity.* Thoreau seemed to me living in the hope to gather this plant, which belonged to him of right." [67] But perceptive as Emerson was, the individualism of Thoreau's life and quest for purity seemed to him to go beyond the limits even Transcendentalism prescribed; not finding its issue in society, it was egoism, like Margaret Fuller's writing, too personal for Emerson. At the time Emerson commissioned Thoreau's essay, his own individualism had been measured by society, and his thought, a few years before so close to what Thoreau now advocated, was becoming more social —as his vocation, too, had been at last accepted.

There were also other seeds buried in the "Natural History" that flowered later in Thoreau's thought. Elaborating the fundamental opposition of nature and society, Thoreau extended its meaning to include that of America and Europe. "Surely good courage will not flag here on the Atlantic border," he wrote, "as long as we are flanked by the Fur Countries. . . . Methinks some creeds in vestries and churches do forget the hunter wrapped in furs by the Great Slave Lake, and that the Esquimaux sledges are drawn by dogs. . . ." The Fur Countries were Thoreau's reference to what remained of the wilderness (the aboriginal nature) of the American continent: it is his first mention of the wild which he defended in "Walking" as "the preservation of the World" and the regenerating power of the West, and which in *A Yankee in Canada* gave him the sense of being "out of the civilized world." "We had only to

---

[66] J, IV, 307.
[67] C, X, 484.

go a quarter of a mile from the road," he said of his Canadian experience, "to find ourselves on the verge of the . . . unexplored wilderness stretching toward Hudson's Bay." [68] This sense of the free and unexplored is what also appealed to him in the Surveys' account of the few remaining bears, wolves, lynxes, and wildcats in Massachusetts—and one of the few passages of excitement in the later *Journals* was Thoreau's account of the Canada lynx in Concord.[69] When he smelled the "strong scent of musk," he said in the "Natural History," he was reminded "of an unexplored wilderness": "Those backwoods are not far off then." And by calling the muskrat "the beaver of the settled States," he was able to remind his readers that Concord was once an important center of the fur trade and that once the Indian (who now first enters the constellation of his writing) was the original inhabitant—and, lest Concord forget, that "there are trappers in our midst still, as well as on the streams of the far West. . . ." [70]

This widening of the meaning of a natural fact by association was Thoreau's essential method in this essay, and, as the "Natural History" first indicated, was prepared for by extensive reading. In *A Yankee in Canada* and *Cape Cod* the show of reading was still greater, often discomfiting the most ardent Thoreauvian. In the "Natural History" it was minimal, however, because Thoreau was still as much an apprentice to books as he was to nature. His reading in natural history was at this time slight; except for Linnaeus, it had been apparently devoted exclusively to birds. He had read Alexander Wilson's *American Ornithology* and Audubon's *Ornithological Biography* at college,[71] and mentions in the essay only Goldsmith and Nuttall. His literary associations, however, were most numerous; and what seems most significant was the extent of his reading in the annals of discovery and adventure. While at Harvard he had begun—with an appetite for the heroic as well as for anthropology—a course of reading in explorations that was only equaled by Francis Parkman. In the college years alone he had read Francis Hall's *Travels in Canada and the United States in 1815 and 1817;* Ross Cox's *Adventures on the Columbia*

---

[68] W, V, 224, 42.

[69] J, XIV, 78-81, 83-87.

[70] The Melvins and Goodwins are used again in the *Week* to contrast the life in nature and the life in society.

[71] Cameron, *Emerson The Essayist,* II, 193, 194.

River, including the Narrative of a Residence of Six Years on the Western Side of the Rocky Mountains among various Tribes of Indians hitherto Unknown; Thomas McKenney's *Sketches of a Tour to the Lakes, of the Character and Customs of the Chippeway Indians* . . . ; Charles Cochrane's *Journal of a Residence and Travels in Columbia during the Years 1823 and 1824;* William Bullock's *Six Months' Residence and Travels in Mexico* . . . ; Mrs. Sigourney's *Traits of the Aborigines of America. A Poem;* John Marshall's *A History of the Colonies Planted by the English on the Continent of North America, From Their Settlement;* John Barrow's *A Voyage to Cochinchina* . . . ; George Waddington and Bernard Hanbury's *Journal of a Visit to Some Parts of Ethiopia;* John Ranking's *Historical Researches on the Conquest of Peru, Mexico, Bogota, Natchez, and Talomeco, in the Thirteenth Century by the Mongols;* Henry Brackenridge's *Journal of a Voyage up the River Missouri;* Charles de Brosses' *Terra Australis Cognita: or Voyages to the Terra Australis, or Southern Hemisphere during the 16th, 17th and 18th Centuries;* and George Back's *Narrative of the Arctic Land Expedition.* . . .[72] This reading, continued more strenuously later, became, whether as metaphor, theme, or substance, a stable thread in the fabric of Thoreau's writing. But he used the anthropological and natural facts he gathered from his reading in just the transcendental way he used his literary facts. He used history to prove the indifference of time and place: the facts that concerned him were either those that showed how man lived in his environment, how he interacted with nature, or those that reported his response to natural facts. The primary conditions and experience of life were the same everywhere. "The history of anything," he wrote, "is only the true account of it, which will always be the same." And "time," he said, "hides no treasures; we want not its *then,* but its now. . . . But one veil hangs over past, present, and future, and it is the province of the historian to find out, not what was, but what is." [73] Accordingly, Thoreau used history to verify his experience, and he used his experience to verify the record of history. His reading was a search for the records of "life." Had he lived to use his many volumes of "facts" about the Indian and nature, he would have written what might have been the most definitive history of

---

[72] Cameron, *Emerson The Essayist,* II, 192-94.

[73] J, I, 325, 268-69.

himself—that natural history of man he suggested at the conclusion of his essay.

The method is obvious in his use of Anacreon's ode on the cicada. Citing his own observation of crickets, asking "Who does not remember the shrill roll-call of the harvest fly?" he wrote that "there were ears for these sounds in Greece long ago, as Anacreon's ode will show." Commenting on the return of spring, he again used an ode of Anacreon, prefacing it with the statement that "the old Teian poet sing[s] . . . as well for New England as for Greece. . . ." The common mussels that he found in the Concord River were as much a fact to him as to the Indian; they form the link of time as well as of association: "In one place, where they [the Indians] are said to have feasted, they [the shells] are found in large quantities, at an elevation of thirty feet above the river, filling the soil to the depth of a foot, and mingled with ashes and Indian remains." Frequently Thoreau used historical fact to another end: to raise his observations to the symbolic level, to permit the play of imagination—what he called "extravagance." Having given the measurements of a dead osprey—that is, the scientific facts— he took from Nuttall, in preference to other data, his commentary from Aristotle and Linnaeus. "The ancients, particularly Aristotle," Nuttall wrote, "pretended that the ospreys taught their young to gaze at the sun, and those who were unable to do so were destroyed. Linnaeus even believed, on ancient authority, that one of the feet of this bird had all the toes divided, while the other was partly webbed, so that it could swim with one foot, and grasp a fish with the other." Thoreau did not discredit these superstitions. As with myth, he accepted them, not for their objective but for their subjective truth. And in the closing sentences of the passage he wrote out his own subjective truth, having moved as far as he could from the barren fact. Returning to the dead bird, he wrote, as if criticizing the unimaginative present, "But that educated eye is now dim, and those talons are nerveless." And then he launched his own verbal flight: "Its shrill scream seems yet to linger in its throat, and the roar of the sea in its wings. There is the tyranny of Jove in its claws, his wrath in the erectile feathers of the head and neck. It reminds me of the Argonautic expedition, and would inspire the dullest to take flight over Parnassus." [74] Similarly, he transformed

[74] His reading in the Greeks was among his earliest and most extensive, and was frequently used as allusion. Usually it signified the "Golden Age," the free life of the senses and a healthy and adventurous intercourse with nature.

the crow into the "dusky spirit of the wood." "I have seen it suggested somewhere," he began with the fact, "that the crow was
brought to this country by the white man; but I shall as soon
believe that the white man planted these pines and hemlocks. He
is no spaniel to follow our steps; but rather flits about the clearings
like the dusky spirit of the Indian, reminding me oftener of Philip
and Powhatan, than of Winthrop and Smith. He is a relic of the
dark ages. By just so slight, by just so lasting a tenure does superstition hold the world ever; there is the rook in England, and the
crow in New England." There follows a poem incorporating some
of the same images and ideas—Thoreau's usual way of working
his verse into his prose. In many cases, though there is always a
relation of theme, the poetry is interlarding. Here it helped Thoreau
carry his extravagance a little higher, but, as in his remark on superstition, the movement of the imagery, all dealing with the aboriginal, was misdirected. For in the poem, the crow is both the
Indian, dispossessed by the Winthrops and Smiths, and Thoreau
himself, the lonely partaker of nature, borne by his bravery, like
the bird,

> . . . above the clouds,
> Over desponding human crowds,
> Which far below
> Lay thy haunts low. . . .

Thoreau's observations in the essay proper were hung on the
frame provided by the Surveys. Taking up the insects, birds, quadrupeds, fishes, flowers, and invertebrate animals, he copied out
and wove together whatever was ready to hand in the *Journal*.
Though the essay has always seemed the work of an accomplished
student of nature, it was actually the work of a novice whose experience and records were few. He used everything he had in the
Journal, and, as in the memorable description of spear fishing, wrote
out freshly what he needed to cover the scope of the Surveys. The
paucity of his experiences is striking; but what he did with them,
the texture of association, hides that fact. Thoreau's studies in
nature, even when they became obsessive, were lamentably poor
science, but only those who want to make him out a scientist are
distressed by this. What he wrote of nature has had its remarkable
appeal just because it wasn't science: he used the Surveys in the
way in which he always used the fact—to advance beyond it to its
human significance. The transcendental aim was not science (and
perhaps his friends were reluctant to have him go to the woods be-

cause they misunderstood his remarks on the bravery of science),
but those personal uses of nature which Thoreau demonstrated in
the essay: the fact-in-the-mind, the fact interacted with and lived
with, assimilated, stained with the colors of human life. Thoreau
said he wanted in books "the hue of the mind." [75] He did indeed fill
his later *Journals* and factbooks (properly so) with natural facts—
and why he did we will see later—but he never used this crude ore
in his writing. Unless he refined it, unless the fact-as-thing became
the fact-as-experience, glowing with the fire of life, it remained in
the workshop. And there these facts, that massive bulk of detail
confronting the mind, remind one of the agonies of assimilation
that Thoreau, beginning so innocently and confidently, had prepared for himself.

The very lack of fact in the "Natural History" made his task
easier. What he took from the *Journal* was already colored by his
mind. When he wrote of insects, there were no facts, but thoughts.
"Entomology," he wrote in the first section, advertising his method,
"extends the limits of being . . . so that I walk in nature with a
sense of greater space and freedom. It suggests besides, that the
universe is not rough-hewn, but perfect in its details." Insects—how
many other associations come to mind—were associated exclusively
with sound: "The sources of the myriad sounds which crowd the
summer noon [and then the cluster forms: the perfect universe,
the sphere music, the summer and noon of inspiration], and which
seem the very grain and stuff of which eternity is made." [76] This
is the thought that prompted Thoreau's use of Anacreon's ode,

> Sweet prophet of summer.
> The Muses love thee,
> And Phoebus himself loves thee
> . . . .
> Almost thou art like the gods.

The cricket's music, which he had noted earliest in his *Journal*, was
the earth song (Anacreon: "Thou skilful, earthborn, song-loving"),
the very pulse of creation, ushering in the seasons. Hearing it in
the autumn, he said, in a passage he omitted, that he felt "the lively
decay of autumn promises as infinite duration and freshness as the
green leaves of spring." [77] The cricket's chant was the primal sound,

---

[75] J, I, 223.

[76] He also associated the cricket with the Indian scriptures, as a "gloss" on
the sacred code (J, I, 267). See also J, I, 276.

[77] J, I, 109.

the audible sphere music. Omitting what was fundamental in his metaphysics of sound, that "the human soul is a silent harp in God's quire, whose strings need only to be swept by the divine breath to chime in with the harmonies of creation," he went on to give the central idea of *The Service:* "Every pulse-beat is in exact time with the cricket's chant and the tickings of the deathwatch in the wall. Alternate with these if you can." [78] He had indeed used entomology to extend the limits of being: he had written his own ode to inspiration.

With birds he was more familiar, but his method was the same. He associated them primarily with the return of spring, with the advent of the summer of inspiration. The birds that remained in winter had his "warmest sympathy," and he listed them, still making them the symbols of his thought if only with an epithet: "the partridge, like a russet link extended over from autumn to spring, preserving unbroken the chain of summers," "the hawk with warrior-like firmness abiding the blasts of winter," "the shrike, with heedless and unfrozen melody bringing back summer again. . . ." The fact was never without some token of response, and his lists had the same artistry as the catalogs of Whitman.[79] One might give them that form:

> The nut-hatch and chicadee flitting in company through the dells of the wood, the one harshly scolding at the intruder, the other with a faint lisping note enticing him on;
> The jay screaming in the orchard;
> The crow cawing in unison with the storm;
> The robin and lark lurking by warm springs in the woods;
> The familiar snow-bird culling a few seeds in the garden, or a few crumbs in the yard. . . .

Always the accurate perception, the thing *seen,* as in the list of migrating birds returning in spring:

> The ducks . . . diving to peck at the root of the lily, and the cranberries which the frost has not loosened;
> The first flock of geese . . . beating to north, in long harrows and waving lines; [80]
> The gingle of the song-sparrow salutes us from the shrubs and fences;

---

[78] J, I, 53.

[79] For shrewd comments on Thoreau's poetic observations, see Stewart, ed., *The American Notebooks by Nathaniel Hawthorne,* pp. 166-67.

[80] Thoreau culled his phrases carefully. See J, I, 177.

The plaintive note of the lark comes clear and sweet from the
  meadow;
The bluebird, like an azure ray,[81] glances past us in our walk.

Then longer treatments of the fish hawk, osprey, and bittern, always
with their calls, until with the "cackle of the flicker . . . summer's
eternity is ushered in. . . ."

The transition from spring to summer was made in terms of
sound. "In May and June," Thoreau wrote, "the woodland quire is
in full tune"—

> Each summer sound
> Is a summer round.

But as summer advances, the migratory birds depart and the
"woods become silent again. . . ." And yet, for the saunterer, there
are birds and sounds enough to reflect his moods. ". . . the solitary
rambler may still find," Thoreau said, "a response and expression
for every mood in the depths of the wood." In *Walden* he asked,
"Why do precisely these objects which we behold make a world?
Why has man just these species of animals for his neighbors, as
if nothing but a mouse could have filled this crevice?" His answer
was the substance of Emerson's theory of language in *Nature*. In
fact, in 1842 he had read G. Oegger's *The True Messiah; or the
Old and New Testaments, examined according to the Principles of
the Language of Nature*,[82] which Emerson had quoted in his treatise. "There seems to be a necessity in spirit," Emerson explained
the correspondence of object and idea, "to manifest itself in material
forms; and day and night, river and storm, beast and bird, acid
and alkali, preëxist in necessary Ideas in the mind of God, and are
what they are by virtue of preceding affections in the world of
spirit. A Fact is the end or last issue of spirit. The visible creation
is the terminus or the circumference of the invisible world." Then
he cited Oegger: " 'Material objects,' said a French philosopher, 'are
necessarily kinds of *scoriae* of the substantial thoughts of the
Creator, which must always preserve an exact relation to their first
origin; in other words, visible nature must have a spiritual and

---

[81] The bluebird and robin were Thoreau's harbingers of rebirth. As one sees
in the "gingle" of the sparrow and in the calls of the other birds, Thoreau was
especially responsive to their sounds—the sounds enriching their return in the
spring, for then they were noisier.

[82] J, I, 320.

moral side.'" [83] Translated into Emerson's subjective idealism, every external fact is a spiritual fact—a fact of consciousness—and the correspondence holds because the external fact is itself an issue of mind, the spirit projected through man. Fact, then, is unconscious mind; to make it conscious, to transform the external into the internal, is the function of man, the way to self-culture—to his own mind and the mind of God. This was Thoreau's answer: "They [animals; external facts] are all beasts of burden, in a sense, made to carry some portion of our thoughts." [84] In this way he gave the reader the clue to his method of using nature, a method already fully employed in the associations that clustered around the facts of his "Natural History." Here he wrote, faintly echoing *Nature,* that "Nature has taken more care than the fondest parent for the education and refinement of her children. . . . When I walk in the woods, I am reminded that a wise purveyor has been there before me; my most delicate experience is typified there."

His approach at this time, however, was wholly subjective, accounting for his limited facts. He did not study nature, as he later did, to pry her meaning from her, amassing facts, living with them, hoping by patience and familiarity to at last find their significance. Indeed, he cast his mind over the fact, and what did not answer to his moods remained outside the range of his interest—there are more insects than the cricket. The failure of his nature studies and the achievement of his writing can both be attributed to this subjective idealism. "It is more proper for a spiritual fact to have suggested an analogous natural one," he wrote in 1841, "than for the natural fact to have preceded the spiritual in our minds." [85] But he also noted at this time that "to give the within outwardness, that is not easy." [86]

Nevertheless he approached nature with the faith he wrote out in "The Inward Morning":

> Packed in my mind lie all the clothes
> Which outward nature wears,
> For, as its hourly fashions change,
> It all things else repairs.

[83] C, I, 34-35.
[84] W, II, 249.
[85] J, I, 175.
[86] J, I, 189.

> My eyes look inward, not without,
> And I but hear myself,
> And this new wealth which I have got
> Is part of my own pelf.
>
> For while I look for change abroad,
> I can no difference find,
> Till some new ray of peace uncalled
> Lumines my inmost mind.[87]

Such a faith, however, depended for its assurance—and here Thoreau was assured—on an unfailing inspiration. It was a faith supported by his early "health" in nature; but in his periods of "decay," guilt filled the void, darkness replaced the dawn. If he provided the garments of nature, he was equally to blame for her nakedness. For he had made Emerson's theory his own mode of communion:

> All things are current found
> On earthly ground,
> Spirits and elements
> Have their descents.
>
> Night and day, year on year,
> High and low, far and near,
> These are our own aspects,
> These are our own regrets.[88]

In time, however, he recognized the responsibility for his "regrets," and saw in Emerson's "A life in harmony with Nature, the love of truth and of virtue, will purge the eyes to understand her text" more than he assumed in his early years.[89] The way to the mountain would not be through the sunny pastures, but through the dark wood. He would have to find the colors in nature herself.

But the youthful Thoreau had colors aplenty. The veery's "clarion," the chickadee and jay

> . . . sing the praise
> Of heroes, and set forth the loveliness
> Of virtue evermore.[90]

And during the "trivial summer days," the veery's call strives "to

---

[87] J, I, 291. For variants see Bode, ed., *Collected Poems of Henry Thoreau,* pp. 74-75. Thoreau wrote in 1843: "How tremendously moral is our life. After all no man can be said to live much in the senses, but every moment is the product of so much character. What painters of scenery we are. We impart to the landscape the perfect colors of our minds" (Houghton. MS AM 278.5).

[88] Bode, ed., *Collected Poems of Henry Thoreau,* p. 83.

[89] C, I, 35.

[90] J, I, 70. Originally not a poem.

lift our thoughts above the street." Thoreau did indeed hear himself: the "Natural History" was not a history of Massachusetts, but
of Thoreau. Thus autumn, because of the return of the birds, is a
"new spring," and the crow the Indian who was already stalking
the colonial forests of Thoreau's mind. The snipe's murmur in
October evenings is "the most spirit-like sound in nature." Of all
the birds he noted, only the loon remained a "fact"—its pursuit on
the retired pond was described (like the spear fishing later in the
essay, showing Thoreau's physical exurberance in nature), but not
yet, as in *Walden,* transformed into the metaphor of thought itself.
Considering this method, one understands, then, why Thoreau
wrote that "I learned to-day that my ornithology had done me no
service." There were bird calls, he said, "which fortunately did not
come within the scope of my science, sung as freshly as if it had
been the first morning of creation, and had for background to their
song an untrodden wilderness, stretching through many a Carolina
and Mexico of the soul." [91] Rewritten in the "Natural History" this
passage was mystified—purposely so to make the reader plumb for
the thought—as in many passages in the published writings that
one finds more clearly expressed in the *Journals* and manuscripts.
"But sometimes one hears a quite new note," he wrote, reminding
one of the function of his famous hound, bay-horse, turtledove
passage, "which has for background other Carolinas and Mexicos
than the books describe, and learns that his ornithology has done
him no service." In effect, he was advising the reader not to take
him literally, and to put away his Wilsons and Audubons. The
records of man were less than the experience of man. He had himself written what the essay was intended to show, that

> My books I'd fain cast-off, I cannot read,
> 'Twixt every page my thoughts go stray at large
> Down in the meadow, where is richer feed,
> And will not mind to hit their proper targe.[92]

The quadrupeds, as we have seen in his treatment of the muskrat,
introduce the "wild" and the Indian, adding another dimension of
meaning, just as geographically they added a margin of wilderness
("the meadow, where is richer feed") to the village life of Concord.
His account of chasing the fox over the snow—again he moved from
winter to spring—also made the wild a present experience. The
original passage, however, was more exhilarating, having in it as

---

[91] J, I, 126.

[92] *The Dial,* III (Oct., 1842), 224.

much of the bounding Thoreau as the bounding fox.[93] Thoreau
tempered this untamableness, as he often did when self-disclosure
might bring reproof, by reducing the "I" of the experience, by re-
casting the passage more objectively. For having begun with innocent pastimes, with insects and birds, he was now working deeper
into the wild itself, and reporting experiences that revealed the
extent of his commitment to it. Chasing foxes, for all the transcendental disclaimers, was not the proper work for a Harvard graduate.
The reader, who had not caught the clue of his method, might misread the essay as he later did *Walden*. Thoreau, of course, was "on
the trail of the Spirit itself which resides in the wood. . . ." What
he was curious to know, he said, was "what has determined its [the
fox's] graceful curvatures, and how surely they were coincident
with the fluctuations of some mind." [94] (He omitted: "Here was one
expression of the divine mind this morning. The pond was his
journal, and last night's snow made a *tabula rasa* for him.") For
the moment, in its "carelessness of freedom," the fox was the hero
of *The Service:* "I give up to him sun and earth as to their true
proprietor. He does not go in the sun, but it seems to follow him,
and there is a visible sympathy between him and it."

In turning to the "fishes," Thoreau was able to begin the final
movement of the essay, to domesticate the wild by returning from
the chase to the quieter studies of flowers and—winter-locked
indoors—of the frost tracery on the window. He was also able to
initiate the themes of the river, the thaw, the flux of nature, themes
that were to become increasingly important in the *Week* and
Walden. "Next to nature," he wrote with fishing in mind, "it seems
as if man's actions were the most natural, they so greatly accord
with her." His moments of ecstasy had often occurred on the water,
drifting in his boat on the pond and river, as imperceptibly a part
of nature as the fishing lines and nets that looked like "new river
weed" in the water. Water and meditation, as Melville said, were
wedded forever, and for Thoreau, as well, the waters of the pond
and river were the depths of being and the symbols of spirit.[95] Once
a fisherman himself, he recalled its delights in terms of inspiration;
and what interested him now was the river itself, its inhabitants,
movement, and life. "Almost nothing is known of their habits," he

[93] J, I, 185-87. The references and spirit here are pagan. See also J, I, 89.

[94] This is comparable to his measuring Walden Pond.

[95] See J, I, 110-12.

said of the fishes, and "methinks I have need even of his [the fish's] sympathy, and to be his fellow in a degree." This was the hint that Thoreau enlarged in the second chapter of the *Week*. In the essay, however, he was more concerned with the thaw, with the breaking of the river's ice, already identifying his "health" with the natural cycles of rebirth.[96] Just as in *Walden* he took assurance from the green weed at the bottom of the frozen pond, so here he felt, because of the fish under the ice, that "there is as good as a mine under me wherever I go." The river's thaw, as one sees in his use of a fragment of "The Thaw," was the measure of his own, but he omitted these suggestions of lapse:

> Fain would I stretch me by the highway-side,
> To thaw and trickle with the melting snow,
> That, mingled soul and body with the tide,
> I too may through the pores of nature flow.
>
> But I, alas, nor trickle can nor fume,
> . . . .[97]

There was no better image of his desire for union, for immersion, not even that of standing "up to one's chin in some retired swamp for a whole summer's day. . . ."[98] But he was not easily dispirited. "In the coldest day," he wrote, "it melts somewhere." The flowing was spirit itself, and its promise. "These motions everywhere in nature," he observed, "must surely [be] the circulations of God. The flowing sail, the running stream, the waving tree, the roving wind,—whence else their infinite health and freedom?" And he had even considered vice and virtue in terms of circulation: "By vice the substance of a man is not changed, but all his pores, and cavities, and avenues are prophaned by being made the thorough-fares [pun?] of vice."[99] So in *Walden* he wrote that "man flows at once to God when the channel of purity is open."[100] Purity and inspiration were one, virtue—physically, intellectually, and morally, as Thoreau wrote in the manuscript version—the key to nature.[101] And sound, the inspirer of heroism and virtue, was also referred to as circulation: "Music is the sound of the circulation in nature's

---

[96] See W, VI, 41.

[97] J, I, 71.

[98] J, I, 141.

[99] J, I, 227-28.

[100] W, II, 243.

[101] See *The Dial*, IV (July, 1843), 60.

veins," he wrote. "It is the flux which melts Nature." [102] No wonder, then, that he said that "who hears the rippling of the rivers will not utterly despair of anything," and that he proposed that "a man's life should be as fresh as a river. It should be the same channel, but a new water every instant." [103]

In the essay, most of these meanings, although already in the *Journal*, are latent. Time and spiritual crises would bring them to light. Only the joy in his description of the thaw indicates its meanings; and in the poem on the Concord River, the lines

> No ripple shows Musketaguid,
> Her very current e'en is hid,
> As deepest souls do calmest rest
> When thoughts are swelling in the breast [104]

show the beginnings of the symbolic transformations of which Thoreau was to make so great a use. At the time he wrote the "Natural History" he was just discovering nature, and he associated it with liberation and joy, not yet with his darkening experiences. The fox-chase and the spear-fishing episodes establish this tone of adventure, the release from the routine of life. Of the latter pastime he wrote: "The dullest soul cannot go upon such an expedition without some of the spirit of adventure; as if he had stolen the boat of Charon and gone down the Styx on a midnight expedition into the realms of Pluto." His experience is contrasted with "what of human life, far in the silent night, is flitting mothlike round its candle"—as in *Walden* the pond and village are contrasted. His pursuits are also contrasted—"the beauty and never-ending novelty of his position"—and in a passage that prefigures "The Village" chapter of *Walden* the meaning of his experience is given. "And when he has done," Thoreau concluded, "he may have to steer his way home through the dark by the north star, and he will feel himself some degrees nearer to it for having lost his way on the earth."

The closing sections of the essay turn from the circulations of nature to the Creator whose spirit they are. At the beginning of the essay, Thoreau had remarked on the perfection of every detail in nature: "Nature will bear the closest inspection. . . . She has no interstices; every part is full of life." Now, in telling of his interest

[102] J, I, 251.

[103] J, I, 293, 347.

[104] J, I, 122-24.

in the motion of snakes, he said that "they make our hands and feet, the wings of the bird, and the fins of the fish seem superfluous, as if Nature had only indulged her fancy in making them." Nature-the-artist fulfills her designs in the simplest way. "Elasticity and flexibleness in the simpler forms of animal life are equivalent to a complex system of limbs in the higher"—and the moral Thoreau added was the moral of spiritual simplicity—"and we have only to be as wise and wily as the serpent, to perform as difficult feats without the vulgar assistance of hands and feet." And nature had other moralities to preach. Her "delicate and fragile features," her "wreaths of vapor, dewlines, feathery sprays" suggested high refinement, grace, and ethereal gentility. Her trees in winter, growing up "regardless of the time and circumstances," suggested the self-reliance Thoreau was endeavoring to practice: "Earth, air, sun, and rain, are occasion enough; they were no better in primeval centuries." And the catkins of the willow, which later became his emblem of spring, expressed "a naked confidence," were his "vegetable redeemers"—"Methinks our virtue will hold out till they come again." Thus, nature-the-artist was "mythical and mystical always," by which he meant symbolic.

But nature was also able to work "with the license and extravagance of genius," her "luxurious and florid style" surpassing art.[105] And here Thoreau adduced what he called "crystalline botany," his observations of the hoarfrost and frost traceries, which were the first phenomena he noted at length in his *Journal*. In them he saw the law that sustained his faith in nature and that in the crucial passage on the sand foliage in *Walden* (where he combined flux and artistry) renewed it. Looking at the hoarfrost, he said that "it struck me that these ghost leaves, and the green ones whose forms they assume, were the creatures of but one law. . . . As if the material were indifferent, but the law one and invariable, and every plant in the spring but pushed up into and filled a permanent and eternal mould, which summer and winter forever, is waiting to be filled." He also added, probably at the time he wrote the essay, what he later elaborated in *Walden:* "This foliate structure is common to the coral and the plumage of birds, and to how large a part of animate and inanimate nature." He had not yet learned from Goethe, as he said in *Walden*, that "the Maker of this earth

---

[105] See J, I, 271.

but patented a leaf." [106] But in turning from the rimed foliage to the crystallizations on the window, he anticipated it. "Vegetation," he noted, "is but a kind of crystallization. . . . Vegetation has been made the type of all growth; but as in crystals the law is more obvious, their material being more simple, and for the most part more transient and fleeting, would it not be as philosophical as it is convenient to consider all growth . . . but a crystallization more or less rapid?" He was looking for the law, he was on the trail of the Spirit: the law, perceived in the smallest detail, felt in the ecstatic moment; the law that would cancel the lapses of time in its own eternal efficacy. His concluding description made time a matter of indifference. "In some places the ice-crystals were lying upon granite rocks, directly over crystals of quartz, the frost-work of a longer night, crystals of a longer period," he wrote, rethinking the material in the *Journal*, "but to some eye unprejudiced by the short term of human life, melting as fast as the former."

"The best poets, after all," Thoreau commented on his studies in 1841, "exhibit only the tame and civil side of nature. They have not seen the west side of any mountain." He did not want this "white man's poetry," but the "Indian's report." He wanted to see nature "from the wilderness as well as the village." [107] The "Indian wisdom" he offered in the "Natural History" was not only the transcendental method of "direct intercourse and sympathy," but a way of life not dreamed of in the parlors of Concord.[108] In nature he had found that he could conform to the fashions of eternity; here was "the very vitality of *vita*" about which the preachers never preached.[109]

III

The heroism of a life in nature was essentially private; for Thoreau its end was individual fulfillment. What prompted the declaration of joy in nature in the "Natural History" was a genuine romantic *Weltschmerz*, the "divine egoism" of which Friedrich

---

[106] W, II, 340.

[107] J, I, 272-73.

[108] In the manuscript diary of Sophia Thoreau one sees the typical sentimental nature lover of the time. Everything "refreshes," the "flowers smile," etc. (HM 957).

[109] J, I, 265.

Schlegel spoke, that desire to mount through the spires of form, to enrich one's experience and cultivate one's uniqueness, and by self-transcendence create a divine self. As we have seen, by going to nature Thoreau was repudiating the expediency and uniformitarianism of society. By 1842 he had found that where friendship would not lift him above himself, nature might. The "perennial threatening attitude" that Emerson admired in Thoreau was merely the sign of his determination for self-preservation.[110] "One does not soon know the trade of life," he wrote in 1841. "That one may work out a true life requires more art and delicate skill than any other work." He was most concerned that "great familiarity with the world" might "win away and bereave us of some susceptibility." He wanted, with something of the old Puritanism, to "walk in the world without learning its ways." [111] Finding that even the life at Emerson's was an "ignoble routine," he determined to "obey the law of nature." The "better road" he sought led to Walden.[112] But meanwhile there were the characteristic complaints: "What . . . can I do to hasten that other time, or that space where there shall be no time, and these things ["I know there is a people somewhere (where) this heroism has a place"] be a more living part of my life, —where there will be no discords in my life?" And: "My life, my life! why will you linger? . . . How often has long delay quenched my aspirations! . . . Can heaven be postponed with no more ado?" [113]

There was always Admetus, however, and always society. The way to the woods was through the pencil factory, and over the fences of the village. And there was a need for love, a human hunger, that even the timeless spaces of nature never satisfied. If Thoreau had found the better road in the "Natural History," it did not solve his problem: every term has its polarity; nature had society. The trade of life was hard. And as his earliest prescriptions for the hero show, he wanted both an inviolable self and "public influence." Even though he protested the ways of the world, he asked Rufus Griswold to include his poems in *The Poets and Poetry of America*,[114] and even though he wrote Emerson that he was

[110] Rusk, ed., *The Letters of Ralph Waldo Emerson*, III, 75.

[111] J, I, 300.

[112] J, I, 332.

[113] J, I, 318, 327.

[114] October 9, 1841. Berg Collection.

"meditating some other method of paying debts than by lectures and writing," he asked him to remember for him "anything of that 'other' sort [that] should come to your ears in New York. . . ." [115] He wanted to be a hero in his place and time; his reading in history had shown him that there had been occasions when heroism had had a place. "If I could help infuse some life and heart into society," he wrote in 1842, "should I not do a service?" [116]

The "Natural History," therefore, was only a partial statement of his desires. It expressed the primary transcendental need, the leisure "to improve his soul's estate." [117] Nature was the source of inspiration and faith, but society was the field of action. The hero was not a solitary, but a man of the world. And when, in 1843, he wrote that "you must store up none of the life in your gift—it is as fatal as to husband your breath. We must *live* all our *life*," he had in mind not only the resources of nature, but the active life he had described in his lecture on Sir Walter Raleigh.[118] For "Raleigh," begun in the months following John's death, was as much a pro- posal for his life as the "Natural History." "The past is only as heroic as we see it," he had written in *The Service;* "it is the canvas on which our conception of heroism is painted, the dim prospectus of our future field. We are dreaming of what we are to do." [119] He had already identified himself with Godfrey of Bouillon; in Raleigh, however, he found a hero who better expressed his needs, who was a hero in a time and place that he had not only mastered in his reading but that in its essential spirit was closer to his own. The martial fantasy of *The Service,* therefore, was now given the foun- dation of actual fact. Raleigh was the hero; Thoreau would judge how well he had learned the trade of life.

"Sir Walter Raleigh" was never published in Thoreau's lifetime. It was given as a lecture at the Concord Lyceum on February 8, 1843, the second lecture he delivered, and it capitalized on the mistakes of the first on "Society" in 1838. Closer to the organization and style of the college essays than anything he ever wrote, it was obviously a literary essay—or a lecture on several personal themes

[115] W, VI, 62.
[116] J, I, 355.
[117] J, I, 118.
[118] HM 13182.
[119] *The Service,* pp. 25-26.

disguised as a literary essay. It was apparently intended to appeal
to his neighbors. Except for his speeches on John Brown, it was
his only venture in biography (Thoreau preferring, as he said, the
presentness of autobiography to the pastness of biography);[120] and,
considering the success of Emerson's lectures on biography in 1835
and the popularity of "lives" in New England, Thoreau probably
hoped that it would launch him as a lecturer—this time more
auspiciously. Even Emerson told Lidian, "Do not fail to tell me
every particular concerning Henry's lecture when it comes—and
the brightest star of the winter shed its clear beams on that
night!"[121] Because Thoreau was not yet an excursionist, "Raleigh"
provided the only materials he could treat in a popular way. Much
of his journalizing had been literary and critical, and continued to
be; and when he lectured again later in the year he did so on the
poetry of Homer, Ossian, and Chaucer.[122]

Though the lecture was probably a tactical success, being nearer
to what was expected of a Harvard graduate, it had its personal
uses for Thoreau—it was autobiography projected on biography.
When Emerson selected his great men for his first lectures he chose
Michelangelo, Luther, Milton, George Fox, and Edmund Burke;
his second list included Plato, Swedenborg, Montaigne, Napoleon,
Shakespeare, and Goethe. Only Napoleon—so he subtitled the lecture—was a man of the world; the others were philosophers,
prophets, or writers, and all were partial men. His preference for
the man of perception determined his choice—he, too, saw the
great man in his own image. When Margaret Fuller, therefore,
wrote that "in the present state of division of labor, the literary man
finds himself condemned to be nothing else," she had Emerson in
mind. "We have the swordsman and statesman and penman," she
continued, "but it is not considered that the same mind which can
rule the destiny of a poem may as well that of an army or an empire. . . . The scientific man may need seclusion from the common
affairs of life, for he has his materials before him; but the man of
letters must seek them in life, and he who cannot act will but imperfectly appreciate action." With most of the critics of her day,
Margaret Fuller believed that the test of literature was character.
"The man of genius," she said, "feels that literature has become

---

[120] J, I, 251.

[121] Rusk, ed., *The Letters of Ralph Waldo Emerson,* III, 129.

[122] See *The Dial,* IV (Jan., 1844), 290-305.

too much a craft by itself. No man should live by or for his pen. Writing is worthless except as the record of life; and no great man ever was satisfied thus to express all his being. His book should be only an indication of himself." Even in an age of specialization, the writer must be a whole man: she was defending, even though she made it the reason for Goethe's failure as a seer, his going to the court of Weimar; for beyond his genius as a writer, Goethe had shown "the culture of the entire man. . . ." [123] Now, it was this wholeness, this ability to rule the destiny of poems and empires, that Thoreau recognized in Raleigh. And this made Raleigh, whose greatness was outside of Emerson's range, the hero in whom he saw his own future projected. "There are few lives," Thoreau said, "so agreeable to the imagination. . . . In a tamer and less healthy age it has a rare poetic interest—his daily life was the stuff of which our dreams are made." [124] Unlike the nineteenth century, Raleigh's was the last age of complete men, of glorious individual greatness —an age, too, that, bursting the confines of medievalism, had looked to the West, had found again an open universe in which adventure was possible. "No one more emphatically represents the heroic character in English history than Sir Walter Raleigh," Thoreau said. "If an English Plutarch were written . . . Raleigh would be the best Greek or Roman among them." [125] Thoreau used him, as he later used himself in *Walden*—the phrase is from Sidney's epitaph—"to shew unto our age a sample of antient virtue."

The character of Raleigh, Thoreau said, was most revealed by "his constant soldier-like bearing and promise": he marched to the music of *The Service*, his motto being *Finem det mihi Virtus*—"Let valor be my end." Like Thoreau in *The Service* he saw in war the necessity of law: "It is in some sense the very genius of law—law creative and active." What "inspiration or conflicts in our breasts" were for Thoreau, battles were for Raleigh. Man is born into "the

---

[123] Wade, ed., *The Writings of Margaret Fuller*, pp. 245, 244, 259. Originally in *The Dial*, II (July, 1841), 1-41.

[124] *Sir Walter Raleigh*, ed. by Henry A. Metcalf, Introduction by F. B. Sanborn, Bibliophile Society, Boston, 1905. I have also used the two manuscript revisions, HM 935 and HM 943. Thoreau probably lectured from the first which numbered 54 pages; the latter, 83 pages in length, and in its final form, was probably the basis of the Bibliophile edition. Metcalf mentions three drafts, probably referring to other fragments in a variety of manuscripts, for part of the Raleigh material was used in the *Week*. All citations are from these sources.

[125] Emerson said that Plutarch was the "Doctor and historian" of the "literature of Heroism . . ." (C, II, 248).

state of war," Emerson had said; he who "assumes a warlike attitude, and affirms his ability to cope single-handed with the infinite
army of enemies" has the "military attitude of the soul we give the
name of Heroism." [126] Raleigh not only filled the outlines of *The
Service,* he filled out Emerson's sketch in "Heroism." For like the
Emersonian hero, he stood above morality, responsive only to the
"secret impulse of an individual character." [127] "The hero," Thoreau
wrote, "is a man of enthusiasm. The world regards less what he
does than how he does it, for his actions unsettle the common
standard. His action had a right to be done however wrong to the
moralist it might be." The enthusiasm Thoreau advocated here was
the same that he had found in nature and had made a theme of the
"Natural History." Speaking of his own ecstasy, he wrote that
"occasionally we rise above the necessity of virtue into an unchangeable morning light, in which we have not to choose . . .
between right and wrong, but live right on and breathe the circum-
ambient air. This is the very vitality of life." [128] Enthusiasm was
inspiration, an influx of spirit more compelling than prudence; it
was not lawless, it was higher law. Accordingly, as Thoreau added,
"all fair action is the product of enthusiasm"; and he had in mind
what he had learned from nature: "Nature herself . . . does nothing
in a prose mood. . . . There is enthusiasm in the sunrise and sunset
. . . there is a thrill in the Spring when it buds and blossoms. . . ."
By these links, the hero was planted in nature. "They are earthborn," Thoreau said, "as was said of the Titans." And Raleigh,
having "*more* nature than other men . . . a great irregular, luxuriant
nature . . . more roots than others," was "one of nature's noble-
men." [129]

The enthusiasm of nature was one thing, the action it quickened
another. "Raleigh" made clear how the joy and health of the "Natural History" might flower in character. Having, as a result of his
communion with nature, "gross health and cheerfulness," and, even
as Emerson also recognized, "a profane levity," the hero was "the
very opposite of the ascetic." He had instead the very things Thoreau admired in Raleigh: a hunger for life, adventure, and scope
of action. "This world," Thoreau said, "seems to be thrown away

[126] C, II, 250.

[127] C, II, 251.

[128] J, I, 265.

[129] It was this titanism that Melville questioned.

on the saint." The hero he was projecting was nearer Natty Bumppo than Holmes's Brahmin with the muscle bred out of him and tamed by books. Raleigh was not a Puritan, but a Renaissance man; and with Hawthorne, Thoreau employed the fuller blooms of the Renaissance to contrast the withered buds of New England. "Certainly to the mind of a New Englander, the descendant or successor of these grim Pilgrims," Thoreau wrote, "mere cheerfulness is a great virtue. . . . To march sturdily through life—patiently and [?]—looking grim defiance at one's foes—that is one way but one cannot help being more attracted by that kind of heroism which relaxes its brow in the presence of danger. . . ." [130] Thoreau, the apostle of joy, was also the apostle of relaxation and leisure— nature was not a place for merchants. What countinghouse mind could relish his comment, so much against the grain of the asceticism of commerce, that "the truly forceful and efficient man does not crowd his day with work, but saunters to his task surrounded by a wide halo ["halo" is a better word than the later use of "margin"] of ease and leisure, and then but does what he likes?" It is only fair to add, appealing as this strain is, that Thoreau was a New Englander who would have liked to find in Raleigh some admixture of the "temperament of George Fox or Oliver Cromwell. . . ." Raleigh's relation to the court, of which Thoreau disapproved, was responsible for this qualification. Still, it indicated the peculiar kind of joy Thoreau prized. Just as the leisure he sought was for the sake of his soul, so his joy was spiritual: the physical exuberance was there, but not quite with the same flavor one finds in Whitman. Thoreau wanted to be "the saint enterprising"—and "the poet active."

And so he took his stand against the ascetic. "The religion of the hero is the very opposite to that of the ascetic," he wrote. "It does withdraw from the world into solitude ["first"—Thoreou noted in pencil] but is the more polished. It makes him more a public man and the less a private. It is not a secret confidor [sic] to him but a message delivered to him. It demands not a narrower cell—but a wider world—so that his presence enhances the beauty and ampleness of nature herself." Thoreau's argument for the public character of the hero, his belief that inspiration tapped a common reservoir and was therefore not subjective, was very much like Emerson's

[130] He also cited Robin Hood, whose ballads were among his favorites, as an example of cheerfulness under all circumstances.

defense of his own use of solitude; so, too, his belief that the hero enhances nature echoed Emerson's notion of the moral beauty of virtue in the section on "Beauty" in *Nature*. This transformation of the private into the public was also a hint for the representative man. Citing Virgil, Thoreau said that the hero lives on "a parallel yet higher course," that he lives with but above the mob. And he quoted Jonson:

> That to the vulgar canst thyself apply,
> Treading a better path not contrary.

In Raleigh, therefore, he saw an individual relying wholly on his own virtues and yet a man of public actions whose voice was "the voice of the commonwealth." Raleigh identified the self and the state; his virtue was a public good. He served, then, as Thoreau tried to serve in "Civil Disobedience"; he had the social conscience Thoreau approved of in John Brown (Thoreau read Raleigh's "The Soul's Errand" as the preface of his funeral speech for John Brown). And Raleigh's hatred of majorities anticipated Thoreau's sentiments in "Civil Disobedience": "But no senate nor civil assembly," Raleigh wrote, "can be under such natural impulses to honor and justice as single persons . . . the honor and conscience that lies in the majority is too thin and diffusive to be efficacious; for a number can do a great wrong, and call it right, and not one of that majority blush for it." Corporations, Raleigh said, have no souls.

Nor did the virtue Thoreau ascribed to the hero have the denying or ascetic aspects of Puritanism: [131] it was pagan virtue, the virtue of self-expansion rather than self-restriction. He said of Raleigh that "the stories about him testify to a character rather than a virtue." Character took the meaning of personality, virtue the more limited religious meaning of "character." Virtue in the religious sense was the limitation of self in accordance with an approved morality; it was obedience, not self-exploration and fulfillment. This explained why Thoreau wanted to be judged as he judged Raleigh: not by his acts but by his aspirations; not by a deed but by his "constant character." "It is not of so much importance to inquire of a man,"

---

[131] See Charles Emerson's views of Shakespeare and Burke in "Notes from the Journal of a Scholar," *The Dial*, I (July, 1840), 14-16. The section on Homer, and in the second installment (*The Dial*, IV [July, 1843], 88-92) the sections on nature, truth, self, and society, are especially close to Thoreau's thought. Thoreau did not know who the author was, but he heartily approved of these articles. See W, VI, 94.

he wrote, "what actions he performed at one and what at another period of his life, as what manner of man he was at every period." Advocating an open or experiential morality he preferred not daring to die, but daring to live—later enacting his preference at Walden. "He will not aspire to a brave deed, but to a brave life," he said in "Raleigh." "Men may act boldly but they cannot live boldly." For the virtue of heroes was exploratory, it tried the unknown: "We are apt to think that there is a kind of virtue," he wrote, "which need not be heroic and brave. But in fact it is only the deed of the greatest. Only the hardy souls venture upon it—for virtue deals with what we have no experience in. How much of mere conformity —though it be to heaven—is there in our idea of virtue. But it [virtue] rather makes others conform to it and compels heaven itself. What else but virtue does the rude pioneer work of the world." Society and religion, conformity and "character," were all one to Thoreau. In "Raleigh" he advised his generation of grim pilgrims to relax its brow, to seek a wider world, to live strenuously. "It would be worth the while," he said, "to remember daily that it is ours to make great demands on heaven and ourselves. . . . The life which will best bear to be considered is not only without sombreness but even without morality."

"It is his praise," Thoreau said of Raleigh, "not to have been a saint or a seer in his . . . generation." Statesman, courtier, naval and army commander, writer, explorer, planter of colonies, prisoner— Raleigh was instead the whole man, the "universal man" of the Renaissance. Living in an age that offered a field of activity for "both the intellectual and physical energies," he participated in the twin enterprises of the time: the Reformation and the exploration of America—the age of reform and of the West. He belonged, Thoreau said, in the age of Columbus, the age of Calvin, Knox, Bayard, Luther, Raphael, Machiavelli, Cabot, Pizarro, Cranmer, Garcilaso, Copernicus, Michelangelo, Ariosto; and he lived in the age of Camoëns, Sidney, Cervantes, Veronese, Tasso, Montaigne, Drake, Halley, Galileo, Kepler, Bacon, Behmen, Jonson, Spenser, and Shakespeare. In that age, whose device Thoreau said should have been an anchor, sword, and quill, Raleigh was a hero in all the affairs of life, active and contemplative, warlike and literary, a worthy among his contemporaries.

But to be a worthy in that generation, Thoreau claimed, he had to be a discoverer; and it was Raleigh's relation to the West that

Thoreau, looking beyond the Alleghenies himself, found most attractive.[132] What Thoreau said of Raleigh could be said for himself: "No one was more familiar with the stories, both true and fabulous, respecting the discovery of the new world. . . ." A contemporary of Drake, Hawkins, Frobisher, and Hudson, he discovered Virginia, explored Guiana, and ascended the Orinoco. Thoreau emphasized this enterprise because it put Raleigh in a better light; he disliked the necessities of the courtier, and the court became for Thoreau the evil influence of Raleigh's life.[133] He would have liked his Raleigh to go on voyages unpatronized, and he said that Raleigh went to Guiana not to win the favor of the Queen but to "secure favor with himself and exercise his genius in fields more worthy of him than a corrupt court." Reading his own desire for the West in Raleigh's, Thoreau said that "it is plain to see that the ideals which as a poet and a hero he worshipped had their dwelling place in the New Continent—and with the ardor and credulity of a child he sought to realize his imaginations." The New Continent was Thoreau's West, inspiring the same pristine hopes, and set, as America had always been, against the decadence of courts, society, and Europe—the "frivolous society of the court. . . ." "The billows of the western ocean were to them [the Raleighs and Frobishers, etc.]," he said, "what the prairies of the same though yet more distant west are to the enterprising youth of the present day." That West, as Raleigh wrote of the New World, was aboriginal nature: "To conclude, it is a country, as yet untouched by the natives of the old world: never sacked, turned, or wrought; the face of the earth hath not been torn, nor the virtue and salt of the soil spent by manurance . . ."—it was Thoreau's cerulean farm, given a geographical place. (And that the Indians liked Raleigh was a significant fact for Thoreau.) "The really fertile soils and luxuriant prairies lie on this [the west] side of the Alleghenies," Thoreau went on, elaborating his own vision, a vision of freedom that had preoccupied him since 1840 and that he later repeated in *Walden*.

I may be a logger on the head waters of the Penobscot, to be recorded in fable hereafter as an amphibious river-god, by as sounding a name

[132] See William Carlos Williams, "Sir Walter Raleigh," *In The American Grain*, Norfolk, Conn., 1939 [1925], pp. 59-62. Of all our contemporary poets, Williams, it seems, is most deeply interested in the annals of the discoverers and the attitudes they had toward the New World.

[133] In *Walden* Thoreau wrote: "The success of great scholars and thinkers ["modern men"] is commonly a courtier-like success, not kingly, not manly. They make shift to live merely by conformity . . ." (W, II, 16; HM 924).

as Triton or Proteus; carry furs from Nootka to China, and so be more
renowned than Jason and his golden fleece; or go on a South Sea exploring expedition, to be hereafter recounted along with the periplus
of Hanno. [This is from the *Journal*, as is the remainder, reduced and
recast for "Raleigh."] These are but a few chances. If I choose I can
move away from public opinion, from government, from religion, from
education, from society—almost from Nature herself, for there are solitudes and [?] of the desert and the sea open to me. There is the
illimitable just as dim and shadowy and unexplored now as when it
floated the fabulous isles of the ancients in its bosom—now indeed
beyond the pillars of Hercules but still Hesperis as the Greeks said is
coincident with the end of the day ["is as remote as the sunset"].[134]

Though Thoreau said that "it is not easy at this day to realize
what extravagant expectations Europe had formed respecting . . .
the new world," he had himself transmuted the gold of its dream
into spirit, its El Dorado into Jerusalem. Some have found it difficult to relate the Thoreau of "Raleigh" with the naturalist, but when
nature becomes the West in his thought and virtue "exploratory,"
the link is clear. Nature is but the new field for discovery, and exploration, now given a metaphysical significance, is what Thoreau
intended his nature study to be. To go to nature, as he had in the
"Natural History," was thereby made a heroic form of action. One
sees in Margaret Fuller's remarks on the solitude of the scientific
man that Thoreau's problem was to make nature itself a proper field
of action. He did this in "Raleigh," and in all his later writings, by
using discovery as a metaphor for his own way of life. And he tried
to secure its significance by making it a recognizable American
assumption: ". . . he had visited the Old World in his free imagination," he said of Raleigh as he might have of Emerson or Whitman
or himself, "and as an unrestrained adventurer the New. . . ." But
his explorations in nature were made in the hope of discovering
Man. The shores of America were nature: the prize was not gold,
but the heroic personality.

That Raleigh was also a writer—a contemplative as well as active
man—extended the spiritual meanings of heroism. Thinking of
Raleigh's imprisonment and perhaps of his own delay, Thoreau said
that "he who contemplates truth and universal laws is free, whatever walls immure his body. . . ." The hero with the pen, Raleigh
was as enterprising in letters as in discovery; he spent his years in
the Tower a "captive knight," replacing the deed with the word,

[134] W, II, 352, 22-23. The passage in J, I, 129-31 is worth consulting in full.

exploring the world of the spirit—"cultivating poetry and philosophy as the noblest deeds compatible with his confinement." His behavior in prison, like the nobility of his death, showed his indifference to and mastery of circumstances: in this respect he was transcendental enough and an earlier John Brown. ("Death scenes of great men," Thoreau said—and his own death and John's come to mind, "are agreeable to consider only when they make another and harmonious chapter in their lives. . . .") This proof of his constant character neutralized the servility of the courtier and, like his ideal friendship with Sidney, canceled the expediency of his relation with Cecil. Though Thoreau especially disliked his service at court, he interpreted Raleigh's relation to the Queen as he would have his own to Lidian. He preferred to think of Raleigh as a knight, not as a statesman or courtier: Raleigh had "the gallantry and grace of chivalry as well as the judgment and experience of a practical Englishman." [135] And as a writer he preferred Raleigh's poems and *History of the World* to his essays on statecraft. "The misfortune and incongruity of the man," Thoreau said, "appear in the fact that he was at once the author of the 'Maxims of State' and 'The Soul's Errand.' "

It was with Raleigh's thought and style as well as his adventures that Thoreau identified himself; for both thought and style were remarkably close to his own, and as a writer rather than freebooter, Raleigh was nearer the actual Thoreau. Already well-read in the literature of the Elizabethan Renaissance, and in the ensuing months at Staten Island to continue his study of the metaphysicals, Thoreau did not find in Raleigh's writing anything new. Raleigh was merely at home in the thought of his time; he was not a "deep philosopher" (though he might have been), perhaps, as Thoreau suggested with all his scorn of effeminacy, because he was tempted by the fastidious taste of the court. And yet because Raleigh was the "whole man" writing and because so many of his sentiments tallied with his own, Thoreau used him to canvass his own themes and his own ideas on the nature of writing.[136] In Raleigh's work he found the idea of the microcosm, the belief in the divinity of the stars and man's participation in their work, the belief in the reality of the unseen and infinite, and an image much like his own Sound

[135] Thoreau added that Raleigh's relation to the Queen was a greater danger than war with Spain or the discovery of America.

[136] Almost all of the substance of his *Journal* entries was used here.

and Silence—"Light is the shadow of God's brightness, who is the light of lights." In Raleigh's poetry—which Thoreau said (as Emerson said of Thoreau's) was the "secret of a man's life"—he also found the distinction between "False Love and True Love" that informed his own view of friendship, the image of virtue and purity in "On Diana" that he used in "The Moon" [137] and in his later studies of moonlight, and the otherworldly heroism of "The Soul's Errand" and "The Pilgrimage" that undoubtedly shaped the crusade motif of "Walking." The only thought of Raleigh's that Thoreau singled out and that ran counter to his own was on the difference between the seasons of man and nature: " 'For the tide of man's life, after it once turneth and declineth, ever runneth with a perpetual ebb and falling stream, but never floweth again; our leaf once fallen, springeth no more; neither doth the sun or the summer adorn us again, with the garments of new leaves and flowers.' " To belie this lapse was the insistent necessity of Thoreau's life.

Raleigh's style was still more agreeable to Thoreau. Here was a man with "a healthy and able body to back his wits," who used the pen as he would an ax or a sword. "The whole man sat down to the writing of his books," Thoreau said, "not some curious brain only." Raleigh was not a Stearns Wheeler or a Charles Newcomb: he was a Thoreau: writing for him was "a stalwart man's work," the labor of a man with "marrow in his back, and a tendon Achilles in his heel." Raleigh's writing, therefore, was related to his manhood as assuredly as the "natural emphasis in his style [to] a man's tread. . . ." For action and labor had removed the "palaver" from his style; he had the organic style "which the best of modern writing does not furnish." He was able to "transfer to his expression the emphasis and sincerity of his action." For he expressed what had to be expressed, that which flowered from his own life and labor, and his expression was not labored, but one with his labor. Thoreau insisted on the necessity of labor: not only was it essential to organic language, but the association of labor and language enabled him to defend his own literary calling as a heroic activity. "The necessity of labor to the scholar," Thoreau wrote, adding his gloss to "The American Scholar," "is not indeed understood. Undoubtedly steady labor with the hands which engrosses the atten-

[137] *The Dial*, III (Oct., 1842), 222.

tion also, is the best method to remove the palaver out of one's style. . . . The scholar may be sure he writes a tougher truth for the calluses on his hands." (He said of his work in the beanfield at Walden Pond that "the labor of the hands, even when pursued to the verge of drudgery, is perhaps never the worst form of idleness. It has a constant and imperishable moral, and to the scholar it yields a classic result." [138] Elsewhere he said that we reason from our hands to our heads.) The writer, then, who knows "many men and things," will write sentences that are "nervous and tough"; his writing will have the supreme virtue of sincerity and the "hue and fragrance" of his mind. For the organic language was really the natural product of character: we are given the clue to Thoreau's own assured tone in his remark that the sure and sound sentence is "spoken firmly and conclusively, as if the author had a right to know what he says."

This was especially what Thoreau valued in Raleigh's *History*. Speaking of the vigor and naturalness of sixteenth-century prose, he said: "You have constantly the warrant of life & experience in all you read. The little that is said is supplied by implication of the much that was done. The sentences are verdurous and blooming . . . because they are rooted in fact and experience." He approved of Raleigh's *History*, therefore, for the very things that the scientific historian does not. The test of history and all other writing was the same for Thoreau—did the writer give a "fresh" experience, could the reader "associate the historian with the exploits he describes?" In Raleigh's case, Thoreau felt "the familiarity and interest of a party and eye-witness," for Raleigh used history as Thoreau did, judging the events of the past by his own present experience, evaluating, for example, the strategy of ancient generals by his own skill. What Thoreau wanted in his own writing and found in Raleigh's work was the author's character. His ultimate test of a book was not literary but moral: its power to move the reader to "commence living on its hint." "What I begin by reading I must finish by acting," he wrote in the *Journal*. "So I cannot stay to hear a *good* sermon and applaud at the conclusion, but shall be half-way to Thermopylae before that." [139] This was but the virtue of biography. Considering Raleigh's life, he wrote that "the relation or sight of any noble life unfits us for all common work. It subsides

[138] W, II, 173.
[139] J, I, 216.

into our very bones and excites us to muscular exertion. We are stronger in the knees. . . . We feel our future deeds hasten themselves within us and move grandly towards a consummation as ships go down the Thames."

"O Friend, never strike sail to a fear!" Emerson wrote in "Heroism," "Come into port greatly, or sail with God the seas." [140] This was not an adjuration to the Bulkingtons of the world, but to Emerson's own fainthearted contemporaries—indeed, behind his general observations on the failure of youth in his times were the figures of his own men of promise.

We have seen or heard of many extraordinary young men who never ripened, or whose performance in natural life was not extraordinary. When we see their air and mien, when we hear them speak of society, of books, of religion, we admire their superiority; they seem to throw contempt on our entire polity and social state; theirs is the tone of a youthful giant who is sent to work revolutions. But they enter an active profession and the forming Colossus shrinks to the common size of man. The magic they used was the ideal tendencies. . . . The lesson they gave in their first aspirations is yet true; and a better valor and a purer truth shall one day organize their belief.[141]

Living at Emerson's, Thoreau took the hint. With his characteristic emphasis on health, he acknowledged that "much of the heroism men praise nowadays is dyspeptic." He, too, wanted to be judged by his aspirations, by the "bloom and halo about the character." With nothing yet to show but his ideal tendencies (ideals which his friend did not further), he wanted to be approved for "a depth of character unfathomed." "Many silent, as well as famous, lives have been the result of no mean thought," he wrote, "though it was never adequately expressed nor conceived. . . ." Thinking of himself as well as Raleigh, he said that "there have been souls of a heroic stamp for whom this world seemed expressly made. . . . Such seem to be an essential part of their age if we consider them in time, and of the scenery if we consider them in Nature." He had the better valor, and, when his servitude was done, would do the heroic deed: what Guiana was to Raleigh, Walden would be to him. Then the world would "witness a heroism which is literally illustrious, whose daily life is the stuff of which our dreams are made. . . ."

---

[140] C, II, 259-60.

[141] C, II, 258-59. In the essay he also spoke directly to Margaret Fuller.

Chapter IV

A WALKER IN THE CITY

> Methinks I should be content to sit at the back door
> in Concord, under the poplar tree, henceforth for-
> ever.
>
> —Thoreau, *Familiar Letters*

I

After the proposals of the "Natural History of
Massachusetts" and "Sir Walter Raleigh," what
need had Thoreau of cities? When one considers
the logic of aspiration in what Thoreau had already written, his interlude at Staten Island in
1843 seems unaccountable, indeed bizarre. He
had already found his way, but it was a way
that, however much it stirred the transcendental
imagination of his friends, did not meet with
their practical approval; where Whitman's declaration of the open road, for example, roused
them, their social timidity kept them from the
"paths untrodden,"

> In the growth by margins of pond-waters,
> Escaped from the life that exhibits itself,
> From all the standards hitherto publish'd, from
>   pleasures, profits, conformities,
> Which too long I was offering to feed my soul. . . .

The symbols of nature and the West were grand,
but too much could be poured into them.

The way to Staten Island had been paved by

Thoreau's friends. It was simply a move from one Emerson household to another, the proximity to publishers making the change advisable. Thoreau's term at the Emersons' had been set at a year; it was not a paying arrangement, and he was in need of money. Unable, as Emerson wrote Margaret Fuller, to find "work such as he has sought for" [1]—presumably writing or lecturing, surveying being a later solution to his problem—Thoreau, damned by dollars as much as Melville, took the practical road to the city, to a tutorship, and to the magazine offices. In fact, he had already been given Godspeed by Hawthorne, who early in the year had him to tea to meet John Louis O'Sullivan, the editor of the *Democratic Review*.[2] O'Sullivan asked him to write for him, and Thoreau promptly complied with "Paradise (To Be) Regained" and "The Landlord." Having already submitted "A Walk to Wachusett" to the only paying magazine in Boston, the *Boston Miscellany*—which it turned out never paid him—Thoreau was forced to seek his "shillings" in New York, where paid writers had been heard of. The money he pursued, however, was more elusive than the spirit, and the pen (he had reason to speak of the necessity of labor for the scholar!) less productive of hard cash than the hoe and the theodolite. He had need for his armor of humor; his letters always referred to his mission—to gather up money before winter—and were sufficiently humorous over his predicament, showing his friends that he was seriously minding the main chance and as jovial as Brother Jonathan. But he must have appreciated the irony of Elizabeth Hoar's farewell gift—an irony, of course, that her tender soul never suspected: an inkstand and pen.

Thoreau's stay at the William Emersons' was not so profitable as his well-wishers expected it to be. He would have been better employed selling pencils. "Everywhere," he told his mother, who did not guess the depth of his banter, "we get soldiers' pay still." He wrote home that "as for money matters, I have not set my traps yet, but I am getting my bait ready." [3] He had indeed set to work writing, and his failure was not so much his own as it was that of the market. When he wrote his mother in August he reported that he might have accomplished "something in the literary way . . .

[1] Rusk, ed., *The Letters of Ralph Waldo Emerson*, III, 91.

[2] W, VI, 51.

[3] W, VI, 91, 86. For his lukewarm response to William Emerson see W, VI, 83, 86.

but for the slowness and poverty of the 'Reviews' themselves." [4] He informed Emerson that he had tried the *Democratic Review, The New Mirror, Brother Jonathan;* that *The Knickerbocker* was "too poor," and that "only *The Ladies' Companion* pays"—and he added in a letter to his mother that "I could not write anything companionable." "As for Eldorado, that is far off yet," he wrote. "My bait will not tempt the rats,—they are too well fed." [5] He had warned Emerson at the beginning of his stay that "you must not count much upon what I can do or learn in New York." [6] Having tried, he now told him that "literature comes to a poor market here; and even the little that I write is more than will sell." He had even tried "sundry methods of earning money in the city": booksellers and publishers had been given a chance to use him, and he had even gone about selling *The Agriculturist*.[7] He had gone down on his knees before Admetus: he had every right to speak firmly of lives of quiet desperation.

The six months at Staten Island and New York, however, yielded some experiences, which, after all, were the genuine compensation, and, as he said of cultivating beans, had imperishable results. For he had learned to know the city: it was his longest stay near one, the only time that he had to make the city a field of action; and the lack of curiosity and disappointment he anticipated before he came were crystallized into permanent disapproval. "Though I know but little of Boston," he wrote Emerson, "yet what attracts me, in a quiet way, seems much meaner and more pretending than there,—libraries, pictures, and faces in the street." [8] In his next letter he told Emerson that "I am ashamed of my eyes that behold it [the city]. . . . It will be something to hate,—that's the advantage it will be to me. . . ." [9] The brick and stone already stretching to 149th Street, with "no 'give' to the foot," the difficulty of making social calls, and the expense for horse cars were too much for his village breeding. But what disturbed him most from the moment of debarking was the anonymity of city life, the great crowds that absorbed his individuality—but which, for him, were still one of

---

[4] W, VI, 105.

[5] W, VI, 107, 108.

[6] W, VI, 78.

[7] W, VI, 107, 105.

[8] W, VI, 79.

[9] W, VI, 82.

the great phenomena, greater in fact than the Great Western, the
Croton Waterworks, and the gallery of the National Academy of
Design which he took the first opportunity to see. He had walked
into Whitman's Mannahatta, and his response was as ambivalent
as when later on he met its bard. The prating about the democratic
multitude was lost in the actual facts of the metropolis. The young
friends of Emerson whom he dutifully looked up—George Ward,
Giles Waldo, William Tappan—fine young men that they were
and "better than the great herd," disappointed him; they were
without direction and goal, caught in the immense tide of an expanding mart, preyed on perhaps by the multiplicity of sensations
that bothered Thoreau (and that more than a half century later
Dreiser used to explain the drifting of the modern man in Lester
Kane). "The pigs in the street," he told Emerson, "are the most
respectable part of the population. When will the world learn that
a million men are of no importance compared with *one* man? . . . I
do not believe there are eight hundred human beings on the
globe." [10] In his *Journal* he noted: "I walked through New York
yesterday—and there is no real and living person." [11]

Fresh from the writing of "Raleigh," Thoreau was unable to
accept the greatest fact of the nineteenth century, that a million
men are more important than one. Excited by "one aspect of the
modern world at least," by the great flow of immigration of westward expansion,[12] his own westering instincts were nevertheless
above, if parallel to, those of his time. And yet, if he did not solve
the most crucial problem of the democratic faith—

> One's-self I sing, a simple separate person,
> Yet utter the word Democratic, the word En-Masse

—by sympathetic absorption or the representative man, he recognized the problem: and recognition was perhaps a tougher approach
than Whitman's social mysticism and Emerson's rationalization for
genius. He loved the laboring man as much as Whitman: he was
one himself.[13] And he knew that the railroad was the trail blazer
of the westward movement, and that the farms of Wisconsin might

[10] W, VI, 82-83, 92.

[11] HM 13182.

[12] W, VI, 96, 110.

[13] He asked his mother to send him the results of the cattle show (W, VI,
111).

make "Counts" of these "respectable but straightened people. . . ." [14]
His democratic faith was sure; even the destruction of Walden
(and by extension, of nature and the West) did not overly disturb
him at this time. "The sturdy Irish arms that do the work are of
more worth than oak and maple," he told his sister. "Methinks I
could look with equanimity upon a long street of Irish cabins, and
pigs and children reveling in the genial Concord dirt; and I should
still find my Walden Wood and Fair Haven in their tanned and
happy faces." [15] Thoreau's love of man was always greater than his
love of nature; he loved nature for its human possibilities—it was
the bulwark against the "shivered heavens" of the city, and the
lamentable depersonalization. [16] Nature ultimately was not "nature,"
but the sum of human aspiration: it was the freedom that Thoreau
found the most significant fact of the nineteenth century, and it
was man's foresight and planning and values, all the directions that
would make the bounty of that freedom fruitful for man. Thus he
cherished the laborer, but not labor; and, transcendentalist that he
was, offered a more practical approach than most of his contemporaries. Emerson and Whitman, of course, appealed to nature and
made man's communion with the cosmos the necessity of self-realization—self-realization being at once the ideal end of the American
experiment and the condition of democratic sympathy. Emerson provided the theory and Whitman a possible stance—man on the open
road; Thoreau, however, demonstrated for scholar and laborer alike
the fine specifications of practical application. Neither Emerson nor
Whitman knew nature as Thoreau did; their relation to nature was
programmatic, Thoreau's an actual interaction. His hatred of the
city, therefore, was more than personal: it not only expressed his
love of man, but an acute awareness of the "expectation of the
land" which the westward movement, in his time as in Crèvecoeur's,
was raising. The West, one of the major dimensions of his thought,
always implied freedom, the possibility of human renewal; the
open land beyond the Alleghenies was merely the geographical
warrant of this possibility. What an expanding and commercial
New York portended he knew: "Let us improve our opportunities,"
he wrote with a sense of urgency in "Walking," "before the evil

[14] W, VI, 110.

[15] W, VI, 116.

[16] W, VI, 82.

days come." [17] He did not need to look beyond Lowell and Acton
to see the Zeniths and Gopher Prairies of the future. The *Week* and
Walden distilled out of his hatred for the city were his offering
toward the reconstruction of man and society. These were the
fragments, still to be written, that he shored against our ruins.

In his first letter home, Thoreau's reaction to New York established this polarity. "I do not like cities," he told his sister. "I want
a whole continent to breathe in, and a good deal of solitude and
silence, such as all Wall Street cannot buy,—nor Broadway with
its wooden pavement." [18] If Whitman's city stifled him, Whitman's
seaside was his recompense. Discovering the sea for the first time,
Thoreau preferred its roar to the "hum of the city." Unable to look
beyond the city to the West, he wrote that "I must live along the
beach, on the southern shore, which looks directly out to sea. . . ."
"The sea-beach is the best thing I have seen," he wrote Emerson.
"It is very solitary and remote, and you only remember New York
occasionally." [19] He had time after his tutoring (from nine until
two) to explore the island, to witness the imposing shipping, and
to make acquaintances more agreeable even than the elder Henry
James or Horace Greeley. His neighbor Captain Smith, an old
fisherman, was more to his taste than the city men: he was the
Staten Island equivalent of Concord's George Minott—the kind of
man in whom Thoreau delighted and later fully described in the
Wellfleet oysterman.[20] The values that Thoreau associated with
Concord, moreover, were transferred to the sea; for the flora of
Staten Island was in advance of that of Concord, and, as always
when he felt this discrepancy, was a phenomenon itself, upsetting
his communion. "I find more of Concord," he told Lidian, "in the
prospect of the sea, beyond Sandy Hook, than in the fields and
woods. . . . I cannot realize that it is the sea I hear now, and not
the wind in Walden woods." [21]

The city, the strange surroundings, were exciting to a man of
perception. (His descriptions of cabmen, immigrants, and Lucretia
Mott reveal a superb skill: he had the makings of a social novelist,
but not a fictive imagination—the moral pressures of New England

[17] W, V, 216.
[18] W, VI, 70.
[19] W, VI, 79, 70.
[20] W, VI, 70, 86.
[21] W, VI, 77.

that turned him to the natural fact robbed us of a novelist. His descriptions, nevertheless, indicate a greater sense of society and people, and a greater compassion than has usually been accorded him.) But the city disturbed the tranquillity and stability—indeed, the routine—that he needed. He had an unbounded curiosity, but he was not by temperament a traveler. He was never to remain long from Concord, always returning with a sense of relief, and the Staten Island interlude, which was his first protracted absence, and one occasioned by uncomfortable necessities, showed him the depths of his roots. No one in his generation had such a hunger for place—unless it was Hawthorne—or knew its values in an age when mobility was becoming a marked characteristic of American life. He had seen the human tide funnel through the Narrows of New York to some purpose. Staten Island, therefore, threw him back on Concord and established it as *his* place. "Methinks I should be content to sit at the back door in Concord, under the poplar tree, henceforth forever," he told his mother. "Not that I am homesick at all,—for places are strangely indifferent to me,—but Concord is still a cynosure to my eyes. . . ." [22] In a letter to his "Friends" that showed more than any other how much the city had laid bare his memory and which, incidentally, was the miniature of the first chapter on Concord in the *Week*, he reminded them that "staying at home is the heavenly way."

My thoughts revert to those dear hills and that *river* which so fills up the world to its brim,—worthy to be named with Mincius and Alpheus, —still drinking its meadows while I am far away. How can it run heedless to the sea, as if I were there to countenance it? George Minott, too, looms up considerably,—and many another old familiar face. These things all look sober and respectable. They are better than the environs of New York, I assure you.

And he went on:

I am pleased to think of Channing as an inhabitant of the gray town. Seven cities contended for Homer dead. . . . In imagination I see you pilgrims taking your way by the red lodge and the cabin of the brave farmer man, so youthful and hale, to the still cheerful woods. And Hawthorne, too, I remember as one with whom I sauntered, in old heroic times, along the banks of the Scamander, amid the ruins of chariots and heroes. . . . And Elizabeth Hoar, my brave townswoman, to be sung of poets. . . . And least of all are forgotten those walks in the woods in ancient days,—too sacred to be idly remembered,—when

[22] W, VI, 99.

their aisles were pervaded as by a fragrant atmosphere [see the life everlasting]. They still seem youthful and cheery to my imagination as Sherwood and Barnsdale,—and of far purer fame. Those afternoons when we wandered o'er Olympus,—and those hills, from which the sun was seen to set, while still our day held on its way.

All this he said he remembered—but he also reminded his friends, who had pushed him into a wider world, that "you are a rare band, and do not make half use enough of one another." [23]

The depth of Thoreau's reaction to the city and the need for vocation that he associated with it were apparent in an illness which began upon his arrival and which he himself felt to be unaccountable. He wrote Emerson that "I have been sick ever since I came here, rather unaccountably—what with a cold, bronchitis, acclimation, etc., still unaccountably." To his sister he wrote: "Tell Mother I think my cold was not wholly owing to imprudence. Perhaps I was being acclimated." [24] He was indeed being acclimated. By July he had another symptom, which he jokingly passed off as the hereditary Jones's affliction: sleepiness. This "skirmishing with drowsiness," he explained, "interferes sadly with my literary projects. . . ." [25] In August he was still trying to keep awake, finding it impossible to work except at rare intervals, and he told Emerson that "I must still reckon myself with the innumerable army of invalids. . . ." "Sooner or later," he said, using the imagery of wakefulness that underlies *Walden*, "I shall awake"; and by the end of August he did. [26]

By that time, however, he had given up his siege of the editors, and had resumed his own private studies. [27] Through his former tutor, Henry McKean, now librarian of the Mercantile Library, he was given a reader's privileges and "several new editions and collections of old poetry" which proved especially restorative to him. [28] For among them he had discovered Quarles and, as he told Lidian, "Enchiridions of Meditation"—and significant for the *Week*, "long poems, almost epics for length . . . interspersed with meditations after a quite original plan. . . ." [29] On into the fall he read Daniel,

[23] W, VI, 92-94. On Sherwood and Barnsdale see J, I, 298-99.
[24] W, VI, 78, 73.
[25] W, VI, 91.
[26] W, VI, 99, 100-101.
[27] He translated *Seven Against Thebes* at this time. See W, VI, 102.
[28] W, VI, 106, 109, 114.
[29] W, VI, 112-13.

Donne, Lovelace, and Ossian, practicing a severe criticism.[30] "I feel as if I were ready," he told Emerson, "to be appointed a committee on poetry, I have got my eyes so whetted and proved of late . . ."; and by the end of the letter he had nicely got at the failure of Emerson's "Ode to Beauty." [31] And when he returned to Concord in November he lectured on Homer, Ossian, and Chaucer, tracing the loss of heroism in poetry and the decline of bardic sternness and fervor. His reading had brought him full circle, face to face again with his own heroic enterprises. He had charted a literary tradition that had domesticated the poet, taking him from "forest to fireside," a tradition of which he disapproved and wanted to repair. And in doing this he had but rediscovered the "primeval aspects, sterner, savager," that were absent in the "white man's poetry," and had dedicated himself to an older tradition of bards who had not come within doors and who "spoke but as they acted." In Ossian he renewed his faith in the heroic life, but it was, perhaps because the city taught him the futility of being a modern Raleigh, much reduced in splendor. The heroic life, he noted in the fragments of the Staten Island *Journal*, "is simple and of few elements." [32] Instead of widening, the city had narrowed Thoreau's alternatives.

II

In May, 1843, Thoreau submitted a review of J. A. Etzler's *The Paradise within the Reach of all Men, without Labor, by Powers of Nature and Machinery* to the *Democratic Review*. But "Paradise (To Be) Regained," as he mockingly called his review, was not quite what O'Sullivan expected of a friend of Hawthorne. O'Sullivan told Thoreau that the "collective we" could not "subscribe to all the opinions," and asked Thoreau for "purely literary" matter. Balked in his first attempt to write for the market, Thoreau immediately turned out "The Landlord," a "short piece," he said, "that I wrote to sell. . . ." [33] The hack work of genius, however, is not necessarily insignificant; and "The Landlord" shows us how Thoreau, who was never a popular writer, faced the major problem

---

[30] HM 13182.
[31] W, VI, 114-15.
[32] HM 13182; J, I, 272-73. See also J, I, 288-89.
[33] W, VI, 102, 111.

of audience. Later on, in the excursions, he managed through his subject matter to find an audience—he wrote a species of travel literature. In "The Landlord," however, he experimented with tone and humor, refusing to forsake his serious themes or to make them subserve narrative. He was not especially successful in this first essay at finding the proper tone, and even in *Walden* the edge of his humor was discomfiting. In fact, in his lifetime he was known by his tone, by a humor sharpened at the expense of the foibles of mankind, a humor that etched his truths all the more sharply.

"The Landlord," therefore, had a muffled seriousness, or a distortion of theme and image—as if Thoreau had rehearsed his serious routines before the mirrors of a Coney Island fun-house. His theme, of course, is serious, that the landlord is the spheral man, the good man, the whole man; but this assertion in itself is paradoxical, challenging the common estimate of tavern- and inn-keepers. In projecting a "man of more open and general sympathies, who possesses a spirit of hospitality . . . and feeds and shelters men from pure love of the creatures," [34] Thoreau was presenting a compensatory image for his own retired life. The landlord was his equivalent of Emerson's Osman, his alter ego, who "had a humanity so broad and deep," and a great heart "so sunny and hospitable in the centre of the country,—that it seemed as if the instinct of all sufferers drew them to his side." [35] Here, balancing the solitude and chill of purity and idea in Transcendentalism, was the heat of the heart, the desire for warmth and sociality: the landlord was the "public and inviting" man. His inn, too, was the nearest to the "entire and perfect house"; for Thoreau—with nature for his reference—claimed that the perfect house should shelter most of humanity, especially "all pilgrims without distinction. . . ." The landlord, then, was a stationary Whitman, minding the open road, greeting the seeker, making him "feel *in* and at home," a host who "is indeed a *host*, and a *lord* of the *land*, a self-appointed brother of his race. . . ." (In this essay Thoreau first began the wholesale use of puns—but the puns drive to the radical meanings of things. Take, for example, "he only can be called proprietor of the house . . . who behaves with most propriety in it" and "there can be no *pro*-fanity when there is no fane behind. . . .") [36] This landlord who

---

[34] All quotations are from W, V, 151-62.

[35] C, III, 154.

[36] He had already resorted to puns in the college essays.

"loves all men equally" and "treats his nearest neighbor as a stranger" (both Emerson and Thoreau preferred to discover their friends anew) was indeed a Whitman: "a man of such universal sympathies, and so broad and genial nature, that he would fain sacrifice the tender but narrow ties of friendship, to a broad, sun-shiny, fair-weather-and-foul friendship for his race; who loves men, not as a philosopher, with philanthropy, nor as an overseer of the poor, with charity, but by a necessity of his nature, as he loves dogs and horses; and standing at his open door from morning till night, would fain see more and more of them come along the highway, and is never satiated." Thirteen years before he met the universal democrat, Thoreau was prepared for his appreciation of Whitman —although in that curious shock of recognition, Thoreau took a darker view of democracy than his host. "We ought to rejoice greatly in him," he nevertheless told his friend Blake. "By his heartiness and broad genialities he puts me into a liberal frame of mind. . . ." "He is very broad, but . . . not fine," Thoreau explained. "He is apparently the greatest democrat the world has seen." [37]

Neither philosopher nor overseer, the landlord was closer to Thoreau at Walden than one at first suspects. "All the neighbor-hood is in his interest," Thoreau said; and his tavern, set in a retired place, offered "a primitive hospitality." In fact, the tavern he had in mind was very much like the hut he later built. "In these retired places the tavern is first of all a house," he wrote, "and warms and shelters its inhabitants. It is as simple and sincere in its essentials as the caves in which the first men dwelt, but it is also as open and public." Furthermore, the landlord was a man-in-nature, a pioneer with ax and spade, making nature supply the wants of many. "To my imagination," Thoreau said, "the Landlord stands clear back in nature. . . . Surely, he has solved some of the problems of life." And surely, the landlord of Walden was not a hermit, even if his girth was not quite that of the portly, "spheral" man. He was not a genius but a man of "health above the common aspects of life," with a "vast relish or appetite" rather than "taste," and with a "certain out-of-door obviousness" in his freely delivered and origi-nal sentiments. "He is not one of your peaked and inhospitable men of genius with particular tastes," Thoreau wrote. "The man of genius, like a dog with a bone, or the slave who has swallowed a

[37] W, VI, 296, 291.

diamond, or a patient with the gravel, sits afar and retired, off the road, hangs out no sign of refreshment for man and beast, but says, by all possible hints and signs, I wish to be alone—good-by—farewell." Not so the landlord, who "can afford to live without privacy," who "sleeps, wakes, eats, drinks, socially, still remembering his race," who "walks abroad through the thoughts of men, and the Iliad and Shakespeare are tame to him," and whose life "is sublimely trivial for the good of men." The landlord, as Thoreau quoted from Chaucer, "of manhood him lacked righte naught." Living an exposed life, standing in "broad and catholic relation" to all men, he was for Thoreau the representative of human nature, and of the sympathy all men want. And knowing the needs of men —their "needs and destiny"—he was "the farthest travelled, though he has never stirred from his door." Finally, he was the "man of infinite experience, who unites hands with wit," and who, because of his public character, deserved, as Menu said of the householder, to be "exempted from taxation and military duty."

The house of the landlord was also as open as himself. Like both Thoreau's hut and the ideal house he described in *Walden,* its privacies were exposed. "All the secrets of housekeeping," Thoreau wrote, "are exhibited to the eyes of men, above and below, before and behind." Even the kitchen, which, in the analogy of man and house, suggested the alimentary functions, did not excite disgust. Kitchens, Thoreau said, "are the holiest recess of the house, the heart of warmth and social life." With Hawthorne in "Peter Goldthwaite's Treasure" and "Fire Worship," and with Melville in "I and My Chimney," Thoreau used the hearth to represent the real self. Kitchens "are the heart, the left ventricle, the very vital part of the house," Thoreau wrote. "Here the real and sincere life which we meet in the streets was actually fed and sheltered. Here burns the taper that cheers the lonely traveller by night, and from this hearth ascends the smokes ["Go then my incense upward from this hearth,/And ask the gods to pardon this clear flame"] [38] that populate the valley to his eyes by day. On the whole, a man may not be so little ashamed of any other part of his house, for here is his sincerity and earnest. . . ." The hut at Walden was dominated by its hearth. Though the hut itself was raised by his friends, Thoreau built the fireplace and chimney himself, and kept its fire burning, ready to share his vital heat with anyone who would take the road to seek it.

[38] "Smoke," *The Dial,* III (April, 1843), 505.

But he was traveler as well as innkeeper. The landlord was not only a projection of his own willingness to offer "himself to the public," but a projection as well of his own need for robust sympathy. By giving his essay the larger significance of religious pilgrimage, he made the innkeeper a symbol of his vision of life. The road itself was the way. And when Thoreau spoke humorously of the landlord's religion, he said that he was "a firm believer in the perseverance of the saints"—of the saunterers, *sainte-terrers*. The tavern, he concluded, compared favorably with the church, for the landlord "gives the wayfarer as good and honest advice to direct him on his road as the priest." His quotation from Chaucer's Prologue to *The Canterbury Tales* helped him establish this metaphor; but his remark that "the great poets have not been ungrateful to their landlords" spoke for the traveler that he had become.

In September, 1843, O'Sullivan accepted "Paradise (To Be) Regained" without any revisions, "having objected," Thoreau reported to Emerson, "only to my want of sympathy with the Committee." [39] Thoreau was always adamantine in his relations with editors— Lowell later revenged himself for Thoreau's reply to his alteration of "Chesuncook" in his unfair essay on Thoreau. And undoubtedly O'Sullivan would have liked to alter the review of Etzler, which struck deeper than the pantheism of "Chesuncook" into the easy assumptions of the American mind. In any case, he solicited nothing more from the youth, who with heavy mockery had ridiculed the quantitative, mechanical utopianism of the time—that "transcendentalism in mechanics," as Thoreau called it, that aimed at a world without exertion, the utopia of the crank—or push button.[40]

In the period of Brook Farm and Fruitlands (Alcott left Concord for Harvard, Massachusetts, on July 1, 1843), of Greeley and the Sylvania Association and Brisbane and Fourierism,[41] Thoreau, by attacking Etzler's still more grandoise humanitarian proposal, showed that all attempts at collective or mechanical reform, worthy of praise as they were as signs of man's hope, were as pearls cast before swine. Transcendentalism in mechanics was one thing, and Transcendentalism in ethics another: the former "will reform nature and circumstances, and then man will be right"; the latter "will

---

[39] W, VI, 107.

[40] All quotations are from W, IV, 280-305.

[41] Of Brisbane Thoreau remarked: "He did not look as if he could let Fourier go, in any case, and throw up his hat" (W, VI, 81). See also W, VI, 96.

reform [man] himself, and then nature and circumstances will be right." Not all of the transcendentalists, however, believed so firmly in self-reform as Emerson and Thoreau, and Thoreau's essay, even more than Emerson's refusal to join Brook Farm, showed them that the transcendental faith in progress and the Emersonian belief in the power of ideas to transform circumstances had some serious disclaimers. In his attitude toward reform and man's possibility of making by invention a "new world, far superior to the present," Thoreau had a deeper and darker view of man's pride that put him in the camp of his friend Hawthorne. "Paradise (To Be) Regained" was a work that relied on Milton for more than its title, and it had its parallels in Hawthorne's "The Celestial Railroad" and "Fire Worship." Hawthorne would have as much to do with "Mr. Smooth-it-away" as Thoreau with the equally optimistic Etzler; the celestial railroad seemed to him more "a sort of mechanical demon that would hurry us to the infernal regions than a laudable contrivance for smoothing our way to the Celestial City." And in "Fire Worship," where he lamented the exchange of the open fireplace for the stove, he wrote: "In one way or another, here and there and all around us, the inventions of mankind are fast blotting the picturesque, the poetic, and the beautiful out of human life." [42]

These were also Thoreau's sentiments, and since Etzler's proposals have come to pass in the age of the bulldozer, radio, and airplane, and we are nearer "shining isles of space" than to heaven or happiness, Thoreau has his vindication—and still speaks to our time. Etzler's proposals for a paradise on earth may have seemed impossible to Thoreau, but not to us: there is more mockery in the historical parody of man's hope than in Thoreau's raillery or the satanism of Mr. Smooth-it-away. Etzler would change " 'the whole face of nature . . . into the most beautiful forms,' " create " 'all imaginable refinements of luxury,' " reduce, nay, eliminate labor, " 'level mountains, sink valleys, create lakes,' " build roads " 'for travelling one thousand miles in twenty-four hours,' " free man from " 'almost all the evils that afflict mankind, except death,' " prolong life—make man indeed the "lord of creation," the master of all the forces of wind, tide, waves, and sun (to say nothing of the energies hidden in the earth), the master of Adams' dynamo, the creator, given the cooperative and collective belt tightening of Etzler's ten-

[42] *The Complete Writings of Nathaniel Hawthorne,* Boston and New York, 1903, IV, 265, 192.

year plan, of a new world, finished and complete for all time. Man would attain heaven by modifying the earth.

But as Thoreau saw, man-made or natural, circumstances remain: "man will always be the victim of circumstances." And even though all labor is reduced to " 'a short turn of some crank,' " some man will have to turn it. And granting everything, and "we . . . finish the outworld for posterity," there would still be a problem no mechanics could solve, what to do with the "leisure to attend the inner" world. The large questions of life that Etzler and other reformers were trying to solve were also Thoreau's, but he approached them from an opposite direction. " *'Any very extraordinary desire of any person may be satisfied by going to the place where the thing is to be had; and anything that requires a particular preparation . . . may be done by the person who desires it'* "—he underlined this passage of Etzler, for it made his essential point. Whatever was unique, individual, and valuable, man would have to do for himself. "No work can be shirked," he said. "Nor can any really important work be made easier by co-operation or machinery. Not one particle of labor now threatening any man can be routed without being performed." The price of virtue still had to be paid in the immemorial way, by the sweat of the brow. Self-reform, which was Thoreau's way of reforming the outward life, emphasized what Etzler minimized, that man himself must do the work: the strong iron rod of Puritanism had a place in his thought.

Thoreau approached Etzler's book in the most untranscendental way: with common sense, that Yankee acuity that made his remarks on economy in *Walden* so telling. The forces of wind, tide, sun, and wave were shown to be less powerful than Etzler had supposed. But this did not trouble Thoreau so much as the ends that they were intended to serve. After all, Etzler had proposed a quantitative heaven, one designed to "minister to our sensible and animal wants," one that aimed "to secure the greatest degree of gross comfort and pleasure merely." Emerson, in the chapter on commodity in *Nature*, had also shown the marvelous forces that work for man: "The wind sows the seed; the sun evaporates the sea; etc. . . . [And] The useful arts are reproductions or new combinations by the wit of man, of the same natural benefactors. . . . he paves the road with iron bars, and, mounting a coach with a ship-load of men, animals, and merchandise behind him, darts through the country . . . like an eagle. . . . how is the face of the world

changed, from the era of Noah to that of Napoleon!" [43] There was
the hint here that Hawthorne needed for "The Celestial Railroad."
But Emerson added what Etzler forgot, "that this mercenary
benefit is one which has respect to a farther good. A man
is fed, not that he may be fed, but that he may work."
The remainder of *Nature* was a manual of self-reform, raising the
sights of men and educating them in the power of perception. And
actually Emerson's examples of the uses of natural forces and inventions were cited to prove a wholly different thesis. As Thoreau
put it, "Already nature is serving all those uses which science slowly
derives on a much higher and grander scale to him that will be
served by her. When the sunshine falls on the path of the poet, he
enjoys all those pure benefits and pleasures which the arts slowly
and partially realize from age to age." Thoreau's quarrel with
Etzler, therefore, was over the mechanical rather than organic use
of nature. "No doubt the simple powers of nature, properly directed by man," Thoreau said, "would make it healthy and a
paradise. . . ." Where Etzler desired to grasp the law of nature and
bend it to the will of man, Thoreau desired to live with the law, to
live in nature, and not transform it. Following Etzler's way, men
dealt "meanly and grossly" with nature, became, in their mono-
mania for power, "the fiercest and cruellest animal," abusing men
and animals alike, cluttering the ground with inventions that are
an "outrage against universal laws," that "insult Nature." And with
an eye to the westward movement, which was but the van of
progress, Thoreau cited the pioneer itch to despoil nature and move
on to " 'better land.' "

This superficial and violent assault on nature was for Thoreau
the most obvious sign of man's want of faith. "Can we do no more
than cut and trim the forest," he asked; "can we not assist in its
interior economy, in the circulation of the sap?" The most important thing he had to tell his generation—and succeeding generations lulled by the placebos of mechanism and association—was
how to live *with* the absolute, abiding laws of nature and man,
that is, how to participate in the fundamental organic processes
that underlie man's best hopes. *Walden* was his counterproposal,
authenticating Emerson's *Nature* by experience, and having for its
immediate target the impractical faith of his time. Why "improve
and beautify the system?" he mocked, "what to make the stars

---

[43] C, I, 13-14.

shine more brightly, the sun more cheery and joyous, the moon more placid and content." Would it not be better and "more heroic and faithful to till and redeem this New England soil of the world" —as he himself would do at Walden—than to move on to the virgin soil of Ohio? "We do not suspect," he wrote, "how much might be done to improve our relation to animated nature even. . . . There are certain pursuits which . . . suggest a nobler and finer relation to nature than we know." He confessed that "sometimes . . . we are so degenerate as to reflect with pleasure on the days when men were yoked like cattle, and drew a crooked stick for a plow. After all, the great interests and methods were the same." His primitivism, like his call for simplicity, was only a way of confronting again the essentials of life: they were means, not articles of faith. Instead his faith was in "a certain divine energy in every man, but sparingly employed as yet, which may be called the crank within . . . the prime mover in all machinery,—quite indispensible to all work." His faith was in faith itself, in the raw material of invention, in the idea and the theory, the dreams of man; and he felt that Etzler failed because he left off dreaming "where he who dreams just before the dawn begins." In the image he later used in *Walden*, he said of Etzler's dream, "His castles in the air fall to the ground, because they are not built lofty enough; they should be secured to heaven's roof."

Thoreau waited until *Walden* to show in detail how to build the foundations of the castle. But in "Paradise (To Be) Regained" he pointed out the building material. "A moral reform," he said, "must first take place"—"the power of rectitude and true behavior" must first be employed. Common sense alone suggested the serious objections to Etzler's scheme: it required time, men, and money; it went begging for the faith of men. Etzler had said that "the execution of the proposals is not proper for individuals. . . . Man is powerful but in union with many. Nothing great . . . can ever be effected by individual enterprise." This was indeed a gross faithlessness. "Alas! this is the crying sin of the age," Thoreau wrote, "this want of faith in the prevalence of a man." Associations could accomplish nothing without "the application of man to the work by faith." To think that one generation would repair what the past ages could not repair was to rely too heavily (and not enough) on the unknown quantity in all human equations. The devil in "Earth's Holocaust" had chuckled over the indestructibility of the human heart. "As for these communities," Thoreau wrote in the *Journal* in 1841, "I think I had rather keep bachelor's hall in hell than go to board in heaven. Do you think your virtue will be boarded with you?" [44] And now he wrote, "Nothing can be effected but by one man. He who wants help wants everything. . . . Faith, indeed, is all the reform that is needed; it is itself a reform."

Hawthorne, whose view of the heart was darker than Thoreau's, would have agreed that "the true reformer does not want time, nor money, nor co-operation, nor advice." He would also have liked to share Thoreau's unqualified belief in the power of love. For Thoreau, translating Etzler's mechanics into ethics in the correspondential manner of Emerson, found instead of the puny forces of physics the incalculable force of spirit. "Love," he said, "is the wind, the tide, the waves, the sunshine." And just as the mechanical forces had not yet been put to ideal uses, so "the power of love has been but meanly and sparingly applied, as yet." It alone, however, was the constant force of the universe, and the most reliable, making "a paradise within which will dispense with a paradise without." Aware, as he said again in *Walden,* of "this restless, nervous, bustling, trivial Nineteenth Century," his plea for a "little patience and privacy, in all our methods" was not antisocial.[45] "Undoubtedly if we were to reform this outward life truly and thoroughly [pun], we should find no duty of the inner omitted," he said. Such a reform "would be employment for our whole nature. . . ." Representatively, with Whitman sharing his discoveries with all men, he

----

[44] J, I, 227.

[45] W, II,· 363. Even his ardently humanitarian family misunderstood him. He said of Charles Lane's writing (Lane was Alcott's partner at Fruitlands) that, though "solid," "I find that I put off the 'social tendencies' to a future day, which may never come" (W, VI, 114). To his sister Helen, who liked the Christian socialism of W. H. Channing, he explained himself and also the basic grounds of his disapproval, later amplified in *Walden:* "You think that Channing's words would apply to me too, as living more in the natural than the moral world; but I think you mean the world of men and women rather, and reformers generally. My objection to Channing and all that fraternity is that they need and deserve sympathy themselves rather than are able to render it to others. They want faith, and mistake their private ail for an infected atmosphere; but let any one of them recover hope for a moment, and right his *particular* grievance, and he will no longer train in that company. To speak or do anything that shall concern mankind, one must speak and act as if well, or from that grain of health which he has left. . . . I have the jaundice myself; but I also know what it is to be well. But do not think that one can escape mankind who is one of them, and is so constantly dealing with them" (W, VI, 118).

would try the private and individual way, to see if spiritual force could be "applied to social ends." And he would not claim perfection, nor cast the universe in one rigid mold. His faith in spirit was not quite a faith in progress, but rather a faith in the power of vision and the novelty of the universe. "The Divine is about to be," he affirmed, "and such is its nature." [46]

III

"The Landlord" and "Paradise (To Be) Regained" were theoretical essays, without the strata of actual experience that gave Thoreau's best work both solidity and form. In "A Walk to Wachusett" and "A Winter Walk," however, he began to make walking the explicit symbol of man's life, and he fully employed in the structure of the essays those archetypal patterns of morning and evening, sunrise and sunset, ascent and descent, mountain and plain, woods and village, summer and winter that became the warp and woof of the *Week* and *Walden*. Though the experiences recorded in these essays were brief, the method Thoreau used in them was essentially that of his best work. Indeed, the method and materials of Thoreau's work remained fairly constant; only the tone and tenor changed, as the method and materials, which were the substance of his life, were tested, and the faith he so easily accepted demanded of him more and firmer resolution and discipline. The faith, of course, never wavered, but the tone changed its pitch; what was at first genial became increasingly strident—faith was tested by works. If "Sir Walter Raleigh," for example, was an earlier "Life Without Principle," "A Walk to Wachusett" and "A Winter Walk," with their espousal of nature, were the earlier versions of "Walking," in which nearly two decades of experience prompted Thoreau to make "an extreme statement" in nature's behalf. Where the earlier essays achieved their effects by their very leisureliness and healthiness, demonstrating the uses of nature, the latter was more declarative and admonishing.

The great fact of "A Walk to Wachusett" [47] was the mountain, that little peak on the western rim of Concord that in its indistinctness and distance was the landmark of Thoreau's destiny. It was also all mountains—Homer's Olympus, Virgil's Etrurian and Thes-

---

[46] Thoreau's example of the shellfish that casts its shell (W, IV, 301) had been used in a letter to Isaiah Williams (Berg Collection).

[47] All quotations are from W, V, 133-52.

salian hills, Humboldt's Andes and Teneriffe; to walk to it was to recover all that mountains had meant in the past, to measure the past by the present experience. Wachusett "served equally to interpret all the allusions of poets and travellers," Thoreau said, thereby universalizing his experience and making, as one always feels in his texture of nature and history, the present of nature the sum of the past. Thoreau went to nature to find the primordial, essential relations of man; searching for the aboriginal, he dug through the layers of time; Homer's Greece and Thoreau's Walden were one; the inviting and unexplored West was not a new world, but an older one, the Golden Age, the undefaced past. One of the curious misinterpretations of Transcendentalism is that which confuses the repudiation of tradition with the repudiation of the past; when Emerson inveighed against history he was only attempting to change subservience to mastery—he was teaching his generation the uses of history, how through consciousness and idea to appropriate the past. In proposing nature as the foundation of America, he was not, with the fervent nationalists, starting from scratch, but offering the past as Henry James did—"we can deal freely with forms of civilization not our own, can pick and choose and assimilate and in short . . . claim our property wherever we find it" [48]—living fully in the memory of man. Nature was not only eternal, but eternal temporally, that is, the fullness of time. Neither Emerson nor Thoreau was a pioneer in the crude sense; they were men of culture who wisely went about their trail blazing with book in hand, looking forward and backward to the eternal—imperishable —experiences of man; they sought in temporality itself, that new dimension of romanticism, the eternal truths of man.

Before the narrative began, therefore, Thoreau provided the perspective in which it was to be seen; nothing was to be taken entirely on the literal level. He had told Emerson in July, 1843, that "in writing, conversation should be folded many times thick. It is the height of art that, on the first perusal, plain common sense should appear; on the second, severe truth; and on a third, beauty; and, having these warrants for its depth and reality, we may then enjoy the beauty for evermore." [49] In his apostrophe to Wachusett he unfolded the meanings to which the essay referred. Wachusett was

---

[48] Letter to Thomas S. Perry, cited by Leon Edel, *Henry James: The Untried Years,* Philadelphia and New York, 1953, p. 264.

[49] W, VI, 94.

first of all associated with the frontier, the West, the primordial—
with silence and with the source of rivers (the "circulations" of
nature): from actual frontier to spiritual frontier. Then, in the
image of a steadfast ship "not skulking [the word Stevenson applied
to Thoreau!] close to land," it was associated with discovery: "Ye
to the westward run,/Until ye find a shore amid the skies." Cool
and blue, the mountain also stood for heavenly purity, and for the
spiritual leisure above time. And in its "unappropriated strength"
and "unhewn primeval timber" it was

> The stock of which new earths are made,
> One day to be our western trade,
> Fit for the stanchions of a world
> Which through the seas of space is hurled.

Then, the mountain was associated with the sun, which, setting for
the poet, had not set for the mountain: "Ye still o'ertop the western
day." For the mountain in the horizon is the "earth's edge." As
Thoreau made clear in the *Week*,

> Through your defiles windeth the way to heaven;
> And yonder still, in spite of history's page,
> Linger the golden and the silver age.

And as he elaborated in "Walking," the West, which is the cardinal
direction of the essay, promised "new dynasties of thought." Finally,
Thoreau identified Wachusett with himself—"May I approve myself thy worthy brother!"—for the mountain "like me/Standest
alone without society." Alone, however, it still served by leavening
everything with its cerulean qualities: it represented the spiritual
experiences the transcendentalist wanted to use to transform his
society. It was in this sense that the mountain (and the poet) was
the "western pioneer . . . /By venturous spirit driven . . . /Up-
holding heaven, holding down earth." With its summit and base,
the mountain was the perfect symbol of the midworld, of spirit
and prudence that the transcendentalist wanted to reconcile.

To go to the mountain, then, was to go westward and heaven-
ward, to experience transcendentally. Thoreau, however, did not
soar immediately; for he had learned from Homer the virtue of
telling how to get there. "When Homer's messengers repair to the
tent of Achilles," he noted in 1838, and adopted as a literary maxim
in his essay, "we do not have to wonder how they get there, but
step by step accompany them along the shore by the resounding
sea." Though the purpose of narrative was to carry the thought—

idea being always the thing he wished to communicate—he was a writer as well as transcendentalist, and he knew the importance of solid ground. He did not so often speak directly from the Over-Soul, from the heights, as Emerson did; and this accounts in large measure for his growing reputation as a writer. The ability to make the fact flower into truth, to perform the flowering, is what gives sinew to his thought. He knew the simple caution of going from the seen to the unseen, and that men reason from the hand to the head. "In the spaces of thought are the reaches of land and water," he advised us of his method, "where men come and go." If, as he went on to say, "the landscape lies far and fair within, and the deepest thinker is the farthest traveller"—hinting that his excursion was in reality an account of a state of mind—he did not forget, as occasionally he did in the *Week*, to take us step by step over an actual sense-awakening landscape. Like the early discoverers whose writing he admired and whose experience he tried to relive, he gave us a genuine territory, adding to it the riches of his experiences, where we, too, can recover the same ground.

Most of Thoreau's excursions were leisurely—that was one of the values he prized. Leisure is but room for thought; and in his writing, allusion, which slowed his pace, was the means. His writing was never hurried: it had the same margin of leisure that his life had. To go to nature, after all, was a special kind of experience. Thoreau never let one forget that it was refreshing, or, in his allusions, that it was universal. "A Walk to Wachusett," therefore, was admirably bucolic, the fragment from Virgil's *Eclogues* fortifying as well as establishing the tone. The narrative, and the initiation into nature, began with the crepuscular hours of a July morning [50] (the morning-evening cycle was deliberately employed), when all the values of the ascent were already available: the morning air was cool (pure) and freshly scented, the bird songs filled the dark woods, "all nature lay passive" and "peace and purity" filled the atmosphere. The walker entered a "solitude with light; which is better than darkness"; he saw dimly, but had an unprofaned privacy. The experience of the cool woods might have taken place anywhere, at any time. The hopfields through which he passed were used to make this point: they were the American vineyards, analogous in culture and use to the grape: they recalled

---

[50] The actual excursion was begun on July 19, 1842, in the company of Richard Fuller. See Rusk, ed., *The Letters of Ralph Waldo Emerson*, III, 75.

Italy and southern France, and the immemorial theme of poets—inspiration itself. And as he went on, he met some mowers in the field who reminded him of the essential transcendental insights that his excursion demonstrated, that all knowledge is private, but that life itself is universal—"that man's life is rounded with the same few facts, the same simple relations everywhere, and it is vain to find it new." Nor are we permitted to forget that man is a "sojourner," a "wayfarer," and that "the path his feet describe is so perfectly symbolical of human life"—"he is treading his old lessons still, and though he may be very weary and travel-worn, it is yet sincere experience." Westering was an ascent; the pilgrimage of man was a search for prospects.

As the traveler came to higher land he found that the pronunciation of names was "truer and wilder," "bred further west." A few leagues' walk from Concord abolished the "tame" and "civil." In brief, then, Thoreau was recounting (and projecting new significance on) the westward movement. By noon he reached the first prospect to the West—the highlands overlooking the valley of Lancaster. Noon, of course, with dawn and sunset, was a time of inspiration; nooning, which accounted later for the philosophical essays of the *Week*, was contemplation. Thus the traveler rested in the shade, read a few pages in the *Aeneid*, and looked out upon Wachusett with its "unchanged proportions" but "less ethereal aspect than had greeted our morning gaze." Reading Virgil, Thoreau felt the similarity of "Italian vales" and "New England hills," but also the difference between "this life so new and modern, that so civil and ancient. . . ." But he read Virgil, he said, "to be reminded of the identity of human nature in all ages"; and even the recognition of differences helped him place all experience in time. Time and space were correlatives: Thoreau blended the two when he spoke of "Virgil, *away* in Rome, two thousand years *off*. . . ." [51] Actually, reading the *Aeneid* reminded Thoreau that "we are both the children of a late age"—that behind Virgil and Thoreau was the Golden Age. The Old World, the past, therefore, was like dim and remote mountains in the rear, still serene and imposing and important, comparable in the dimness and remoteness to Wachusett in the West, marking the future. Past and future were East and West, but the attraction of remoteness was the same, and it was this that stood behind Thoreau as he faced west. He was not

[51] My italics.

leaving the Old World behind, but as his appropriation of Virgil tells us, taking it with him. Since all time was experientially the same, even the differences in space were obliterated: the West had the significance of the past, just as inspiration wherever attained, on Wachusett or Olympus, was the same.

As the traveler descended into the valley of the Nashua, he felt the lack of coolness, and everywhere the scent of the vegetation was dry. The heat of the day, the afternoon, and the descent represented the inevitable lapse from inspiration. At this stage in his career, Thoreau accepted its necessity without guilt; he recalled the lament of Hassan in the desert, and he cited the experiences of colonial explorers who had been made faint by the heat. By walking in the shadows, bathing his feet in the streams, and loitering into late afternoon, however, he was able to recover his "morning elasticity." And he was refreshed at evening, when he reached Sterling, and smelled the pines and heard the roar of water.

For a Concordian, Sterling was a western town, a frontier settlement. As Thoreau also said of the woodman's hut in "A Winter Walk," it was civilization that made nature look wild. "Left to herself," he wrote, "nature is always more or less civilized, and delights in a certain refinement. . . ." So the raw settlement reminded him of both the West and the wild, and of the glaring disharmony of man in nature. "Each one's world," he moralized, is "but a clearing in the forest. . . ." When he himself had cleared a place for his hut at Walden, he hoped, as he said in "A Winter Walk," that nature would overlook "the encroachment and profanity of man"; for he knew that nature would accept his hut in time, and build around it—"flowers as well as weeds," he said, "follow in the footsteps of man." [52] Whether this would be the case with Sterling, or with the inroads of civilization in nature, were other questions. His faith in the self-sufficiency of the frontier towns and in the possibility of their respect for nature was darkened by the fact that the greatest gift the Sterling innkeeper could give him was the Concord newspaper. At the base of the mountain, Sterling did not improve its opportunities: it looked to the East. And the Stillwater River, along which Thoreau made his way to the summit, had been dammed, like the town it served, for a "career of usefulness."

The ascent of Wachusett gained in significance by its contrast with the pursuits of the plain, most immediately with the complacency of Sterling. Thoreau left the inn before the village was

[52] W, V, 172-73.

stirring, in the morning twilight, "after it had been hallowed by the night air. . . ." The ascent, of course, was an act of purification, and one is reminded by Thoreau's "lofty prudence" of similar rituals in the *Week* and *Walden:* "the traveller who ascends into a mountainous region should fortify himself," he wrote of his own practice, "by eating of such light ambrosial fruits as grow there [he gathered raspberries]; and, by drinking of the springs which gush out from the mountain sides,[53] as he gradually inhales the subtler and purer atmosphere of those elevated places, thus propitiating the mountain gods, by a sacrifice of their own fruits." Ascent was discipline, the regimen of "Higher Laws"—"the gross products of the plains and valleys are for such as dwell therein." Wachusett was not very high; from its summit one saw Monadnock and still higher mountains to the northwest, but it was high enough to remove one "from all contagion with the plain." It was a transcendental place, like Walden Pond, "a place where gods might wander, so solemn and solitary. . . ." And it is significant for an understanding of the complex meanings of civilization *vs.* nature, which were so much in the thought of Thoreau's generation, that he felt himself, in the haze that shut down on every side, in a "blue Pacific," and that he compared his position to that of "voyagers of an aërial Polynesia. . . ."

While waiting for a "clearer atmosphere," Thoreau read Wordsworth's "Peter Bell," citing in the essay those lines on the Cheviot hills and Yorkshire dales that corroborated his own experience. He dreamed, too, that one day Wachusett would be a Helvellyn or a Parnassus, a mountain memorialized by his pen, a worthy addition to the "new annals in the history of man."[54] And as evening condensed the haze, and the landscape became visible, he quoted directly from Virgil's *Eclogues,* using the older poet's words to describe what he had seen. Finally, as the landscape to the east was covered with shadow, and the sun set, he had this benediction: "The sun's rays fell on us two alone, of all New England men." Even at night, on the bleak summit, with the fierce cold wind and the moonlight, he recognized the seal of the destiny he had been seeking, in the stars, in that alliance with the laws of nature which never fail.

---

[53] Thoreau used the springs as Hawthorne did, as symbols of heavenly purity.

[54] Though Thoreau had responded to the call for a national literature in his college years, his experience with editors in New York, especially with O'Sullivan, undoubtedly strengthened this sentiment. During the 1840's New York was a battleground for this issue.

This experience of inspiration was private, and though the inspiration of the sunrise on the next morning was equally private, it was given a social value. For Thoreau made his account of the sunrise a brilliant image of the discovery of Massachusetts: "When the dawn had reached its prime, we enjoyed the view of a distinct horizon line, and could fancy ourselves at sea, and the distant hills the waves in the horizon, as seen from the deck of a vessel. . . . At length we saw the sun rise up out of the sea, and shine on Massachusetts. . . ." He had indeed discovered the land, from this prospect above it. "We began to realize the extent of the view," he wrote, "and how the earth, in some degree, answered to the heavens in breadth, the white villages to the constellations in the sky." Noting the correspondence of earth to heaven, invoking the image of the stars that "were given for a consolation to man," Thoreau used the remainder of the essay to consider the relation of heaven and earth, to show the uses of heaven *on* earth. With the sunrise, he turned to the land; the time to descend had come. But before he descended, he surveyed his state, "spread out before us in its length and breadth, like a map," and read in the lay of the land the destiny of America. The "grandest feature" was Monadnock, the height of land separating the valleys of the Merrimack and the Connecticut rivers—valleys "teeming with Yankee men" who might misread the destiny symbolized by the mountain ranges to the west. For these ranges seemed to Thoreau to have been shaped by a "comprehensive intelligence": "the hand which moulded their opposite slopes, making one to balance the other . . . was privy to the plan of the universe." The lesser ranges of New England, the Alleghenies, the larger streams, the coast, and the bank of the ocean itself ran northeast to southwest, determining not only the course of the wind and the migration of birds, but the migrations of men. The "improvements of civilization," however, filled the valleys. The ranges themselves were barriers to "prejudice and fanaticism," and the ultimate value of the mountains for Thoreau was the fact that they might keep the West purer, that, if the pioneer used the peaks instead of "petty landmarks," the westward movement might justify the hopes of America. "In passing over these heights of land," he wrote, "the follies of the plain are refined and purified; and as many species of plants do not scale their summits, so many species of folly no doubt do not cross the Alleghenies. . . ." Thoreau was

asking his generation to follow law rather than expediency, to ally
the westward movement with a larger spiritual destiny.[55]

His essay, in fact, was written to show how men, living "the
desultory life of the plain," can "impart a little of that mountain
grandeur into it." His excursion, like the *Week* and *Walden,* had
been only the objective correlative of inspiration.[56] "This level life
too has its summit," he explained, "there is elevation in every hour,
as no part of the earth is so low that the heavens may not be seen
from, and we have only to stand on the summit of our hour to
command an uninterrupted horizon." Not everything was lost,
therefore, when he descended to the "abodes of men" and plodded
the dusty roads of the plain where his thought became passive and
mechanical. The "ethereal hues" of the mountain still measured his
progress, and walking eastward, back into the past, his old environment now had an "unexpected refinement" and "classic appearance." Inspiration had taught him the lesson of time. Still further
in the past, he remembered the Indian wars and Mrs. Rowlandson's capture, the "dark age of New England," now as remote as
the "irruption of the Goths." From the mountain he had looked
into the future, but modern America was at Sterling, classic America
at Concord, and the dark ages in the memory of Philip and Standish
and Lovell, a heroic age that he would later find not shadowy but
golden, a counterpoise, like the West, to the serenity and civility
of Concord. Furthermore, he had learned on the summit the lesson
of space, that nature was ample and roomy, that there was plenty
of room to go alone. Looking back to Wachusett once more, from
the magnificent prospect at Harvard, and feeling the repose of the
evening, he had the experience he wanted to communicate to his
contemporaries: "we could not help contrasting the equanimity of
nature," he said, "with the bustle and impatience of man." Here,
again, in terms of the conduct of life was the significance of the
mountain and the plain. Having once had this inspiration, the
plainsman need not despair. He could live in the view, if not on the
summit, of the mountain. And every hour might still have its summit, as Thoreau went on to relate in greater detail in the *Week* and
Walden.

[55] The mountain prospect of America might be compared with Whitman's
continental soaring. And Thoreau's example of the bird that finds its way by
the peaks suggests the same spiritual value as Bryant's "To a Waterfowl."

[56] The subjectivism of romantic self-expression was "objectified" in two ways,
by public symbolism and by allusion—both universalizing the experience.

There were many ways to symbolize the transcendental values. In "A Winter Walk," for example, the spatial distinction of mountain and plain could as easily be made by contrasting Concord woods and Concord village, and the inner values of inspiration, associated with the cool peaks, could be transposed to the cold of winter. "A Winter Walk," therefore, has the general structure of "A Walk to Wachusett"—the purpose of walking is the same, and the morning-evening cycle is employed again.[57] This walk, however, was localized: with much of the natural detail of the "Natural History," it was a canvass of the resources of the Concord woods, written perhaps with an eye to his neighbors (it was printed in *The Dial* where Thoreau said it belonged) and as a preliminary survey of the Walden vicinity. Composed in the first month of Thoreau's Staten Island residence, in May, 1843, it showed the depth of his need for the Concord environment; that a winter's walk was described might also have been due to an unconscious wish to live in any season but that of Staten Island, to go back in memory to his last season at home.

Winter, however, had special advantages. It was a most unseasonable time to walk the woods, thereby emphasizing the heroic aspects of the enterprise, contrasting Thoreau's "inward heat" with the house-bound warmth of the villagers, and dramatizing his essential insight that whatever the season, nature is a constant source of inspiration. The cold, of course, opened up a wide range of special associations—purity, chastity, virtue, self-reliance—and winter itself, offering the sharpest contrast with the other seasons, provided the best test of his faith in the abiding life of nature. In this essay—and in this stage of Thoreau's communion with nature—winter was not a season of discontent, not even a time of self-communion and appraisal. He was not looking ahead to spring; there was as yet no need in his spiritual economy for rebirth. The essay was happily external, inspiration was taken for granted, and its fullness made for a summer assurance that obliterated winter, eliminated the outer seasons, and led, in the writing, to easy and perhaps confusing transitions from season to season.[58]

[57] All quotations are from W, V, 163-83.

[58] In preparing the essay for publication Emerson tried to eliminate what he called "mannerisms" and tricks of rhetoric, i.e. the inversion of values, "to call a cold place sultry, a solitude public, a wilderness *domestic* (a favorite word), and in the woods to insult over cities. . . ." These mannerisms, however, were the essential Thoreau, so deeply a part of the essay that Emerson could not effectively remove them (W, V, xiii).

In the economy of nature, winter is the season in which all life hibernates, when the earth slumbers and men retreat inward to their hearths. Commonly, winter is the cruelest season, the bleak dormant time; and Thoreau began the essay with these associations, especially those of sleep. The "snug cheer within," however, he will seek without, and while the villagers sleep he will bestir himself in the winter morning. More than any, this essay gives one a sense of solitude and loneliness, and suggests the ease with which one can leave routines behind for strange adventures merely by awakening at an unaccustomed hour. In the snowy twilight before dawn, Thoreau silently left the house; this action dissociated him from the village as ascent had from the plain. He achieved the sense of wonder in the transition by describing it in "Tartarian" and "Infernal" terms. The landscape under the leaden sky was "dim and spectral . . . like the shadowy realms"; the sounds he heard were infernal—"all seem to come from Pluto's barnyard and beyond the Styx"—suggesting instead of melancholy, however, something "too solemn and mysterious for earth." The dark was the underworld, like winter to spring, but it was also a deeper primeval nature which, as the tracks of the night animals reminded Thoreau, was still alive. Even though it was winter, then, sunrise brought some of the virtues of spring.

The smoke from the chimneys was another indication of awakening. Smoke, Thoreau explained, "is a hieroglyphic of man's life, and suggests more intimate and important things than the boiling of a pot." Smoke, thought, inspiration—these were the signs of spiritual life; the smoke was given an added religious connotation by the reference to "matins." And the way in which the smoke rose from the houses, first sluggishly, then in "wreathed loiterings," as if with "uncertain purpose," symbolized the half-wakened farmer's sluggish thoughts. The smoke, however, was also the "emissary," the "earliest, latest pilgrim," a "venturous wreath"—like Thoreau abroad on that winter morning—seeking its "heavenward course," "exploring in the dawn,/And making slow acquaintance with the day." The early-morning sounds also reinforced the inspirational, religious meanings: "clear and bell-like," they came from greater distances and with greater purity because the winter air, unlike summer's, "conveys only the finer particles of sound . . . with short and sweet vibrations." Indeed, the icy air was "refined and purified by cold" and the "tense sky [seemed] groined like the aisles of a cathedral."

The rising sun—magnificently described both visually and aurally as the "faint clashing swinging sound of cymbals"—began the process of melting which marked the course of the day and the essay. But Thoreau, as the sounds and smoke had hinted, already had from the cold the "increased glow of thought and feeling," the "inward heat," that made him indifferent to seasons. At this period in his life he would anticipate rather than await the seasons; he felt that by conforming to nature and adopting a pure and simple diet, he could live as well as the plants and animals, at home in every season.[59] "A healthy man," he wrote, "is the complement of the seasons, and in winter, summer is in his heart. There is the south." What he found most pleasing in winter, however, was "the wonderful purity of nature. . . ." Everything he witnessed—"the clean napkin of snow," the "fineness and purity" of "the cleansed air"— was merely the outward evidence of his own state. "In the bare fields and tinkling woods," he wrote, "see what virtue survives." All contagion was swept away, and only virtue remained—"whatever we meet with in cold and bleak places, as the tops of mountains, we respect for a sort of sturdy innocence, a Puritan toughness." He was describing his own "pure and steadfast virtue": when "all things . . . seem to be called in for shelter," he wrote, "what stays out must be part of the original frame of the universe, and of such valor as God himself." His virtue, therefore, was the "subterranean fire," like that of nature, which never went out, and the outward thaw was but the symbol of his inner heat and spirit. "In the winter," he said, "warmth stands for all virtue," a virtue equivalent to the sun; for the "warmth comes directly from the sun, and is not radiated from the earth, as in summer. . . ." Thus the walker, inspired by the cold and warm with health, found winter warm. "This subterranean fire," he explained his play on warmth, "has its altar in each man's breast, for in the coldest day, and on the bleakest hill, the traveller cherishes a warmer fire within . . . than is kindled on any hearth."

And for the walker, who had left the "gadding town," the woods, still "glad and warm . . . as genial and cheery in winter as in summer," were the proper place to find a comparable virtue. Always concerned with the conditions and sources of inspiration, Thoreau

[59] The daring of this excursion was that he was going to put the bleakest nature to use. But when he tested the geniality of winter by going out into the snow "without greatcoat or drawers" he became ill with bronchitis (J, I, 201, 214).

wanted to remind his neighbors of their dependence on nature. "We borrow from the forest," he pointed out what he would demonstrate in *Walden*, "the boards which shelter, and the sticks which warm [physically and spiritually] us. . . . What would human life be without forests? . . . Our humble villages in the plain are their contribution." Unaware of the life still stirring in the woods, the villagers were spiritually dead. They did not see the snow melting at the bases of trees, the growing winter rye, the frolic of the squirrels and rabbits, the tracks of the fox, or the larvae of the caddis worms. Unacquainted with the "self-subsistent valor" of insects and animals, they were shut off from "the simplicity and purity of a primitive age, and a health and hope far remote from towns and cities." They had lost what Thoreau had found, "reflections of a richer variety than the life of cities," a life "more serene and worthier to contemplate."

They had lost what Thoreau had lost at Staten Island and was trying to summon again in the remainder of the essay: a heroic virtue, a life in the woods, and the margin of leisure and spontaneity that the walk itself, with its freedom from petty goals and its richness of experience, afforded. The scenes Thoreau described became the scenery of his life: Walden Pond, Fair Haven Cliffs and Bay, and the Concord River. And the deserted woodman's hut he visited suggested not only the rude shelter he later built, but the life it would permit him to live. "The hemlocks whispered over his head," he imagined, "these hickory logs were his fuel . . . yonder fuming rill in the hollow . . . was his well. . . . through this broad chimney throat . . . he looked up to learn the progress of the storm, and, seeing the bright stars of Cassiopeia's chair shining brightly down upon him, fell contentedly asleep." Sitting in the hut, while the eaves were dripping with melted snow, with the lisp of the titmouse and the warmth of the sun at the door, he was already enjoying "the friendship of the seasons" that he described in "Sounds" and "Solitude" in *Walden*.[60] And Walden Pond itself— here referred to only as a woodland lake—now for the first time appeared in his writing, already full of personal significance. The lesson it symbolized was the same one he had learned at Staten Island—" 'sitting still at home is the heavenly way; the going out is the way of the world.' " [61] Instead, Walden Pond was a spiritual

---

[60] W, II, 145.

[61] See W, VI, 93.

traveler. "In its evaporation," Thoreau said, "it travels as far as any" —an idea he later developed in "The Pond in Winter," where the ice was harvested for Bombay and Calcutta, and "the pure Walden water is mingled with the sacred water of the Ganges." [62] The pond was only identified with Thoreau in this way and not yet explicitly with his real self, but it still had in Thoreau's mind the permanent associations of purity and ecstasy. "The sins of the wood," he said, "are washed out in it." Sedentary but not idle, its basic function in the economy of nature was purification: "the sun comes with his evaporation to sweep the dust from its surface each morning, and a fresh surface is constantly welling up; and annually, after whatever impurities have accumulated herein, its liquid transparency appears again in the spring." "In summer," he said, "a hushed music seems to sweep across its surface." Not only all natural signs, but his deepest needs directed Thoreau to this "mirror in the breast of nature." [63] The breaking up of the ice, however, was not associated with Walden in this essay, but with Fair Haven Bay. The thunderous booming of the ice, of course, had the same meaning: caused by tides more subtle than those of the oceans, "every sound is fraught with the same mysterious assurance of health. . . ." As in *Walden*,

> Methinks the summer still is nigh,
> And lurketh underneath. . . .

The final episode, an afternoon's skating on the river, suggested some of the associations used in the *Week*. The river, which "flows in the rear of towns," was the transcendental highway, a way of seeing all things "from a new and wilder side." It was, like the mountain, "the outside and edge of the earth," a perspective from which the "violent contrasts" of civilization and nature were no longer offensive. The flow of the river suggested "the law of obedience," the ease with which obstacles were overcome by yielding to the law; in fact, here was the fundamental idea and structure of the *Week*: "From the remote interior, its current conducts him by broad and easy steps, or by one gentle inclined plane, to the sea."

---

[62] W, II, 329.

[63] One does not know how much the value of Walden woods was increased in Emerson's mind by what Thoreau had written. But Emerson bought fourteen acres on the shore of the pond in October, 1844. William Emerson thought his brother had purchased the land for Alcott (see Rusk, ed., *The Letters of Ralph Waldo Emerson*, III, 262-63). But it turned out to be the only piece of speculation from which Thoreau benefited.

Thoreau proposed it as "the path for a sick man. . . ." As a highway, too, it proved that "no domain of nature is quite closed to man at all times," a lesson that one could also read in the abundant life beneath its icy crust. For the ice was "superficial," the springs that really fed the stream were "below the frost." This, of course, was the burden of the essay—and what Thoreau discovered again when he plumbed the depths of Walden in winter.

In "A Winter Walk" this assurance of subterranean life was enough. Only later would the necessity of rebirth demand an actual spring. But some of the meanings of winter in *Walden* were nevertheless anticipated in the essay. Winter, he said (the essay was approaching evening and the snow was again covering the landscape), was the best time "to inspect the summer's work"—winter was the season of reflection and contemplation, when one studied his "dormant buds." Returning to the village and the earlier meaning of inwardness, he said that "in winter we lead a more inward life. Our hearts are warm and cheery, like cottages under drifts . . . but from whose chimneys the smoke cheerfully ascends." This "quiet and serene life," the "boreal leisure" at the chimney side, where Thoreau felt his pulse in the sounds, was the interior life that, in *Walden* too, was symbolized by withdrawing to the hearth.

Thoreau, however, did not let this image of contentment stand for the final meaning of the essay. Contentment could too easily be misconstrued by hearth-bound villagers; heroism, the rewards of which were serenity and contemplation, was the moral he explicitly drew. He preferred the fisherman on the ice who had sacrificed the "sprightliness and vivacity of towns to the dumb sobriety of nature," who moved "deliberately," as a part of nature; and he compared this man-in-nature with the natives early navigators had seen at Nootka Sound and on the northwest coast. Like them (and like Raleigh), "he belongs to the natural family of man, and is planted deeper in nature and has more root than the inhabitants of towns"; and like them, fishing through the ice, he was "a worshipper of the unseen." His symbol of winter, furthermore, was not that of the almanac, "an old man, facing the wind and sleet, and drawing his cloak about him," but rather "a merry woodchopper, and warm-blooded youth, as blithe as summer." This woodchopper, of course, was the winter walker with an ax, another Thoreau; and he was proving that the "good Hebrew Revelation takes no cognizance of this cheerful snow." "We know of no scripture," Thoreau wrote, "which records the pure benignity of the gods on a New England winter night. Their praises have never been sung, only their wrath deprecated." He was sporting, as in the *Week* and *Walden,* with the faith of the fathers. "The best scripture," he added, "records but a meagre faith." Instead of the reserved and austere lives of the saints, he proposed a heroic life that, in its inexpressible joy, would repudiate the cheerlessness of religion. "Let a brave devout man," he concluded, "spend the year in the woods of Maine or Labrador, and see if the Hebrew Scriptures speak adequately to his condition and experience, from the setting in of winter to the breaking up of the ice." There was no need, however, to go so far: "A Winter Walk" showed that the experiment could be tried in the Walden woods.

Chapter V

THE ELYSIAN FIELDS

> No wonder need be then excited in our minds, when we occasionally hear of the young spirit, to whom the costliest education has been afforded, and before whom the whole world invitingly lies as a beautiful unexplored garden, every path free to his foot, turning, after a little experience, his course from the city towards the woods.
>
> —Charles Lane, "Life in the Woods," *The Dial,* 1844

I

The interval at Staten Island, which sharpened in Thoreau's mind the images of a Walden life, did not mitigate the sense of crisis with which he had begun it. Hoping "to make a new experience however mean . . . the basis of his manhood's success," he had failed; he had solved none of his problems. "What am I at present?" he had asked in January, 1843. "A diseased bundle of nerves standing between time and eternity like a withered leaf. A more miserable object one could not well imagine." [1] Later, in October, when the Staten Island experience was drawing to an end, he noted in his *Journal:* "Though I am old enough to have dis-

---

[1] Houghton. MS AM 278.5.

covered that the dreams of youth are not to be realized in this state of existence, yet I think it would be the next greatest happiness always to be allowed to look under the eyelids of time and contemplate the perfect steadily with the clear understanding I do not attain to it." [2] At Staten Island he had entered a dark tunnel; New York had brought him low; failure had even clouded his faith.

And yet, as his writing during this period showed, the present experience was projecting another; there were other ways to try his manhood's success. If he returned to the village from the city a defeated Franklin without the conqueror's gold pieces, he had at least steeled his resolution with defeat and closed off one plan for his life by opening up another. After all, the Staten Island proposal had not been his. He did not believe, with Ellery Channing, who was soon to try New York himself, that he "ought not to see Concord again these ten years," that he "ought to grind up fifty Concords" in his mill.[3] On the contrary, Staten Island drove him deeper to his Concord fundament, to a place where the dreams of youth could be realized. The marrow of his faith had not been touched; he still believed that "there is an ideal or real nature, infinitely more perfect than the natural as there is an ideal life of man"; and he would stake his life on it, for he had no other alternative. "Where nature ceases to be supernatural to a man what will he do then?"—here is faith distilled from despair.[4] "Of what worth is human life if its actions are no longer to have this sublime and unexplored scenery? Who will build a cottage and dwell in it with enthusiasm if not in the elysian fields?" [5]

When Thoreau returned to Concord and the pencil factory, and —judging from the sudden silence of his *Journals*—had passed his least fruitful year, Channing gave a different advice that helps one fill the empty pages. "I see nothing for you in this earth," he wrote, "but that field which I once christened 'Briars'; go out upon that, build yourself a hut, and there begin the grand process of devouring yourself alive. Eat yourself up; you will eat nobody else, nor anything else." [6] As for Emerson, he remained as silent as Tho-

---

[2] HM 13182.

[3] W, VI, 120.

[4] "The heroic actions are performed," he said, "by such as are oppressed by the meanness of their lives" (Houghton. MS AM 278.5).

[5] November 2, 1843. HM 13182.

[6] W, VI, 121. In the manuscript of *Walden* Thoreau answered Channing

reau about his friend's affairs in that empty year. His only comment, however, was a sufficient account of Thoreau's determination to live only in the Elysian fields:

Henry said that the other world was all his art; that his pencils would draw no other; that his jackknife would cut nothing else. He does not use it as a means. Henry is a good substantial Childe, not encumbered with himself. He has no troublesome memory, no wake, but lives *ex tempore*, and brings to-day a new proposition as radical and revolutionary as that of yesterday, but different. The only man of leisure in the town. He is a good Abbot Samson: and carries counsel in his breast. If he cannot show his performance much more manifest than that of the other grand promisers, at least I can see that, with his practical faculty, he has declined the kingdoms of this world. Satan has no bribe for him.[7]

This appraisal, of course, was ambivalent, and should be considered with Emerson's desire for the practical man in mind. He had written Sam Ward (soon to take his place in Emerson's galaxy as the representative man of the world) that "I read Napoleon's memoirs lately & could not help grudging to Europe that grand executive faculty which in this vast empty Eden of ours with so many fine theories & so many white-robed candidates, might consolidate, organize, & put in action, so much."[8] He had been looking to Thoreau to do this work—the engineering he himself had hoped to do—but Thoreau had returned to a sturdier self-reliance. Emerson's doctrines were directed to the end of power, Thoreau's to the end of joy.

This might explain the curious omission from Emerson's *Journals* and letters of any mention of Thoreau's experiment at Walden Pond. Although Emerson had written at this time of "the new man": "His duties are to omit and omit, to show you the back of his hands, to do nothing as you would have him. His prudence is a new prudence, his charity a new kind, his temperance original, his whole wealth of virtues are undescribed varieties"[9]—though he was searching for the new man, he did not recognize him in Thoreau, and though he gave him the use of his Walden acres, he apparently did not approve of his experiment. He did not especially care to see the

with a saying of Pythagoras: "*Cor ne edito*" ("Eat not the heart"). And in his own words he commented, "You must eat something else to be sure" (HM 924). Appropriately, this was originally in "Solitude."

[7] Emerson, J, VI, 515.

[8] Rusk, ed., *The Letters of Ralph Waldo Emerson*, III, 268.

[9] Emerson, J, VII, 180-81.

backs of the hands of his friends; self-reliance was more easily admired from a distance. "Thoreau sometimes appears only as a *gendarme*," he complained in 1847, "good to knock down a cockney with, but without that power to cheer and establish which makes the value of a friend." [10] Instead his sympathies were with Ellery Channing, the "incomparable companion" whom he had helped to send to Europe to complete his "poetic education" [11] at the same time Thoreau was completing his at Walden, and with James Elliot Cabot, a tougher scholar than the late Stearns Wheeler, who had begun to be of intellectual service to him. The chill in the friendship of Emerson and Thoreau was in the core and did not disturb their lifelong intercourse so much as it did the pages of their *Journals;* they rendered each other valuable services, even though each rubbed the other against the grain and never satisfied the deepest claims that each had made on the other. After the Staten Island episode they met, not as Thoreau and Alcott did with the spirit for a boon companion, but rather with the specter of resistance between them. When Thoreau paid his tribute to his friends in *Walden,* measuring them by their conviviality and willingness to seek him at his hut, he gave the palm to Channing and Alcott. Of Emerson he wrote: "There was one other with whom I had 'solid seasons,' long to be remembered, at his house in the village, and who looked in upon me from time to time; but I had no more for society there." [12]

The grounds of this difference were not only temperamental but intellectual. By 1844 Emerson had tempered the unrestricted self-reliance of the revolutionary addresses of the 1830's; his view of nature was also gradually shifting from that of a beneficent monitor to that of an evolutionary force, and his concern with society and "culture" was increasing.[13] The nature he invoked was more pro-

---

[10] Emerson, J, VIII, 303.

[11] Rusk, ed., *The Letters of Ralph Waldo Emerson,* III, 267, 327.

[12] W, II, 297-98. This was his constant objection, that with Emerson he never reached the tableland of friendship where both met in God, i.e., had "society."

[13] There is a social side to Emerson's thought that has been neglected, perhaps because it was not adequately represented in his published work. A part of his success as a lecturer was due to the fact that he spoke of "the times." He was an acute social historian and commentator. In 1844, for example, he gave a course of lectures on New England that did for New England what *English Traits* did for England. See Rusk, ed., *The Letters of Ralph Waldo Emerson,* III, 233.

grammatic and conceptual than actual: he did not need to go to
Walden Pond to find it. This growth in his thought, furthermore,
unraveled a fundamental knot in the transcendental dialectic, that
of nature and society. He had once put nature against society—
there had been personal and intellectually strategic reasons for this
—but now he was seeking a reconciliation closer to that of Alcott,
a position admirably represented by Alcott's friend, Charles Lane,
in his essay on "Life in the Woods." [14]

Whether the "free life in the woods" was "savage, barbarous, and
brutal," and whether the "refined, polished, and elevated . . . housed
life" of civilization was better, were the questions that Lane had
tried to answer. He assumed, of course, as one sees in the way he
set up his propositions, that the natural was better than the civilized
life: this was the assumption of his transcendental contemporaries,
an assumption strengthened by the line of thought from Locke to
Rousseau. Civilization was erected, Lane claimed, not against the
harm of nature, but against "human rapacity." It was not fair,
therefore, to speak of the man of the woods as a "barbarian" or
"savage" in contrast to the "civilian" of the cities; Lane preferred
to call the man in nature the "sylvan" man, and even cited David
Brainerd's lament over the Indians to prove that the savage was
indeed sylvan, a man who, by means of his direct intercourse with
nature, had "the heights of mind, elevation of thought, purity in
sentiment" of the civilian. In fact, the sylvan man took on all the
attributes Thoreau implied when he spoke of "Indian wisdom" in
the "Natural History of Massachusetts," and he filled out the sketch
of the kind of man Emerson had suggested in *Nature:* here was
the transcendental life—one without disease, one of the senses, one
that provided an immediate intercourse with nature and in which
man lived in the "process" and knew sympathetically; an intuitive,
inward life as well that led beyond the "circumferential science"
of mere intellect to the organic unity at the center; a life, finally,
in which man did not need to despoil nature or man to get un-
essentials, but in which nature, the benevolent mother, filled all his
needs. All this was put in the balance in favor of nature. But that
one found this nature in the woods was taken for granted by Lane;
he did not test that assumption at Walden Pond, nor did he go to
Maine to see if the Indian were sylvan.

---

[14] *The Dial,* IV (April, 1844), 415-25. All subsequent quotations are from
this article.

If these were the antitheses, however, who could reject the sylvan life? All the positive values were to be found in the woods; civilization, or rather city life, was merely a negative fact. Civilization, Lane wrote, getting deeper into the dilemma of his logic, "secures no vital *progress* to the soul"; he would only concede that it was "some *improvement* in social arrangements. . . ." Though, with Alcott, he wanted nothing of the woods, his argument led to an invitation to further the soul by looking "in some other, some new direction"; and in the civilized nineteenth century that direction was, as Thoreau wrote in "Walking," to the southwest, to the wild. Given Lane's argument, then, "No wonder need be . . . excited in our minds, when we occasionally hear of the young spirit . . . turning, after a little experience, his course from the city towards the woods." The way and the justification, it seems, were prepared for Thoreau's experiment.

But Lane, like Alcott, with whom he had tried the experiment at Fruitlands, was a philosopher of the hearth, and he had granted too much.[15] Though he had found the sylvan life equally civilized and full of spirit, he did not think that it was the proper goal of the white man. "Such a life," he said, "and the notion of entering on it must be considered merely an interesting dream." Nature had now become the intellectual counter so readily manipulated by his friends; it was the dream, the values they would wrest for their time, but against the actual fact of civilization it was patently visionary. "The experiment of a true wilderness life by a white person"—with this stroke he turned the Indian into a man of straw—"must, however, be very rare. He is not born for it; he is not natured for it. He lacks the essential qualities as well as the physical substance for such a life. . . ." Even though Lane knew "of some individuals, on whom the world might hopefully rely to become eminent even amongst the worthy, betaking themselves from the busy haunts of men to a more select and secluded life"—he was undoubtedly thinking of Thoreau, the only champion of the wild in the Concord Circle—he wondered if they would succeed "in wrestling against their increased natural needs, and their remaining civic wants, diminished as these may be?" Speaking from his own social bias as well as from inexperience, Lane closed off the road to nature he had opened by saying that "on trial, as on due considera-

---

[15] Concerning the "beautiful liberty of the sylvan life," he confessed that "we have on this occasion perhaps too strongly tended. . . ."

tion, it will be found that this is not a very promising course." The actual experiment, he thought, would be too time-consuming: "By the time the hut is built, the rudest furniture constructed, the wood chopped, the fire burning, the bread grown and prepared," he objected, "the whole time will be exhausted, and no interval remain for comfortably clothing the body, for expansion in art, or for recreation by the book or pen." If Emerson could not join gardening and intellectual labor, this wholesale attempt to go to nature was, as Lane concluded, not the mode "by which the simple and pure in heart shall escape the pressures and burdens, which prevent the full and happy development of the soul."

This argument is hardly convincing, but it was nevertheless the kind of argument that Thoreau had to disprove by actually going to the woods; and perhaps with Lane in mind, the close details of his economy to the end of spirit had special significance. For Thoreau was not only addressing his neighbors in Concord in *Walden,* he was addressing the friends who had been skeptical of his experiment.[16] They did not take Lane's first objection, however, so seriously as his second, the disapproval of solitude. For solitude, the "recluse life," the renunciation of society, was the crucial point. Solitude, Lane claimed,

is not a condition in which human beings can be brought into the world, and it is rarely a condition in which they should attempt to remain in it. . . . an association of some kind seems more suitable, as it is evidently more natural. It is natural, not only in the sense of harmony with the human affections, which out of social intimacy must painfully wither, but also it is natural to the interior or spirit life. The highest virtue can be promoted by friendship and fellowship. If even God himself may have a favorite disciple upon whose bosom he can recline; the spiritually minded surely cannot commit a very great error in adopting the aid of co-support, when they are so fortunate as to find it, or still more fortunate to be able to bestow it.

Though Lane had extolled the Indian in defining the sylvan life, he now went on to show that this child of nature did not live "an isolate life," that, on the contrary, "he moves in a circle much more social than modern cities can boast." In fact, the tribe, with its communal property relations, became his model of the "universal family"—that "new and superior phalanx" by which he hoped to

---

[16] In the *Week* Thoreau replied to Lane and Alcott: "Gardening is civil and social, but it wants the vigor and freedom of the forest. . . ." The entire chapter on "Sunday" developed the theme of civilization *vs.* nature (W, I, 55).

marry the sylvan and civilian. The point he continued to emphasize, however, was that of the white man's unfitness for a return to the Indian life—"The pure oxygen which the Creator provided is suitable to the red man, while the white is only happy in steam, or some other self-generated atmosphere." When the white man tried to return to the Indian life, moreover, he did not find the saving tribal society, he found isolation; and therefore he did not solve the problem of the "true life" because he did not reconcile the sylvan and civilian. To live at either of these poles, Lane said, was "human selfishness. . . ."

Emerson, of course, did not approve of phalanxes, whether Fourieristic or Alcottian; but he agreed with his friends that solitude as an end rather than as a means was not the proper course for the transcendentalist. He persisted in thinking of Thoreau as a hermit who had retired from the great occasions of life; and one of the most dramatic episodes of Transcendentalism did not receive his blessing. Perhaps to his mind going to Walden was as ineffectual a protest as Thoreau's refusal to pay his taxes: Emerson's resistance was not civil. He put these resistances together in his Funeral Speech only as examples of Thoreau's "original judgment" and intransigent self-reliance, and though he said of the Walden episode that "this action was quite native and fit for him," he continued to think of it as a "solitude." Walden was not an important event in his account of Thoreau's life, for it represented to the Emerson who had witnessed it Thoreau's abdication from society, the decisive choice for a private life. "Had his genius been only contemplative," Emerson explained, "he had been fitted to his life, but with his energy and practical ability he seemed born for great enterprise and for command; and I so much regret the loss of his rare powers of action, that I cannot help counting it a fault in him that he had no ambition. . . . Pounding beans is good to the end of pounding empires one of these days; but if, at the end of years, it is still only beans!" [17] Other commentators on *Walden* were to make more of the beans, but most agreed with Emerson that solitude was selfish, and many pointed out that Thoreau had cheated in his experiment by borrowing what he needed and by sneaking into town. They did not see that Thoreau's experiment—even though the terms were somewhat modified—tried to further Lane's recon-

---

[17] C, X, 457-58, 480. "Farmers far and near," Thoreau noted, "call it the paradise of beans" (J, I, 423).

ciliation, "to combine the hardiness of . . . savages with the intellectualness of the civilized man." [18] And they misread the magnificent rhapsody on "Solitude"—which Thoreau used to counter Lane's objection—as the primary message, and overlooked the social meanings of the book. With Thoreau's friends, they saw only its most dramatic feature, the symbolic act of withdrawal.[19]

II

"In 1845 he built himself a small framed house on the shores of Walden Pond," Emerson said, "and lived there two years alone, a life of labor and study. . . . As soon as he had exhausted the advantages of that solitude, he abandoned it." [20] It is true, of course, that among the immediate prudential reasons for Thoreau's withdrawal was the need to find an economy that would give him the leisure and privacy to get on with his work as a writer. He had learned at Staten Island that he had made a false start. And he had also learned there the extent of his need for the woods. When he returned to Concord, however, he could not resume the free life of the apprentice at the Emerson household. Staten Island had released him from that arrangement, and the discontinuation of *The Dial* cut the strongest tie he had with Emerson. He came back, therefore, to find only the same pile of debts: so he went to the pencil factory to earn his freedom.[21] The silent year of 1844 was a year of servitude, and Thoreau learned at first hand the economy of desperation. When he spoke of man's slavery to things and of the lifelong drag of property in *Walden*, the struggle of his own family was before him: in 1844 he had himself helped his father build the Texas house. But coming home was not his solution either. He needed Concord but not the gossip of his mother's house; and now, instead of finding a refuge at Emerson's, he needed to free himself from the intellectual gossip and biases of his friends.[22] In 1844 he was trying to make his relations with Concord on his own terms, and the experiment at Walden Pond made this possi-

[18] W, II, 14.

[19] Even Ellery Channing repudiated Thoreau's social ethics (*Thoreau: The Poet-Naturalist,* Boston, 1873, pp. 297ff.).

[20] C, X, 457-58.

[21] In his autobiographical record all Thoreau said of 1844 was "made pencils in 1844" (J, VIII, 66).

[22] See J, I, 364.

ble.[23] If Channing said that it was the result of economic fore-
thought, solving temporarily his vocational necessity, he forgot to
say that his vocational necessities were more than economic.

Going to Walden for Thoreau was comparable to Melville's going
to sea, an economic act, certainly, but more profoundly an attempt
to recast his own life: to measure society, to find himself, and, above
all, to meet the ungraspable phantom of life. A proper motto for
the book might be, "Rather than love, than money, than fame, give
me truth." One feels in the silence of Thoreau's friends the rupture
that such an experiment required; and on Thoreau's part, as well
as Melville's, one recognizes the reflex in the heroic stance. One
would have to relate all of Thoreau's life to show adequately his
reasons for going to the Pond, to explain, for example, his simple
statement, "My purpose in going to Walden Pond was not to live
cheaply nor to live dearly there, but to transact some private
business with the fewest obstacles. . . ." [24] And one would have to
strip the original intentions Thoreau had in going to the Pond
from those that were overlaid in the following years when the
Walden experiment itself began to become a symbol for him. For
he no more expected a *Walden*, a peak in achievement, from his
experiment than Melville expected a *Moby-Dick:* both were folded
many times thick, and that was the work of time.

Several intentions, nevertheless, were the same because, like Melville's going to sea, they had a symbolic value that was so fundamental that they enclosed whatever Thoreau added. "I wish to
meet the facts of life—the vital facts, which are the phenomena or
actuality the gods meant to show us—face to face, and so I came
down here." [25] This was Thoreau's second entry in the *Journal* of
that period, a kind of spontaneous utterance, helping him to settle
his purpose. "Men nowhere live as yet a natural life," he wrote in
1843. "The poets even have not described it. Man's life must be of
equal simplicity and sincerity with nature, and his actions har-
monise with her grandeur and beauty." [26] This natural life, he
believed, would enable him to reflect the aspects of nature, to live
with "the great facts of his existence"—"The life of men . . . will

[23] Alcott, for example, said that he could "have" Thoreau "if I will betake
me to Walden," just as he could have Emerson "at the Road Forks . . ."
(Shepard, ed., *The Journals of Bronson Alcott,* p. 194).

[24] W, II, 21.

[25] J, I, 362.

[26] Houghton. MS AM 278.5.

deserve to have the sun to light it by day and the moon by night, to be ushered in by the freshness and melody of spring, to be entertained by the luxuriance and vigor of summer, and matured and solaced by the hues and dignity of autumn." [27] This natural intercourse was for Thoreau the lasting attraction of farming, and the advantages he once saw in the Hollowell farm he found he could have at less cost at Walden. His economy, of which so much has been made, was only a means; he had indeed to live cheaply, but not so much for the purpose of making ends meet (which was crucial, of course, in explaining his life to his neighbors) as for testing against the bounty of nature the essentials of civilization: within two months he began to write out his reflections on shelter and dress. Actually, the economic facts of his life, which he himself found novel enough to use as lectures in 1847,[28] diminished in importance in his *Journals,* as they did in *Walden.* They were necessarily strategic and introductory, but prudential; and he was more concerned with conveying the joy of spirit that he had achieved by such slight means—using his economy not for prescriptive ends but as an example of the ease with which any man can alter his life. The value of the Walden *Journal* is not in its entries, most of which were later used in *Walden,* but in the sudden perspectives it opens on the original experience there. His economy does not seem so purposeful; rather the fact that seems so glorious and that filled Thoreau with joyous wonder was his liberation from "this grovelling life." He had escaped the thralldom of Admetus, he had left the workshop and suddenly found "a fresher auroral atmosphere"; freed, at last, he was Apollo, with no acrimony in him for his failures, happily surprised that by simple prudence he had broken such heavy chains.[29]

Ellery Channing once suggested to Thoreau that he "might be something, if he would only take a journey through the Everlasting

---

[27] J, I, 367; Houghton. MS AM 278.5. It is at this point, the question of the fewest obstacles, that the two strains Thoreau found in himself were joined: "I find an instinct in me conducting to a mystic spiritual life, and also another to a primitive savage life" (J, I, 384). The primitive brought him face to face with spiritual reality.

[28] Emerson recorded that Thoreau lectured on "his housekeeping at Walden Pond. . . ." As the manuscripts of *Walden* also indicate, this was the content of Thoreau's lectures on the "History of Himself," delivered on February 10 and 24, 1847 (Rusk, ed., *The Letters of Ralph Waldo Emerson,* III, 377).

[29] J, I, 361.

No. . . ." [30] Thoreau, however, had already made the journey into
the abyss; never having found "his own occasion in himself," [31]
having felt the "bloom" of his life fade, he knew the darkness that
even his faith was powerless to relieve. After telling how he had
lived by his imagination, he wrote in the manuscript of *Walden,* "If
the reader thinks that I am vainglorious and set, I assure him that
I could tell a pitiful story respecting myself . . . could encourage
him with a sufficient list of failures. . . ." [32] And in the *Week,* he
wrote that

> . . . since we sailed [in 1839]
> Some things have failed,
> And many a dream
> Gone down the stream.[33]

But he did not intend, any more than Emerson, to communicate his
doubts or grief. *Walden,* he said, was not to be an ode to dejection.
How could it be, when in fact it was the exception to Alcott's comment on "experiments"—"None of us were prepared to actualize
practically the ideal life of which we dreamed." [34] In his first
month at the Pond Thoreau wrote: "What was seen true once, and
sanctioned by the flash of Jove, will always be true, and nothing
can hinder it. I have the warrant that no fair dream I have had
need fail of its fulfillment." His sense of relief and satisfaction in
this renewal of his faith—the Walden period was his most extended
ecstasy—prompted him to write that "sometimes, when I compare
myself with other men, methinks I am favored by the gods. They
seem to whisper joy to me beyond my deserts, and that I do have
a solid warrant and surety at their hands, which my fellows do
not." [35] No longer did he think of "eternities delayed." [36] "In my
father's house are many mansions," he wrote out of the unusual
contentment of this period. "The borders of our plot are set with
flowers, whose seeds were blown from more Elysian fields

---

[30] Cited in F. B. Sanborn, *Henry D. Thoreau* (American Men of Letters),
Boston, 1882, p. 210.

[31] J, I, 377.

[32] HM 924; J, III, 293.

[33] W, I, 16.

[34] Cited by Annie Russell Marble, *Thoreau: His Home, Friends and Books,*
New York, 1902, p. 111.

[35] J, I, 365.

[36] J, I, 407.

adjacent." [37] In going to the woods, he had not eaten himself up nor fallen deeper in the abyss. Instead, he had given himself up to an experiment with God, he had let out his divinity, and, in the fullness of the Everlasting Yea, had been more prodigal with the spirit than with his dollars and cents.[38]

This sense of spiritual release and abandon, this sense of unreserved powers, was the dominant note of this period of his life. Everything that he had dreamed of in *The Service* had come to pass, and he lived in the delightful surprise of its continuation. His economy, and the beanfield especially, which provoked his neighbors' scorn, seemed heroic to him, and he relished it because it came to be that "strict behavior" by means of which

> I could elicit back the brightest star
> That lurks behind a cloud.[39]

He wanted the heroic life that had always been necessary to his sense of worthiness. "What doth he ask?" he wrote in "The Hero,"

> Some worthy task,
> Never to run
> Till that be done,
> That never done
> Under the sun.
> Here to begin
> All things to win
> By his endeavor
> Forever and ever.
> Happy and well
> On this ground to dwell,
> This soil subdue,
> Plant, and renew.[40]

The social demands of heroism were already in his thought—to plant and renew—and before his crop was harvested he wrote: "I will not plant beans another summer, but sincerity, truth, simplicity, faith, trust, innocence, and see if they will not grow in this soil with such manure as I have, and sustain me." He had not, as his friends believed, let solitude betray him; ecstasy had not driven him from men but to them, and, with Whitman, his own self-realization helped him perceive their common divinity. "I would

---

[37] J, I, 374-75.

[38] See J, I, 386.

[39] Bode, ed., *Collected Poems of Henry Thoreau*, p. 139.

[40] J, I, 403.

not forget," he wrote, "that I deal with infinite and divine qualities in my fellows. All men, indeed, are divine in their core of light. . . ." [41] Even his own joy called him back to the world:

> Yet some mighty pain
> He would sustain,
> So to preserve
> His tenderness.
> Not be deceived,
> Of suff'ring bereaved,
> Not lose his life
> By living too well,
> Nor escape strife
> In his lonely cell,
> And so find out heaven
> By not knowing hell.

He did not wish to be "once for all, forever, blest," nor "from his heart to banish all sighs. . . ." For he wanted again the exhilaration of renewal, the advent of a "new fate." A "risen man," he wrote, "never returns to where he began." Thus, he welcomed the lapse that would renew his humanity:

> Some smiting by God,
> Occasion to gain
> To shed human tears
> And to entertain
> Still demonic fears.

And most of all, in wanting to share man's fate he wanted to assure himself that his wonderful ecstasy would not harden into aloofness; not only would he keep the hero's armor bright by use, he would keep his tenderness. For his deepest need, like Whitman's, was

> Forever to love and to love and to love,
> Within him, around him, beneath him, above. [42]

Communion had released the spring in the rock.

And communion also taught him, as it would Whitman, the value of the uncommitted life; his success in achieving it made it the essential advice he had for his neighbors: ". . . I would say to my fellows, once for all, As long as possible live free and uncommitted." [43] He, too, believed that life was a pilgrimage, and proposed the open road as the path for the hero.

---

[41] J, I, 382.

[42] J, I, 403-5.

[43] W, II, 93.

Is there no road
This way, my friend?
Is there no road
Without any end?
Have you not seen
In ancient times
Pilgrims go by here
Toward other climes,
With shining faces
Youthful and strong
Mounting this hill. . . .[44]

In the *Week*, the heroism of the early settlers became a permanent dimension of his thought, a fixed gauge by which he measured the stalwartness of his neighbors and himself. Not only their commitment to worldly uncommittedness but their hardiness appealed to him: they were heroes of his own stamp. By going to Walden to begin from scratch he felt that he was re-enacting the settlement; considered socially, he was testing the Massachusetts soil for its virtue—to see if once again it could sustain a man.[45] Most immediately, however, it satisfied his own hunger for the strenuous life, for the joys of action that his townsmen had forgotten in their quest for ease. "Why not live a hard and emphatic life, not to be avoided, full of adventures and work, learn much in it, travel much, though it be only in these woods?" In the summer of his first year at the Pond, this suggestion startled him into an awareness of the symbolic meaning of his new life. "I sometimes walk across a field with unexpected expansion and long-missed content," he wrote in the most memorable passage of the Walden *Journal*,

as if there were a field worthy of me. The usual daily boundaries of life are dispersed, and I see in what field I stand. When on my way this afternoon, Shall I go down the long hill in the rain to fish in the pond? I ask myself. And I say to myself: Yes, roam far, grasp life and conquer it, learn much and live. Your fetters are knocked off; you are really free. Stay till late in the night, be unwise and daring. See many men far and near, in their fields and cottages before the sun sets, though as if many more were to be seen. And yet each *rencontre* shall be so satisfactory and simple that no other shall seem possible. Do not repose every night as villagers do. The noble life is continuous and unintermitting. At least, live with a longer radius. Men come home at night only from the next field or street, where their household echoes haunt, and

[44] J, I, 406.
[45] Perhaps his interest in colonial history began in this endeavor.

their life pines and is sickly because it breathes its own breath. . . . But come home from far, from ventures and perils, from enterprise and discovery and crusading, with faith and experience and character. Do not rest much. Dismiss prudence, fear, conformity. Remember only what is promised. Make the day light you, and the night hold a candle, though you be falling from heaven to earth[,] "from morn to dewy eve a summer's day." [46]

All of Thoreau's purposes took the hue of this adventure, and when he wrote the *Week* in the years at the Pond, the ecstasy of his youth blended with the ecstasy of the present, and the *Week* itself seemed to him the best way to express his discovery of ecstasy and joy. For in the *Week* he found the "myth" which joined together his ecstasy, his sense of winning it day by day, and his heroism. "My days were not days of the week," he said in *Walden*, fully aware that "this was sheer idleness to my fellow-townsmen. . . ." And yet, he continued, "my life itself was become my amusement and never ceased to be novel." The *Week* was offered as proof, testifying to his faith: "Follow your genius closely enough, and it will not fail to show you a fresh prospect every hour." [47]

One of the important things Thoreau discovered by going back to the great facts of existence was the universality of myth. From the start, his house at the Pond was associated with the auroral atmosphere of "the halls of Olympus"; and he identified himself with the heroic tradition—"I too sit here on the shore of my Ithaca, a fellow-wanderer and survivor of Ulysses." [48] Ulysses, however, was never his "hero," and, unlike most "romantics," he did not appropriate the *Odyssey*. When he spoke of Homer, it was almost always exclusively in terms of the *Iliad*. That book was Greek literature for him—though he translated *Prometheus Bound* and *Seven Against Thebes*, Pindar and Anacreon. Furthermore, the Greece he inhabited in his mind was not that of the city, the great age of Athens and Pericles, but that of the Golden Age, the heroic time of Achilles and Hector and the siege of Troy, and the more pastoral times that led him back to the exploits of mythical heroes and gods. He could read Homer in the woods because in essentials Walden was Greece; and living the history of man anew, he could find

[46] J, I, 385-86.

[47] W, II, 124-25.

[48] J, I, 361, 363. The friends who watched his departure in the *Week* were "the last inhabitants of Ithaca" (Berg Collection).

suddenly revealed to him those archetypal truths of human life that myth contains.

In the summer of 1845 Thoreau began the study of myth that was so important in the composition of the *Week* and *Walden*. Hard at work on the *Week*, his first book, he was troubled by the transcendentalist's usual difficulty—consecutiveness. Perception was not his problem: he had stored enough in his *Journals* to make several books. Speaking of the "inspirations" in his *Journal*, and the winnowing of them into lectures and essays, he wrote that "at last they stand, like the cubes of Pythagoras . . . like statues on their pedestals, but statues rarely take hold of hands. There is only such connection and series as is attainable in the galleries." And knowing the importance of this book in his attempt to win an audience, he added, "And this affects their immediate practical and popular influence." [49] (Society was not out of his mind: he was merely preparing to meet it again more advantageously.) His problem as a writer, then, was to extend the principle of perception to structure: to create fables as well as symbols, or to make the structure itself symbolic. In perception, Emerson said, one discovers "the analogy that marries Matter and Mind"—perception unites sensation and idea, so that "every fact is related on one side to sensation and on the other to morals." [50] This correspondence, however, was also the value of myth. "The ancients probably saw the moral significance of nature in the objects," Emerson wrote, "without afterthought or effort to separate the object and the expression." [51] It was for this reason that Emerson called mythology "the literature of reason" and said that "fable has in it somewhat divine," that is, the permanent, universal truth that placed it among the "scriptures." [52]

Thoreau was probably familiar with the correspondential claims of myth. When he read Alexander Ross's *Mystagogus Poeticus, Or The Muses Interpreter*, a handbook of mythology which also attempted to uncover the universal truth by providing several interpretations of each fable, he did not think the "hidden significance . . . the ethics running parallel to the poetry and history" very remarkable. As a writer, of course, he wanted just this multisignificance: "The fable," he noted, "which is truly and naturally com-

---

[49] J, I, 413.

[50] C, I, 36.

[51] Emerson, J, III, 558.

[52] C, II, 108-9.

posed, so as to please the imagination of a child . . . is to the wise
man an apothegm and admits his wisest interpretation." The fable
was only important because of this "higher, poetical truth." In his
early "Walks" he had already joined the sensation and the idea;
now he was looking for a fable that would do the same for the many
ideas he had for the *Week;* and what struck him in reading Ross
was "the readiness with which they [myths] may be made to express
any truth." "They are the skeletons of still older and more universal
truths than any whose flesh and blood they are for the time made
to wear," he explained. "It is like striving to make the sun and the
wind and the sea signify." [53] In this sense, the elemental similes of
Homer and Ossian were myths, were "fossil poetry," and fulfilled
Thoreau's specification for *"scripture,"* for the written word: "A
word which may be translated into every dialect, and suggests a
truth to every mind. . . ." [54] Emerson had written in *Nature* that
"as we go back in history, language seems more picturesque, until
its infancy, when it is all poetry; or all spiritual facts are represented
by natural symbols." It was for this reason that, in proposing a regeneration of language, he advised the writer to "hold primarily on
nature," to "pierce this rotten diction and fasten words again to
visible things. . . ." [55] The power of language was its universality,
and this was only achieved by using natural symbols: if Whitman
made the leaf signify, and Melville the sea, Thoreau made the sun
and the river; with Whitman and Melville, he found that to secure
this power he had to live with the elements of language, and that
to make the structure of his work equally symbolic he had to find
an action that was also as simple, elemental, and universal. Though
he saw in the myths he was reading many that spoke to his condition—that of Apollo and Admetus, those on the origins of music,
and those that related the invention of the practical arts of life—he
did not, as so many contemporary authors do, use the myth itself
for his structure. Instead, like Whitman and Melville, he created his
own by going back to the original conditions of myth. When he
finally saw that a boating excursion on the Concord and Merrimack
was symbolic, as much so as leaving the house for the open road
or going to sea—when he saw that this simple event could freight

---

[53] J, I, 392-93.

[54] J, I, 370. In HM 13182 Thoreau wrote: "Old poems seem as universal as
the subsoil."

[55] C, I, 29-30.

his thought, he was at last ready to write his book. And he would have this advantage in creating his own myth, in reporting, as Whitman said, "all heroism from an American point of view" [56]— that the reader would not need to turn to his library, but only to his experience, that by enacting the mythic process [57] rather than appropriating a myth, what was native would also be universal. Perhaps the greatest value of the Walden experiment for Thoreau as a writer was this discovery, that Walden was as good as Greece, the Concord River as good as the Scamander, that by reducing his life he was also reducing his thought to essentials. "Carnac! Carnac!" he exclaimed at Walden, "this is Carnac for me. . . ." [58]

III

A Week on the Concord and Merrimack Rivers, the happy product of Thoreau's life at the Pond, was the first version of *Walden,* his first attempt to find a form that would express his life; and, like *Walden,* it tallied the materials of that life. The germinal idea was the same for both—as it was, obviously, the program for all of his writing. In 1841 Thoreau proposed to write a poem called "Concord." "For argument," he wrote, "I should have the River, the Woods, the Ponds, the Hills, the Fields, the Swamps and Meadows, the Streets and Buildings, and the Villagers. Then Morning, Noon, and Evening, Spring, Summer, Autumn, and Winter, Night, Indian Summer, and the Mountains in the Horizon." [59] As time and experience made them meaningful, he took what he needed from this catalog of symbols; and he began with the river because, even more than the pond, it was deeper in his thought. Both, of course, helped him dramatize the growth of the self, and he identified both with his destiny. The river, however, was associated with his nativity, the pond at first with a visit to Concord in his childhood. Of the river he wrote:

I was born upon thy bank, river,
My blood flows in thy stream,

---

[56] Section 6, "Starting From Paumanok," *Leaves of Grass.*

[57] At this time Thoreau was especially interested in Ovid's retelling of the myths of creation. See Ethel Seybold, *Thoreau: The Quest and The Classics,* New Haven, 1951, Chap. III.

[58] J, I, 376.

[59] J, I, 282.

> And thou meanderest forever
> At the bottom of my dream.[60]

And the river was also associated with actual youthful joys, with John, and considering this friendship, with an excursion more memorable than Walden: the river had none of the associations of solitude and retirement of the pond; it was not the scene of trial or experiment; it was not private; nothing depended on it—instead, it was the scene of adventure and friendship, of the irrecoverable abandon of youth. The river was holiday, an escape like Huck Finn's from town and school, never the stern destiny of the ensuing years.

Fortunately, the Walden years, by providing another though more mature communion, helped Thoreau materialize this earlier experience. His present joy was the perspective from which he recollected the earlier experience, and this helped him keep its hue as well as transform it in keeping with his more profound sense of heroic enterprise. For like all his major writing, the *Week* was a work ripened by recollection. He did not understand how important recollection was in his own creative process at the time he was composing the *Week;* why, for example, with a desire to write, he could make nothing of the original excursion in 1840. Later on, however, he recognized that *time* distances as well as the haze and prospects with which he was familiar: "How is it," he wrote, "that what is actually present and transpiring is commonly perceived by the common sense and understanding only, is bare and bald, without halo or the blue enamel of intervening air? But let it be past or to come, and it is at once idealized. . . . so the fact remembered is idealized. It is a deed ripe and with the bloom on it. It is not simply the understanding now, but the imagination that takes cognizance of it. The imagination requires a long range. It is the faculty of the poet to see present things as if, in this sense, also past and future, as if distant or universally significant." [61] It was a characteristic of his life that he idealized—or symbolized—his own spiritual goals by projecting them into the future; this was as much

---

[60] J, I, 438. See also his early poem, "I Love A Careless Streamlet," Bode, ed., *Collected Poems of Henry Thoreau*, p. 87. Theodore Brown, reminiscing on Thoreau, spoke of "the river that runs all through his life" (A. and W. Ricketson, eds., *Daniel Ricketson and His Friends*, p. 214). The river, not the pond, was mentioned in his review of Howitt.

[61] J, XIII, 17. One use of history was to provide this distance.

his strategy as Whitman's.[62] But it was a characteristic of his life as a writer, as it was of Melville's, that he idealized his occasions by letting them become memories. At Walden Pond, therefore, he could not have written *Walden:* his experience was too close to him, too bare and bald, usable, perhaps, for his lectures on economy or a still later lecture on self-reform, but as yet, in the largest sense, not idealized, not symbolized. This is not to say that the Walden experiment was fallow: it refracted the earlier experience and those of the intervening seven years. Though he did not know it then, the Walden period was the richest fulfillment of his life. In fact, it gave us two books—the *Week*, which preserved the actual ecstasy of that time, and *Walden*, which, in his years of decay, was written to summon it again.

When he went to Walden Thoreau was reaching his maturity— he was twenty-eight years old. In 1839, the year the *Week* looks back to, he was only two years out of college, at home in nature but without much transcendental familiarity with her, and without the pressing need to make nature a part of his life. But after many crises, the years that followed had led to liberation; he was now free, as he said in "Economy," "to adventure on life now, his vacation from humbler toil having commenced." [63] And that sense of release became the tenor of the *Week*. Having found a full communion with nature, his golden age was at hand, his sensitivity was exquisite and rewarding, and those shadows of decay he had already known were, in the imagery of *The Service*, dissipated by strong light. Everywhere was the effulgence of light and sound that filled him with ecstatic inspiration. Time had indeed become timeless, like the river, and his life in nature, "outside to time, perennial, young, divine, and in the wind and rain which never die." [64] If he was aware, as he must have been, of the cost he had paid for his Elysium, he did not tabulate it in the *Week*. What, after all, was economy? Having earned his soul's leisure he could forget it, at most symbolize the discipline, the action necessary to contemplation, in the pleasures of boating. His sense of serenity was better expressed by the placid river than the building of a hut; only later, in the years after Walden, those years of deepening despair, did he need to show *how* he had earned it. For *Walden* commemorated

---

[62] The West was his most amorphous symbol of this.

[63] W, II, 17.

[64] W, I, 7.

his later search for the regenerative forces of nature. Now, however, he had his soul's necessities; he lived in a communion with
nature that was as close as the boat and the river, a communion as
easy as the launching of his boat on its waters—and as yielding.
He felt the oneness of nature, not its otherness—he was not wresting
his life from nature, but living in it. Writing of Carlyle's works
during these years, he found omitted what he himself wanted to
express, "the Easter vacations, when all men submit to float on the
full currents of life." [65] Vocation for Thoreau had become vacation
—that leisure, as George Ripley said, "to live in all the faculties of
the soul." [66]

Faithful to the 1839 excursion and the Walden years, Thoreau's
first book was the record of an outing of the spirit, a soul's voyage
gaily taken on the tides of youthful hope. ". . . Life went a-maying/
with Nature, Hope, and Poesy,/When I was young!" Coleridge recalled in "Youth and Age"; "We Poets in our youth begin in gladness," Wordsworth wrote in "Resolution and Independence," "As
if life's business were a summer mood." And this, too, was the
experience to which Thoreau was faithful in writing the *Week*.
Childlike and pure, nature for Thoreau was still "one and continuous everywhere"; [67] time had not yet raised the noble doubt, and
without suspicion he could contemplate the twigs and leaves of
the stream which mirrored his life. His life was "constantly as fresh
as this river," every instant "a new water" flooding his channel.[68]
As he wrote in his poem on "Manhood," he was on departure, "a
long-lived child/As yet uninjured by all worldly taint/ . . . whose
whole life is play." On his return, however, and the intimations
came as fast as the last day's voyaging, he was the "mature soul of
lesser innocence," for whom the leisure, once taken as the free gift
of nature, had become a commodity in his spiritual economy and,
therefore, of his vocational striving. Then, he would prefer the
brave man "who from the sad experience of his fate" had won "the
ripe bloom of a self-wrought content" [69]—here was the hero of
Walden. Confronting this fact as well as his joy at Walden, Tho-

---

[65] W, IV, 347.

[66] O. B. Frothingham, *George Ripley* (American Men of Letters), Boston,
1882, p. 125.

[67] W, I, 372.

[68] W, I, 137.

[69] Bode, ed., *Collected Poems of Henry Thoreau*, p. 225.

reau wrote that "we can conceive of nothing more fair than something we have experienced." Thus, he said, "We linger in manhood to tell the dreams of our childhood. . . ." [70]

The joyousness of the *Week* was the result of Thoreau's earlier purity and present healthy wholeness. Every day had brought its ecstasy; every morning—the *Week* is composed of mornings and the day's promise, and of the rewards of "silence"—was as pristine and dreamlike as the Sunday awakening he described at such devoted length. It was the first dawn of his voyage, ushering in a day without blemish, a Sunday morning, he said, "summing up their week. . . ." [71] The day was perfectly calm and transparent, fulfilling the needs of inspiration. Nature supplied the perfect mirror for his untarnished soul—a "natural Sabbath," he wrote, all intensely still, the air "elastic and crystalline," the landscape seen through it, ideally remote and perfect, and the water and air so undisturbed that "the flight of a kingfisher or robin over the river was as distinctly seen reflected in the water below as in the air above." Every "twig and blade of grass," he wrote, "was so faithfully reflected; too faithfully indeed for art to imitate. . . ." [72] Reflection, of course, was nature playing at the game of correspondence, but for Thoreau it was also the symbol of his own confident subjective idealism, of the ease with which, in those days, everything radiated meaning. "I have found all things thus far," he said, "persons and inanimate matter, elements and seasons, strangely adapted to my resources." [73] The days of the *Week* were days like this, days in which the morning lingers into twilight, and the splendor hardly fades before another dawn. "My days were not days of the week," Thoreau said in *Walden*, having explained the philosophy of the morning that underlay both books. " 'Renew thyself completely each day,' " was the Oriental wisdom he followed there, " 'do it again, and again, and forever again.' " [74] But in the *Week* he followed Gower—

[70] W, I, 406.

[71] W, I, 48.

[72] W, I, 44-45, 47.

[73] W, I, 312. This was appropriately followed by "The Inward Morning." How far he went in putting consciousness before fact can be seen in his remark: "It seemed a strange phenomenon to us that the two rivers should mingle their waters so readily, since we had never associated them in our thoughts" (W, I, 81).

[74] W, II, 98, 124.

> I thynke for to touche also
> The worlde whiche neweth everie daie,
> So as I can, so as I maie.[75]

For the *Week* was truer to Gower's invitation than to the injunction to purity in *Walden*. Nowhere in Thoreau was there so much light, so much day, all so readily accepted, as if inspiration were a natural and a permanent state; nowhere such "fertile idleness." [76]

In the *Week* Thoreau wrote out his faith in nature: in the possibility of sympathetic correspondence. He was certain that nature would sustain him as easily as the stream. For nature was the stream, that grand circulation he saw in every thing, flowing in "rivers of sap," in "rivers of stars, and milky ways," in "rivers of rock" and "rivers of ore"—flowing as well in his thought.[77] Like Emerson on the bare common with the circulations of being flowing through him, Thoreau—as the metaphor of the book revealed —had launched himself on the flux and become one with it. He did this with *élan*, like a schoolboy shoving off the Concord shore to adventure in the elements. Compared with the earnestness of the beginning of *Walden*, the *Week* is easy, high-spirited, unedged. In it the satire and argument Thoreau was already employing were not barbed. And compared with the misanthropy and suspicion of Ishmael in the beginning of *Moby-Dick*, here was a young man, as much in search of truth, who had a hope of life, not a premonition of death, who felt that nature would not betray him. The ambience of this assurance always remained; and this assurance, more than anything, distinguished him from Melville. For all of his strictures on society, for all of his individualism, Thoreau never seems an outcast or isolato because, unlike Melville, he never felt he was. And if, later on, he had to earn that assurance, he never lost the sense of invitation in nature to which he responded in the *Week:* "Come, come, my lovely fair, and let us try/Those rural delicacies." [78]

Unfortunately the *Week* has been forgotten in the praise of

---

[75] W, I, 121.

[76] J, I, 136. Here he first began to recollect the excursion. Edwin Morton preferred the *Week* to *Walden*. The latter was "that somewhat Dantean wood, after this pleasant river excursion" ("Thoreau and His Books," *Harvard Magazine*, [Jan., 1855], reprinted in Jones, ed., *Pertaining to Thoreau*, p. 69).

[77] W, I, 353. See also C, I, 44.

[78] Francis Quarles, "Christ's Invitation to the Soul," which Thoreau used as the epigraph for the first day (W, I, 12).

Walden. It is said to be an inferior work, a hodgepodge of old poems and translations, of essays in history, criticism, and ethics; and its joyfulness has been overlooked in preference to the desperate economies which have long been identified with the stereotype of Thoreau. But *Walden* was only a half of Thoreau's experiment on life. Without the *Week* we would scarcely know the first chapters of what amounts to his *Prelude;* and we would underestimate the hard-won, the conscious and resolute, affirmations of *Walden.* Indeed, *Walden* was the book it was, because the *Week* anticipated it: not only in ecstasy, but in theme and organization. For its central theme, like that of *Walden,* was the problem of inspiration, the organic life and the quest for being; and its special plea was made, if not so insistently as later, in behalf of this spiritual vocation. Its expression and organization, which have been most severely criticized, were also as natural and organic. If one sees the *Week* and *Walden* as a continuing narrative of Thoreau's life—as companion books covering nearly fifteen years of transcendental experience— then the framework of days which ostensibly gives unity to the *Week* is more than a convenience. The day, the dawn, the morning —these had been from the beginning of his *Journal* the symbols of Thoreau's ecstasy; and he used the day to organize the *Week* because it was the natural unit of his inspiration. The day, moreover, was as essential to Thoreau's experience of the availability of influx in his periods of health as the seasons were in *Walden* to his transcendence of decay. "The prospect of the young is forward and unbounded," he wrote, "mingling the future with the present. In the declining day the thoughts make haste to rest in darkness, and hardly look forward to the ensuing morning. . . . The same hopes and prospects are not for him who stands upon the rosy mountaintops of life, and him who expects the setting of his earthly day." [79] In the *Week* his prospect was forward and unbounded; he knew the mountaintop. But in *Walden* his daily renewal had lengthened into a trial of discipline, endurance, and hope, like that of outlasting winter for spring. *Walden* moved with the seasons because Thoreau had necessarily to harness his hope to a slower cycle. And its tremendous assurance came from his success in finding in that slower cycle "something even in the lapse of time by which time recovers itself." [80]

[79] W, I, 138.

[80] W, I, 374.

In the *Week*, however, while time was lapsing to the ocean, its eternal reservoir, it was also recovering itself in the day. Daily the sun gathered the mists to the mountain, renewed and purified the stream of time at its source; these were the waters the "gods distill." [81] For Thoreau, who spent six days ascending the Concord and Merrimack and one day in descent, this river of time was a permanent element of his adventure, flowing ahead and behind, into the future and into the past, measured, as the eternally timeless always is, by the transient progress of each day, by the inspiration of the present moment. The river and the day—these symbols of time and of Thoreau's consciousness of time—provided him with a conceit for the *Week*. The spiritual milieu of the *Week* was time and the river, and Thoreau made certain that these dimensions of his experience were recognized. The Concord River, he wrote at the beginning, was "as old as the Nile or Euphrates"; it was the river universal and time timeless, as motionless, gentle, and "scarcely perceptible" as his native stream. [82] As the eternal, the river was the background against which history was enacted, and, as we shall see, a dimension by which it was judged. For once launched on it, history lived in the everlasting present of Thoreau's consciousness. For him the Concord was the Xanthus and Scamander, the Mississippi, Ganges, and Nile—the inlet to the "ancient reservoir" and the "constant lure" to the "voyageur" whose real object in following the river road into the interior of continents was the discovery of its source. [83] To ascend the river to its fount was to get to the beginning or youth of time, to the summit where water was mist and mingled with light, and all was a golden age. Thoreau was retraveling time to his springtime, and it was against the sense of this achievement that the descent was so rapid, that suddenly his golden age had turned to autumn.

The river was not only this stream of consciousness, the continuity of experience, it was for Thoreau what the sea was for Melville: the only place for exploration left to the spiritual pioneer. Although in a different key, the first chapter of the *Week* recalls Melville's

---

[81] W, I, 85-86. This imagery was used as early as 1837 in "I Love A Careless Streamlet." Of course it was conventional, having been used by Bryant in his poems and Cole in his paintings. The waters distilled by God also anticipate Walden Pond, which also renewed itself and which Thoreau called " 'God's Drop.' "

[82] W, I, 3, 7. See also p. 380.

[83] W, I, 10-11.

musings on the sea in *Moby-Dick:* both river and sea were the
brink of the unknown, and, as Thoreau pointed out, they provided
an equal experience.[84] Size did not matter: there was just as much
wetness, danger, shipwreck, new men and things; both represented
the possibilities of novelty and action, and of heroism. And both
represented the world of mind—"as every one knows," Melville
said, "meditation and water are wedded for ever." [85] The "mystical
vibration" on going to sea that Melville spoke of was that something
irresistible in water for Thoreau, that something so spiritually akin
to him that he felt himself called to it "by a natural impulse" and
beckoned to "accompany [its] currents. . . ." [86] Certainly, for Melville and Thoreau, the constant lure was the quest for a reality that
had been encrusted by time and landed conventions, a reality to be
regained by experience outside of time—that is, by immersion in
its flux. Looking at objects through the haze over the water, Thoreau said that he saw them "in their eternal relations," that "the
superficial and apparent" were no longer of any importance. Listening to the waves breaking on the shore, he felt that he was "absolved
from all obligations to the past. . . ." Launched on his adventure,
beyond the "firm lands of Concord," time had indeed become the
stream he went a-fishing in.[87]

The river had become the way of communion with the eternal.
As Emerson wrote much later in "Two Rivers,"

. . . sweeter rivers pulsing flit
Through thee, as thou through Concord Plain.

Thou in thy banks are pent:
The stream I love unbounded goes
Through flood and sea and firmament;
Through light, through life, it forward flows.

. . . .
Through years, through men, through nature fleet,
Through love and thought, through power and dream.[88]

---

[84] He spoke of the river, with its headlands, capes, and ports, as one would
the sea, and united both in "voyageur," which punned on "voyager," but
which also identified his voyage with that of the early French explorers of
rivers (W, I, 13-19).

[85] "Loomings," *Moby-Dick.*

[86] W, I, 11.

[87] W, I, 383, 14.

[88] C, IX, 248.

For Thoreau, too, who made the literal river yield this adventure in the spirit, the Concord and Merrimack were all rivers and the life on their shores all life. Along their banks "dwelt the subject of Hebrew scriptures, and the Espirit des Lois. . . ." "All that is told of mankind," he said, "of the inhabitants of the Upper Nile, and the Sunderbunds, and Timbuctoo, and the Orinoko, was experienced here." To excursion in time was to excursion in history; and the idea which illuminated Thoreau's method was the result of his awareness of the fact that "as men lived in Thebes, so do they live in Dunstable to-day." [89] What he fished for, then, was the universal and timeless. Just as Melville had freed himself and gained a perspective, so Thoreau gained in the detachment of river life a perspective from which experience could be universalized. "We discover infinite change in particulars only," he remarked, "not in generals." [90] The particular river, the particular events, were only the heavier element used "to float the lighter." He built his book as he built his boat, the one the vehicle of his thought, the other of his experience. "If rightly made . . . [it would be] a creature of two elements"—of water and air, fact and spirit; and like man, for whom life was both river and being, his experience could only be fully described in "reference to the two elements in which [he] was to spend [his] existence." [91]

The river, then, like the ocean for Melville, was merely the literal medium of a spiritual adventure. "I had often stood on the banks of the Concord," Thoreau recalled, "watching the lapse of the current, an emblem of progress, following the same law with the system, with time, with all that is made. . . ." Everything that floated past on this gentle current seemed to him to be fulfilling its fate; and because he saw in these objects something analogous to himself, something of "singular interest to me," he "resolved to launch myself on its bosom, and float whither it would bear me." [92] In Melville's vocabulary, Thoreau was now a loose-fish, an abandoned soul, ready to be caught on the sharp hook of reality. But for Thoreau, the bosom on which he floated *was* reality, and he launched his soul with faith in its beneficence. "Surely the fates

[89] W, I, 127-28. Thebes, of course, shows Thoreau's concern with Greece, and the Orinoco with Raleigh. The Xanthus, in the earlier quotation, was Zeus's river (God-derived).

[90] W, I, 128.

[91] W, I, 12-13.

[92] W, I, 11.

are forever kind," he wrote, "though Nature's laws are more immutable than any despot's, yet to man's daily life they rarely seem rigid, but permit him to relax with license in summer weather." [93] His experience supported this belief, and during the summer of the *Week* he never doubted that

> . . . thro' the ages one increasing purpose runs,
> And the thoughts of men are widen'd with the process of the Suns.[94]

The river and the sea, however, were not to be equated as symbols of this assurance, as Thoreau himself learned later at Cape Cod. At sea, only the intervals of calm were transcendental, and he was never able to make the sea, as he was the river, the symbol of his profoundest needs and experiences. Recovering the ground of the 1839 excursion on his carriage trip to the White Mountains in 1858, he recaptured both the joy and the symbolic values which, in the *Week,* the river had for him.

What a relief and expansion of my thoughts when I came out from that inland position . . . to this broad river's shore! This vista was incredible there. Suddenly I see a broad reach of blue beneath, with its curves and headlands, liberating me from the more terrene earth. What a difference it makes whether I spend my four hours' nooning between the hills by yonder roadside, or on the brink of this fair river, within a quarter of a mile of that! Here the earth is fluid to my thought, the sky is reflected from beneath, and around yonder cape is the highway to other continents. This current allies me to all the world. There my thoughts were confined and trivial. . . . Here they are expanded and elevated, and I am charmed by the beautiful river-reach. It is equal to a different season and country and creates a different mood. As you travel northward from Concord, probably the reaches of the Merrimack River . . . will be the first inspiring sight. There is something in the scenery of a broad river equivalent to culture and civilization. Its channel conducts our thoughts as well as bodies to classic and famous ports, and allies us to all that is fair and great. . . . It is just wide enough to interrupt the land and lead my eye and thoughts down its channel to the sea. A river is superior to a lake in its liberating influence.[95]

If the river was the way, the process of the suns—the days—was the length of time and kind of time Thoreau needed to reach his goal. Without the pulse and duration of the days one would not

---

[93] W, I, 34.

[94] W, I, 129. See also W, I, 19.

[95] J, XI, 4. Like his experience on Ktaadn, his experience with the ocean gave him a terrifying sense of otherness, of a primordial nature apart from the interests of man, and not easily conquered by thought.

appreciate the eternal, for the days are the pulse of the eternal. Instead of writing from within the eternal, as Emerson usually did, Thoreau made the reader spend himself with him on his pilgrim's progress.[96] He knew with Emerson that the hodiernal cycle of day and night was the cycle of inspiration, that the day was the advent of the eternal, its splendor the moment of eternity we knew, and its fading the lapse into darkness, the mother of time. Each day, therefore, like the transcendental dialectic of thought, was to bring its wider prospects, those new and unsuspected reaches in the river that suddenly seemed to Thoreau to be oceans and inland lakes. The movement of the actual narrative of the excursion was linear, but the actual was broken by transcendental surprises. Each day, like the advancing Emersonian circle, was a renewal of eternal concerns; so, too, each chapter, which advanced the basic themes of the book. For the *Week* was not only an excursion in deed but in thought, and in it Thoreau created one of the finest examples of "transcendental" form. Where *Walden* supplied a form for the growth of consciousness, the *Week* supplied a form for thought itself—and that is why it was Thoreau's most contemplative book.

It is true, of course, as Professor Canby has said, that the *Week* is "perilously like a library of the shorter works of Henry Thoreau." [97] Indeed, almost everything he had previously written was used in it again. And it is true, as Emerson explained to Evert Duyckinck, that "the narrative of the little voyage, though faithful, is a very slender thread for such big beads & ingots as are strung on it." [98] This has been the critical consensus, and criticism of the *Week*, finding it sufficient, has stopped here: the *Week* is an "anthology carried upon a frame of story"; [99] it is not an organic expression. Even Mr. William Drake, who recognized that the *Week* is "an exploratory journey into thought," has said that "one feels too strongly the simple alternation between one level and the other," that Thoreau's difficulty "lay in making the poetry and

---

[96] There are perhaps suggestive parallels with Bunyan's *Pilgrim's Progress,* which Thoreau thought "the best sermon which has been preached" from the New Testament (W, I, 72).

[97] *Thoreau,* p. 272. George Whicher called it a "Transcendental Miscellany" (*Walden Revisited,* Chicago, 1945, p. 33); and it might be called, as F. O. Matthiessen called *Mardi,* "A Source-Book for Plenitude."

[98] Rusk, ed., *The Letters of Ralph Waldo Emerson,* III, 384.

[99] Canby, *Thoreau,* p. 272.

speculation about friendship, favorite authors, Christianity, and the art of writing, develop naturally out of the context of the experience on its naturalistic level." [100] All this perhaps is just. And yet there is a unity—the same kind of unity one finds in "Song of Myself" and even in *Walden*. As Mr. Drake pointed out, "It is not only the narrative that holds *Walden* together, but also the singleness of the problem explored, the definiteness of aim. . . ." [101] If one accepts Thoreau's structural metaphor—

> Hei sayled by thought and pleasaunce
> Without labor east and west,
> Alle was one, calme and tempest [102]

—if one accepts the day and its manifold associations, then there is a unity of theme, and the "miscellaneous" speculations one finds on this level are all concerned with the problem of inspiration. If the theme of *Walden* was how to become spiritually awake, the theme of the *Week* was wakefulness itself and what to do with it. One cannot agree with Lowell (who properly cited Izaak Walton's "rivers . . . were made for wise men to contemplate and fools to pass by without consideration") that "the great charm of Mr. Thoreau's book seems to be, that its being a book at all is a happy fortuity." [103] In spite of his preference for the *Week* rather than *Walden*, Edwin Morton was nearer Thoreau's actual achievement: "The author . . . divided his book according to the days of the week, discussing topics somewhat appropriate to each day, as well as the scenes through which they were passing. This he has very successfully done; and in this light his book is an artistic and beautiful performance,—more so, I think, than 'Walden.' " [104]

[100] *A Formal Study of H. D. Thoreau*, Master's thesis, University of Iowa, 1948, pp. 18, 21, 25. This study, though brief and introductory and perhaps not well enough grounded in transcendental epistemology, is a valuable contribution. It is the first to consider Thoreau-the-artist in terms of the development of his metaphors, symbols, imagery, and dramatic situations.

[101] Drake, *A Formal Study*, p. 29.

[102] W, I, 338. "I who sail now in a boat, have I not sailed in a thought? *Vide* Chaucer" (J, I, 442). He omitted the following from the final version because he made it the metaphor of the book: "As if we had launched our bark in the sluggish current of our thoughts, and were bound nowhither" (J, I, 136).

[103] *Massachusestts Quarterly Review*, III (Dec., 1849), 46.

[104] Jones, ed., *Pertaining to Thoreau*, p. 58. Favorable criticisms of other aspects of the *Week* can be found in Rusk, ed., *The Letters of Ralph Waldo Emerson*, III, 377, 384, and in Shepard, ed., *The Journals of Bronson Alcott*, pp. 213-15.

As his own essays on writing in the *Week* explain, Thoreau was trying to write a deliberate book, a scripture, a myth. He wanted not only an out-of-doors book—a book of inspiration and "superfluity of life"—but one that to be read required the very leisure that he was extolling in the *Week*. He despised the "fluent" writing of his day, and preferred books that did not rush on, that afforded digressions, that lingered over details—and his river ran that way.[105] Homer, for whom all is present and worthy of interest, might have been a model; or perhaps the oldest scriptures, for, as he said of the *Veeshnoo Sarma*, "The story is as slender as a thread on which pearls are strung. . . . It seems as if the old philosopher could not talk without moving, and each motion were made the apology or occasion for a sentence, but, this being found inconvenient, the fictitious progress of the tale was invented." [106] Thoreau did not invent a tale (though he took liberties with the actual excursion) because he believed that the basis of all writing should be "life," the experience of the writer.[107] But he did set up as a philosopher, and wrote the kind of contemplative book he thought a philosopher should write. He liked in Francis Quarles, whom he discovered in 1843, the "quintessence of meditation," "his Morning Muse"; [108] and when he found, in his studies of metaphysical poetry, a suggestion for his book in Sylvester's translation of Du Bartas' *Divine Weeks*, he took with it the spirit of meditation. As has been frequently noticed in other respects, the *Week* is a seventeenth-century book.[109]

And yet, because he worked from experience and wanted to show how ideas were rooted in places and actions, he maintained an excellent balance between thought and occasion, making each occasion yield *its* thought, each place, what Henry James might have called its value. In fact, to this end he was artful, preparing every context and transition, and placing his longest contemplations in the "nooning" periods of the day. Nothing was fortuitous, and

[105] W, I, 102-6, 153.

[106] J, I, 346; W, I, 153.

[107] This was why he thought *Sartor Resartus* Carlyle's best book. The *Week*, incidentally, was compared to this book.

[108] W, VI, 112.

[109] It has been suggested by Lawrence Sidney Willson (*The Influence of Early North American History and Legend on the Writings of Henry David Thoreau*, Doctoral dissertation, Yale University, 1944, p. 204) that the form of the *Week* is that of old chronicles, like those of Hakluyt and Purchas.

what seems so remarkable is that so slender a thread could carry so much without breaking, that he found one in his experience that could do all he wanted. Compared with Goethe's *Italiänische Reise*, which Thoreau said "jogs along at a snail's pace, but always mindful that the earth is beneath and the heavens are above," [110] it was equally the record of how much a remarkable man can see. Compared with *Mardi*, which appeared in the same year, it was better organized because it was better conceived—because Thoreau had learned the lesson of symbolism that Melville apparently found instructive when he read the *Week*.[111] And compared with Margaret Fuller's *Summer on the Lakes*, which was published in 1844, in time to suggest an approach, it was not only better description and thought, but genuinely organic: its seams were tight.

Those who expected a book of descriptive narrative misunderstood Thoreau's avowed intention of traveling in thought. How, otherwise, one might ask, could Thoreau have expressed his ecstasy, which was not an empty rapture but a perception and contemplation of ideas? Lowell, in a review of Henry James, said that the ancient traveler "saw with his bodily eyes, and reported . . . the outside and appearance of things. . . . The modern traveller . . . travels in himself, and records . . . the scenery of his own mind. . . ." [112] Thoreau, however, was noteworthy in doing both. When he wrote to Emerson about his lecture on Ktaadn in 1848, he said that it contained "many facts and some poetry." [113] Always trying to find the balance of outer and inner, he admired the exact description of the early travelers and discoverers, and, unlike the sentimental travel writers of the time, made the one the adequate condition of the other. Not only was he trying to present the landscape so exactly that subsequent travelers would find him true, but he was trying to re-create the process of thought; he was, by means of the voyage, trying to give it heroic and epic proportions.[114]

[110] W, I, 347.

[111] Melville borrowed the *Week* from Evert Duyckinck in 1850. See Merton M. Sealts, "Melville's Reading," *Harvard Library Bulletin*, IV (Winter, 1950), 100.

[112] *Function of the Poet*, ed. by A. Mordell, Boston and New York, 1920, p. 112.

[113] W, VI, 150.

[114] With his details of colonial history, Thoreau was also trying to give the American landscape poetic associations. He fulfilled Samuel Knapp's desires: "The waters of those American rivers are as pure and sweet, and their names

He recognized this problem as he composed the book at Walden, and he measured his aims as a writer against the genius of the age. Of Emerson he said that the "divine in man has had no more easy, methodically distinct expression." But he noted that "Emerson does not consider things in respect to their essential utility. . . . His probes pass one side of their centre of gravity." [115] What he meant he explained when he said that Emerson's essays were not poetry,[116] when, in the *Week*, he admonished his "rare Contemporary" to "let epic trade winds blow, and cease this waltz of inspirations." [117] With Margaret Fuller, who complained that Emerson "did not lie along the ground long enough to hear the secret whispers of our parent life," Thoreau wanted not only the oracular light but the facts that contained "the juices of life." [118] "What though we lose a thousand wise responses of the oracle," he asked, "if we may have instead some natural acres of Ionian earth?" [119] As he said in a different context of Carlyle's *French Revolution*, "We want not only a background to the picture, but a ground under the feet also." [120]

In Carlyle, however, he found more sturdiness and the kind of heroism that was absent in Emerson; indeed, here was the writer to whom he felt more akin.[121] Because of this he wrote a discerning essay of appreciation, "Thomas Carlyle and His Works." It was written during the Walden period, given as a lecture in 1846, and published in 1847. Though Thoreau was fully aware of what "the young of this generation" owed "his manly, brotherly speech," aware that his was "the richest prose style we know of" and that the transcendental philosophy needed the leaven of his humor "to render it light and digestible," he added some disclaimers that, true as they were of Carlyle, defined better his own literary intentions.[122]

would be as poetical, were they as familiar to us in song, as the others, which have been immortalized for ages" (*Lectures on American Literature*, New York, 1829, p. 189).

[115] J, I, 432-33.

[116] HM 13182. Poetry, scripture, and myth were synonymous.

[117] W, I, 104.

[118] Wade, ed., *The Writings of Margaret Fuller*, pp. 393, 68.

[119] W, I, 104.

[120] W, IV, 343. See also Alcott on Emerson and Thoreau, Shepard, ed., *The Journals of Bronson Alcott*, pp. 253-54.

[121] See William Ellery Channing, *Thoreau: The Poet-Naturalist*, revised edition, Boston, 1902, p. 50.

[122] All quotations are from W, IV, 316-55.

Carlyle, he believed, was not a poet, and because he was not a poet, the heroes he described as projections of himself were not what America needed. In this essay Thoreau was writing out his program for the American writer, a disguised preface to his own work, worthy of comparison with Melville's essay on Hawthorne's *Mosses* and Whitman's 1855 Preface to *Leaves of Grass.*

Though Carlyle represented the reformer and drew innumerable sketches of the hero as a man of action, Thoreau said that he was "not a Reformer in our sense of the term"—to what extent his vocation was consonant with his life disturbed the New England economist at Walden who believed that "philosophy practised is the goal of learning. . . ." Carlyle's writing, however, was perfectly suited to the practical issues of English life; for "the condition of England," Thoreau wrote, pushing his distinction, "demands a hero, not a poet." But if England needed heroes and the "Titanic" voice—as Emerson also recognized in *English Traits*—America, "where there are potatoes enough," needed poets, who instead of startling and provoking would inform, and who instead of writing humor would write scripture. Thoreau felt that Carlyle's humor, which he found the main attraction of his books and the characteristic of his style, would not wear well, no more than a joke. And though Thoreau himself believed that humor was "allied to every, even the divinest faculty," and was the most humorous of the transcendentalists, he asserted that "SCRIPTURE . . . is WRITING, *par excellence.*" "Humors will not feed a man," he wrote in the *Journal;* "The heart is not a humor, nor do they go to the heart, as the blood does." [123]

Carlyle's writing satisfied Thoreau's hunger for conversation, but not this deeper New England need for meditation. The humor that characterized the style was also the characteristic of the man. His writing was flame, "apt to be incommoded by heat and smoke," rather than light, and indicated a depth which Carlyle had neglected to fathom. It was essentially superficial: Carlyle, Thoreau said, was not "*seer,* but a brave looker-on and *reviewer*"; and, unlike Emerson, he failed because "he never consults the oracle, but thinks to utter oracles himself." Poetry, however, was the achievement of the seer "who retires behind the truth he utters" [124]— "Poetry," Thoreau wrote, "is the only life got, the only work done,

[123] J, I, 336.
[124] J, I, 336.

the only pure product and free labor of man, performed only when
he has put all the world under his feet, and conquered the last of
his foes." This was what he found wanting in Carlyle; this made
his writings less than works of art. "We know very well the nature
of this man's sadness," Thoreau said of Carlyle (as he might have
of Melville), "but we do not know the nature of his gladness. . . .
We want more of his inmost life; his hymn and prayer more; his
elegy and eulogy less; that he should speak more from his character,
and less from his talent. . . ." And with his own work in mind
Thoreau went on to say, "There is no calm philosophy of life here,
such as you might put at the end of the Almanac, to hang over
the farmer's hearth, how men shall live in these winter, in these
summer days. No philosophy, properly speaking, of love, or friendship, or religion, or politics, or education, or nature, or spirit. . . . no
contemplation of man's life from the serene oriental ground, nor
yet from the stirring occidental." [125]

In stating his case for the poet, Thoreau had apparently renounced the heroic life of the man of action that Emerson had
hoped for him; he had even taken the new line of vocational defense
that Emerson established in "The Poet"—that to utter thoughts is
action. And yet it was quite clear that if Thoreau did not want to
be the Carlylean hero, neither did he want to be the Emersonian
"observer." If he were to utter thoughts it would be by living them.
"To live like a philosopher," he said, "is to live, not foolishly, like
other men, but wisely and according to universal laws." Making
philosophy take the step of conduct, finding the universal laws by
going to nature, was heroic enough. Thus, in citing Carlyle's translation of Schiller's remarks on the artist, Thoreau was speaking for
his own achievement and sense of vocation during the Walden
years: " 'Let some beneficent divinity snatch him, when a suckling
. . . and nurse him with the milk of a better time, that he may
ripen to his full stature beneath a distant Grecian sky. And having
grown to manhood, let him return, a foreign shape, into his century;
not, however, to delight it by his presence, but . . . to purify it.
The matter of his works, he will take from the present, but their
form he will derive from a nobler time; nay, from beyond all time,
from the absolute unchanging unity of his own nature.' " [126] This

---

[125] Thoreau's belief that the hero hides his struggles accounted for the kind
of books he wrote, for their themes and tone.

[126] How appropriate Schiller was may be seen perhaps in Henry James's

hero, the hero he worshiped, belonged to neither Carlyle's nor Emerson's camp; men of action like Luther and Cromwell, and thinkers like Plato and Goethe, were partial and expressed the limitations that Thoreau found in the writing and character of their champions. By putting "their worthies together," however, Thoreau hoped to get "a pretty fair representation of mankind"; those sides of himself and those literary qualities that he admired in Carlyle and Emerson he would reconcile by creating a complete hero. For not only had Carlyle and Emerson omitted Jesus, and slighted "the peaceful practical hero, whom Columbus may represent"—Columbus, who was so important to Thoreau's conception of the hero as spiritual discoverer—they had forgotten "the Man of the Age, come to be called workingman. . . ." Anticipating Whitman in demanding that the hero be a usable "stock-personality," Thoreau added that "none yet speaks to his condition, for the speaker is not yet in his condition." But having known the condition of the workingman himself, and having had the heroism to surmount it, Thoreau directed the *Week* to the needs of America. By giving the condition of his thought, by making it perceptible in experience, he would give his age an epic of inspiration. He would translate the transcendental oracle into a pattern for conduct: he would not only utter it, he would demonstrate it. Even Jesus, he said, "taught mankind but imperfectly to live; his thoughts were all directed toward another world." And speaking for his own gospel, he continued, "There is another kind of success than his. Even here we have a sort of living to get, and must buffet it somewhat longer. There are various tough problems yet to solve, and we must make shift to live, betwixt spirit and matter, such a human life as we can." [127] If Emerson also recognized that this midworld was best, he could not make its claims felt in his writing. It was left for Thoreau, with his tougher grasp on life and dramatic experience in nature, to do that.

Betwixt spirit and matter—here was the fundamental problem

identification of Schiller and Thoreau. See Matthiessen, ed., *The James Family*, p. 431. In the context of the Carlyle essay this passage was used to support Thoreau's belief that Carlyle was not an innovator in form. But the last line suggests the inner form derived from experience, and the passage fits Thoreau's withdrawal and return so well that it must have appealed to him for other than the reason he acknowledged: the passage says more about the nurture and mission of the artist than about form.

[127] W, I, 74. This suggests a point at which the *Week* and *Walden* merge.

f Transcendentalism, whether in conduct or style. Carlyle lacked the one, Emerson the other; and Thoreau knew that their common failure lay in not living the organic life. A style that would have the strengths of Carlyle and Emerson would have to be the expression of an organic life: the groundwork of his book could not be any "matter"; it, too, had to be the theme or idea enacted dramatically. Thus both the *Week* and *Walden,* and even the lesser excursions, had for their basis a life in nature and showed in action what they affirmed in thought. As in Whitman's and Melville's writing, the Emersonian stance of spiritual explorer was actualized. "Walking," which summarized Thoreau's defense of nature, confirmed as well his most typical mode of action or participation. When one turns to the *Week,* therefore, he realizes how far Thoreau had advanced beyond Margaret Fuller, whose *Summer on the Lakes* was not the best situation for her thoughts, or even Emerson, whose essays had only a dialectical unity, with nothing in action to support them. Thoreau did not collect his essays as he might have, and if he was wiser in treating their themes less formally in *Walden,* he did not fail to the extent most critics maintain. In fact, the transition from action to thought, from rowing to contemplating, was as natural as Thoreau had known it in his experience: the open road of the *Week* opened into thought. *To perceive is to be* was the transcendentalists' contribution to philosophy: perception was the permanent experience, and the *Week* was essentially the record of this experience.

The organization of the *Week,* therefore, was not haphazard but deliberately organic. It was unified on both literal and spiritual levels, and the one was adequate to the other. Moreover, it was a bold attempt to create a new form, to adventure beyond the safe beaten paths of literature, where, at best, "'the talent pleases us most which submits to shine with new gracefulness through old forms.'" [128] But deliberate as it was, it did not sacrifice the principle of unconsciousness which, for Thoreau, was the essential requirement of organic art. Thoreau recognized that Goethe's style was "the best that can be successfully cultivated" if one wished to "pioneer into unexplored regions of thought," [129] but he was not content to be the conscious artist that he believed Goethe was.

---

[128] W, IV, 338.
[129] W, IV, 331-32.

Goethe—and Thoreau undoubtedly intended the pun—was "too *well-bred* to be thoroughly bred." Having benefited from Margaret Fuller's brilliant essay on Goethe, Thoreau reduced all transcendental criticism of the most towering writer of the age to the essential point: "Goethe's whole education and life were those of the artist. He lacks the unconsciousness of the poet. . . . the fault of his education is, so to speak, its artistic completeness." Thoreau elaborated this distinction between artist and poet (or genius) in terms of his own education. Goethe lived "the life of a city boy, whose toys are pictures and works of art"; everything he saw, Goethe himself had admitted, was " 'with reference to art.' " This, as Margaret Fuller had driven home, was a fault of character as well as of writing—Goethe had betrayed his genius by going to Weimar and, as Thoreau put it, by aiming "to secure a rank in society that would satisfy his notion of fitness and respectability." For Goethe himself had written that the sublime was only found in " 'the undefinable, wide-expanding feelings of youth and of un-cultivated nations' "; he recognized that in "the woods without the gates" one found the condition of the sublime, one lived an organic life which, when translated into aesthetics, taught one that " 'The laws of Nature break the rules of Art.' " For only the man of nature —the poet, the genius—could create an organic form. "The Man of Genius may at the same time be, indeed is commonly, an Artist, but the two are not to be confounded," Thoreau explained. "The Man of Genius . . . is an originator, an inspired or demonic man, who produces a perfect work in obedience to laws yet unexplored. The Artist is he who detects and applies the law from observation of the works of Genius, whether of man or nature." That is to say, the genius relies on the unconscious: "The unconsciousness of man is the consciousness of God." [130] At Walden, therefore, Thoreau not only believed he was the Man of the Age, but that he was the Genius, living beyond the gates. Unlike Carlyle, he would "retire behind the truth he utters"—he would appear "in the attitude of a man with ear inclined, who comes as silently and meekly as the morning star, which is unconscious of the dawn it heralds, leading the way up the steep as though alone and unobserved in its observing, without looking behind." [131]

It is significant that the problem of the artist for Thoreau was a

[130] The above quotations on Goethe are from W, I, 348-51.
[131] J, I, 336.

question of depth: his ideal was the poet, who pierced the surface
of life to its interior laws, who discovered the organic law of the
universe itself. The organic principle he sought was deeper than
that of craft: without this principle the formal niceties of the artist
were mechanical. Thoreau did not carry the distinction of genius
and artists any further into the problem of craft because it did
not disturb him. One could always organize a book, but whether
the principle of organization were genuinely organic was the important distinction. The genius was not lawless, and what he beheld
the artist might use to fashion his work. Greater than organizing
his insights, which he succeeded well enough in doing, was the
fundamental problem of insight: how to keep his unconsciousness.
Reason and Understanding, Imagination and Fancy, Genius and
Talent were not at war in Thoreau; they were not opposites so
much as higher and lower faculties. The failure of a writer, as he
showed in his remarks on Emerson, Carlyle, and Goethe, was in
his *condition*, in his refusal or inability to fall back on nature. It
was ultimately a failure in character. Indeed, this was the way in
which he viewed the difficulties of his own later years; for him
the problem of perception was ethical.

Now the *Week* was organic in both senses: its form, or shaping
symbols of river and day, grew out of the perception of law, and
its narrative basis was an experience in nature. Granted Thoreau's
specifications for art, he could only write a book on nature; in fact,
nature would always remain the condition of his major work. There
was another spiritual law, however, that Thoreau was able to in-
corporate in the structure of the *Week*. "The life of the wise man,"
he wrote, "is most of all extemporaneous, for he lives out of an
eternity which includes all time." The *Week* with its successive
dawns had this extemporaneous character. It exemplified Thoreau's
awareness of the necessity of spiritual renewal. In the inner world,
he said, man has no credit or capital: "He must try his fortune again
to-day as yesterday." [132]

Thoreau introduced the reader to his method and the law of the
book in "Saturday," the day of departure. Having already discussed
the lure of voyaging in a short opening chapter on the Concord,

---

[132] W, I, 332. "We must learn," he said in *Walden*, "to reawaken and keep
ourselves awake, not by mechanical means, but by an infinite expectation of
the dawn . . ." (W, II, 100).

he now considered the water life of his native environment: he spent most of the chapter describing fishes. Obviously, he was not concerned with the fish themselves,[133] but with "the fish principle in nature. . . ." "There are fishes wherever there is a fluid medium," he said, "and even in clouds and melted metals we detect their semblance." Fishes were worthy of attention because they were "forms and phases of the life in nature universally dispersed." Speaking of fishes, Thoreau was in effect speaking of thoughts, of a mode of the spirit, and the "sense of the grand security and serenity of nature" that they gave him was equally true of his belief in unfailing inspiration. The fishes, indeed, were a catalog of thoughts: the bream, the most common fish, easily caught by closing the fingers about it, a "perfect jewel" in its "native element"; the common perch, also caught in the hands, but half grown; the chevin, a rarity, inhabiting the darker, swifter waters, and the test of the complete angler, for catching this "denizen of the water wholly" was like inspiration itself—"suddenly by a coincidence never to be remembered, emerges this fabulous inhabitant of another element, a thing heard of but not seen, as if it was the instant creation of an eddy, a true product of the running stream"; the shiner, which first nibbles the bait, but is not easily caught; the pickerel, the swiftest, wariest, and most voracious, "a solemn, stately, ruminant fish, lurking under the shadow of a pad at noon"; the horned pout, tenacious of life; the sucker, not often caught by the "mere angler," reminding Thoreau of something foreign, of the "fertility of the seas"; the eel, now rare because of the dams,[134] always working upstream, wasting and dying in preference to returning, suggesting to Thoreau a "tragic feature . . . worthy to be remembered with Shakespeare's description of the sea-floor"; and the shad, once abundant, once caught by the Indians and colonists but now kept from migrating up the river by the dam at Billerica and the factories at Lowell. Of all these fishes, the shad was Thoreau's hero. He felt that they were his contemporary; he identified his river life and destiny with theirs. "When Nature gave thee instinct, gave she thee the heart to bear thy fate?" he asked, thinking of the shad's persistent, innocent, and brave determination to

---

[133] During the Walden period Thoreau began to collect specimens for J. E. Cabot and Louis Agassiz. In a letter to Cabot he lists the fishes to be found in Concord (W, VI, 126-28).

[134] See W, VI, 127.

fulfill its "higher destinies." "I for one am with thee," he wrote, "and who knows what may avail a crow-bar against that Billerica dam?" The shad heeding its "instinct" was a transcendental fish, the dam that tried to "reason" with it the artificial, prudential, utilitarian obstacles to the actual life. Always in the background of Thoreau's voyage, the dam represented all of the ominous forces that had destroyed the wild, the possibilities of natural and spiritual life in America. The poor shad, Thoreau said, "knowest not where men do *not* dwell, where there are *not* factories, in these days." [135]

Considering also the life of the fisherman, it was possible for Thoreau to describe his own vocation, the life of contemplation. Fishing, he said, was "a sort of solemn sacrament and withdrawal from the world"—as Izaak Walton had said, a contemplative man's recreation. And science, Thoreau went on to say, thinking of science in terms of the Indian wisdom of the "Natural History" and of his own study of the fishes, was "only a more contemplative man's recreation." Thinking of vocations in light of the transcendental notion of the ages of man from out-of-door life to consciousness, he claimed that every age had its characteristic vocation, that in the spring of history, man was a fisher and a hunter.[136] One's vocation, therefore, placed him in time: to fish, or to excursion on the river, was a recreation appropriate to the Golden Age, a vocation that Thoreau subtly transformed, however, by blending the out-of-door life with the life of the mind. Because fishing belonged to the natural era, it also provided Thoreau with a historical reference by which to judge the present. In fact, he had begun the chapter by holding up against the heroism of Concord in the past the ignoble lives of the present; and the lone fisherman whom he passed as he left Concord not only suggested what followed of fish and fishermen, but stood as a symbol of the quiet heroism of his own undertaking. When he thought of the shad, he remembered a militia company called "The Shad," and the colonial days when men were fishermen by trade and fed their families in this way. Tracing the degeneration of this vocation, he described an account book, dated 1805, of a fisherman who had succumbed to rum—a fisherman very

[135] All quotations are from W, I, 23-32, 35-36. Thoreau's treatment of fish as symbol, even his moralizing of fact, might have helped Melville. For an example see W, I, 36. The dams were also mentioned at the very beginning of the book. See also J, V, 110.

[136] See W, II, 235.

much like the ne'er-do-well Goodwin whose hardy participation in nature Thoreau preferred to the "civil politic life" of the villagers. "Some men," Thoreau wrote, speaking for his pursuits as well as those of the Goodwins, "are judges these August days, sitting on benches . . . judging there honorably, between the seasons and between meals," while the fisherman lives in the seasons, "stands in three feet of water . . . amid the fragrance of water-lilies, mint, and pontederia, leading his life many rods from dry land, within a pole's length of where the larger fishes swim." In defending the vocation of the Golden Age, Thoreau was defending his own: the villager and the Walden experimenter were already projected, the specialized and the whole man, the man cut off from and the man within the tides of life. In the image of the fisherman and the judge were all the values of Whitman's "When I Heard the Learn'd Astronomer," the belief in knowledge by contact and communion, the vitalistic idea of a living world, in which fish and water, thought and flux were one, and in which the goal of living intensely was but the meeting with this flux at its creative moment, when by immersion in it one shared the "spirit." It was in this sense that the fisherman represented Thoreau's vocation: he would get his living, like the colonists of Concord, from nature—and his life.[137]

"Saturday" was not one of the *days* of Thoreau's week, merely the day of departure. Its place in the book was properly introductory, establishing the book's dimensions and themes, providing the necessary lesson in symbolic interpretation, and doing for the reader what it had for Thoreau—immersing him, whetting his vision, as Thoreau punned on his fluvial experience, "for the sights it was to behold."[138] And not only did it function in relation to the rest of the book, but within itself it was admirably composed, doing in the simplest terms what had to be done if the book were not to be dull—making the literal as luminous as possible, leading the reader by means of the actual adventure to an adventure in spirit. Thus, Thoreau began with the actual departure, but by describing the perfect adaptation of his boat to the elements hinted at a soul's voyage. With his gift for seeing the large in the small, he was able to suggest the unusual enterprise of going to sea; and as he left behind "the firm lands of Concord" and drifted slowly past the battleground, he was able, by this natural transition, to

[137] All quotations are from W, I, 21-23, 32-34.
[138] W, I, 38.

draw on the amplitude of history and time, and relate his excursion
to the heroic lives of colonial times; he, too, was a discoverer, a
voyageur. As the placid river carried him beyond Concord, he had
already found the leisure for meditation; he had left the past behind, entered a new world of luxuriant nature, floated, in fact, from
"past to future." Effortlessly he had achieved the sense of outward
movement, the expectancy of "new scenes and adventures." [139] At
this point the lone fisherman, who was the last landmark, provided
the transition for the discussion of fisherman and fishes—that is
to say, for his major theme of vocation. And at the conclusion of
that passage, which closed with the moralizing on the thwarted
destiny of the shad, he mentioned the farmers of Wayland, Sudbury, and Concord, whose flooded pastures were also a tribute to
the dam. This not only made the privileges of the "dam proprietors"
a practical issue, but afforded a return to the narrative level, to the
actual sight of men haying in the fields. "That was a long pull from
Ball's Hill to Carlisle Bridge," [140] Thoreau wrote of the distance he
had covered in thought and in fact, thereby enabling him to close
the chapter with the actual preparations for camp. But here again,
the novelty and adventure of the experience were made themati-
cally meaningful and prefigurative. At last completely alone, surrounded by the dark, as if in a primeval wilderness, the mast of his
boat etched against the sky reminded him of "the first encroachment of commerce on this land." "That straight geometrical line . . .
stood for the last refinements of civilized life," this new explorer
wrote, "and what of sublimity there is in history was there symbolized." And the breathing of the wind, and the sounds of a still-
living nature that echoed in the silence of the darkness, excited his
heroism and heralded the spiritual promise of the dawn.[141]

Each chapter, each day, more or less fully, developed and crystallized these themes. Running through his course of days, Thoreau
was trying to push his themes in every direction, trying to discover,
as he said of the hunter and fisher in *Walden*, what his proper pursuit should be. "He goes thither at first as a hunter and fisher, until
at last, if he has the seeds of a better life in him," he wrote, "he

---

[139] W, I, 17-20.

[140] W, I, 37.

[141] W, I, 39-41. Most of the days end in this way. Here, however, Thoreau
prepared for his extensive treatment of sound and silence in "Monday."

distinguishes his proper objects, as a poet or naturalist it may be, and leaves the gun and fish-pole behind." That is to say, he arms himself with perception, and tries to get his living in that way. And in the *Week* he was exploring this life, and trying to find its vindication in its rewards: by taking stock, he would prepare himself for the final day, when the summer of life changed to autumn. For he expected, and planned the *Week* to that end, that with evening coming on, "other parts of our day's work will shine than we thought at noon, and we shall discover the real purport of our toil." [142] "Sunday," for example, was built around the morning or sun-day vocation, developing Thoreau's ideas on the variety of ways of worshiping on the natural Sabbath; "Monday" contrasted the poet's "nooning" or contemplative pleasures with those of the restless Yankees, and carried the theme of contemplation *vs.* action back to the Oriental scriptures, especially the *Bhagavad-Gita*,[143] and Thoreau's own embodiment of that wisdom in "Sound and Silence"; "Tuesday," beginning in the fog, which for the faithful Thoreau hid the "bright day" as silence harbored sound, enacted the sense of high destiny of the previous chapter in one of Thoreau's finest accounts of the quest for inspiration; "Wednesday," after the solitude of inspiration, was something of a social chapter, its easy and leisurely tone set by the Arcadian life of the humble people on the shore, and its long discourse on friendship appropriately fitted to Thoreau's concern with sharing his life; "Thursday," the last day of upward travel, was devoted once more to the sufficiency of nature, and to the vocation of traveling as spiritual exploration, the only kind left now that the physical frontier was gone; and "Friday," the day of return, on which autumnal thoughts gathered

---

[142] W, I, 133.

[143] Emerson was reintroduced to the *Bhagavad-Gita* by J. E. Cabot in 1845; his excitement was great, and undoubtedly Thoreau caught it (Rusk, ed., *The Letters of Ralph Waldo Emerson*, III, 288ff.). Thoreau's interest, however, was practical: the problem of contemplation *vs.* action was his own during these years. The *Bhagavad-Gita* was the most highly praised book in the *Week*, especially because it did complete justice to contemplation; but Thoreau, with his desire for heroic action, could not accept its counsels of passivity and fate.

Of the Oriental scriptures he wrote: "You will not have to pierce far into the summer day to come to them. In the New England noontide are more materials for oriental history than the Sanscrit contains." Indeed, nature was before the Vedas, and in nature Thoreau was closer to his materials than in any book (HM 956). This idea was the basis of the chapter on "Sounds" in *Walden*.

around the homeward traveler, was a recapitulation and assessment, turning on the concerns of the poet and his need to transmute his experience in nature into art and the art of life—it brought the *Week* to an evening close, just as it brought the maturing traveler face to face with his proper object, to the very life he was living at Walden.

In this way the chapters of Thoreau's journey unfolded his spiritual course from youth to maturity, and each chapter carried the weight of the preceding ones. "Sunday," obviously, defined the kind of day that composed the *Week*. Opening with a rhapsody on the dawn, it established the notion of sunny day ("Rightly named Suna-day, or day of the sun. One is satisfied . . . to bask in his beams —to exist barely—the live-long day") [144] or day of inspiration. Sunday, Thoreau said in *Walden*, should not be "the conclusion of an ill-spent week" but "the fresh and brave beginning of a new one"— and he made it the beginning of his own, which, as he had announced in his "Commencement Address," would be "his Sabbath of the affections and the soul. . . ." [145] An anti-Sabbitarian who believed that "there is no infidelity so great as that which prays, and keeps the Sabbath, and founds churches," [146] his *Week* had indeed reversed the order of things; his very idea of a day was in itself the revolution that the *Week* in its entirety described. For not only was his Sunday the beginning of a week of *leisure* in nature, it was *pagan:* Thoreau worshiped the sun. His day had "more of the auroral rosy and white than of the yellow in it, as if it dated from an earlier than the fall of man [i.e. the Golden Age], and still preserved a heathenish integrity. . . ." [147] Inspiration—light—would be, after all, a natural Sabbath, and for the transcendentalist inspiration would be genuine worship. With this natural religion in mind, Thoreau read his contemporaries a lesson in religion (and civilization), beginning with a historic account of the determination of the people of Bedford "'to be eased of [their] burden on the Sabbath,'" that is, their belief that they could serve God at home, without traveling to Concord. [148] Then, with the history of Bedford as his occasion, he turned to the Indian and the "wilder," more

---

[144] J, I, 29.
[145] W, II, 106; W, VI, 9.
[146] J, I, 309; W, I, 77.
[147] W, I, 42.
[148] W, I, 51.

natural forms of worship, to Greek myths and gods—to Memnon,
for example, the "son of Morning." [149] In myth, Thoreau said, was
"an aproach to that universal language which all men have sought
for in vain"—it preceded noonday or evening thought, it was the
expression of the "matutine intellect," of the "auroral atmosphere,"
and thus the fitting gospel of the Golden Age.[150] Having, in this
way, introduced his favorite scripture—and, incidentally, prepared
for his discussion of the transcendentalist's proper work—and
having acknowledged that in "my Pantheon, Pan still reigns in his
pristine glory [and] is not dead, as was rumored," Thoreau took up
"the Christian fable" and discoursed on the ways of Unitarians, on
Christ, on the variety of bibles. Of Christianity he concluded: "It
has dreamed a sad dream, and does not yet welcome the morning
with joy." [151]

By this time it was noon, and Thoreau had reached the middle
of the chapter. The remainder, however, was still auroral. Turning
now to the vocation of the poet, to the problems of organic language
and bookmaking, he demanded as the test of books that they stand
"unobstructed sunshine and daylight," and the first writer he tried,
naturally, was Homer, the heroic bard of the Golden Age, the poet
of the rosy-fingered dawn. The *Iliad*, Thoreau wrote, was worthy
of being remembered "in our wisest hours" (it was his reading at
Walden) because it "embodies still all the sunlight that fell on
Asia Minor." In turning to books, however, Thoreau had not forgotten that his theme was worship; he reminded the reader, as he
did in *Walden*, where reading was one of his disciplines, that "there
are those, the wisdom of whose reading is their worship. . . ." He
discussed, too, the "true, sincere" books and the efforts of native
Americans to write them. These books, he said, will be hewn from

[149] W, I, 58. He also used as examples the South Sea islanders, who had
afforded Melville the material for the same contrast. Lowell favorably compared the *Week* to *Typee*.

[150] W, I, 61. Matutine intellect was taken from Emerson's "morning knowledge, *matutina cognitio*"—knowledge of God (C, I, 73, 413).

[151] W, I, 65, 67, 78. The popularity of the *Week* suffered because of
Thoreau's attack on Christianity. George Ripley, for example, thought Thoreau's
preference for Indian scriptures rather than the Bible neither "good sense or
good taste," and was offended by his "misplaced Pantheistic attack on the
Christian Faith." Lowell approved his "fine, intelligent paganism," but Edwin
Morton, otherwise a most sympathetic critic, disliked Thoreau's preference for
Buddha rather than Christ. "Transcendentalism," he wrote, "thy name is
Brahm!" (Jones, ed., *Pertaining to Thoreau*, pp. 1-10, 13-31, 51-72).

life, will be "a stalwart man's work," and will "record the story of the day. . . ." The harvest of man's morning work, these books will shed the light of a labor that in itself is worship; their language, like life, will be organic. And this mode of worship will make the week-long a natural Sabbath in the sun.[152]

The *Week* was just such an extended Sabbath devoted to a voyage to the headwaters of inspiration. Ecstasy, as we saw, was its dominant tone; and in "Tuesday" Thoreau used an experience of the summer of 1844 as the basis of his finest anecdote of inspiration. "Tuesday" began "long before daylight" in the "earlier sunshine" of the mist,[153] and prefigured the cloudy sea into which Thoreau would soon take the reader. "Though we were enveloped in mist as usual," he wrote, "we trusted that there was a bright day behind it"—with hardly a paragraph's delay he recounted the experience that sustained this faith, an experience which condensed all of Thoreau's previous excursions to the mountains. Like Dante, he had entered a wood and come to the foot of a hill where the valley ended; and like Bunyan, too, he had his 'pilgrim's way to make.[154] "My route," Thoreau began, giving his experience an archetypal pattern, "lay up a long and spacious valley . . . sloping up to the very clouds. . . . a stream ran down the middle of the valley. . . . It seemed a road for the pilgrim to enter upon who would climb to the gates of heaven." [155] But unlike Dante or Bunyan—although Thoreau took pains to show how unusual his climb was—he was on a holiday. Even so, Thoreau did not ascend the mountain by the easiest path, as the boys from Williams College did; he determined, he said, "to find my own route up the steep, as the shorter and more adventurous way." And he proudly asserted, as he did many times in contrasting his way and his vocation with those of the multitude, that "they never went by the way I was going." [156] En route, after he had passed the last house, Thoreau was accosted

---

[152] W, I, 94ff.

[153] There was actually a fog that day (HM 956). Thoreau was as faithful to the original experience as he could be; he prepared the way for this "digression" with: "As we cannot distinguish objects through this dense fog, let me tell this story more at length" (W, I, 189).

[154] All quotations are from W, I, 189-200.

[155] The *Week* in its entirety has the same archetypal pattern. See the poem that prepares for this experience, W, I, 188.

[156] One wonders if he had in mind Hawthorne's "The Celestial Railroad." In any case, this would have been the transcendentalist's reply.

by a man who mistook him for a peddler and who counseled him, as one Yankee to another, to take the longer but easier path. ". . . nobody ever went this way," he was told, "there was no path" and the way was "as steep as the roof of a house." But for Thoreau the "ascent was by no means difficult or unpleasant," and quicker besides, and he stopped to moralize on the fact that people who live in the mountains ought to follow their common sense and realize that "it takes only more time and patience . . . than to travel the smoothest highway." Full of transcendental assurance, Thoreau knew that "it is very rare that you meet with obstacles in this world, which the humblest man has not faculties to surmount." He knew, as he explained at length in *Walden,* that in a transcendental universe one was not alone if he stood by himself; and if the anecdote displayed his hardiness and uniqueness, it only did so to show that if all shared his faith a similar experience would be theirs.

There was much of the Yankee in Thoreau's ascent: the pilgrimage itself was a spiritual undertaking, but its execution was prudential. The long cold night on the mountaintop was the prudential price Thoreau paid for the dawn—just as the price of the journey up the Merrimack was the labor of rowing against the current, or the price of the Walden experiment, listed for his literal contemporaries to the fraction of a cent, was the labor of domesticating oneself for inspiration. This price had to be paid, and, accordingly, having reached his goal before sunset and having taken "one fair view of the country before the sun went down," Thoreau postponed the spiritual reward until morning. "I was too thirsty," he remarked matter-of-factly, "to waste any light in viewing the prospect, and set out directly to find water." Perhaps to prove that he was "more used to woods and mountains" than his neighbors, but also to insist on the prudential necessities—and leisure in all things—he lingered with Homeric patience over the details of digging his well, making his fire, and preparing his supper. And no doubt, sitting alone on the top of a mountain, he seemed as ridiculous to his readers as he did to his neighbors at Walden. But once Thoreau got up there he had truly ascended, and the world below was beneath him, a world to be judged from this peak. He had attained the permanent: he could take his ease before the fire to pass the evening reading newspapers, or rather "scraps of newspapers" that former picnickers, unmindful of the use to which this pilgrim would put their transient wrappings, had left behind. A trip to a mountain,

Thoreau added later, should be an education: "Every visit to its summit would, as it were, generalize the particular information gained below, and subject it to more catholic tests." And so it was in this instance and in the *Week* as a whole: Thoreau read the old newspapers "at a vast advantage," looking for enduring information, not the "whimsical and crude, and one-idea'd" matter that people "down below" prize most. The advertisements interested him most because they suggested the poetry of commerce—the "Lumber, Cotton, Sugar, Hides, Guano and Log-wood" that were later amplified into an apostrophe in *Walden*. But this was only a short diversion. He returned abruptly to the cold mountaintop and his preparation for sleep, to the blanket of boards in which he encased himself (an earlier version, perhaps, of his hut) and to his only companions, the mice.

The dawn and Thoreau's ascent into being were contrasted with this hardy preparation. Before daybreak Thoreau perched himself upon the top of the Williams College observatory; he delayed once more, however, to tell how even here he had to listen to the "stale humdrum" of an "untamable fly"—taking the reader back to the discussion of the *Gita* in "Monday," where he had cited Warren Hastings on the exercise of abstracted contemplation, and how, in separating the mind from the senses, " 'even the buzzing of a fly will sometimes have the power to disturb it.' " [157] But then the dawn broke:

As the light increased I discovered around me an ocean of mist, which reached up by chance exactly to the base of the tower, and shut out every vestige of the earth, while I was left floating on this fragment of the wreck of a world, on my carved plank in cloudland. . . . As the light in the east steadily increased, it revealed to me more clearly the new world into which I had arisen in the night, the new terra-firma perchance of my future life. There was not a crevice left through which the trivial places we name Massachusetts, or Vermont, or New York, could be seen. . . . All around beneath me was spread for a hundred miles on every side, as far as the eye could reach, an undulating country of clouds, answering in the varied swell of its surface to the terrestrial world it veiled. There were immense snowy pastures apparently smooth-shaven and firm, and shady vales between the vaporous mountains, and far in the horizon I could see where some luxurious misty timber jutted into the prairie; and trace the windings of a water course, some unimagined Amazon or Orinoko, by the misty trees on its brink. As there was wanting the symbol, so there was not the substance of impurity, no spot or stain.

[157] W, I, 143.

It was a favor for which to be silent to be shown this vision. The earth beneath had become such a flitting thing of lights and shadows as the clouds had been before. It was not merely veiled to us, but it had passed away like the phantom of a shadow . . . and this new platform was gained. As I had climbed above storm and cloud, so by successive days' journeys I might reach the region of eternal day. . . .

Certainly, for Thoreau, this was the sea of his adoption. When the sun arose "on this pure world," Thoreau found himself "in the dazzling halls of Aurora . . . playing with the rosy fingers of the Dawn, in the very path of the Sun's chariot, and sprinkled with its dewy dust, enjoying the benignant smile, and near at hand the far-darting glances of the god." With the dawn had come the Golden Age. "Only that day dawns," Thoreau said at the end of *Walden*, "to which we are awake." And nowhere else had he recorded so well his wakefulness, and his faith in what Melville would call the theoretic bright side. "The inhabitants of earth," Thoreau said, "behold commonly but the dark and shadowy underside of heaven's pavement. . . ." But they were not awake.

Soon, however, the clouds began to lift, and before the sun could reach its zenith, it was *stained* by them. This was owing to "some unworthiness in myself," Thoreau said, to "my wavering virtue"; and without delay he descended, or, as he put it, "sank down again" to the "'forlorn world.'" There he found himself "in the region of cloud and drizzling rain," and like a traveler from another world was told that, down below, the sun had never shown itself. If this experience of inspiration was characteristic of the flowing of ecstasy and the ebbing of decay, and of the fact that decay was the result of impurity, still there was never the tone of despair. Striving and discipline and purification would again prepare the pilgrim. On the evening of his ascent, Thoreau had noted "the summits of new and yet higher mountains . . . by which I might hope to climb to heaven again. . . ." [158]

This experience of the day gathered every strand of the *Week* together. This was the experience that he had lingered to tell. In an early draft of the *Week* he had written of early-morning courage: "In the morning we do not believe in expediency, but will start afresh without botching. . . . To our neighbors who have

[158] See "The Delights of a Discoverer," Sanborn, *Life*, p. 69: ". . . if one hill is not lofty enough to afford him a prospect of his El Dorado, he mounts another. . . . A glorious discovery awaits him, the dazzling splendor of which casts into the shade all his previous trials and difficulties." See also C, III, 75.

risen in mist and rain, we tell of a clear sunrise and the singing of birds, as some traditionary mythus. I look back to those fresh but now remote hours as to the dawn of time, when a solid and blooming health reigned, and every deed was simple and heroic." [159] And at the end of the *Week*, his mountain experience reminded him of his major theme, that "men nowhere . . . live yet a *natural* life," that man "needs not only to be spiritualized, but *naturalized*, on the soil of the earth." "When we come down into the distant village, visible from the mountain top," he wrote, "the nobler inhabitants with whom we peopled it have departed, and left only vermin in its desolate streets." What his experience had taught him, however, was that "we live on the verge of another and purer realm," that all one needed to do to enter it was "to develop these divine germs called the senses"—for "we are provided with senses as well fitted to penetrate the spaces of the real, the substantial, the eternal, as these outward are to penetrate the material universe." Wanting most of all to teach his generation the difference between the narrow common-sense view and the "infinitely expanded and liberating one," he wrote that "we need pray for no higher heaven than the pure senses can furnish, a *purely* sensuous life." "We are comparatively deaf and dumb and blind," he said, "and without smell or taste or feeling. Every generation makes the discovery, that its divine vigor has been dissipated, and each sense and faculty misapplied and debauched. The ears were made, not for such trivial uses as men are wont to suppose, but to hear celestial sounds. The eyes were not made for . . . grovelling uses, but to behold beauty now invisible. May we not *see* God? Are we to be put off and amused in this life, as it were with a mere allegory? Is not Nature, rightly read, that of which she is commonly taken to be the symbol merely?" Thus the explorer, who had found an unimagined Orinoco in the correspondence of the clouds, told his generation of the new America he had discovered for them. "It is easier to discover another such a new world as Columbus did," he wrote, "than to go within one fold of this which we appear to know so well; the land is lost sight of, the compass varies, and mankind mutiny; and still history accumulates like rubbish before the portals of nature." He had discovered more than the shores of America; he had taken the stream into the interior of the continent. He had discovered depth: "There is a nature behind the ordinary, in which we have only some

[159] HM 13195.

vague preëmption right and western reserve as yet. We live on the outskirts of that region." [160]

In this account of inspiration Thoreau had answered the question he would put in *Walden:* "By the blushes of Aurora and the music of Memnon, what should be a man's *morning work* in this world?" [161] The search for inspiration and its subsequent transformation into poetry—this morning work was the transcendental vocation and religion. Art, he informed his readers, is a vocation and a religious work, one unfortunately submerged in a bustling America, wasting itself in the frenzy to possess trifles. This was another aspect of the dominant theme of the *Week*, for, after all, a week's boating excursion was an affront to the multitudes who had other, more serious things to do. Almost all whom Thoreau passed—even boatmen—had a querulous curiosity. His leisure was a novelty, as unconventional as the life at Walden Pond; and his pursuit of contemplation, his abandonment to the stream, was a criticism of "restless Yankee men," and of the endless activity and toil of their lives.[162] He had already made this point explicit, when in praising that "strange, and heretical, and unpopular" book, the New Testament, he cited the text, "'Seek first the kingdom of heaven.'—'Lay not up for yourself treasures on earth.'—'. . . For what is a man profited, if he shall gain the whole world, and lose his own soul?'" "Think of this, Yankees!" he had written, a veritable devil quoting scripture.[163] Thoreau, of course, knew the figure he cut in the world: his humor was chiefly an awareness of this; he did not need Lowell to caricature him. Everywhere in the *Week* (as also in *Walden*), he contrasted his occupation with those of his neighbors—with the judge, the farmer, the lockman, the boatman, the minister—and he broadly hinted that had they his courage, the courage of their ancestors, they would make an adventure of life. He tenderly struck home when he told of little Nathan, a model farmer's son, whose eyes sparkled with eagerness to share in his adventures and who, accordingly, "wished himself already his own

---

[160] W, I, 405-13.

[161] W, II, 40.

[162] W, I, 226. Josh Billings said of the Yankee: "The buty ov a river tew him iz its capacity for a steamboat; its sloping banks checker into bildin lots, and its poetry waters might do the drudgery ov a cottin mill." See also Emerson, J, VII, 299.

[163] W, I, 73. He used scripture in the same way in *Walden*.

man." But like grown men, Yankee men, "Nathan was still his father's boy, and had not come to years of discretion." [164]

The motif of vocation, however, was even more organic. The river itself was its structural symbol, and on the river Thoreau pursued his vocation. Like the Sudbury road, leading to the southwest, to the adventurous frontier, the river was the way to the mountains, to the "fountainhead and source of rivers," to equally original and undefiled springs. "The river," Thoreau wrote, "is by far the most attractive highway," not only because it was the way to his spiritual goal, but because its unexpected reaches and changing scenes prevented routine. It freed the traveler from the "Conscience . . . bred in the house," and, like the mountain, it gave him perspective, and now and again the prism of thin haze that blended the particular and separate into the flux of eternal relation.[165] It was, therefore, the suitable path for the transcendentalist who did not want the "distinct" and "limited," but the encouragement to his imagination to exaggerate the natural into the sublime.[166] "Roads," he said in "Walking," "are made for horses and men of business. I do not travel in them much, comparatively, because I am not in a hurry to get to any tavern or grocery or livery-stable or depot to which they lead." [167] As the path, then, that fulfilled his needs, the river was preferable to the civilized routes that often paralleled its course: it offered a "much fairer, more wild and memorable experience than the dusty and jarring one" of the highway.[168] And although Thoreau knew that the river had been replaced by the "true and main stream," the railroad whose source was the factory and whose whistle the scream of progress, and had become only the waste water of the mills, he believed that it was still a "pleasant course" for small vessels and transcendental wayfarers.[169]

Thus the river became the true way, always for Thoreau the symbol of the transcendental direction he opposed to the apparently destined course of America. Like innumerable symbols

[164] W, I, 307-8. The same function was served in the discussion of visitors in *Walden*, and little Nathan became the handsome sailor who told Thoreau, "Sir, I like your notions" (HM 924).

[165] W, I, 201, 204, 75.

[166] W, I, 202.

[167] W, V, 213-14.

[168] W, I, 204.

[169] W, I, 89-90. On the push of civilization (or Anglo-Saxon energy) at the expense of the Indian and nature see Hawthorne's "Main Street."

in American literature—like Hart Crane's bridge, for example
—Thoreau's stream was at cross purposes with American life:
once the way into America, Americans no longer followed
its leadings. When, after the unwilling leisure of their un-
natural Sabbath, they struck out on Monday on *their* "un-
attempted adventures," they did not journey up the stream,
but in the early morning began "to cross the ferry on the
business of the week." This ferry, Thoreau appropriately described in the chapter on "Monday," was as busy as a beaver dam,
and all the world seemed anxious to get across the Merrimack
River at this particular point, waiting to get set over,—children
with their two cents done up in paper, jailbirds broke loose and
constable with warrant, travellers from distant lands to distant
lands, men and women to whom the Merrimack River was a
bar. . . . Many of these Monday men are ministers, reseeking their
parishes with hired horses, with sermons in their valises all read
and gutted, the day after never with them. They cross each other's
routes all the country over like woof and warp, making a garment
of loose texture; vacation now for six days." [170] Thoreau was reminded of Charon and the River Styx, of John Ledyard, of the
Wandering Jew—men "transiting all day." And on the ferry he
commented, "it is only a *transjectus*, a transitory voyage, like life
itself, none but the long-lived gods bound up or down the stream."
To indicate his course he added, making the contrast clearer between the ministers and himself, "Good religious men, with the
love of men in their hearts, and the means to pay their toll in their
pockets. We got over this ferry chain without scraping, rowing
athwart the tide of travel,—no toll from us that day."

Thoreau had prepared for this moral by telling of an event of
the previous evening. Then, two men, having been "waylaid by the
Sabbath," tried to take passage with Thoreau, whose smoothly
gliding boat seemed to them an available ferry come to help them
in their distress. But, already overloaded, Thoreau denied them
passage, and watching their frantic attempts to get across was
"struck by the seeming, though innocent indifference of Nature to
these men's necessities, while elsewhere she was equally serving
others." [171] This was, of course, a parable of self-reliance in relation

[170] W, I, 122-23. In one respect the railroad served the same purpose in
Walden. See W, II, 135-36.
[171] W, I, 115-17.

to prudential and spiritual laws: the stream was nature, was Spirit, the servant of Thoreau's necessities only because he had yielded to it and was going its way; to his anxious fellow men it would forever be an obstacle.[172]

It was fitting that the remainder of "Monday" extended this contrast in purposes and vocations. The contrast was made in several ways, in terms of the qualities of vocations—contemplation *vs.* action, leisure *vs.* busy-ness; in terms of American experience— the Indian and the colonial past *vs.* industry and its possible future; in terms of universal history—East *vs.* West, Orientalism *vs.* Occidentalism. Like a fundamental contrast in Emerson's thought, that of Works and Days, Thoreau's supported a similar moral. "Works and days were offered us," Emerson wrote, "and we took works. . . . [But] He is only rich who owns the day." [173] The reconciliation Thoreau saw for himself and for the nation was that between a wise passivity and a purposeless activity—"a struggle between the oriental and occidental in every nation," a struggle between those who "would be forever contemplating the sun, and [those] who are hastening toward the sunset." [174] The danger he saw was not so much in hastening toward the sun to prolong the day; the danger was that "unless we do more than learn the trade of our time, we are but apprentices, and not yet masters of the art of life." [175]

This, of course, was the whole burden of *Walden* as well as of the *Week*. Toward the mastery of life he emphasized the need for contemplation, the political and institutional implications of which were self-reform. If the West was active and restless, its philosophers were still too passive in regarding the law. They followed the expedient, forgetting that "the absolutely right is expedient for all." [176] The immediate practical issue of contemplation for Thoreau, therefore, was finding that mode of life "by which a man may put bread into his mouth which will not prejudice him as a companion and neighbor." [177] And the ultimate social value of self-

---

[172] The transcendental conception of necessity was first stated by Thoreau in *The Service*. It was the central idea of an organic conduct of life—that whether or not one subscribes to Spirit, one must go with the current of life, not against it. Here the wisdom of Lao-tzu would have supported Thoreau.

[173] C, VII, 168.

[174] W, I, 147.

[175] W, I, 129.

[176] W, I, 138.

[177] W, I, 136.

reform was its example: "He who eats the fruit [of past wisdom], should at least plant the seed; aye, if possible, a better seed than that whose fruit he has enjoyed." Explaining one of his own motives for going to Walden, he said, "Defray thy debt to the world; eat not the seeds of institutions, as the luxurious do, but plant it rather, while thou devourest the pulp and tuber for thy subsistence; that so, perchance, one variety may at last be found worthy of preservation." [178] The seed he was planting, however, was of the transcendental variety, compacted of insight and the integrity of living in harmony with it. His seed "expanded in the warm day" like the melon in Emerson's *Nature;* it grew by contemplation and leisure, by postponing "the practicalness of life" to hear the locust sing, by allying every hour to the "morning of creation." [179] While he was composing the *Week,* he lived this life of contemplation, and transferred it to the river. He suggested that "we might lead a dignified oriental life along this stream. . . ." [180] And in both instances, he was the rare Western philosopher who knew, in the Oriental sense, "the significance of Contemplation." [181] There was no better proof than "Monday" itself, which began in the hustle of enterprise and ended with the famous rhapsody on sound. What he wished most to communicate in the flow of his book was the sense of communion that came with calm and lingered at the heart of contemplation. The reward of the soul's leisure was to rest beside a stream, "becalmed in the infinite leisure and repose of nature." And such was the reward of the *Week:* "we contemplated at our leisure the lapse of the river and of human life; and as that current, with its floating twigs and leaves, so did all things pass in review before us, while far away in cities and marts on this very stream, the old routine was proceeding still." [182]

One sees more clearly in the *Week* than in *Walden* that this man in nature was hardly a primitive. Nature properly read was the repository of laws and the best guide into the history that men had written on her face. She was the permanent and the transient, the

---

[178] W, I, 129-30.

[179] W, I, 145-46, 164. See C, I, 59. Thoreau's eating of a melon prompted his discussion of seeds, but since the melon was the fruit of the East, it also became a symbol of contemplation and lesiure (W, I, 129-30).

[180] W, I, 130.

[181] W, I, 143.

[182] W, I, 128, 130.

source and tide of life: to see her law enacted in time one had to be the historian of man as well as nature. Even if one recognized the permanent, "primitive" essentials of all human life, one could not return to the static timelessness and unconsciousness of primitive existence. The primitiveness Thoreau championed, therefore, was at best a symbol of the need for an organic life, one whose functions grew out of law, and it asked more of man than "civilization" did: that he live by his highest consciousness, that he transform a physical communion with nature into a spiritual one. With Emerson, he wanted to make his generation take the step from commodity to spirit.

Except for the literal interludes, Thoreau rarely left the lands of contemplation. All passed in review—all time, history, books, the contents of his mind. The light of everlasting day shone steadily; but the shadows were gathering. "Continued travelling," the traveler himself said, "is far from productive . . . ere long it will wear a man clean up, after making the heart sore into the bargain." [183] Unless the traveler is reborn by traveling, by passing the frontiers of old experience, unless expectation ends in ecstasy, he sickens in his despair. That this note entered the *Week* was due to Thoreau's truthfulness to the inevitable crises of transcendental experience: the day was followed by evening, and by night. In the sterner insistence of the last chapter, which brought the traveler home, the previous joys of his life merged with those of Walden, and the themes of *Walden* were anticipated. For if Thoreau found his river going in a direction his fellow men did not recognize, he also found that "go where we will on the *surface* of things, men have been before us." The true frontiers, he realized, "are not east or west, north or south, but wherever a man *fronts* a fact, though that fact be his neighbor, there is an unsettled wilderness between him and Canada, between him and the setting sun, or further still, between him and *it*." Thus the determined note absent at the beginning of the *Week*, and the injunction: "Let him build himself a log-house . . . where he is, *fronting* IT, and wage there an Old French war for seven or seventy years, with Indians and Rangers, or whatever else may come between him and the reality, and save his scalp if he can." [184] When the goal of the *Week* was attained (in "Thurs-

---

[183] W, I, 326. "All travelling grows out of a wish to return home and stay at Rome [the Eternal City]—if the traveller can find it" (HM 13195).
[184] W, I, 323-24.

day"), summer became autumn, and with it, as Thoreau said, "the fairies all gone or concealed." With the cottagers on the stream for whom "the Fall [on the transcendental level this was a pun] had commenced," Thoreau at the close of the *Week* was "retreating inward to the haunts of summer." [185]

Now, in this season of inwardness and harvest, he was concerned with the actual tensions of his vocation as a poet, with finding a permanent basis in his life for those values he had found in the abandonment of the excursion. He believed that the artist and his work were one, that to be a hero-bard like Ossian or Homer one had to live like one. The crucial problem was to make a life in which those "rare intervals [when] we rise above the necessity of virtue into an unchangeable morning light, in which we have only to live right on and breathe the ambrosial air" were more than adventitious.[186] And this problem, as he now saw it, was one of purification—for it was only by purity that inspiration and union with the IT were possible. The unworthiness that clouded the sun once more seemed to him to signalize his descent into autumn. "When a shadow flits across the landscape of the soul, where," he asked, "is the substance?" If decay, or impurity, were the answer, there was, however, still this compensation: "the constant abrasion and decay of our lives makes the soil of our future growth." His faith, like his faith in the compost of the wilderness, was in organic renewal. "The wood which we now mature," he wrote, "when it becomes *virgin* mould, determines the character of our second growth." In the transcendental spiritual economy, decay and change were inevitable, not only from day to day, but from youth to age, from season to season. Thoreau knew that "every man casts a shadow . . . this is his grief; let him turn which way he will, it falls opposite to the sun; short at noon, long at eve." In the language of *The Service*, he added that the shadow was "no greater than his own opacity"; and he proposed the remedy of purity: "The divine light is diffused almost entirely around us, and by means of the reflection of light, or else by a certain self-luminousness, or, as some will have it, transparency, if we will preserve ourselves untarnished, we are able to enlighten our shaded side." [187] Autumn,

---

[185] W, I, 357. Thoreau spoke of his return as a descent, as a "continually dropping downward" (W, I, 361).

[186] W, I, 394.

[187] W, I, 375-76. My italics.

for all of its suggestions of loss, with its sharp, clear air, "cleansed of all the summer's impurities," was not without the promise of more heroic adventures of the spirit.[188] In a passage that prefigured his later autumnal themes, Thoreau wrote with restraint and eloquence of what he himself had harvested in the rapid downward travel of the last day: "The moon no longer reflects the day, but rises to her absolute rule, and the husbandman and hunter acknowledge her for their mistress. Asters and golden-rods reign along the way, and the life-everlasting withers not. The fields are reaped and shorn of their pride, but an inward verdure still crowns them. The thistle scatters its down on the pool, and yellow leaves clothe the vine, and naught disturbs the serious life of men. But behind the sheaves, and under the sod, there lurks a ripe fruit, which the reapers have not gathered, the true harvest of the year, which it bears for ever, annually watering and maturing it, and man never severs the stalk which bears this palatable fruit." [189]

Assured of this true harvest, braced by the challenge of autumn, and resolved on purity, Thoreau felt himself equal to the requirements of genius, to the highest standards of ethics and art. All the riches of his verdurous season had now become the goal of his heroic endeavor, and he felt that "by his greater strength and endurance his fainting companions [would] recognize the God in him." Fed by "the genuine nectar and ambrosia of the gods," invigorated by the "thrills of inspiration," his life, he said, would be preserved "to a serene old age." The "simple, fibrous life" would sustain him.[190] Thus he wrote with hope,

> So fast we hasten to decay,
> Yet through our night glows many a star,
> That still shall claim its sunny day.[191]

As the traveler returned in the autumn evening, he was especially sensitive to the larger context, to the background, of his inspiration. He had spent the day in contemplating the methods of the poet, in marshaling his forces for another assault on fact. And even though his thoughts were preoccupied with "life's wasting day," he felt too strongly to despair the assurance he heard in silence, the "universal refuge":

[188] W, I, 377.

[189] W, I, 404.

[190] W, I, 362, 365, 368. These pages show his hunger for fame.

[191] W, I, 378.

> I hear the sweet evening sounds
> From your undecaying grounds. . . .[192]

With the knowledge of decay there was a newly gained maturity, and a conscious awareness of his relation to the perpetual forces of the universe. But knowing that these forces never fail, he gladly leaped ashore and fastened his boat to the wild apple tree, which, he said, "still bore the mark which its chain had worn in the chafing of the spring freshets." A cycle of life and experience had been completed: putting the final period to his youth, Thoreau, now living his simple, fibrous life at Walden, was the *voyageur* who was "rowing homeward to find some autumnal work to do, and help the revolution of the seasons." [193]

[192] W, I, 416, 417, 418.
[193] W, I, 420, 415.

Chapter VI

THE VOCATION OF PURITY:
OR, LIFE WITH PRINCIPLE

> It is the marriage of the soul with Nature that makes
> the intellect fruitful, and gives birth to imagination.
>
> —Thoreau, *Journal*, 1851

I

Thoreau was equivocal about his reasons for
leaving Walden Pond. In the *Journal* of 1852 he
wrote of his reasons, "I do not think that I can
tell." And then he added, "I have often wished
myself back. . . . Perhaps if I lived there much
longer, I might live there forever." Still, he felt
"a little stagnation," and that "a ticket to Heaven
must include tickets to Limbo, Purgatory, and
Hell." [1] Looking back to Walden in 1852, he had
reasons aplenty for wanting to return; but remembering the actual experience and its place
in his maturing destiny, he knew well enough
what other lives he had to live. The experiment
at Walden had been effective therapy: he had
renewed his faith both by living there and by
writing the *Week*, and armed with his manuscript he was again ready to return to the world.
The exact moment of his return, it seems, was
determined by Emerson's departure for England

[1] J, III, 214-15.

in October, 1847, and by Lidian's invitation—not Emerson's, apparently—to spend the winter with her.[2] Except for the fact that he was now the man of the house, the old pattern of his life was resumed. He was confident again, and, as he told Emerson, whom he at last called Waldo, the lectures began to multiply on his desk.[3] Now, perhaps, he could be the writer and have the recognition Emerson had hoped for him.

He managed, in fact, to begin a new trial of lecturing immediately, delivering his account of the 1846 expedition to Ktaadn in January, and his "The Rights and Duties of the Individual in Relation to Government," the early version of "Civil Disobedience," in February, 1848. The lecture he had prepared on "Friendship" was wisely reserved for the *Week*.[4] Not yet depressed over the difficulty of finding a publisher for the *Week*, he was willing, awaiting the day of wider renown, to get his wares ready and try them on the Concord Lyceum. And when, after much delay, the *Week* was published in 1849, *Walden* was announced as forthcoming—not, of course, the *Walden* we know, but one probably comprising the lectures he had given in 1847 on housekeeping (a large portion of "Economy"), the lectures he delivered under Hawthorne's auspices at Salem in 1848 and 1849 on economy, on reading and sounds, the lecture he delivered in 1849 on "White Beans and Walden Pond," and perhaps another lecture of 1848, unnamed in the records of the Concord Lyceum, which included the material on dyspeptic humanitarian reformers and self-reform later divided between "Economy" and "Conclusion."[5] Thoreau's prospects seemed promising during the lecture season of 1848-49: he had been warmly reviewed for the humor and satire of "Economy," his Ktaadn lecture had appealed to men and boys, and he had learned a lesson that continued popularity demanded: that allegory chills an audience. And the twenty-dollar fee (Emerson's price)[6] that he was paid for

[2] Rusk, ed., *The Letters of Ralph Waldo Emerson*, III, 415.

[3] W, VI, 154.

[4] W, VI, 145, 150, 154, 156.

[5] Hoeltje, "Thoreau as Lecturer," pp. 485-94. The records of the Concord Lyceum list only one lecture for 1848, and that without a title. We know from Thoreau's letters that he gave two, and internal evidence and oral quality in the manuscript on reform suggest a third. Thoreau may have lectured at Portland and Bangor in 1849. See Canby, *Thoreau*, p. 248.

[6] Hoeltje, "Thoreau as Lecturer."

each lecture undoubtedly was welcome, as a prospect of self-sufficiency and a sign of fame.

The *Week*, however, was Thoreau's bid for fame, finished in one form and ready for publication in the summer of 1846. Writing to Newcomb in July, Emerson said that "in a short time, if Wiley & Putnam smile, you shall have Henry Thoreau's 'Excursion on Concord & Merrimack rivers,' a seven days' voyage in as many chapters, pastoral as Isaak Walton, spicy as flagroot, broad & deep as Menu." [7] As his interest in Thoreau renewed itself, Emerson reported the "good American book" to Carlyle and Margaret Fuller in February, 1847, and in March wrote Evert Duyckinck of Wiley & Putnam explaining the book he had advised Thoreau to send him, "that it may have a good edition & wide publishing." [8] But Wiley & Putnam did not smile, nor, as Thoreau wrote Emerson in England in November, Munroe, Harpers, or Crosby & Nichols. None of these publishers would print it at his risk, only at the author's, and Thoreau, following Emerson's advice, would not accept these terms. "If I liked the book well enough, I should not delay," he wrote, "but for the present I am indifferent." [9] This, however, was a brave indifference, for he wrote Elliot Cabot that "you can imagine the effect of delay on an author's estimate of his own work." [10] If the delay forced him to mend the book, it did not help his sense of self-esteem, and Emerson, with fine wisdom, wrote from England, "I should print it at once, nor do I think that you would incur any risk in doing so that you cannot well afford." [11] Emerson knew the cost of delay, how much Thoreau's long-postponed success depended on this book; but he did not count on the poor sale, nor on the many years it would take Thoreau to heal his pride. He mistook Thoreau's refusal to publish *Walden* immediately for obstinacy; but it was self-defense—and once again the delay gave us a better book. Of the *Week*, published at last at the author's risk by James Munroe in May, 1849, only 294 copies of an edition of 1000 were sold or given away; the remaining copies were returned to Thoreau four years later, and in November, 1853, when *Walden* was about

[7] Rusk, ed., *The Letters of Ralph Waldo Emerson*, III, 338.
[8] Rusk, ed., *The Letters of Ralph Waldo Emerson*, III, 376, 377, 384.
[9] W, VI, 139.
[10] W, VI, 156.
[11] W, VI, 156n.

ready for the press, Thoreau reported that his debt to his publisher had finally been settled.[12]

The years between the publishing of the *Week* and *Walden* were very much like the years following Thoreau's first residence at the Emersons: there was a promise of success in the intermittent and widening demand for lectures, a few articles had been sold, but there was no real success, no self-sufficiency in these vocations. When he left the Emersons in July, 1848, he returned home to take up the family business which had begun to prosper, and which more and more, during his father's illness, needed him. He was to serve Admetus for the rest of his life, and when the call to lecture was not frequent enough, was to add to his servitude the chains of the surveyor. The failure of the *Week*, like the failure at Staten Island, closed the last opportunity for freedom; and this time he had no Walden Pond to go to, only a more staggering debt to pay off and increasing family responsibilities. And he was older: the bloom of life was fading; there were already indications in recurring illnesses of the slow deterioration of his vigor. In the last decade of his life the problem of vocation was nothing compared to the problem of retaining his vital heat. His heroism, now, was needed to maintain his condition as a poet, to bring about again that "marriage of the soul with Nature that makes the intellect fruitful, and gives birth to imagination." [13]

For the harmony of relations, the organic life he had known at Walden, was behind, and breakdown before him. The unity of his life was fragmented by the necessity of laboring for other men, by the coarsening of his life and the sense of impurity, by a growing recognition in the lapse of inspiration and the feeling of the otherness of nature (which he had learned on his first visits to the Maine woods and Cape Cod), of the abyss beneath unity, and by the importunities of a society that, increasingly revealing its expediency in the Mexican war and the fugitive slave law, destroyed his felicity and drew him away from the solution of his private problems. Everything he wrote after the Walden years bore the marks of his difficulties: the satire sharpened, the tone became urgent and strident, the preaching on the absolute that began in 1848 in his letters to Harrison Blake carried over into his other writing. Like Emerson, he had not known the extent of his stake in self-reliance

---

[12] J, V, 459, 521.

[*] J, II, 413.

until he was assailed; then, however, he did not give quarter, and with an individualism which has properly become a fixed point in the American mind stood his ground to the end. In 1851 he recorded the resolve that crystallized *Walden* for him and that became the incentive of his remaining work:

> That way of viewing things you know of . . . take that view, adhere to that, insist on that, see all things from that point of view. . . . Do not speak for other men; speak for yourself. . . . Though you should only speak to one kindred mind in all time, though you should not speak to one, but only utter aloud, that you may the more completely realize and live in the idea which contains the reason of your life, that you may build yourself up to the height of your conceptions, that you may remember your Creator in the days of your youth and justify His ways to man, that the end of life may not be its amusement, speak—though your thought presupposes the non-existence of your hearers—thoughts that transcend life and death.[14]

Driven back on himself, he made his individualism programmatic; the superiority that had lurked in his college essays and that had been somewhat softened in his early writing now became his last weapon, glittering in the air for the first time in the sharp logic of "Civil Disobedience." A champion of principle, the spokesman of conscience, he would war on expediency in any form. And he would live by his law—"I must be good as I am made to be good"—he would exploit his uniqueness to the full. Man, he said, was "not to be referred to, or classed with, any company. He is truly singular. . . ." He discovered again in trying Emerson's experiment of inverting the head that every man had a unique angle of vision and that for this reason the wisdom of his elders did not necessarily apply to his condition. "There is life," he wrote, "an experiment untried by me, and it does not avail me that you have tried it. If I have any valuable experience, I am sure to reflect that this my mentors said nothing about."[15] And as he felt all the more the autumn of his life, he had no time to waste: he would speak for himself, and tell his valuable experiences.

One of the valuable experiences he had to tell was how he had dodged the pressures of economic life by the easy calculus of simplicity—though few who have taken this Thoreau for their ideal have seen the extent to which his repudiation of materialism was also a repudiation of expediency, and how much simplicity or

---

[14] J, III, 157-58. See W, I, 363.
[15] J, III, 263, 286-87, 291, 294-95.

poverty, as he called it, was a condition of conscience and virtue. He could utter his strong words against the state in "Civil Disobedience" because, as he pointed out, he had no property to protect; and he could show how wealth, rather than leading to virtue as Poor Richard claimed, leads to its sacrifice. Of course the participation in spirit and the unity of life were the most valuable experiences he had to communicate, but the means by which they were achieved, that is to say, the obstacles that had to be pushed aside to attain them, became more significant for him as he grew older. Sooner or later, in one form or another, the actual would invade his freedom; he could not set up the transcendental experiment in a vacuum, and the transcendental assumption that idea shapes circumstance would have to meet the test of society. More and more, in the various forms of servitude—at first as vocation, then in forms he could not so easily determine, reform, slavery, war —the actual bore down on him. And then he recognized that all freedom was one, that the freedom to make his life depended on a freedom from the innumerable coercions he did not seek but which nevertheless had to be faced and disposed of. He could not honestly write a manual of self-reform in *Walden* until he had practically, as well as theoretically, defined the terms on which a man is free to pursue his life. Even in the *Week,* where he first mentioned his night in jail, he knew that to live by the law in his relation to nature required that he live by the law in all of his relations—in all those relations that were covered by tradition, institutions, and the custom of mankind.

"The Rights and Duties of the Individual in Relation to Government"—the title of the lecture that he delivered in 1848 and printed as "Civil Disobedience" in 1849 [16]—was a part of his larger thought on man and institutions in the *Week;* and if the original title was not so dramatic, it was a more exact one for a statement of principles that appeared again and again, wherever Thoreau faced the general problem of society. The act of civil disobedience was not the most important thing, though it was, of course, the most vivid example of Thoreau's attempt to abide by his principles. As for so many readers, for Thoreau himself it was a courageous act that caught his imagination; and he dwelt on it in the *Week* and *Walden,* as well as in this essay, because it confirmed for him his identifi-

[16] Originally published in Elizabeth Peabody, *Aesthetic Papers,* Boston, 1849. All quotations are from W, IV, 356-87.

cation with the hero. In fact, the public profession of his principles, like his pleas for John Brown before his timid neighbors, was a more significant political act than the refusal to pay his poll tax: it was a public "signing off," more forceful even than his written statement when he cut his tie with the church, a call to conscience, indeed an *act*.[17] Civil disobedience was merely one form of conscientious objection, one way of announcing and making felt one's preference for justice. For Thoreau did not insist on passive resistance, which has been too commonly construed as passivity or passiveness.[18] He was resisting, he was acting in the only way, or perhaps in the simplest, most available way, he could, without, as he said later, violating the laws of his own nature. Most men, he wrote in the *Week*, live with " 'too passive a regard for the laws,' " and he even cited Krishna's advice to Arjuna in the *Bhagavad-Gita*, that " 'action is preferable to inaction.' "[19] The kind of passive resistance he had in mind—and the kind of situation in which it was to be employed—was represented for him in Antigone's adamant defense of " 'the unwritten and immovable laws of the gods.' "[20] He took his cue from her; those scenes between Antigone and Creon personalized the issue, dramatized for him the belief that government was a matter of men and conscience, and showed him the positive way in which an individual could produce a counterfriction and clog the machinery of government.

One did not rebel, however, at the expense of one's own nature. The most important thing Thoreau had to say was that the ultimate health of the state depended on conscience, that the reason it must preserve rather than destroy "the wise minority," and must even allow a few "to live aloof from it," was to keep alive the sources of virtue. Above all, there must be somewhere some repository of law; and for Thoreau, who could never find it in the *machinery* or the *association* of government, the individual alone was the "higher

---

[17] Alcott, for example, who had also refused to pay his tax, did not declare himself in this way. He thought Thoreau's lecture on "Civil Disobedience" an admirable statement (Shepard, ed., *The Journals of Bronson Alcott*, p. 201), and in 1854 he took an active and almost foolhardy part in the Anthony Burns affair. Emerson thought Thoreau's refusal to pay his tax "mean and skulking" (*The Journals of Bronson Alcott*, p. 183). See also Emerson, J, VII, 186, 219-22.

[18] Passive resistance carried far enough usually provokes violence.

[19] W, I, 137, 140.

[20] W, I, 140.

and independent power, from which all its own power and authority are derived. . . ." "The mass of men," he said, "serve the state . . . not as men . . . but as machines, with their bodies." They relinquished the free exercise of their moral sense—and corporations, as he had learned from Raleigh, had no conscience. But the heroes, as they were now defined in political terms, "serve the state with their consciences also, and so necessarily resist it for the most part; and they are commonly treated as enemies by it."[21] Thoreau's view of government, of course, was of a piece with his view of reform; to schemes like Etzler's, to the do-goodism of philanthropists and governments, to the inevitable compromise and expediency of associations and majorities, he had only one reply: you must eventually rely on "the vitality and force of a single living man. . . ." By all means, then, the individual must not abdicate what for Thoreau was the only political obligation, the right of conscience; nor should he, in his attempt to reform the state, use any means that would violate this law of his being. No other social act was more important; indeed, he believed that by preserving the conscience, by leavening "the whole lump" of society, he was serving the state, he was giving himself entirely to his fellow men. He knew, however, that in doing this he would appear "useless and selfish," but this was the way in which he interpreted social usefulness, and it was because of this that for him, guarding and cultivating the seeds of virtue, *Walden* was a social book, an outright gift of the man himself.

Writing of Mirabeau, who said, "I reason without obeying, when obedience appears to me contrary to reason," and who took to highway robbery to test the courage of his opposition to society, Thoreau said, "A saner man would have found opportunities enough to put himself in formal opposition to the most sacred laws of society, and so test his resolution, in the natural course of events, without violating the laws of his own nature. It is not for a man to *put himself* in such an attitude to society, but to *maintain* himself in whatever attitude he finds himself through obedience to the

---

[21] Thoreau listed Christ among the political heroes and rebels. In the *Week* he said that "Christ is the prince of Reformers and Radicals," and that the New Testament, which he also offered as a guide to legislators in "Civil Disobedience," was "remarkable for its pure morality," that "all mortals are convicted by its conscience." Thoreau gave another meaning to the "day" when he said of the practical, humane reform of Christ, that then "the day began" (W, I, 141-42).

laws of his being, which will never be one of opposition to a just government." [22] The civil disobedience Thoreau practiced was irreproachable only when it rested on and did not violate justice, and he practiced it only because the state was unjust and because it was the least expected weapon, a weapon of incalculable spiritual force because it destroyed the assumption of absolute social right and authority. It raised the issue of conscience and justice, and thus undermined the foundations of expediency.

Thoreau had no intention of being passive; even at college he had encountered the problem of expediency and justice in Paley and Stewart, and had learned from Cicero's *De Officiis* that expediency is not law and that passivity may be a connivance with injustice.[23] And Thoreau had no intention of not serving the state— greatness, he believed, depended on public influence. The tone of the final pages of "Civil Disobedience" in fact was mollifying; Thoreau declared that from "a lower point of view" the government, even the Constitution, was admirable, that he had no wish to quarrel, that he would be "but too ready to conform. . . ." He confessed that he willingly paid his highway and school taxes, that he was "desirous of being a good neighbor. . . ." But he drew the line when conformity and passivity became a connivance with injustice, and there was no inconsistency in his thought when he championed the bloody ways by which John Brown upheld the law. Blood was a price he was willing to pay: he was not speaking entirely metaphorically when he said, "But even suppose blood should flow. Is there not a sort of blood shed when a man's conscience is wounded?" A stickler for complicity, he knew that by aiding Brown he was helping him to shed it. The refusal to pay his poll tax was the least of his resistances; he had also forwarded fugitive slaves

[22] J, II, 332-33. This was used in *Walden* (W, II, 355) to justify his own example of self-reform, his belief that the private man can radiate society by the influence of character. In the manuscript version he added: "We would not have a rabid virtue that will be revenged on society, and descends on it, not like the morning dew to refresh it, but like the fervid noon day sun to wither it" (HM 924).

[23] Gruber, *The Education of Henry Thoreau*, pp. 111-12, 141-47. In his essay on "Titus Pomponius Atticus" he had written, "We may not conform ourselves to any mortal pattern, but should conform our every act and thought to Truth." And he had criticized Atticus because in trying to hold to truth he withdrew and avoided offending others. This was passive connivance, and for Thoreau, for whom truth was a weapon that called for use, one could not choose the way of inaction (Sanborn, *Life*, pp. 183-85).

in defiance of the law; he had, in his way, contributed to Harper's Ferry. When, as Alcott complained, "How little is the social compact understood, or felt! Is it not one tissue of selfishness, fraud, and corruption?" [24]—when the state could not purge itself, someone had to further it by the lever of resistance. And this was to act against it. Thoreau could plead for John Brown, could extol his heroism, because he felt that in his own way he had taken comparable risks. He defended Brown as a man of principle.

The justification for such action was not hard to find in a transcendental philosophy that had made Truth the absolute measure of all things. Expediency and conscience were the pivotal terms of Thoreau's essay—expediency represented by Paley, conscience by Thoreau—terms which merely defined politically the larger dualism of Prudence and Spiritual Laws. Though the transcendentalist was a seeker after Truth, who, living in the flux of experience and life, knew that he could never wholly fix it; though, through this very faculty of perception, he had raised men to new dignity and enlarged the scope of democracy, he was nevertheless an absolutist; for him there was a moral law, absolute Truth, Justice, Right. "In politics," Theodore Parker said in the most brilliant clarification of the issues between the sensational philosophy and transcendentalism, "sensationalism knows nothing of absolute right, absolute justice; only of historical right, historical justice." [25] Appealing to human history rather than human nature, the sensationalist considered absolute justice "a whim"; the only right or justice he knew was "political expediency," which, as Thoreau also said, amounted to the rule of might rather than right, and reduced all to the majority principle of the greatest good for the greatest number. And this good, Parker said, "may be obtained by sacrificing the greatest good of the lesser number,—by sacrificing any individual,—or sacrificing absolute good." Transcendentalism, on the other hand, starting from human nature, "appeals to a natural justice, natural right; absolute justice, absolute right." The source of these absolutes, Parker explained, was "the conscience of God,"

---

[24] Shepard, ed., *The Journals of Bronson Alcott*, p. 149.

[25] All quotations from Parker are from his essay, "Transcendentalism." Probably written in the 1850's, it is reprinted in Parker's *Collected Works*, Boston, 1907-10, VI. See John E. Dirks, *The Critical Theology of Theodore Parker*, New York, 1948, p. 77n. It can be more conveniently found in *The Transcendentalist Revolt Against Materialism*, ed. by George F. Whicher, Boston, 1949, pp. 65-83.

—in man, the moral sense or conscience "which is our consciousness of the conscience of God."[26] Instead of making expedient laws, of legislating pragmatically in terms of what had proved serviceable in the past, instead of seeking guidance in historical precedents and facts, the transcendentalist legislated in terms of the idea, he tried to fashion laws that were just because they were a human translation of the divine laws. To defend one's position on historical grounds, to say, as the southern spokesmen did, that slavery had always existed in the history of man, was to deny the transcendentalist's claim that idea anticipates history, that man need not surrender the future to tradition, that he was free to work toward, if not immediately realize, the ideal of justice.

The defense of minority rights, which was one of the contributions of Transcendentalism to democratic thought, was merely a part of a still greater conception of government: that government is moral, a positive agency in the furtherance of justice, that its ultimate test is not the protection of property but the extension of human rights. Everything that Randolph Bourne was later to hammer out in his study of the state was already in "Civil Disobedience," and only the force of denying expediency and coercion made these individual protests appear to be anarchical statements of the theory of negative government. That government is best which governs least was not the real issue—as Thoreau's own belief in the collective spirit of our institutions and his social proposals for lyceums and natural preserves showed.[27] Instead the issue was the end to which the *instrument* of government should be put, to the end of greed or human fulfillment, to material or spiritual uses. In behalf of this view both Parker and Thoreau cited the American Revolution, Parker claiming that "the authors of the American Revolution, as well as the fathers of New England, were transcendentalists" because they had faith in ideas rather than history. They did not yield to tradition. Reading American history in the transcendental way George Bancroft had popularized, Parker said: "The American Revolution, with American history since, is an attempt to

---

[26] See Whitman, "Great are the Myths" (1855):

　　Great is Justice!

　　Justice is not settled by legislators and laws; it is in the soul. . . .

[27] On Thoreau's awareness of the positive uses of government, see John C. Broderick, "Thoreau's Proposals for Legislation," *American Quarterly*, VII (Fall, 1955), 285-90.

prove by experience this transcendental proposition, to organize the transcendental idea of politics. The idea demands for its organization, a democracy—a government of all, for all, and by all [Lincoln immortalized this phrase, but also adopted the notion of "proposition," the view of American history, and the belief which followed in government as the agency of the divine law]; a government by natural justice, by legislation that is divine as much as a true astronomy is divine, legislation which enacts law representing a fact of the universe, a resolution of God."

As for the rights and duties of the individual in relation to government, they were all reduced to the single need "to be co-ordinate with justice." "Only the absolutely right is expedient for all," Thoreau said in the *Week;*[28] and Parker brought his logic to the same conclusion when he wrote, "Legislation must represent that [the immutable morality], or the law is not binding on any man." Man's primary allegiance—the unspecified premise of Thoreau's essay—was not to the state but to nature. For the conscience of the individual, the ideas he was to bring to bear on society, had their source in nature. As one sees in other proponents of natural rights, in Cooper's Natty Bumppo, for example, nature is opposed to the state, the individual to society—man is considered outside of society, free to leave it when it jeopardizes his integrity (free, that is, if there is still open territory in the West) or free to act on it. But he hardly acts within it. The social virtues of the eighteenth century were minimized; one did not conciliate, one reformed society in the interests of justice, and failing this, he had every right to leave it. So Parker said: "By birth man is a citizen of the universe, subject to God; no oath of allegiance, no king, no parliament, no congress, no people, can absolve him from his natural fealty thereto, and alienate a man born to the rights, born to the duties, of a citizen of God's universe. Society, government, politics come not from a social compact which men made and may unmake, but [as Natty and Thoreau attempted to demonstrate] from a social nature of God's making; a nation is to be self-ruled by justice." [29] When man entered the state, therefore, he did so through the portal of justice, binding himself only because the laws were just. "Justice," Parker wrote, "is

---

[28] W, I, 138.

[29] Melville wrote at the end of "The Sermon," *Moby-Dick:* "top-gallant delight is to him, who acknowledges no law or lord, but the Lord his God, and is only a patriot to heaven."

the point common to one man and the world of men, the balance-point." And when he extended this idea to individual ethics which, of course, underlay the social ethics, and wrote the democratic law of human relations so important to Thoreau and Whitman (and to Natty)—"I am to respect my own nature and be an individual man, —your nature and be a social man"—he said, "a scheme of morals . . . demands that you be you—I, I; balances individualism and socialism on the central point of justice . . . puts natural right, natural duty, before all institutions, all laws, all traditions."

This, of course, was a program for the American democratic sentiment. But there was this difficulty: Could one be sure that his ideas had the warrant of conscience? Did all men in their proposals for reform really act from a sense of right? Might not the transcendental politician "take his own personal whims," as Parker warned, "for oracles of human nature?" Might not the Ethan Brands, Ahabs, and Hollingsworths act rashly, "ignore the past, and scorn its lessons," and so destroy society? The danger of the position Parker had outlined was that "the transcendental moralist" might "abhor the actual rules of morality," that in his impatience with the necessity of compromise and the tardiness of social change might resort to absolutism in practice as well as in idea. Transcendental madness was the danger: to "take a transient impulse, personal and fugitive, for a universal law; follow a passion, and come to naught; surrender his manhood, his free will to his unreflecting instinct. . . ." "Men that are transcendental-mad," Parker said, "we have all seen in morals; to be transcendental-wise, sober, is another thing." There were Ahabs by the score at the Chardon Street conventions, few Captain Veres. As far as other reformers went Thoreau was aware of the danger of legislating one's dyspepsia into law, and what saved Thoreau from this predicament was his refusal to use coercion in behalf of his ideas. He was not a reformer in this sense; persuasion and example were his only weapons. For him good government, like Paradise, began at home; social ethics were personal ethics, and the only valuable reform was self-reform. One could avoid the dangers of transcendental madness by limiting reform to oneself. Fortunately for the American, he wrote in *A Yankee in Canada,* the government still let one *"speculate* without bounds." [30] There was still a West as close as Walden Pond, where one could experiment in new worlds, could be the true reformer and dis-

[30] W, V, 83.

coverer of social ideals. It was sufficient for one who would not violate his nature (or another's) to try the experiment and publish the results, letting his character and ideas leaven the lump.

"I had gone down to the woods for other purposes," Thoreau explained his night in jail in *Walden;* "But wherever a man goes, men will pursue and paw him with their dirty institutions, and, if they can, constrain him to belong to their desperate odd-fellow society." [31] When he spoke of the quiet desperation of the mass of men, he said it was not a characteristic of wisdom to do desperate things. But society, as he depicted it in a John Field, Flint, or Deacon Spaulding, was desperate, bound by the routine of custom and tradition, forgetful of "the true necessaries and means of life. . . ." [32] His night in jail had probably been the most unexpected occurrence of the Walden period, and it drove the wedge of society deep into his life and thought. It led to his strictures in "Civil Disobedience," and, what was even more important, provided him with the social framework in which to set his private experiment at Walden, in which, in fact, to make it count socially. Had he not gone to jail, *Walden* might well have been only an account of his spiritual rebirth; as it was, however, placed between "Economy" and "Conclusion," his experiment in renewal became an example of what he considered a true social reform—so much so that the social aspects of the book were more often remembered than the personal ones. Nevertheless, it should be noted that the "other purposes" were primary and that, in his writing, Thoreau subscribed to Margaret Fuller's dictum that the greatest art reveals the course of the aspiring soul.

Walden began with the established social situation, with the long chapter on "Economy"; it ended with an appeal to self-reform, with Thoreau's gift of an ideal prospect and with the greatest of all transcendental gifts, the reminder that "the universe is wider than our views of it," that its fullness and novelty were invitations to a better life, and that men should "not repeat the old error, but leave life as free to those who are to come. . . ." Having himself begun to learn the lesson of his maturity, that "before many summers these things will wear a different aspect," that "incredible changes take place

[31] W, II, 190.

[32] W, II, 9. Thoreau associated desperation with society, wisdom with nature; he began and ended *Walden* with catalogs of desperate behavior.

within the experience of every man," he did not want, any more than Whitman in "Song of Myself," to impose a way of life, but instead to show its larger conditions and to enjoin the reformers, eager to change one fixture for another, not to "stiffen the current of life. . . ." [33] He began with society, therefore, and ended with the individual-in-nature—that is to say, free from any institutional ties; and he began on the surface ("I perceive," he said, "that we inhabitants of New England live this mean life that we do because our vision does not penetrate the surface of things"), turning inward as he fought the duel of his own life, until at the conclusion he approved of the hero who went inward, who explored his "private sea" and the "folds of being." [34] In an age of transcendental-mad reformers he sketched a different reformer, his new hero who explored the sea of being; who by standing outside of society had a fresh perspective and a *"point d'appui"* for his fulcrum. Finding again the natural substratum of things and the immemorial necessities of human life, he could show that all institutions were but impermanent and inadequate attempts to stabilize the movement of life and that they were always behind the needs of the present generation. If nothing else, he could temper the zeal of the social mechanics by forcing them to see the difference between the transient and permanent; and to those who were really bent on reforming their mean and sneaking lives he could show the way, the open road before them.

He had all this in mind when he wrote, sometime between 1848 and 1851, a lecture on reform and self-reform, which seems to have been intended to explain the stand he had taken in "Civil Disobedi-

[33] W, II, 353; Houghton. MS AM 278.5.

[34] The remark on "surface" concluded the introductory sections of *Walden* (W, II, 107) and prepared for the memorable lines: "Let us settle ourselves, and work and wedge out feet downward through the mud and slush of opinion, and prejudice, and tradition . . . till we come to a hard bottom and rocks in place, which we can call *reality* . . ."—lines that explained the experiment he had undertaken and that provided dimensions equivalent to society and the individual-in-nature. In "Conclusion" he again brought this distinction to the reader's attention: "Most have not delved six feet beneath the surface. . . . Yet we esteem ourselves wise, and have an established order on the surface" (W, II, 365). In "Life Without Principle" he used the same imagery. In society "Surface meets surface" and "we do not ourselves rest on an underpinning of granitic truth, the lowest primitive rock." As for self-reform, he now used the imagery of gold mining, as much a phenomenon of the time as South Sea explorations: "Why *I* might . . . sink a shaft down to the gold within me, and work that mine."

ence." [35] Divided between the section on reformers in "Economy" (pp. 80-88) and the section on self-discovery in "Conclusion," this essay, in its essentials, was incorporated in *Walden;* it became the social framework of the book. "He does a service to mankind," Thoreau began the essay, "who shows the insignificance and transitoriness of all institutions compared with a man, and that they should be his tools and utensils, not his law and master." The error in social thinking—the superstition he wished to eradicate—was that of institutional permanence, inviolability, and authority; and the error for which he pilloried the reformers, and which was a part of their madness, consisted "in seeking to establish and give permanence to that which will not establish and perpetuate itself." Acting from within society, legislators and reformers were "the subjects and servants of it," and having "no resting place without it," they were, accordingly, incapable of moving it. Thus Thoreau began by indicating the need for a wider perspective: he would not speak of society from within it, nor even "consider the life of man only within certain limits"; instead, he would "take in the prospect as far as I can see," he would stand outside on the rock of nature, he would see how other men as well as himself had lived in respect to the permanent, believing that by showing the "transitoriness of the partial and false" he would help to "establish the solid and true." He would be radical, as he had been in "Civil Disobedience," by getting to the root or principle of the thing.

Looked at as candidly as the scientist studies astronomy, looked at by "a thoughtful and original man, though solitary," government, he said, had "a very problematical existence." Commonly thought to stand for positive virtue and respectability, it was, for Thoreau, the sum of man's desperation, "a last resort," expressing "the extreme needs of men. . . ." "We are wont to speak of society—of civilized society, at least," he said, "as some great success, and a result to be admired by all men, but consider what a failure and abortion it is." Judged by the result of the experiment—the "respectable and lawful ruin of the individual"—a "civilized human society" was an unrealized dream. It transferred to itself the virtue and respecta-

---

[35] These dates seem likely in view of internal evidence—allusions to the Mexican war and Oregon, and a *Journal* passage of the later date. According to information added to the manuscript by W. A. White in 1904, the two drafts of the essay were versions of "Life Without Principle." This, however, seems to be an error. The manuscript is in The Houghton Library, MS AM 278.5, and all quotations are from this source.

bility found only in individual men, and it forgot that the "character of society when its institutions are freest can only be just as good as the average character of its members, and of course any worthy man is better authority and more respectable." If one considered, then, the character of the man "who has migrated to this New World," considered, as Thoreau did with telling effect, the northern man with southern principles, he would have to grant the conclusion that led Thoreau to civil disobedience: "Under the name of order and civil government we are all made at last to pay homage to and support our own meanness." For government, he explained, "not only murders but it executes [pun]," and, of course, "it never executes justice upon itself, for that would be suicide, but only on those who oppose it." Thus, out of fear, it raised its presumptions of authority and divine sanction, which it took the brave man with "a clear and far seeing eye to discover . . . [were] not wholly divine in their origin or continuance."

Government, furthermore, was a piece of machinery, long since removed from the state of nature with which it was supposed to have begun, no longer limited to "the simple laws of man and nature" but ensnarled in "precedents and succedents," in all manner of fiscal, domestic, and foreign affairs; so complex, as the familiar argument of Paine had once made clear to another revolutionary generation, that it "trips itself up" in its "train of precedents," and requires specialists to arrange and learn "the errors of the fathers." [36] And how distant, to the proponent of simplicity and principle, its true function was! How artificial, how unnecessary, to one who thought of social problems in terms of individual relationships, who believed, along with Emerson and Whitman, that man was the sum of his relations and that he could freely enter into those relations that fulfilled his needs. No wonder, then, that Thoreau was

[36] Like Bourne, Thoreau made the issue one of the elders, of fathers and sons. Of the conservatives, whom he admired in other respects, he said: "He is a dutiful son but a tyrannical father, and does not foresee that unimaginable point of time when the rising generation will have attained to a level with the risen. Rather he is himself a son all his days, and never arrives at such maturity as to be informed that he and such as he are now mankind and the latest generation, the occupants and proprietors of the globe, but he feels it to be his chief duty to preserve the law and order which he finds existing."

For a brilliant gloss on the psychology of authority and liberty, so important to Thoreau's generation, see David Riesman, *Individualism Reconsidered*, Anchor Books, New York, 1955, p. 207, where he links reverence for the past with those views which make much of original sin.

contemptuous of involuntary intercourse, of fire societies, internal and external improvement societies, religious societies, political and civil societies (the latter being reduced in importance by their place in such a series), and asked "of what use these enactments running like cobwebs from man to man, and forming a net work called order of society, when every instant a living man travels from himself, and your cobwebs are left hitched to so many posts." The last and best, the "rarest" of all societies, Thoreau said, was "what is emphatically called good society—or good company— which is the greatest success on this line, & the society movement carried through." He was not thinking of the associative life, but of friendship: "If we will think deeply & from our interest & experience as individuals . . . we shall find that society has no permanent place or existence, but takes place whenever man meets man, and that then there is more of it, in proportion as there is less of what is commonly called society, or the forms and conventions which have grown out of previous meetings. The meeting with a man on friendly terms . . . will be the instantaneous establishment of good institutions and the annihilation of all bad ones."

Thoreau, whom Alcott called "the independent of independents . . . the sole signer of the Declaration, and a Revolution in himself," [37] was not set against reform—for Emerson had said that man was born to be a reformer—but only against those reformers who invented "superior prison disciplines." For how could one reform men by shutting out the light, by directing attention to the rottenness and corruption of institutions, when what was needed was a report of the "soundness and vigor . . . which are the more prevalent & universal facts," when what men needed was a "serener truth" than that of society? Reformers, unfortunately, had "consoled the fears [rather] than satisfied the free demands and hopes of men." What was needed—and it was in meeting this demand that *Walden* served Thoreau's notion of reform—was the record of "a simple and irrepressible satisfaction with the gift of life, a memorable and unbribed praise of God." "When we can praise God," Thoreau said, "we shall not find fault with ourselves nor with mankind."

The infidelity of reformers, however, was but the principal reason for their failure; there were others. If they were sick of tradition and conformity and looked "forward to coming springs with hope," still they submerged the individual in the "We" and "Our." To

[37] Shepard, ed., *The Journals of Bronson Alcott*, p. 238.

advance the "Great Causes" they solicited the cooperation of energetic men like Thoreau, meanwhile enjoying the distinction of speaking brave words which their audiences knew they never intended to enact—for the audience, too, as Thoreau knew, was phlegmatic and "agreed to be the audience," going to the Lyceum night after night, not to be "excited to violence" but "for entertainment and a pleasurable excitement merely." "The modern Reformers," Thoreau said, "are a class of improvvisánti more wonderful and amusing than the Italians." Indeed reform itself had settled into an institution, with its society dinners and its lecture circuits, and its meetings at which resolutions thickened the air but nothing was resolved. But the passage that Thoreau could not refrain from elaborating when he adapted it for *Walden* reduced the motive for reform to dyspepsia: "If anything ail a man so that he does not perform his function [the bowels, he added in *Walden*, are the seat of sympathy]; especially if his digestion is poor, though he may have considerable nervous strength left; if he has failed in all his undertakings hitherto; if he has committed some heinous sin and repents, that is, having done it, is now pretty well aware that he has done it,—what does he do? Why he sets about reforming the world. Do ye hear it, ye Moloffs, ye Patagonians, ye Tartars, ye Nez Percés? The world is going to be reformed, formed once for all. Presto—change!" He could not spare the ridicule, knowing himself how much health was a matter of self-reform, knowing its disciplines, and how much easier it was to meddle with "the exposed roots of innocent institutions" than with his own—and knowing that affliction of the elders, the affirming of "essential disease & disorder to the child who has just begun to bathe his senses and his understanding in the perception of order and beauty. . . ." Before one preached the doctrines of despair and recommended institutions for other men, before one spoke easy words, Thoreau suggested that he cure *his* ailment and that he represent "one pretty perfect institution in himself, the centre and circumference of all others, an erect man." And besides his words he wanted some sample of his wares.[38]

---

[38] Thoreau understood the private reasons for social coercion, the secret sources of moral indignation, even though he spoke of them as dyspepsia. Hence his insistence on the *free* gift, the gift of the healthy man. He did not see, however, that in his attempt to reform friendship he was equally coercive: he asked for the inner life of another, and was willing to expose the sacred privacy of individual life. (It was customary for transcendentalists to circulate

The great benefactors, among whom Thoreau placed himself in this lecture, had of course been "single and singular and not successes of men." Like Thoreau's philosopher in *Walden*, they had been "the progenitors of a nobler race of men" [39]—such benefactors as Minerva, Ceres, Neptune, Prometheus, Socrates, Christ, Luther, Columbus, Arkwright. They had not wasted themselves on petty causes (the so-called "Great Causes" of their day) nor had they chosen their callings "out of those enterprises which society has to offer." They had not become "a spindle in the factory of Society" or shepherds of "the flocks of Admetus." Instead they had obeyed the call of their "divine gifts"—a call which Thoreau knew, since he was speaking for himself, would not "be whither your neighbors and kind friends and patrons expect or desire. . . ." And yet this single and singular way was of the greatest social usefulness, for society needed an "animating soul," and in every society, according to Thoreau's theory of the great man, there must be "at least one individual, its founder and leader, who does not belong to it, but who imparts to it whatever life and efficiency it has. . . ." There must be someone who, respecting the mystery and privacy of human life, makes his life and work a blessing to mankind, who, following his positive inspiration, offers society "some pure product . . . some life got in this old trade of getting a living—some work, done which shall not be a mending, a cobbling, a reforming." What this pure product was, *Walden* was intended to show: the divine gift of morning light, sunset, the hilarity of spring, the serenity of joy of summer, autumn's ripeness, and winter's abundance in silence: [40] the gift of an open world, the freshness of an unexplored nature. The gift Thoreau laid at the feet of society was that of a new world, the actual and imaginary West of men's dreams.[41]

This new world, moreover, was the individual's real self—the permanent soil of man. The westering he advocated, like the reform he preached, was spiritual; the frontier that compelled him was that of the human personality, and he wanted all men to be, as he

their private journals among themselves.) Thoreau would have lost nothing by retaining his manners; indeed, he would have come nearer to the human intimacy he desired. Only in his social thinking, only when forced into relations he didn't need, did he insist on the preservation of privacy.

[39] W, II, 16.

[40] This was also used in HM 924.

[41] See the parable of the artist of the city of Kouroo, W, II, 359-60. Another example was the sun in its orbit, shedding its beneficent light on the world.

too was trying to be, "grown entire to man's estate sound in limb & in spirit, undaunted[,] equal to his hopes." The open nature to the west, fortunately, was the bounty of America that made the new man possible; it stood for the "virgin mould," for the primordial conditions of renewal. But it was also the symbol of new human territories. Westering and exploration, heroic and grand as they were in fact, were still more heroic and grand in a spiritual sense. The blossoms and fruits, "what public and private advantages may push up through this rind we call a man," were the El Dorado he sought. And this new world was as close as Walden; the frontier was wherever a man fronted IT, wherever he enjoyed an original relation to the universe. "Those who dwell in Oregon and the far west," he explained, "are not so solitary as the enterprising independent thinker, applying his discoveries to his own life." The farthest west was "a simple, independent, original, natural life." Thus when he advised as his measure of reform a deepening of roots, he had in mind both the actual and the metaphorical meanings of nature, and since one was the condition of the other, they were indeed inseparable: "Let your roots like those of the willow wander wider[,] deeper[,] to some moist fertile spot in the earth," he wrote, "where are the fountains of life. . . ." But this moist and fertile soil was also the soil of the self, and how inseparable it was from nature could be seen when he contrasted it with the wasteland of society: "Be . . . rooted withall in your native soil of originality and independence, your virgin mould of inexhausted strength and fertility. Nor suffer yourselves ever to be translated again into the foreign and congenial regions of tradition and conformity, or the lean and sandy soils of public opinion."

To explore this new world, finally, was to go inward; the original relation to the universe was the occasion of consciousness, of self-discovery. In keeping with the metaphor of discovery, "Know thyself" became, in *Walden*, "Explore thyself"; and the allusions to geographical discovery, with all they implied of open worlds, suggested a still wider world, the last and always open frontier, the private sea. "Every man is the lord and governor of a realm how infinite in its resources, how unexplored in its length and breadth," Thoreau affirmed. "How infinitely trackless yet impassable we are. Is not our own interior white on the chart? like Central Africa? Here is the centre of Central Africa. Forward is a direction which no traveller has taken." The metaphor was congenial to him, identifying him with the hero he most admired, and now, with the necessity of explaining his own life, it gave his life the grandeur and social value he believed it deserved. He was Melville's solitary mastheader discovering new worlds, venturing out of sight of land, scanning his private sea. But unlike his neighbors he was not "outward bound" in the sense of living "out and out," but "inward bound, retiring in and in, further & further every day," withdrawing deeper "within the folds of being," where, he said, "you may discover it all [all that can delight and astonish] in yourselves." Such exploration, however, demanded "the eye and the nerve": cowards went outward, heroes went inward; few were willing to "fight a duel with [their] lives. . . ." (The spiritual crusader of *The Service* had at last found the enemy.) And when he mentioned the South Sea exploring expedition, he not only hoped to make his metaphor clear in terms of contemporary history, but to draw again the distinction between the safe associative and the dangerous individual life: "What after all was the meaning of that Exploring Expedition, with all its passell[?] [42] and expense, but a recognition of the fact that there are continents & seas in the moral world to which every man is a passage and inlet, all unexplored by him; but that it is easier to sail many thousand miles through cold & storm & savage cannibals, in a government ship, with 500 men & boys to steer & sail for one, than it is to explore the private sea, the Atlantic & Pacific oceans of one's being alone." And though he added in *Walden*, "Be rather the Mungo Park, the Lewis and Clarke and Frobisher, of your own streams and oceans. . . . Nay be a Columbus to whole new continents and worlds within you, opening new channels, not of trade, but of thought," his idea of the reformer was abundantly clear. "It is natural that we should be enterprising," he wrote in the *Journal*, "for we are descended from the enterprising, who sought to better their fortunes in the New World." [43] Thoreau believed himself to be one more such illustrious spiritual explorer, and if he did not leave a "pile of empty cans sky-high for a sign [to guide . . . successors]," he left *Walden*.[44]

II

The *Walden* we know was not the work of the Walden period. Critics, understandably, have assumed that it was from its assured

---

[42] In *Walden* he used "parade" (W, II, 354).

[43] J, III, 270.

[44] W, II, 353. "To guide your successors" was in the manuscript, HM 924.

and affirmative tone. Like Thoreau's autumnal work, however, it was the product of the last decade of his life, a decade of increasingly frequent crises, the testimony of which was all too clear in the thirteen *Journals* of the years from 1850 to 1861. These *Journals* record the desperation of the spiritual seeker who has lost his communion, and fully explain the sense of loss which Thoreau intended to convey in the allegorical passage on the hound, the bay horse, and the turtledove. Elsewhere in *Walden* he confessed that he had become "coarse" and "callous," that he was never awakened by the cockerel, that his seeds of virtue had lost their vitality and did not come up. Even in the chapter on "Sounds," the celebration of ecstasy is of the past and Thoreau had become aware of the owls, of the darker moods they reflected, those of lost hope and "the mortification of all healthy and courageous thought." [45] *Walden* does, of course, memorialize the period of his greatest spiritual success. But like the *Week* it is a work of recollection: it was formed and tempered by the experiences that had followed his success, and it became the kind of book it did because these experiences of loss helped him realize how great and fleeting his success had been. Where the *Week* captured that ecstasy in its freshness, *Walden* captured it in retrospect, and its affirmation, accordingly, was in a different key. It was affirmative—nothing that Thoreau published directly disclosed the gathering despair of his life. But the affirmation was prospective, in the promise rather than the achievement of aspiration. Even the Walden experience to Thoreau in these later years seemed to have been translated into a future possibility. He did not see it so much as an actual success as the way to success. "I know of no more encouraging fact," he wrote, setting the tone of resolution in the book, "than the unquestionable ability of man to elevate his life by conscious endeavor." [46] By 1854 the Walden experience had been altered, not only by the *Journal* materials Thoreau added until the last moment but by the lengthening perspective of despair. Educated by failure, determined now by conscious endeavor to find the way back to his golden age, his affirmation in *Walden* was that of one who had known the darkness but would not submit, who took instead the last refuge of optimism, the faith in faith itself.

When Thoreau wrote *Walden* he was the god in ruins that Emer-

---

[45] W, II, 240, 31, 141, 181, 139.

[46] W, II, 100.

son described at the end of *Nature*. "Once he was permeated and dissolved by spirit," Emerson explained. "He filled nature with his overflowing currents. Out from him sprang the sun and moon. . . . The laws of his mind, the periods of his actions externized themselves into day and night, into the year and the seasons. But, having made for himself this huge shell, his waters retired. . . ." [47] So had it been for Thoreau; at Walden he had had, he said, "my own sun and moon and stars, and a little world all to myself." [48] But in the years following Walden his universe no longer corresponded to him —then, as Emerson said in his fable, "the world lacks unity, and lies broken and in heaps. . . ." But Emerson was not aware when he wrote *Nature* of the dilemmas of subjective idealism; in his heady idealism he believed that "Nature is not fixed but fluid. Spirit alters, moulds, makes it. The immobility or bruteness of nature is the absence of spirit; to pure spirit it is fluid, it is volatile, it is obedient." And he had gone on to proclaim the faith that Thoreau had tried to enact at Walden: "Every spirit builds itself a house, and beyond its house a world, and beyond its world a heaven. Know then that the world exists for you. For you is the phenomenon perfect. What we are, that only can we see. . . . Build therefore your own world. As fast as you conform your life to the pure idea in your mind, that will unfold its great proportions." [49] Emerson was to learn, and Thoreau too, that nature had an existence independent of the mind, that though it was beneficent, its economy also allowed for a spendthrift heedlessness of life. Thoreau, in fact, began to see that nature sacrificed life in order to advance life and that this was the sign of her "health." "I love to see that Nature is so rife with life," he said, "that myriads can be afforded to be sacrificed . . . that tender organizations can be so serenely squashed out of existence like pulp. . . ." [50] The *life* of nature, like the *tendency* of nature for Emerson, became for Thoreau the new anchor of his faith: man might fail, but the tides in nature never failed; season advanced upon season, and life was forever renewed from death and decay. While he recognized the independence of nature, he did not give up his belief in the correspondence of man and nature. If he could no longer so easily cast his mood over nature

[47] C, I, 71.
[48] W, II, 144.
[49] C, I, 73-74, 76.
[50] W, II, 350.

and have freely those inspirations which made nature the source of spiritual life, it did not occur to him to put the blame on nature and thus abandon the theory of nature in which he had invested his life. Instead he accepted Emerson's explanation that "the ruin or the blank that we see when we look at nature, is in our own eye." He took upon himself the burden of guilt and set about to make himself worthy of nature. "The problem of restoring to the world original and eternal beauty," Emerson wrote, "is solved by the redemption of the soul." [51]

The problem of the marriage of the soul with nature, however, was not to be solved only by the redemption of the soul. Now, because the mind did not make nature, one had also to study her phenomena more closely. For when one could no longer project his mood *on* nature, he had instead to find his mood *in* her; he had to know her ways so intimately that he could anticipate them; he had to know the whole of her economy and the laws that governed her changes, so that, anticipating them, he could find in their occasions what was needed by the mind. Thus when the components of his sympathetic union were divided, Thoreau found it necessary, as he had not in his youth, to work at both of them. More and more he became a scientist studying nature for herself, though his pursuit of objectivity was always tempered by a revulsion from the scientific method; and at the same time he practiced a severer asceticism and discipline to the end of purifying the channels of perception. Both were needed. The lesson of the renewal of the seasons, which strengthened his faith and provided the structure of *Walden*, rested on the patient work of the scientist, who after 1850 began the staggering task of charting every change and every phenomenon in the hope of finding in the cycle of the year correspondences to the seasons of man. His ultimate goal, of course, was not scientific, and when he complained that he was becoming a scientist at the expense of the poet, he was not so much lamenting his nature studies (which became more arduous and elaborate) as his inability to humanize them. And this inability, he felt, was due to his own impurity. "What a faculty must that be," he wrote in 1851 in the passage on the marriage of the mind and nature, "which can paint the most barren landscape . . . in glorious colors! It is pure and invigorated senses reacting on a sound and strong imagination. Is not that the poet's case?" [52] He had learned from Emerson that

[51] C, I, 73.

[52] J, II, 413. See also the revealing passage in J, III, 233-34.

purity or virtue was a condition of reading the hieroglyphics of
nature and that "a man's power to connect his thought with its
proper symbol . . . depends on the simplicity of his character. . . ." [53]
For this reason the chapter on "Higher Laws" was the most personally revealing addition to Thoreau's thought after the *Week*. All
he could advise there was the avoidance of uncleanness by working
earnestly, an ascetic of simplicity fortified by labor, like his own
discipline in the beanfield. The unconscious intercourse with nature
of the *voyageur* of the *Week* and of the hunter and fisher (here he
recapitulated his own history) was gone. Now his conscious endeavor was tilling the seeds of virtue, the proper object of the
mature man of lesser innocence; and if this also represented a way
into the processes of nature that was not scientific but sympathetic
and intimate, helping him catch nature in her dishabille, it was
still more valuable as a discipline that controlled "the generative
energy." That energy, Thoreau said, "when we are loose, dissipates
and makes us unclean, when we are continent invigorates and
inspires us." [54] He had always glorified the senses; indeed, it was
here that he contributed so much to the barren landscape of New
England culture. But the problem he faced as he grew older was
that of keeping his senses pure, and in his exasperation over the
fact that they had a health of their own ("we may be well, yet not
pure") it almost seemed, from his images of slimy bestial life, that
the Puritan had returned to extirpate them. Fortunately, he did
not propose to close off the senses, but to purify them. It was simply
that his life had deepened, and that just as he had recognized the
darker sounds of nature, her internecine wars, and wastefulness of
life, so he recognized the reptile in man himself. He did not think
of purity as denial; otherwise he would not have sung the raptures
of joy that his "pagan" life had brought him. Purity, instead, was
but a necessity of the perception and joy for which he lived: "How
watchful we must be to keep the crystal well that we were made,
clear!—that it be not made turbid by our contact with the world,
so that it will not reflect objects." [55] The corollary of this *Journal*
entry of 1853 was his statement in "Higher Laws" that "man flows
at once to God when the channel of purity is open." What he had
not needed to say, but what was implied in the innocence of youth,
now became essential to the innocence of maturity. "Chastity which

[53] C, I, 29. See also C, III, 28.
[54] W, II, 243.
[55] J, V, 453.

includes all temperance or purity," he wrote in the manuscript of this chapter, "is the secret of genius." [56]

The writing of *Walden* became a form of self-therapy, the expression in words of what Thoreau could never again express in deeds, an attempt to create a cosmos. As artist he was attempting to do what Emerson had recommended in "Beauty" (in *Nature*), to embody for contemplation and renewal the idea he had discovered in his experience in nature; and what was so remarkable, when one follows the many courses of his thought in his *Journals* and *Letters*, was his power to do this. In the *Journals* his world was indeed broken and in heaps, but there were already in the correspondence he began with Harrison Blake in 1848 the beginnings of an effort toward redintegration. Those letters were the first crystallization of what he would say in *Walden*, letters which were unsparingly confessional, insistently—truculently—aspiring, and uncompromisingly moral, the bare nerves and compressed spirit of conscious endeavor, a welcome dialogue with himself that, softened somewhat by amplification and dramatization, he later addressed to his neighbors. To know the temper of his mind and the iron resolution of the years following Walden, and the inflexible Spartanism he used to shield his own distress when forced to speak of his life, one must go to his letters to Blake, and for the last years to his letters to Daniel Ricketson; but to understand the necessity of the militancy that offended Emerson, that held his willing disciple Blake in awed submission, and that wounded the more tender-souled Ricketson, one must go to the *Journals*. And there one will find a tragedy of aspiration, a tragedy no less tragic because it was "romantic"—because it was all internalized and played out within the self—and one will excuse, as his friends would have had they known the enormous demands he had made on himself, and as one always does in the presence of bravery, the outward hardness that he offered them.

Perhaps one notices most in taking up these *Journals* a sense of time-serving and waiting. The entries are longer, looser, more anecdotal, more often of the past, and not, as in the first *Journal*, healthily prospective. Though there is more natural description and classification, and an enlargement of social thinking, there is also less of the literary quality of the earlier *Journal*, which is to say,

---

[56] HM 924.

not that his interest in his literary pursuits had flagged, but that he was now literally using his *Journal* to store the raw material of thought. Both the unformed (or uninformed) bulk of the *Journals* and the sense of the past, the nostalgic tone of memory, were the measure of the change that had overtaken him. So, too, were the ascetic and otherworldly strains, and the most apparent sign that he had passed into the autumnal stage of life, the transference of his values to the symbols of dryness, coolness, and night, symbols of purity and the concentration of "intellect" rather than of the luxury and expansiveness of sense.

These years, of course, were not without their upsurge of spirit and moments of ecstasy, but the sad consequence of these gains was a sublime regret, a greater sense of loss, a reminder of the longer periods of vastation and a poignant awareness that, where the seeds in nature were stirring and pointing to flower and fruit, he had "lain fallow long enough." [57] He did not know exactly why this was so, only that he was inspired less frequently and for shorter seasons, and that nothing was so miraculous as the remembrance of his youth.[58] This may account for the fact that, though he was preoccupied with autumnal and winter symbols, in *Walden* the emphatic symbol is spring; certainly, the contrast between his youth and his maturity accounted for the otherwise almost inexplicable sense of impurity (who, one wonders, could have been purer?), and since purity, along with inspiration, had been his in his youth, for the lingering over the springtime itself. For the question he asked as the seasons fulfilled themselves year after year was "shall not a man have his spring as well as the plants?" [59] That he did not seemed to him to be due to the inevitable growth of self-conscious-ness. "After the era of youth is passed," he wrote, "the knowledge of ourselves is an alloy that spoils our satisfactions. . . . If I could wholly cease to be ashamed of myself, I think that all my days would be fair." [60] And again he enjoined in a passage that has its echo in *Walden*, "Remember thy Creator in the days of thy youth; *i.e.*, lay up a store of natural influences. Sing while you may, before the evil days come. He that hath ears, let him hear. See, hear, smell, taste, etc., while the senses are fresh and pure." [61]

---

[57] J, II, 101, 213.

[58] J, II, 33.

[59] J, II, 34.

[60] J, II, 77.

[61] J, II, 330. See the last paragraph of "Natural History of Massachusetts."

Why did he lament again and again "those youthful days!" and wish again to be a child? [62] What was it that he felt that he had lost when he wrote "how much—how, perhaps, all—that is best in our experience in middle life may be resolved into the memory of our youth!" [63] An entry like the following which was more extensive but still typical may tell us:

Methinks my present experience [ecstasy] is nothing; my past experience is all in all. I think that no experience which I have to-day comes up to, or is comparable with, the experiences of my boyhood. . . . Formerly, methought, nature developed as I developed, and grew up with me. My life was ecstasy. In youth, before I lost any of my senses, I can remember that I was all alive, and inhabited my body with inexpressible satisfaction. . . . This earth was the most glorious musical instrument, and I was audience to its strains. To have such sweet impressions made on us, such ecstasies begotten of the breezes! I can remember how I was astonished. I said to myself,—I said to others,— "There comes into my mind such an indescribable, infinite, all-absorbing, divine, heavenly pleasure, a sense of elevation and expansion, and [I] have had nought to do with it. I perceive that I am dealt with by superior powers. This is a pleasure, a joy, an existence which I have not procured myself. I speak as a witness on the stand, and tell what I have perceived." The morning and the evening were sweet to me, and I led a life aloof from society of men. . . . The maker of me was improving me. When I detected this interference I was profoundly moved. For years I marched as to a music in comparison with which the military music of the streets is noise and discord. I was daily intoxicated, and yet no man could call me intemperate. With all your science can you tell how it is, and whence it is, that light comes into the soul? [64]

With all our science, of course, we are as incapable as Thoreau was of accounting for what assuredly had been—so genuine are its accents even in memory—an authentic experience of "grace." And though in dealing with an experience beyond the tools of analysis, and never wholly explicable from the outside, one is indeed irreverent and presumptuous, one can at least try to cover the lapse from ecstasy by giving it a name. We do not know why his God had forsaken him, but that He had is evident, and we can say simply, because Thoreau himself had formulated the conditions of

[62] J, V, 75. His compassionate interest in little Johnny Riordan, brave and innocent, seems to have been a part of his own preoccupation with childhood. See J, III, 149-50, 241-44. His friendship with Alcott may also have been strengthened by this, for the child, as unadulterated innocence, was at the center of Alcott's thought.

[63] J, IV, 460.

[64] J, II, 306-7.

experience in these terms, that he had passed from subjective to objective idealism. In doing so, his loss had been overwhelming. If the change did not destroy the possibility of correspondence, it destroyed for Thoreau the way in which that perception had been an experience of ecstasy.

> Packed in my mind lie all the clothes
> Which outward nature wears. . . .

Proud as this assertion of the projection of mind on nature may seem, for it is a statement of the belief that man makes nature and that the correspondences are in this *act*, one should not overlook the fact that what one projects is not his trivial mood or self, but the spirit of God through him. He is acting, as Emerson said in *Nature*, as the finite agent of God's creative power. Idealism was not in question; the primacy of mind and the symbolic nature of reality remained in either version of idealism. What was in question, however, was the kind of experience for which Emerson's *Nature* was the rationalization, that is, the assimilation of God, the inner appropriation of spirit, the sharing of the circulations of Being. In that experience correspondence could be taken for granted; to read the symbolic character of nature was secondary to the experience that made it possible, merely the proof of the experience, the visible sign of spiritual grace—that sacrament Thoreau, working the problem in reverse, hoped *Walden* would become. One sees this in Emerson's treatment of "Language," where his first two propositions on language are proved by the third—"Nature is the symbol of spirit." [65] And one sees this in the most distinctive aspect of his treatise, the need to go beyond "Idealism" to "Spirit," to find the way out of the splendid labyrinth of one's perceptions by not only claiming the presence of ideas in the mind, but the reality as well to which they correspond. The experience of God's presence almost made projection gratuitous.[66] That was why in his early years Thoreau was less concerned with reading the meaning of natural facts and his writing was less concrete; his life was then an ecstasy, and, as he said, "nature developed as I developed, and grew up with me." But though he read and humanized natural facts

[65] C, I, 25.

[66] Coleridge (*Anima Poetae*, ed. by E. H. Coleridge, London, 1895, p. 136) wrote: "In looking at objects of Nature . . . I seem rather to be seeking, as it were *asking* for, a symbolical language for something within me that already and forever exists, than observing anything new."

with brilliant success for the rest of his life and was undoubtedly
a better writer, he no longer had the *experience* or *life* they had
once occasioned. His inability to see significance effortlessly or
relate his mood to natural fact he correctly accounted for as a
want of inspiration, and a systematic search for meaning—of an
intelligibility in nature that was apart from him—could not recapture it. Where once God had put forth nature through him and
he had possessed God in that experience, he was now trying to find
God *through* nature; though the transcendental triangle of God-
man-nature remained the same, the experience was one way and
not reversible. Once God had set the flow of experience in motion,
now Thoreau had to; and with his growing sense of the otherness
of nature the tides of spirit ebbed, and, no longer living within its
presence, his feeling of emptiness was genuine.[67]

He spoke of his failure as having lost his senses, but it should be
clear that they never failed, or that the only sense that failed him
was not in his vocabulary, the sixth sense of Edwards that opened
the way to the spiritual "sense of the heart." Without this sense, he
could only think the other senses "sensuous," and because, for all
their vitality, they no longer excited him, he began to distrust them
and determined, by purifying them, to make them worthy instruments again. The difficulty here as well as in the externality of
nature was the need for conscious activity. Everything that had
been unconscious and passive had now to be critically overseen,
and the more intensely he disciplined himself and the more de-
mandingly he went in search of the secrets in nature, the more he
lost the blessed passiveness, that sense he so accurately described,
of being acted on by "superior powers," of having "nought to do
with it." That unconsciousness by which he had formerly characterized genius he now replaced with chastity, and he preached conscious endeavor because it was the only way he knew to be true to
his aspirations. He hoped that "this faith and expectation" would
"make to itself ears at length," and that he would at last catch the
strain that "always retreats as I advance." [68] His "fall" from the
paradise of subjective idealism had, of course, not been due to any
willfulness or disobedience, even though the former ecstasy had
been the basis of the pride of self-reliance. Nevertheless, becoming

[67] Thoreau, unknowingly, traced this movement in "Prayers," *The Dial*, III
(July, 1842), 77-81.
[68] J, X, 128-29.

conscious of his own impotence he tried to be more obedient; and just as he recognized that beyond the sounds he heard there was silence, so he became aware of what had been an easy assumption, that "God is silent and mysterious." [69] And even though he learned from his enterprise that he might yet develop with nature, he also knew that what he wanted most required the abdication of activity.

The symbol in terms of which he told this spiritual history was the telegraph harp. The telegraph had been installed in 1851 upon the completion of the Fitchburg railroad, and in the remaining years of Thoreau's life it carried messages for him for which it was never intended. "At the entrance to the Deep Cut," he wrote in 1851, "I heard the telegraph wire vibrating like an aeolian harp. It reminded me suddenly,—reservedly, with a beautiful paucity of communication, even silently, such was its effect on my thoughts,—it reminded me, I say, with a certain pathetic moderation, of what finer and deeper stirrings I was susceptible. . . ." It told him "conclusively and past all refutation, that there were higher, infinitely higher, planes of life. . . ." Such was the message it always bore him: "'Bear in mind, Child, and never for an instant forget,'" Thoreau recorded its communication, "'that there are higher planes, infinitely higher planes, of life than this thou art now travelling on. Know that the goal is distant, and is upward, and is worthy all your life's efforts to attain to.'" [70] But if the telegraph harp reminded him of the stirring music of the spheres of *The Service*, telling him the direction of his march, it also measured his faltering steps. "Few are the days," he wrote in 1852, "when the telegraph harp rises into a pure, clear melody. Though the wind may blow strong or soft, in this or that direction, nought will you hear but a low hum or murmur, or even a buzzing sound; but at length, when some undistinguishable zephyr blows, when the conditions not easy to be detected arrive, it suddenly and unexpectedly rises into melody, as if a god had touched it. . . ." [71] And it was the same with the soul for which the harp had become the transparent image. "So it is with the lyres of bards," Thoreau noted. "Are not inspiration and ecstasy a more rapid vibration of the nerves swept by the inrushing excited spirit, whether zephyral or boreal in its character?" [72]

[69] J, II, 100.

[70] J, II, 496-97.

[71] J, III, 247.

[72] J, III, 247, 175.

In this analogy to inspiration, the passivity of the experience was apparent, but as he extended the analogy the tension of the wire was also seen to play its part. "There is every variety and degree of inspiration," he said, "from mere fullness of life to the most rapt mood. A human soul is played on even as this wire, which now vibrates slowly and gently . . . and anon the sound swells and vibrates with such intensity as if it would rend the wire, as far as the elasticity and tension of the wire permits. . . ." [73] There were still moments when the sound of the harp "melted" him, times when "I have been intently, and it may be laboriously, at work, and am somewhat listless or abandoned after it, reposing, that the muse visits me. . . . It is from out the shadow of my toil that I look into the light." [74] But these occasions were few, and more often the sound did not excite rapture but a sense of loss. In time he associated it with spring and with Greece, in both cases because it prophesied "finer senses, a finer life, a golden age." [75] It reminded him that one needed healthy senses, that nature was only for the virtuous. "It occurred to me," he wrote, "when I awoke this morning, feeling regret for intemperance of the day before in eating fruit, which had dulled my sensibilities, that a man was to be treated as a musical instrument, and if any viol was to be made of sound timber and kept well tuned always, it was he, so that when the bow of events is drawn across him he may vibrate and resound in perfect harmony. A sensitive soul will be continually trying his strings to see if they are in tune." [76] But when he tried his strings he found that he was not in tune, that seldom did the "favorable conditions occur, and the indescribable coincidence" take place, and "then there is music." [77] Instead he reported of the harp that "it is very fitful, and only sounds when it is in the mood" and that "the wire will perhaps labor long . . . before it attains to melody." [78] By 1852 he knew why he had not heard its strain all summer: "Its string is rusted and slackened, relaxed and now no more encourages the walker. I miss it much. So it is with all sublunary things. Every poet's lyre loses its tension. It cannot bear the alternate contraction

[73] J, II, 497.
[74] J, VI, 194.
[75] J, III, 219, 224, 342; J, IV, 458; J, V, 43.
[76] J, IV, 80; J, V, 424.
[77] J, III, 248.
[78] J, IV, 473.

and expansion of the seasons." [79] And finally in the spring of 1854, when *Walden* was in press, he wrote of his despair of plucking his own strings into music by tightening them and seeking the plectrum in nature. "We soon get through with Nature," he began this terse and memorable confession of failure. "She excites an expectation which she cannot satisfy. The merest child which has rambled into a copsewood dreams of a wilderness so wild and strange and inexhaustible as Nature can never show him. . . . How many springs shall I continue to see the common sucker . . . floating dead on our river! Will not Nature select her types from a new fount?" He continued, however, to describe the impasse of objective idealism in terms of the subjective idealism he could never give up. (He had written elsewhere of those youthful days "when the walker does not too curiously observe particulars, but sees, hears, scents, tastes, and feels only himself,—the phenomena that show themselves in him,—his expanding body, his intellect and heart. No worm or insect, quadruped or bird, confined his view, but the unbounded universe was his. A bird is now become a mote in his eye." [80]) Now:

This earth which is spread out like a map around me is but the lining of my inmost soul exposed. In me is the sucker that I see. No wholly extraneous object can compel me to recognize it. I am guilty of suckers. I go about to look at flowers and listen to the birds. There was a time when the beauty and the music were all within, and I sat and listened to my thoughts, and there was a song in them. I sat for hours on rocks and wrestled with the melody which possessed me. I sat and listened by the hour to a positive though faint and distant music, not sung by any bird, nor vibrating any earthly harp. When you walked with a joy which knew not its own origin. When you were an organ of which the world was but one poor broken pipe. I lay long on the rocks, foundered like a harp on the seashore, that knows not how it is dealt with. You sat on the earth as on a raft, listening to music that was not of the earth, but which ruled and arranged it. Man *should be* the harp articulate. When your cords were tense.[81]

Thoreau became aware of his slackening tension in the breakdown of perception. He went about looking at flowers and listening to birds, and even though he enjoyed nature and seemed "more constantly merged in nature," he did not have many spiritual experiences and felt that "Nature is as far from me as God. . . ." [82] When

---

[79] J, IV, 206.
[80] J, V, 75.
[81] J, VI, 293-94.
[82] J, III, 66; J, II, 47.

the robins no longer awakened him, he wondered if he were at fault, and when the spring landscape suddenly "looked uncommonly bare and dry," he read in this his own unworthiness and was encouraged when he was unexpectedly struck by the beauty of a natural object. For now he believed that "the perception of beauty is a moral test." [83] There were times when, sick of his self-concern, he felt that "it is salutary to deal with the surface of things"—"Why have we ever slandered the outward?" he asked. "The perception of surfaces will always have the effect of miracle to a sane sense." But like the moral test of beauty, this miracle merely spoke for his susceptibilities.[84] Thus he wrote that "we begin to die, not in our senses or extremities, but in our divine faculties. Our members may be sound, our sight and hearing perfect, but our genius and imagination betray signs of decay." [85] These signs of decay were everywhere, in the fact that the winter did not "blue" his soul as before, that sounds no longer found any "answering depths" in him, that with every year the lapse was greater, "the mornings are further between; the days are fewer." [86] And when he reviewed his daily work in the *Journal*, there was fact, not insight, to tell him that for all his ardor he had not known nature with the "Indian wisdom" of his youth.

He attributed his decay to many things, but most immediately to the fact that "the world is too much with us, and our whole soul is stained by what it works in, like the dyer's hand." [87] Not only was surveying, which had almost become his profession in these years, trivial and coarsening—he complained that it forced him "to live grossly or be inattentive to my diet"—it kept him from working with and for his nobler faculties.[88] Behind his strictures on economy in *Walden*, and in his insistence on living now, was his own need to make his life whole again by getting his living while living. "A man had better starve at once," he wrote, "than lose his innocence in the process of getting his bread." [89] To him vocation

---

[83] J, IV, 180, 126.

[84] J, IV, 312-13. This effect of nature was physical; Emerson described it in "Beauty" (*Nature*), adding that "the presence of a higher, namely, of the spiritual element is essential to its perfection" (C, I, 19).

[85] J, VI, 80.

[86] J, VI, 165; J, IV, 144, 198.

[87] J, V, 454.

[88] J, VI, 20-21.

[89] J, V, 454. See "Life Without Principle," where this strain of the thought of these years is best expressed.

had always meant getting his life, not his living—that was the driving truth of "Life Without Principle"; he saw his vocation in the grandest terms, and was true to it in *Walden*, to show men how to live. But unable to work with equal industry at his writing because he could not find employment as a lecturer, he wondered while he served Admetus if he had succumbed to "the difficulties of life like other men?" and he asked, "How can a man be a wise man, if he doesn't know any better how to live than other men?" [90] Surveying was the trade he had in mind when he said in *Walden* that trade curses everything it touches, and he had even been harsher in the *Journal* where he wrote that "nothing is so opposed to poetry . . . as business. It is the negation of life." [91] He preached simplicity because it helped preserve his vigor, but also because "no *trade* is simple, but artificial and complex. It postpones life and substitutes death." [92]

He said in his account of his former ecstasy that he had "led a life aloof from society of men. . . ." Now, however, his ties with society were many and stronger, and what he wrote in *Walden* about the snares of society and the freedom of solitude was sharpened by his desire to make a memory a present reality. It was not only the treadmill of routine or the fact that the virtue of men in society was like that of "pigs in a litter" or the mammon worship that disturbed him, but that intercourse with society made one "thoroughly prosaic, hard, and coarse." [93] When he wrote "The Village" he made his point with broad humor, for how could one take seriously the pursuits of men, even their politics, which were so "frivolous" and "trivial," so superficial and secondary? [94] Indeed it was their politics that had begun to pursue him, until, as he said of reformers who called him by his first name and rubbed him "continually with the greasy cheeks of their kindness" and covered him with "slimy benignity," he feared that he "should get greased all over with it past restoration. . . ." [95] It was when he thought of this and the expediency of society that he made the distance from society a condition of purity; but he could no longer travel that distance to Walden, because his own interest in social justice had

[90] J, IV, 246; J, VI, 208-9.

[91] J, IV, 162.

[92] J, V, 445.

[93] J, IV, 397; J, V, 506.

[94] J, III, 461.

[95] J, V, 263-65.

tied him to society. Slavery in all its forms, whether in the over-worked Irish girl or the brutalized farmer or the Negro, disquieted him, and in these years the "hermit" of Walden collected money for the poor Irishman and, as he wrote in *Walden,* harbored and forwarded fugitive slaves.[96] He had been beset with the problem of slavery from the time of the Mexican war—and even earlier if one recalls that his home was a hotbed of abolitionism—and it had been increasingly distracting him, until in the Anthony Burns affair the slavery of Massachusetts itself became unbearable. His native soil, in which he hoped to plant the seeds of virtue, had flowered with rank weeds of injustice. ". . . what signifies the beauty of nature when men are base?" he asked on returning from his usual morning walk. "We walk to lakes to see our serenity reflected in them. When we are not serene, we go not to them. Who can be serene in a country where both rulers and ruled are without prin-ciple? The remembrance of the baseness of politicians spoils my walks. My thoughts are murder to the State; I endeavor in vain to observe nature; my thoughts involuntarily go plotting against the state." [97] The expediency of society made him prize the virtue of nature and hunger for her solitudes, but he was still insufficiently the hermit. When he saw the lily springing from the slime, and drew the analogy of nature and society, he also drew a moral for his own life: "This fragrance assures me that, though all other men fall, one shall stand fast. . . ." Here was a symbol of the "resurrec-tion of virtue," reminding him that, like the lily, he must "enhance the . . . sweetness of the atmosphere. . . ." He could not flee society when the value of life was being depreciated, for he had learned that "life itself being worthless, all things with it, that feed it, are worthless." [98]

Thoreau, then, was unsettled by an age without repose that put society between him and his objects. The "restless, nervous, bus-tling, trivial Nineteenth Century" he made sport of in *Walden* had infected him, if only by making him feel the need to champion principle. But his correspondence with nature was also intermitted by the failure of a society still closer to him, the society of friend-ship. Emerson had found friendship restorative when, with his loss of vigor, nature did not whip his top. Thoreau, however, having

---

[96] J, V, 234, 438.

[97] J, VI, 358.

[98] J, VI, 355-56. All the above was used in "Slavery in Massachusetts."

neither the passport of fame nor Emerson's gift of using men, found that although the perception of natural beauty increased his desire for society, it diminished his fitness for the actual life of parlors.[99] Like the other beatitudes of his life, friendship lived only in memory. "I have an ideal friend," he wrote, "in whose place actual persons sometimes stand for a season. The last I may often miss, but the first I recover when I am myself again." [100] This fine self-reliance, however, was merely the bravery of loss, and, since he did not recover himself so easily as before, did not heal his deepest grief. "To attain to a true relation to one human creature," he said, "is enough to make a year memorable." [101] But he did not attain to any such relations; instead the one on which he had all his life set his heart continued to fail him. Of Emerson he wrote:

Ah, I yearn toward thee, my friend, but I have not confidence in thee. We do not believe in the same God. I am not thou; thou art not I. We trust each other to-day, but we distrust to-morrow. Even when I meet thee unexpectedly, I part from thee with disappointment. Though I enjoy thee more than other men, yet I am more disappointed with thee than with others. . . . Here I have been on what the world would call friendly terms with one fourteen years, have pleased my imagination sometimes with loving him; and yet our hate is stronger than our love. Why are we related, yet thus unsatisfactorily? . . . when I consider what my friend's relations and acquaintances are, what his tastes and habits, then the difference between us gets named. I see that all these friends and acquaintances and tastes and habits are indeed my friend's self. In the first place, my friend is prouder than I am,—and I am very proud, perchance.[102]

Both were proud, indeed, and the criticism of each other that they had once confined to their journals they apparently could no longer withhold. "He finds fault with me, that I walk alone," Thoreau wrote, "when I pine for want of a companion; that I commit my thoughts to a diary even on my walks, instead of seeking to share them generously with a friend; curses my practice even. Awful as it is to contemplate, I pray that, if I am the cold intellectual skeptic whom he rebukes, his curse may take effect, and wither and dry up these sources of my life, and my journal no longer yield me

[99] J, IV, 258-59.

[100] J, II, 48.

[101] J, II, 173.

[102] J, III, 61-62. Much of Thoreau's treatment of the difficulties of friendship is in his poetry, and that is perhaps why Emerson said that his biography was in his verses.

pleasure nor life." [103] But Thoreau was equally hard though honest. After his magnificent tribute to Alcott in *Walden*, he wrote, for all his neighbors to read, of "one other with whom I had 'solid seasons' . . . at his house in the village . . . but I had no more for society there." [104] The enigmatic closing phrase referred to the "old settler" or God, the third party who had made his friendship with Alcott a "society." He had missed this society—that was really his quarrel with Emerson—and even Lidian, who had been the surrogate for his love, was no longer "the morning star or the evening star." [105] The extent of his anguish could be seen in his typical but terrifying withdrawal to the Ideal, in his tortured remarks to Blake on love and chastity,[106] remarks that underlay his concern with "Higher Laws," and in his strange belief that women live closer to their "animal instincts" than men and that one would find "more sympathy in the intellect and philosophy of man than in the refinement and delicacy of woman." [107] One wonders what solace he could find in the belief, so contrary to his needs, that "the heart is only for rare occasions; the intellect affords the most unfailing entertainment," or in a final version that disclosed his real loss, "The pleasures of the intellect are permanent; the pleasures of the heart are transitory." [108] For there was little comfort in the entry on the estrangement of friends and on the value of keeping a journal that followed, that "my thoughts are my company." [109]

Thoreau, of course, was not a cold intellectual skeptic even though he had begun to place his trust in intellect—in the cold and the purity of the Ideal. If spring was a time of love, then winter was the season of his discontent, with this compensation, however, that it was a season of cold and purity and thought. Nevertheless, this gain was accompanied by loss, and finding, as he said, "no fields . . . so barren to me as the men of whom I expect everything but get nothing," the sources of his life began to wither and dry up. "By myself I can live and thrive," he continued, "but in the society of incompatible friends I starve. To cultivate their

[103] J, III, 390.
[104] W, II, 297-98.
[105] J, III, 82.
[106] W, VI, 197-209.
[107] J, II, 116.
[108] J, III, 168, 216.
[109] J, III, 217.

society is to cherish a sore which can only be healed by abandoning them." [110] He did not mean that he could live without friendship, but that in nature he could find solace, and there, by contracting the friendship of the gods, compel the friendship of men. [111] For he wanted most to reconcile his love of nature and of man, the high aspirations that he preserved for himself in nature and the human need to share his life with men. Nothing, however, was more recalcitrant than his friendships; they remained the one relation, notwithstanding the warm descriptions of his friends in *Walden*, that he could not accommodate in his otherwise organic world. His dilemma was shaped by his growing awareness that "those qualities which bring you near to the one estrange you from the other." [112] Unable to accept friendship on anything less than his ideal terms, he chose to give himself entirely to nature, but even here he found in the poverty of perception that he had cut his own roots. As he tried to kindle nature with his own life, he discovered that "Nature must be viewed humanly to be viewed at all; that is, her scenes must be associated with humane affections. . . ." Nature, he found, "is most significant to a lover," and that that lover was "preëminently a lover of man." How bleak his world had become could be seen in the logic of his concluding question and answer: "If I have no friend, what is Nature to me? She ceases to be morally significant." [113]

Under the strain of the stresses of friends and society Thoreau began to lose his vigor, that "vital heat" that was also being rapidly dissipated by ill health. Vital heat, as he used the phrase in *Walden*, stood for physical life and inspiration, for both had been intimately related in his experience, and undoubtedly the organic world of his youth had been held together by his uncommon vigor. He had written in 1852 that "as long as the bodily vigor lasts, man sympathizes with nature," [114] but this only showed that he had become aware of the problem. He tried to solve the problem by seeking his "health" (which again combined the physical and spiritual) outdoors; he wanted again that "abundance of life or health" that had charged his senses when he was young and that had contributed

---

[110] J, V, 86-87.

[111] J, II, 33.

[112] J, III, 400.

[113] J, IV, 163.

[114] J, IV, 155.

to his "intoxication." [115] But his pursuit of nature became so strenuous, and, as Lewis Mumford suggests, his diet so inadequate to his life, that he literally consumed himself.[116] There was irony in the fact that, while he kept "out of doors for the sake of the mineral, vegetable, and animal" in him, knowing that "health requires this relaxation, this aimless life," his life in nature was anything but aimless and relaxed.[117] He might have used nature for health if he had been able to keep, as he once noted with returning confidence, a "meteorological journal of the mind." [118] But now the very possibility of such a journal, which was to become his work in these years, depended on nature; to have his seasons he had to know hers.

The Thoreau who committed his thoughts to his diary even on his walks was the naturalist in search of the seasons of nature who in time even purchased a telescope.[119] Had Emerson read these field notes he would have been disappointed; and it is clear, in any case, that even though Emerson had recorded a comparable ebbing of spirit as early as "Experience," he did not understand the terrible necessity of Thoreau's last years. He described Thoreau's practice accurately enough from the outside, missing entirely the grandeur of the attempt to prove his own philosophy true. And when he called Thoreau cold and intellectual (the very things he himself had once been called!) he was right again, except that he attributed to Thoreau's personality what was truer of his new method of naturalizing. For many of the reasons already related nature had become barren, and the method which Thoreau now adopted in order to find her meaning, in spite of all the fruit it bore in analogies, did not bear any significant crop of inspiration. In fact it was over this method, which he unwillingly used, that he pondered most what had happened to him. If he had been a cold intellectual skeptic he would have found it adequate, and if he was skeptical at all it was over his recourse to the science that murders to dissect, which he found "inconsistent with the poetic perception. . . ." [120]

[115] J, IV, 218-19.

[116] *The Conduct of Life*, New York, 1951, p. 272.

[117] J, IV, 409-10. See also J, IV, 432.

[118] J, II, 403.

[119] J, VI, 166. During these years Thoreau began to use the facilities of The Boston Society of Natural History.

[120] J, VI, 452.

This is not to say that the method of the naturalist is a bad method, but rather that for Thoreau's purposes it was the wrong method, and that his distrust of it, indeed the guilt he felt in consciously employing it, banished the "presence" that he hoped to find.

How far he had come can be seen by returning to the "Natural History of Massachusetts," where he had belittled "measurement and minute description" and had proposed the method of enthusiasm instead of the laborious method of science. "Wisdom," he said there, "does not inspect, but behold. . . . we cannot know truth by contrivance and method" but "by direct intercourse and sympathy." With his "finer organization" he did not need a telescope or herbarium, nor Gray or Linnaeus, and instead of record books he had had "a deeper and finer experience." This finer experience had, of course, been one of ecstasy, an empowering influx the seal of which had been an integrity of impression and an ability to relate fact to human life. Both powers constituted the superiority of poetry over science, and that was why, aware that he was failing in them, he wrote that "every poet has trembled on the verge of science." [121] For he was beginning to be a "microscopic" observer himself. "I fear that the character of my knowledge is from year to year becoming more distinct and scientific," he wrote; "that in exchange for views as wide as heaven's cope, I am being narrowed down to the field of the microscope. I see details, not wholes nor the shadow of the whole." [122] In 1852 he was so absorbed in details that he wrote the year off as one of "observation." He knew, however, that "Nature is reported not by him who goes forth consciously as an observer, but in the fullness of life," that "to such a one she rushes to make her report," [123] and he spoke of this difference in terms of the familiar distinctions between insight and observation and fullness and outline that he had learned from Emerson. "If you would obtain insight," he warned, "avoid anatomy." [124] He knew that he needed a "true sauntering of the eye," or, as he rephrased it, to look "only with the side of his eye." [125] For this had been his method in those youthful days when

[121] J, IV, 239.

[122] J, III, 336-37.

[123] J, IV, 174-75. He wrote that "no mere willful activity whatever . . . will produce true poetry or science." What really mattered was "how much alive you are" (J, VI, 237).

[124] J, IV, 9.

[125] J, IV, 351; J, V, 45.

"no worm or insect, quadruped or bird, confined his view, but the unbounded universe was his." [126] Now he reported that "I have the habit of attention to such excess that my senses get no rest, but suffer from a constant strain." [127] And now instead of "color" there was only "outline," and instead of the "whole truth" only a "particle of it." [128] He had overworked his senses, partly as discipline but also in order to regain his sympathy with nature, and the very thing for which he was striving he lost by striving, that "integrity of impression," that unified vision and sense of relatedness that Emerson had said distinguished the "stick of timber" from the "tree of the poet." [129] Beginning to fall over the verge, he was aware that his knowledge, like that of the man of science, was becoming "timber collected in yards," good, perhaps, for "public works" but not sufficiently humanized for the good of men.[130]

Though his nature study continued without abatement, it is significant that he did not emphasize it in *Walden*, but exemplified instead the kind of observation he had practiced in his youth. If he worked in his beanfield it was to participate in the natural process and to create the conditions in which he could look out of the side of his eye—to recapture in some measure the kind of life he found so admirable in Therien, the woodchopper, and in all "ignorant" men who knew the human uses of things.[131] And if he observed his brute neighbors more closely and measured the pond, it was always for the "tropes and symbols with which to describe his life." [132] What he deplored in the scientist was the inability or refusal to "relate his facts to human life." [133] He did not, as he said in the "Natural History," "underrate the value of a fact," and even though he now realized how true it was that "we must look a long time before we can see," he still labored in the hope that one day the fact would "flower in a truth." [134] That nature did "*fable*" in *Walden*, and every natural phenomenon took the color of his ex-

---

[126] J, V, 75.

[127] J, IV, 351.

[128] J, III, 301, 232.

[129] C, I, 8.

[130] J, II, 138.

[131] J, II, 138.

[132] J, V, 135.

[133] J, II, 138.

[134] W, V, 130-31. In J, IV, 116 he spoke of facts that "fall from the poetic observer as ripe seeds."

perience, must have seemed to him a glorious success.[135] For it proved that he could at least bring his *past* life to the fact, that even if he did not achieve the old ecstasy, the foundations of correspondence were still there, and he could still write the natural history of man. By making this his work, he saved himself from science; and as he learned to accept the inevitability of his loss he limited his ardor to more realizable goals. In effect, he went to nature now, not expressly for his life, but to give it his life (hoping, of course, in this way to earn his ecstasy indirectly), and in doing this he not only humanized the fact, but, as all his writing from *Walden* on testified, humanized himself.

In spite of his gifts for nature study, Thoreau was not a good naturalist, belonging, as he said, to the *"Miscellaneous* Botanophilists" in Linnaeus' classification.[136] The reason, obviously, was that he was never objective, that even when he recorded observations without their effect on him, he was true to his subjective intention by indicating that *he* saw or tasted or smelled, etc. He remained as highly critical of scientific surveys as he had been in his review of them in the "Natural History," reading them only to learn their language.[137] And one suspects that he began his habit of night walks in these years, not only because he frequently spent his days surveying or because he identified night with coolness and purity, but because, as Hawthorne had said of moonlight, it stimulated the play of his imagination. "I am less conscious than in the presence of the sun," he wrote of these excursions; "my instincts have more influence." [138] And if these walks restored his unconsciousness they also helped him, as did his trips to the mountains, to justify his belief that "the idealist views things in the large." [139] Indeed, where all the conditions of his former experience in nature had changed, one thing remained—his belief in the primacy of the mind. And though at times he seemed to speak with all the fervor of the subjective idealist, it was simply because he had found that the work he would have done as a poet, in any case, could still be done. When he was mistaken for a naturalist by a villager who offered him a two-headed calf, he was overcome with disgust, and

[135] J, V, 135.
[136] J, III, 309.
[137] J, V, 42; J, VI, 265.
[138] J, V, 278.
[139] J, VI, 129.

asserted: "I am not interested in mere phenomena, though it were the explosion of a planet, only as it may have lain in the experience of a human being." [140] And when he took up this idea a few weeks later he wrote out his faith: "There is no such thing as pure *objective* observation. Your observation . . . to be significant, must be *subjective*. The sum of what the writer of whatever class has to report is simply some human experience, whether he be poet or philosopher or man of science. The man of most science is the man most alive, whose life is the greatest event. Senses that take cognizance of outward things merely are of no avail. It matters not where or how far you travel . . . but how much alive you are. . . . All that a man has to say or do that can possibly concern mankind, is in some shape or other to tell the story of his love,—to sing; and, if he is fortunate and keeps alive, he will be forever in love." [141]

As always, however, the problem was keeping alive; and when he presented the case in this way he could only recall that once he overflowed with life and was rich in experience, and "pray for such inward experience as will make nature significant." [142] "If you are really a sick man," he acknowledged, "you cannot accomplish so much as if you were well." [143] Nevertheless, he also recognized that science "sees everywhere the traces, and it is itself the agent, of a Universal Intelligence," [144] that if the spirit did not play through him, he could find its laws outside of himself. Year after year he compounded his facts, growing so familiar with them that they did indeed flower into truth. He discovered the law of the seasons, and with it a foundation for either of his conflicting moods: the cycle of the seasons, with the promise, represented by spring, of spiritual renewal; and the linear movement of growth and maturation, represented by the close of the year, which if in no way comparable in joy to germination, still bore the fruit of his original seed. Thus he was able to join his youth and age in a natural continuity and find a tough satisfaction in one of the profoundest truths of man and nature, that ripeness is all. He learned that all things have their seasons, even his lapse, that intellectual contem-

---

[140] J, VI, 206. In 1837 he had written Helen: "What are the convulsions of a planet, compared with the emotions of the soul?" (W, VI, 13).

[141] J, VI, 236-37.

[142] J, V, 135.

[143] J, VI, 237.

[144] J, VI, 4.

plation might well replace ecstasy, and that by obeying this law he was still in the hand of God. For if the inexorable seasons often seemed to be his undoing, and he hoped sometimes to transcend them, he also recognized that by accepting this fate, these human limitations, he might have the compensation of fulfillment.

III

Natural phenomena, as Emerson reminded his generation in *Nature*, have always provided the richest analogies for human life; language, myth, and ritual have sprung from man's interaction with nature. With this Thoreau, of course, was familiar; from the time he read Howitt he had grounded his work in nature. His later work, in fact, might be considered an extension of Howitt's *The Book of the Seasons*, for he too, if more elaborately and less sentimentally, spent his last years preparing a calendar of nature. The comparison, however, serves best to show how far Thoreau had come since his college days, how solidly he had surpassed the nature genre of Howitt. But even more, it helps us see what might easily be overlooked in Thoreau, that though the seasons are the most obvious analogy for the life of man and one which literature has made a common inheritance, Thoreau had to discover the *analogies* for himself. Indeed, it was during his years of crisis, from 1850 on, that he made this his work; and although he published only a fraction of the riches of his *Journal*, it was from this work that he reaped the structure (and its meaning) of *Walden* and the framework of all that he still hoped to do.

Thoreau had always spent his life in nature, but never so purposively as in the years following the Walden experiment. His reasons for the intensification of nature study in these later years were connected, of course, with the breakdown he was undergoing; this is to say that they were complex and that just as he never resolved his subjective and objective idealism, so he never resolved the several purposes of this enterprise. In part, he went to nature for solitude, to heal his social wounds. He also went "to store up influences"—for if he now found it easier to "expand" in his chamber, he still recognized that he had to "lay up a stock of experiences" for his writing times.[145] He went for "health," and even as a naturalist tried to bring himself into the "sound" condition. As a naturalist he was looking for the signs of seasonal change,

---

[145] J, II, 338, 456.

for the order of creation, hoping that the "fits and starts" [146] of each season would find a corresponding mood in him, that familiarity would help him anticipate the occasion, that a year of observation would be followed by a year of insight. His hope here was to "so live that there should be no desultory moment in all my life! that in the trivial season, when small fruits are ripe, my fruits might be ripe also! that I could match nature always with my moods! that in each season when some part of nature especially flourishes, then a corresponding part of me may not fail to flourish!" [147] By means of his science he was trying to prepare the conditions for the unconscious ecstasy of the subjective idealist. "I would fain explore," he wrote in a passage reworked for "Brute Neighbors," "the mysterious relation between myself and these things. I would at least know what these things unavoidably are, make a chart of our life, know how its shores tend, that butterflies reappear and when, know why just this circle of creatures completes the world. Can I not by expectation affect the revolutions of nature, make a day to bring forth something new?" [148]

Initially, his goal was not to chart the seasons only, but to find in every provocative change the permanence of spring. Closer study and the failure of "expectation," however, taught him that natural development was cyclical. "For the first time," he wrote in 1852, "I perceive this spring that the year is a circle." [149] As this bespoke renewal he was heartened, but when it forced him to draw the analogy presented by the "dead stems of the tansy, goldenrod, johnswort, asters, hardhack, etc.," he could only insist that man was not an annual plant, that the cycle did not wholly apply to him.[150] He was to find plenty of evidence of spring even in winter and signs of second growth in fall, but nothing would gainsay the fact that if the round of the seasons brought renewal for nature, it brought only the fruition and withering of the species—that in the cycle, life grew from death. At last he felt that permanence was not to be found in the terrestrial, but only in the celestial order, that the heavens were the proper background for life and that only the sky was permanent. Thus, as we shall see, the image that

[146] J, III, 483.
[147] J, II, 391.
[148] J, III, 438; W, II, 249.
[149] J, III, 438.
[150] J, III, 188.

distilled his faith in the chapter on "Spring" in *Walden* was that of "the transparent pond already calm and full of hope as in a summer evening, reflecting a summer evening sky in its bosom, though none was visible overhead, as if it had intelligence with some remote horizon." [151] His greatest desire was to transcend the inevitable course of life, to have his immortality now; and the artistic victory of *Walden* was that by living through that course with resolution he had earned a new spring, had brought new life out of his decay.

The years from 1850 to 1854 were especially important for the development of Thoreau's attitudes toward the seasons in *Walden* and for the emergence of its leading symbols. The hunger for spring and renewal was the result of these years, but so was the acceptance of autumn and winter, the latter of which at least had often been terrifying to him. One would have expected Thoreau to dramatize the arrival of spring by projecting it against the season of man's discontent. But the winter of *Walden* was a season seemingly as equable as any other, demonstrating Thoreau's belief that for the healthy man all seasons were good, that a man living in harmony with nature would find his fruits in every season. Indeed, it was during the winter that he angled for the pond itself and found the law that, prophesying, sustained his faith in the regeneration of life. That winter became a season of content at all betrayed one of the most significant changes in Thoreau's later years, a growing preference for the autumnal phases of life. Most of his work through the *Week* had exalted the day and the summer, and even in *Walden* he remained true to the experience of "those youthful days" by placing his easiest and grandest communions in the summer season. From *Walden* on, however, his work turned toward night, toward autumn and winter—from the season of sensations to the season of their intellectual harvest. This change was acceptable to Thoreau because, from one point of view, it helped him exchange the lost values of inspiration for those of maturity and expression, and because, from another, autumn and winter had become associated with purity, and their trials with the purification he felt he needed to bring in the spring.

Of all the seasons, summer seems to have been the least attractive during these years. He had, it is true, an upsurge of spirits in the summer of 1851, and after the bleak winter of 1851-52 he wel-

[151] W, II, 344.

comed the spring and summer when he could again immerse himself in sensations. But summer was also his time for surveying, and it began, therefore, to be the season when he felt his impurity most. As he charted the changing seasons more closely summer was associated with heat and dryness and hardness—"Summer," he reported in 1853, "is one long drought" [152]—or it was associated with the sensuousness of rank growth or with the hazy atmosphere that seemed to correspond to his own obstructed vision.[153] "In summer," he wrote of himself, "the animal and vegetable in him are perfected as in a torrid zone; he lives in his senses mainly." [154] By May there was already oppressive heat, all was in full leaf, and the "slimy reptile life" was wide awake; by mid-June in 1852 the drought had begun, and by the end of June the dryness had set in.[155] The freshness and clearness of spring were followed by a sultry, misty atmosphere, and if the earth seemed a paradise, Thoreau still felt the loss of his view of the heavens.[156] "Our view is confined, the horizon near, no mountains," Thoreau wrote of the hazy June weather. "We are more of the earth, farther from heaven, these days. We live in a grosser element. . . . Even the birds sing with less vigor and vivacity. The season of hope and promise is past; already the season of small fruits has arrived. . . . We are a little saddened, because we begin to see the interval between our hopes and their fulfillment. The prospect of the heavens is taken away, and we are presented only with a few small berries." [157] In midsummer, he added later, "we are of the earth,—confounded with it,—and covered with its dust." [158]

By 1854 summer had indeed become the season of lapse, "the trivial season." It made him look back to spring with regret and forward to autumn with longing, for both were seasons of coolness and clarity, the one a season of invigoration, the other of restoration. This preference for spring and autumn was, one suspects, due in part to his ill health which made the heat and heavy atmosphere unbearable (and perhaps explains why at the height of his illness

[152] J, V, 328.
[153] J, IV, 63.
[154] J, III, 70.
[155] J, V, 161; J, IV, 98, 140.
[156] J, IV, 41-42.
[157] J, VI, 361-62.
[158] J, V, 427.

he sought the milder climate of Minnesota). During these years, moreover, he began his search for coolness as an antidote for everything he associated with the hot, sensuous days. He preferred spring mornings and autumn evenings, and welcomed the summer night for the same reasons. For having found his days trivial, he turned to the less profaned night, and he did so not "to skulk in darkness" but because he relished its dewy purity, the "silent, spiritual, contemplative" moonlight, and the "divine suggestions," the strengthening of his "impulses to purity, to heroism, to literary effort even. . . ." [159] These impulses, he now claimed, were never "day-born," and night, the novelty of which seemed to him a new-found "season," became "sacred and glorious," the "long past season" of which he dreamed.[160] Moonlight, in fact, took on the values he had once attributed to the dawn; it was "the earliest and dewy morning light," and now, instead of heralding day, the dawn reminded him of night.[161] As the long past season, night became the time of unconsciousness, identified also with Greece and the wild and the mountaintop. At the same time, however, in terms of the present rather than the past season, the special value of night, as of autumn and winter, was that its coolness enabled him to "collect and concentrate" his thoughts.[162] With his growing distrust of the senses, he began to insist on the intellect, on the "cooler moments" when sensations (inspirations) could be worked into art. For with Emerson, who distinguished the receptive and constructive phases of the mind, Thoreau, in these years when his ecstasy yielded "so little fruit," would have given anything for concentration, for the power to report his experiences in "gold-leaf," if not in "solid gold." [163] To the lecturer and writer, furthermore, the seasons served immediate vocational needs: summer, at best, was a time to store up influences, autumn and winter the time for making them yield their expression. A "noctivagus," then, his walks were "pernox but not perniciosus," [164] one sign merely of the gradual shift in his life toward the seasons of maturity. "The morning hope is soon lost," he had found, "in what becomes the routine

[159] J, II, 265, 306; J, III, 273; J, II, 249, 284, 286-87.
[160] J, II, 287, 284.
[161] J, II, 249-50.
[162] J, V, 358. See also J, II, 390.
[163] J, II, 468-69.
[164] J, III, 273.

of the day, and we do not recover ourselves again until we land on the pensive shores of evening, shores which skirt the great western continent of night. At sunset we look into the west. For centuries our thoughts fish those grand banks that lie before the newfoundland, before our spirits take up their abode in that Hesperian Continent to which these lie in the way." [165]

The day, of course, was the epitome of the year, and noting this correspondence, Thoreau had written that "after middle age man ceases to be interested in the morning and in the spring." [166] He retained his interest in spring, however, to the extent that he never lost his hopefulness. The spring never failed to invigorate him, especially after the long imprisonment of winter; for, in spite of its many associations with inwardness, thought, self-reliance, and purity, winter also reflected the horror of his own barrenness. "Now a man will eat his heart, if ever," he wrote in November, "now while the earth is bare, barren and cheerless. . . ." [167] Even the cricket, whose chant symbolized for Thoreau the eternal earth song, ceased its singing when the ground began to freeze with the approach of winter.[168] There were compensations, however, in this season in the inner and indoor life of thought: "The seasons were not made in vain," Thoreau argued. "The winter was made to concentrate and harden and mature the kernel of his brain, to give tone and firmness and consistency to his thought. Then is the great harvest of the year, the harvest of thought." [169] There was the suggestion, too, of purity and the courage to undertake a new start: "Is the great snow of use to the hunter only, and not to the saint, or him who is earnestly building up a life?" [170] But when he stirred out of doors it was not so much for the special glories of winter as it was to find the signs of hardiness and the earliest signs of spring. Whenever he found green grass, lichens, or other green-leaved plants he was delightfully shocked; but the phenomena which excited him most and which became major symbols in *Walden* were the return of the bluebirds, robins, and sparrows, the thaws, and the breaking up of the ice. All three represented the

[165] J, VI, 53.
[166] J, V, 385, 393.
[167] J, V, 520. See also J, IV, 405.
[168] J, III, 109.
[169] J, VI, 85.
[170] J, VI, 43-45.

hidden intelligence of nature, the unfailing operation of law, a responsiveness to changes more subtle than Thoreau could observe. "Birds are the truest heralds of the seasons," Thoreau wrote, "since they appreciate a thousand delicate changes in the atmosphere which is their element, of which man cannot be aware." [171] He recognized that birds and flowers were the real harbingers of spring, and in one description of the seasons he went on to identify summer with leafing and shade, and autumn with fruit—a scheme to which he added the distinctions of color, atmosphere, and the stages from youth to manhood. In another description, however, spring was identified as the season of water—"the reign of moisture"—summer of heat and dryness, winter of cold; [172] and it was as symbols of moisture that the melting earth and ice attracted him. A December or January thaw, which he first recorded in the winter of 1851-52, and which increasingly interested him, always seemed a miracle to him, a relenting of the gods in the midst of winter.[173] He associated this phenomenon with the deep cut through which the railroad passed on the southwest shore of Walden Pond, and with the telegraph which followed the right of way. From his first entry, that "the artist [God] is at work in the Deep Cut," and from later observations, he created in *Walden* the richest symbol of the renewal of life, a symbol, however, that spoke for his rebirth as well as nature's: "The clay in the Deep Cut is melting and streaming down, glistening in the sun. It is I that melts, while the harp sounds on high, and the snow-drifts on the west side look like clouds." [174] And it was the same for the breaking up of the ice: "Walden [he reported in 1853] is melting apace. . . . It is glorious to behold the life and joy of this ribbon of water sparkling in the sun. The wind blows eastward over the opaque ice . . . till it slides on to the living water surface, where it raises a myriad brilliant sparkles . . . an expression of glee, of youth, of spring. . . . It is the contrast between life and death. There is the difference between winter and spring." [175] He had, of course, been aware of the "circulations" before, but now, when he reflected on the fact (and its correspondence to him) that in summer the rushing waters ceased

[171] Houghton. MS AM 278.5.

[172] J, V, 328.

[173] J, III, 161.

[174] J, III, 226.

[175] J, V, 28-29.

and the streams became narrow and turbid, the clear and sparkling floods of spring became one more symbol of the vigor and purity of his youth.

Spring was always the season of hope, when life awakened to a gentle warmth, like a hard, closed pine cone which had resisted all other attempts to open it.[176] Not yet oppressive, the spring warmth bore the fragrance of flowers and moist earth and made him feel young again, if only by restoring the vitality of his senses. In the spring of 1852, and again in the spring of 1853, whose glories were transcribed in *Walden*, he felt again the complete correspondence between himself and nature. "It is a genial and reassuring day," he recorded in the spring of 1853. "The softness of the air mollifies our own dry and congealed substance. I sit down by a wall to see if I can muse again. We become, as it were, pliant and ductile again to strange but memorable influences; we are led a little way by our genius. We are affected like the earth, and yield to the elemental tenderness; winter breaks up within us; the frost is coming out of me, and I am heaved like the road; accumulated masses of ice and snow dissolve, and thoughts like a freshet pour down unwonted channels." [177] For a brief interval, at least, there was no need to lament, as he had in "The Thaw," that "I, alas, nor trickle can nor fume," for now he did indeed "thaw and trickle with the melting snow" and mingle "soul and body with the tide" and "through the pores of nature flow." [178] And it was at such times that he was encouraged to "set out once more to climb the mountain of the earth. . . ." [179] Phenomenon after phenomenon in that memorable spring, from the faint peep of the reviving hyla to the opening willow catkins (which in still later years became a major symbol), challenged again the spiritual pluck of the old soldier of *The Service*. "Men were born to succeed, not to fail"— that was the answer he found in the spring to "despair and postponement." [180] He awakened earlier now in a joyful and expectant mood, having, he said, "an appointment with spring"; and it was a double awakening, from his nocturnal and diurnal slumbers. "We burst through the thallus of our ordinary life with a proper ex-

---

[176] J, IV, 495.
[177] J, V, 34.
[178] Bode, ed., *Collected Poems of Henry Thoreau*, p. 107.
[179] J, V, 35.
[180] J, V, 36.

ciple," he said, "we awake with emphasis." [181] Such mornings were truly "mornings of creation," when the world seemed to be beginning anew, when, he said, "men are new-born" and "have the seeds of life in them," when he no longer felt impelled to look back into the night, but "to a dawn for which no man ever rose early enough." [182] Then he felt "as if we had migrated and were ready to begin life again in a new country, with new hopes and resolutions"—he launched his new boat, he heard the telegraph harp more frequently now that the boisterous winds of winter had ceased, and once again he resolved not to be a scientist.[183]

This ecstasy was prospective, however, like his resolutions, a strengthening of himself for the inevitable heats to come. For he had studied the year sufficiently to know that his best seasons were brief: spring and autumn were each of two months' duration, summer and winter of four.[184] And if he always felt the barrenness of winter, after the genial seedtime and sprouting of spring, he felt a comparable horror of the long months of heat and growth. When he was young there had been some satisfaction in growth, but now he associated it with the lapse of hope, with hardening and coarsening, with impurity and sin. Emerson had written that "what we are, that only can we see," and Thoreau's awareness in these years that "filth and impurity are as old as cleanliness and purity," that "to correspond to man completely Nature is even perhaps unchaste herself," must have seemed to him a reading of his own unworthiness.[185] By May he feared that the sound of the toads would no longer be musical, knowing now that it could be traced to "slimy pools," and that all their singing had been about "toad-spawn." [186] He recognized, too, the obvious phallic form of mushrooms and toadstools; and the excessive luxuriance of some flowers—the flower itself being a sexual organ—led him to the heart of his personal testimony on chastity in the letter to Blake, that "fertile flowers are single, not double." [187] Many of the signs

---

[181] J, V, 36.

[182] J, IV, 478.

[183] J, V, 37, 39, 43, 45.

[184] J, IV, 404. He tried to shorten winter by making December an autumn month and February a spring month (J, VI, 112).

[185] C, I, 76; J, III, 255. See also J, IV, 126, 149.

[186] J, V, 161, 112; J, IV, 31.

[187] J, III, 324. In the letter to Blake he wrote: "The *luxury* of affection—there's the danger." He had a suspicion also that his relation to Lidian was

of manhood, of which surveying was one, made him feel that "Pegasus has lost his wings; he has turned a reptile and gone on his belly." [188] Indeed, the reptilian imagery of *Walden* (as well as the imagery of carrion) dates from these years of surveying, when, living "this slimy, beastly kind of life, eating and drinking," he felt that he had become "the very sewers, the cloacae, of nature." [189] With all the horror of Roderick in Hawthorne's "Egotism; Or, The Bosom Serpent," he felt that once he had swallowed a snake. "Is there not such a thing as getting rid of the snake which you have swallowed when young," he asked, "when thoughtless you stooped and drank at stagnant waters, which has worried you in your waking hours and in your sleep ever since, and appropriated the life that was yours?" His renewed interest in Oriental purification rites, in bathing, contemplation, and disciplines, was his attempt to catch the snake "boldly by the head and draw him out," curled though it might be about his "vitals." [190] Part of the anxiety, of which these images were bred, was due to his sense of stagnation, of being muddied: "My nature may be as still as this water," he wrote, "but it is not so pure, and its reflections are not so distinct." [191] To keep his crystal well pure, he felt that he had to bestir himself; when the summer became tropical, slumbering like "a serpent that has swallowed its prey," activity itself became a mode of cleanliness, a way of avoiding the mosses, algae, lichens, and fungi that "plant themselves on all quiet surfaces"—a way of remaining "awake." [192] "Sometimes," he wrote, "the one side of a man is pasture for fungi . . . he being partially rotten." [193]

Just as Thoreau had looked with increasing eagerness for the signs of spring in winter, so now, by July, he was looking for the signs of autumn in summer. To autumn—the actual season of his life—he transferred many of the values of spring, even finding

not entirely pure, and he asserted that "man is capable of a love of woman quite transcending marriage," that the end of this relation was not "propagation, but rather the maturation of the species." He also related this pure love to spring (W, VI, 207; J, II, 184-85).

[188] J, III, 5.

[189] J, II, 9.

[190] J, II, 393.

[191] J, III, 404.

[192] J, V, 328; J, III, 246. Activity was also a way of energizing the mind (J, II, 472).

[193] J, V, 503.

more satisfaction in the later season because in this "rejuvenescence," this "sort of attempt at a spring," his restoration had been earned by the summer's ordeal.[194] The presage of fall reminded him of "the end of life," but it also reminded him that the true end of life was maturity, that the fruit was to prove the flower of spring, that even the idle summer had been necessary because the richer colors of autumn were "the fruit of the dog-days, heats of manhood or age, not of youth." [195] The rising waters of the river, the clearing of turbid pools, the returning birds that filled the summer's silence, the coolness and the crystalline atmosphere, and the blooming autumnal plants—all these were the phenomena of a second spring, signs of regained purity. And this purity was not that of the late-flowering tobacco pipe, the protected whiteness of which turned black in the sun—its "untried virtue cannot long stand the light and air"; instead it was the tried and seasoned virtue of the pokeweed, all brilliantly purple, "beautiful both with and without berries, all afire with ripeness." Here was the "emblem of a successful life. . . ." "It excites me to behold it," Thoreau wrote. "What a success is its! What maturity it arrives [at], ripening from leaf to root! May I mature as perfectly, root and branch, as the poke!" [196] For he was seeking now not "the purity of infancy," as he said of the partridge, but "a wisdom clarified by experience." [197] Like " 'the dry, pearly, and almost incorruptible heads of the Life Everlasting,' " the purity he sought was not in the bud of youth, but in the fruit of asceticism, "beyond change and decay, not lusty but immortal. . . ." [198]

The wood thrush, whose "pure and unmatchable melody" filled the summer woods and symbolized his longing for wildness, now vied with the "serene and cool" sound of the cricket.[199] When he heard its chirp in the spring, "not so wildly melodious, but . . . wiser and more mature than that of the wood thrush," he was already advised of autumn: "With this elixir I see clear through the summer now to autumn, and any summer work seems frivolous. . . . At one leap I go from the just opened buttercup to the

[194] J, II, 99.
[195] J, IV, 267, 108.
[196] J, V, 347-48, 393-94.
[197] W, II, 251.
[198] J, IV, 307.
[199] J, V, 254, 292-93; J, VI, 327.

life-everlasting. . . . the summer is for time-servers." [200] Again, in
the following spring, the crickets suggested "lateness"—

but only as we come to a knowledge of eternity after some acquaintance
with time. It is only late for all trivial and hurried pursuits. It suggests
a wisdom mature, never late, being above all temporal considerations,
which possesses the coolness and maturity of autumn amidst the aspiration of spring and the heats of summer. To the birds they say: "Ah! you
speak like children from impulse; Nature speaks through you; but with
us it is ripe knowledge. The seasons do not revolve for us; we sing
their lullaby." . . . It is no transient love-strain, hushed when the incu-
bating season is past, but a glorifying of God and enjoying of him forever. They sit aside from the revolution of the seasons. Their strain is
unvaried as Truth.[201]

This ripeness and wisdom, like the crickets' song, was the reward
of the evening, increasing with the year, becoming the foremost
sign of autumn; it was associated with the reddening of the year,
with October or the sunset month, and with the sunset itself, which
Thoreau now observed with more devotion because it symbolized
for him the purifying of the day. Both earth and sky, the earth
song of the cricket and the western blaze, had the same essential
meaning for him, that of having attained at last a serenity im-
pervious to the changes of time. "I think," he wrote, "you never see
such a brightness in the noonday heavens as in the western sky
sometimes, just before the sun goes down . . . like the ecstasy which
we [are] told sometimes lights up the face of a dying man. That
is a *serene* or evening death, like the end of the day.[202] Then, at
last, through all the grossness which has accumulated in the atmosphere of the day, is seen a patch of serene sky fairer by contrast
with the surrounding dark than midday, and even the gross atmosphere of the day is gilded and made pure as amber by the
setting sun, as if the day's sins were forgiven it." [203] He added

[200] J, V, 158.

[201] J, VI, 290-91.

[202] He seemed reconciled to this: "May my life be not destitute of its Indian
summer, a season of fine and clear, mild weather in which I may prolong my
hunting before the winter comes, when I may once more lie on the ground
with faith, as in spring, and even with more serene confidence. And then
[the imagery is Bryant's] I will [wrap the] drapery of summer about me and
lie down to pleasant dreams. As one year passes into another through the
medium of winter, so does this our life pass into another through the medium
of death" (J, II, 481-82). Thoreau's reflections on death begin at this time.

[203] J, III, 159.

elsewhere that "in proportion as I have celestial thoughts, is it necessary for me to be out and behold the western sky before sunset. . . . That is the symbol of the unclouded mind that knows neither winter nor summer. . . . That is the hue, that the purity, and transparency, and distance from earthly taint of my inmost mind. . . ." [204]

He felt better in the autumn, and the radiance of health and activity, of course, did much to glorify the season. "Fair thoughts and a serene mind make fair days," he said. "As the skies appear to a man, so is his mind." [205] But the days were also fair because he had himself reached the season of fruits and had found a ripeness in himself. When he closed the chapter on "Solitude" in *Walden* with his praise of the restorative powers of nature, of spring and morning air, he took his inspiration from the passage on the beautiful maturity of the pokeweed. Out of his sense of having successfully passed through "the irresistible revolution of time," out of his deepening awareness that "everything is done in season" and that everything has its appointed time, he could accept the necessity of each season, however barren, and even gladly welcome his response to these changes as a sign that he had not hardened irreparably into old age.[206] He could now say that " 'nature' is but another name for health," that one should "live in each season as it passes; breathe the air, drink the drink, taste the fruit, and resign yourself to the influence of each. . . . Grow green with spring, yellow and ripe with autumn." [207] If at times he despaired of his lost hopes, as in the familiar passage on the youth who gets his materials together to build a bridge to the moon or a palace or temple, and in middle age concludes to build a woodshed with them, he also recognized in the fact that trees have two growths in the year—a spring and an autumn growth—a hardier hope. "So is it with man," he said, thinking of the trees checked in their growth by the cold of winter and the drought of summer: "most have a spring growth only, and never get over this first check to their youthful hopes; but plants of hardier constitution, or perhaps planted in a more genial soil, speedily recover themselves, and, though they bear the scar or knot in remembrance

[204] J, III, 200-201.

[205] J, III, 201.

[206] J, IV, 336, 317, 240; J, III, 363, 366.

[207] J, V, 394. See also J, III, 70.

of their disappointment, they push forward again and have a vigorous fall growth which is equivalent to a new spring." [208] And when he carried the analogy to the reddening plants of fall, he said that this "second flowering" of the whole plant was "to celebrate the maturity of the fruit." "The first," he explained, "to celebrate the age of puberty, the marriageable age; the second, the maturity of the parent, the age of wisdom, the fullness of years." [209] His hope in the spring, to be worthy of reporting the glory of the universe, was still alive in the fall, when, feeling the rich heaviness of his honey and his wax, he again affirmed that his profession was "to be always on the alert to find God in nature, to know his lurking-places. . . ." He was still searching for "the springs of life," and because he was, he could write a book vibrant with spring in the autumn of his life. [210] Though the cycle from spring to autumn, with its griefs and scars, was sufficiently tragic, and he had paid for his ticket to heaven by going through limbo, purgatory, and hell, there was still enough glory in the autumn to make possible the writing of *Walden,* especially when the coarser flour of his experience had been sifted into "Life Without Principle." Indeed, in these years the writing of *Walden* was the ripening of his fruit and a harvest which did not fail when the drought destroyed the corn. [211]

---

[208] J, IV, 227-28.

[209] J, IV, 308.

[210] J, III, 351; J, II, 470-72.

[211] I have borrowed this metaphor from J, VI, 486-87, where Thoreau spoke of preparing his lectures as the threshing of his grain: "The lecturer must commence his threshing as early as August, that his fine flour may be ready for his winter customers. The fall rains will make full springs and raise his streams sufficiently to grind his grist." In this work of preparing his "crop of experience" for market, Thoreau was able to use his lesser inspiration and find in this the reward of his autumn years.

Chapter VII

WALDEN: OR, THE METAMORPHOSES

My mind is bent to tell of bodies changed into new forms. Ye gods, for you yourselves have wrought the changes, breathe on these my undertakings, and bring down my song in unbroken strains from the world's very beginning even unto the present time.

—Ovid, *Metamorphoses*, I, 1-4

. . . there is but one great poetic idea possible to man—the progress of a soul through the various forms of existence.

—Margaret Fuller, "Goethe," *The Dial*, 1841

Some men's lives are but an aspiration, a yearning toward a higher state, and they are wholly misapprehended, until they are referred to, or traced through, all their metamorphoses.

—Thoreau, *Journal*, 1851

I

What Thoreau finally published on August 9, 1854, some seven years after his experiment at the Pond, was a fable of the renewal of life. The intervening years had given him much to say; he wanted, among other things, to provide a guide for students and a manual for self-reform, to record his actual experience in the woods and to defend his vocation, and to write a modern epic of farming. But most of all he wanted to set to rights again all his relations with men, society, and nature, to create again out of the chaos of his life a cosmos, to bring in again the eternal spring of the Golden Age. Written in the years of his decay, in the realization that "spring will not last forever," *Walden* was Thoreau's attempt to "drain the cup of inspiration to its last dregs." [1] Whatever its public intention, its personal intention was therapeutic: if it was his attempt to say his say once and for all, to give the world, as he said when he contemplated the unspoken wisdom of Bill Wheeler's life, "the benefit of his long trial," it was also his attempt, in Schiller's phrase, to "keep true to the dream of thy youth." [2] By enacting his aspiration in words, he was trying to sustain himself against loss. "What can be expressed in words," he told Blake, "can be expressed in life." [3] He was still haunted by the stirring injunctions of Emerson's *Nature:* idea alters circumstance, and by conforming one's life to the idea in one's mind, one builds his own world. That, indeed, was the dream of his youth, and as he looked back over the years of trial the benefit he felt he had to give the world was not the present fact of his inability to express it in life, but rather the glorious fact that he once had, and that he might again by resolution, discipline, and heroic hope. "Did you ever hear of a man," he asked Blake, "who had striven all his life faithfully and singly toward an object and in no measure obtained it? If a man constantly aspires, is he not elevated?" [4] *Walden* was a fable for renewal, a book of metamorphoses, a record of earning one's life, simply because what Thoreau was actually expressing in words he was expressing in his life. In fact, *Walden* was not so much an account of a past ecstasy—though of course it was that—as it was an account, actualized in terms of his former life in the woods, of his aspirations, of his desire for self-transcendence and self-union.

The book that finally appeared was obviously not the book that had been announced for publication earlier. [5] For as a work of

[1] J, III, 221.

[2] J, III, 195-98.

[3] W, VI, 163.

[4] W, VI, 162.

[5] In the preface to the manuscript version (HM 924) Thoreau wrote: "Nearly all of this volume was written eight or nine years ago in the scenery

recollected experience (and not recollected in tranquillity) it had a second growth, germinating slowly in the *Journals* of the years following his experiment. New material, of course, had been added, but something more important had happened: the original Walden experience had become a symbol, an experiment, an action, that he could use to bind together the many things he had to say. The value of keeping a journal, its function for the writer, was that it helped him perform this symbolizing process—as the critic who sorts the entries in Thoreau's fashion discovers. "Each thought that is welcomed and recorded," Thoreau said, "is a nest egg, by the side of which more will be laid. Thoughts accidentally thrown together become a frame in which more may be developed and exhibited. . . . Having by chance recorded a few disconnected thoughts and then brought them into juxtaposition, they suggest a whole new field in which it was possible to labor and to think." In this way, he found, "my own writings may inspire me and at last I may make wholes of parts." [6] We have already seen the new fields that the *Journals* of the years following Walden opened to him; they suggest that the original *Walden* might only have been another more elaborate excursion, faithful, as all his writing was, to his own experience and to his belief that the themes of literature are always close by, but not that greatest literature which records "the world of thought and of the soul"—the "permanent" literature that all transcendentalists hoped to write.[7] At most, it would have been another *Week*, which belongs in the "permanent" class, but which is too much a static ecstasy, a trip to heaven without the tickets to limbo, purgatory, and hell, a book that speaks almost directly from the soul and that does not carry the soul through its various forms of existence. Indeed, it was out of his knowledge of these forms of existence that *Walden* took its final form.

& under the circumstances it describes, and a considerable part was read (at that time as lectures) before the Concord Lyceum. In what is now added the object has been chiefly to make it a completer & truer account of that portion of the author's life." According to the records of the Concord Lyceum, however, Thoreau lectured twice, in February, 1847, on the "History of Himself" (Emerson noted that he spoke about his housekeeping at the Pond), and in January, 1849, on "White Beans and Walden Pond" (see Hoeltje, "Thoreau as Lecturer," p. 491; Rusk, ed., *The Letters of Ralph Waldo Emerson*, III, 377-78). In the interest of establishing the truth of his narrative, Thoreau, of course, claimed more than a close study of the book will bear. Much was added after his experiment, not only completing but transforming the book.

[6] J, III, 217.
[7] J, III, 212.

Though Thoreau was always "sincere"—his test of a writer—he did mislead many readers by adhering to another rule for writing: that the hero hide his struggles.[8] He criticized reformers for not opening the prospects of hope, and he said that he did "not propose to write an ode to dejection. . . ."[9] But this did not mean, as many still infer, that he could not have written such an ode, that he did not have the materials for one in his life. We are inclined today to make much of the metaphysical principle of evil, even to use it as a critical measure of writing—to say that an Emerson or Thoreau did not know evil, as if this evil came in a shape other than lapse, inadequacy, or vastation, to say nothing of what Emerson called the Whiggish facts; as if anyone, especially men of such acute sensibility, could avoid it, could mount their hope on any less substantial foundation. How could we read them at all, if we thought that they did not speak to our condition, and out of the inevitable human condition? Now if he had wanted only to report his ecstasy, Thoreau might have given, as he proposed many times, an account of one day well spent in nature. But he was more concerned with telling how ecstasy was earned, how life was got, how, in the *absence* of these necessities, one deliberately remade his life. The loss behind *Walden* could only be inferred in this change from having to getting, in the pitch of resolution, in "Higher Laws," in his attribution of desperation to his neighbors (he remarked at the end of "Spring" that "through our own recovered innocence we discern the innocence of our neighbors"),[10] and, most of all, in the structure of the year.

It was, of course, a book of hope, of seasoned hope, and for his purposes the year provided a better structural pattern because it was larger and included, in a way impossible to the day, the actual details of the seasons of man, all sorts of details of growth and development and striving, the metamorphoses which now seemed to him the most important fact of life, the new basis of hope. He could have all the symbolic equivalents of the day—and, indeed, he made as much of the morning as he had in the *Week*, the significant difference now being his insistence on wakefulness. At the same time he could be true to his new knowledge of trial

[8] He admitted that he could tell a tale of failure but that he put a brave face on things.
[9] W, II, 94.
[10] W, II, 346–47.

and discipline and seasonal weather by using symbols of gradual transformation: ice-thaw-flux; seed-flower-fruit; grub-chrysalis-butterfly; symbols, too, that in every case carried the change from lower to higher forms, from fixity to fluidity, from innocence to ripeness, from larval sensuality to aerial purity. He could spend a day in rapt contemplation as Whitman did in "Song of Myself"— "Sounds" was his record of such a day—but, what was more important, he could actually participate in the processes of building and renewing his world. Planting his seeds and harvesting his crop, clearing his land and building his hut—these were the solid activities of renewal, a history in brief of the course of agriculture from "a state of nature to the highest state of cultivation," and a literal foundation on which a number of spiritual truths could be raised.[11] A day was sufficient, of course, as a symbol of the experience of possessing the world, but now that he had to make a new world, a day was not long enough. *Walden* was written in the awareness that eternity is purchased in time, that, as Emerson said, "the years teach much which the days never know." [12]

When Thoreau, "for convenience," put the experience of two years into one, when he saw that his experience was "a fable" with a moral and that such a fable would make wholes of parts, the *Walden* we now have was finally under way.[13] Making wholes of parts had always been the most difficult thing for the transcendental writer who obeyed his genius rather than his talent, and Thoreau saw his own problem magnified in 1852—the year in which he seemed most preoccupied with the problems of composition—when he heard his friend Channing deliver "the most original lecture I ever heard," a lecture, however, that desperately needed some controlling idea. "How much more glorious if talent were added to genius," he remarked of the lecture, "if there [were] a just arrangement and development of thought, and each step were not a leap, but he ran a space to take a yet higher leap!" [14] Only the day before he had pondered on the need for "the true cement" for his thoughts and had concluded that the best solution was a fable with a moral. "The truth so told," he explained, "has the best advantages of the most abstract statement, for it is not the less

[11] J, III, 328.
[12] C, III, 69.
[13] W, II, 93-94; J, III, 239.
[14] J, III, 249. See J, III, 108.

universally applicable." [15] He was thinking, as he had during the composition of the *Week*, of the much-needed "myth," of that action which would give his thought concreteness as well as universality and at the same time make the thoughts of different periods in his life cohere. He had succeeded relatively well in finding one for the *Week*, and he was to do even better in *Walden*, for the myth he used not only served as the frame and foundation of truth, but put his thoughts in those natural relations in which he had found them.[16] One compensation of his years of decay was that he was forced to rely more on his talent, and his talent, as Channing justly recognized, was architectural. "The impression of the 'Week' and 'Walden' is single, as of a living product, a perfectly jointed building," Channing wrote; "yet no more composite productions could be cited." Both books, and later writing like "Wild Apples" and "Autumnal Tints," possessed "this unity of treatment," were products of his "constructing, combining talent." [17] For unlike most of the earlier work and the excursions, where the unity was provided by the experience itself, the later and major writing had an imaginative unity; they were the only works in which Thoreau took the liberty to alter the experience to suit his convenience, the only works in which symbol was below as well as above the texture, the very structure itself.

As a lecturer and a writer, Thoreau's experience had been similar to Channing's: he had never found an audience willing to give the needed close attention or to follow him on his own ground. He had only scorn in the *Week* and *Walden* for easy books, and in his exasperation he said that his generation hated "any direct revelation, any original thought," as "it hates virtue." [18] Prophets or transcendentalists were not wanted by the lyceums. He found, however, that his facts, if not his allegory, were often welcome, and he learned by the time he was writing *Walden* that the facts that flowered in the field would flower in books. But although he recognized the importance of the fable and admitted the need for a more orderly presentation, he did not intend to meet his audience by descending to partial truths—things "said with references to certain conventions or existing institutions, not absolutely." Instead,

---

[15] J, III, 239.

[16] On the need for a "rounded" truth see J, III, 465.

[17] *Thoreau: The Poet-Naturalist* (1902), p. 39.

[18] J, III, 119.

he said that he would speak with still "deeper references" and that to understand his words the reader himself would have to be "translated." [19]

The problem here, of course, was at the very heart of the transcendentalist's vocation as writer: how to get the reader to take the spiritual view. In the concluding pages of *Walden* Thoreau remarked that "in this part of the world it is considered a ground for complaint if a man's writings admit of more than one interpretation." [20] At the very beginning he had teased the curiosity of his neighbors (and has since teased many scholars) by telling them in allegory and whimsey something of how he had spent his life. But he teased with a purpose: he was instructing them in how to read his book, in how to cure their "brain-rot"; for the truth he wanted to express, "his facts," would be "falsehoods to the common sense." "I would so state facts," he said, "that they shall be significant, shall be myths or mythologic." [21] This is what he meant in *Walden* when he wrote that "I fear chiefly lest my expression may not be *extra-vagant* enough. . . ." [22] Extravagance, or exaggeration as he sometimes called it, was his way to truth. "It is only by emphasis and exaggeration," he wrote in his criticism of Gilpin, "that real effects are described"—and the kind of exaggeration he was considering here he employed in his description of the pond in "Where I Lived, and What I Lived For." [23] In a letter to Blake he warned, "I trust that you realize what an exaggerator I am,—that I lay myself out to exaggerate whenever I have an opportunity,—pile Pelion upon Ossa, to reach heaven so." [24] His most difficult problem in *Walden* was to get the reader above the level of common sense, that is, to see from the inside rather than the outside, to get beyond his frame of reference. To do this, he did indeed lay himself out, not only by creating a structural perspective by incongruity in the opposition of civilization and nature, but by his use of history, anthropology, and reading, by paradox, humor, irony, ridicule, and

---

[19] J, III, 85-86.

[20] W, II, 358. See Canby, *Thoreau*, p. 243, where Thoreau's Aunt Maria is quoted as saying: "I do love to hear things call'd by their right names, and these *Transcendentalists* do so transmogrophy . . . so transmogrophy their words and pervert common sense that I have no patience with them."

[21] J, III, 99. See also W, VI, 94 on levels of meaning.

[22] W, II, 357.

[23] J, IV, 339.

[24] W, VI, 220. See also J, I, 411-12; J, VI, 100.

scorn, by philological puns, by parables, by dramatization, by utopian prospects, by emphatic polarities, by every variety of symbolic statement.

All this was merely to say that fact alone was not truth but the means to truth, and that, like his contemporaries Emerson, Hawthorne, Melville, and Whitman, he wanted the "volatile truth" that betrayed "the inadequacy of the residual statement." [25] He would have considered *Walden* a failure if it served only to communicate an eccentric's refusal to go along with society, as it did to most reviewers in his day, or if his "faith and piety," the fragrance of his words, were reduced to pap, as in our day, for tired businessmen long since beyond the point of no return. He told his readers not to look into the ashes for the sublimates, he reminded them that the verses of Kabir had four levels of meaning, and, like Whitman, who compared the untranslatable natural expression of his barbaric yawp to that of the hawk, Thoreau said that it was a "ridiculous demand . . . that you shall speak so that they can understand you," that "neither men nor toadstools grow so." [26] His protestation was defensible because, symbolist though he was, his symbols were not private: mystery, not mystification, was his goal. He wanted his residual statement to be natural, to translate itself and the reader as easily as any natural fact. Even his "deeper references" were natural—the reality in nature—and he was justified in believing that his residual statement, the actual record, would translate itself because nature was a universal language whose correspondences were guaranteed by the very structure of the universe. If his fable, as he claimed, was not obscure ("my shallow meaning is but too clear"),[27] its deeper meanings were; and not because he did not do everything he could, but because, as all symbolist writers discover, his readers had to be taught to read. To read *Walden* the reader had to learn how to read nature, as Thoreau pointed out in the chapters on "Reading" and "Sounds." He had little sympathy for mass culture: "Why level downward to our dullest perceptions always," he wrote, "and praise that as common sense?" He intended to speak "like a man in a waking moment, to men in their waking moments" [28]—though he did his best to use *Walden* to awaken his

---

[25] W, II, 357.

[26] W, II, 356, 358; HM 924.

[27] HM 924.

[28] W, II, 357.

readers. And had he taught them to read he would have taught them as well all that he was attempting to do in *Walden*—and what Emerson had tried to do in *Nature* and Whitman would try to do in "Song of Myself"—to stand in an original relation to the universe and to read its meanings for themselves: "How to live. How to get the most life. . . . [How to] go in search of the springs of life. . . ." [29]

II

In *Walden* Thoreau followed his advice to Channing: he ran a space in order to take the higher leap. He began with surface before he spoke of depth, with the transient rather than the permanent, with complexity before simplicity, disease before health, tradition and routine before the free, uncommitted life— with society and commodity before self and spirit. He wrote Blake that "to set about living a true life is to journey to a distant country, gradually to find ourselves surrounded by new scenes and men"; but before he told of the new country he had discovered, he described the old.[30] Like Emerson in *Nature* he began with the prudential, rising through the progressive uses of nature to spirit. Indeed, most of Emerson's treatise was embodied in *Walden:* "Commodity" in "Economy"; "Nature" and "Beauty" in "Sounds" and "Solitude"; "Language" in "Brute Neighbors"; "Discipline" in "Reading," "The Beanfield," and "Higher Laws"; "Idealism," "Spirit," and "Prospects" in "The Pond in Winter," "Spring," and "Conclusion." For that matter, Emerson's "Experience," which accounted for the philosophy of *Nature* in psychological terms, as a dialectic of spirit, was also embodied: Illusion, Temperament, Succession, Surface, Surprise, Reality, Subjectiveness—all the "lords of life" were there, as well as a similar progression from spiritual emptiness and that suspicion of "our instruments" which Emerson attributed to the fall of man, to that miraculous moment, born of engaging in actual everyday life, when life again revealed "its inscrutable possibilities." [31]

Thoreau began *Walden* on the familiar ground of "Economy," at the actual point at which he found his neighbors and himself. Here he rehearsed his own history, both past and present, of getting a

---

[29] J, II, 470, 472.

[30] W, VI, 160.

[31] C, III, 75, 53.

living. He began his book with a genuine, practical, Yankee problem; but his concern with economy, though Yankee in its means, was spiritual in its ends. The problem, he told Blake, "is not merely to get life for our bodies, but by this or a similar discipline to get life for our souls; by cultivating the lowland farm on right principles, that is, with this view, to turn it into an upland farm." [32] Indeed, the sting in his whole treatment of economy was the determination not to get a living in the accepted but rather in the spiritual sense, with its assumption that there were necessities of the soul that were not being satisfied by the instituted ways of life, that "the country is not yet adapted to *human* culture, and we are still forced to cut our *spiritual* bread far thinner than our forefathers did their wheaten." [33] He had found, he wrote Greeley, that to have time for writing he did not need to earn his bread by the sweat of his brow, that six weeks of manual labor would support him in his simple life for a year.[34] He had also found that one need not accept the servitudes of economy any more than the servitudes of politics, that one could be free, if daring and hardy enough, to use society rather than be used by it.[35] And he had found—and this was perhaps an even more direct blow—that work itself, even the discipline of cultivating his beans, was not a duty, the penalty of man's fall, as the Puritans supposed, but a form of joy, a way to personal growth. "There is no play in them," he said of the desperate, "for this comes after work." [36]

Thoreau was assailed by reviewers in his day not only for his withdrawal from society and for making work a pastime but for his doctrine of simplicity, which seemed to them a renunciation of all the goods of a civilization whose progress was measured by the increasing flow of things. In our time, however, we have almost made the virtue of simplicity *the* moral of *Walden*, accepting it, at least when goods are scarce, in the narrowest sense Thoreau had in mind when he wrote: "The unlimited anxiety, strain, and care of some persons is one very incurable form of disease; simple

---

[32] W, VI, 212.

[33] W, II, 44.

[34] W, VI, 170-71.

[35] In "Civil Disobedience" (W, IV, 381) he said: "I will still make what use and get what advantage of her [the state] I can, as is usual in such cases."

[36] W, II, 9.

arithmetic might have corrected it. . . ." [37] The economic anxiety for which he prescribed simplicity, however, was merely the most obvious symptom of still deeper anxieties, of the fact that life had lost its savor and purpose, had become fixed and external; and he himself had simplified his life, not in the spirit of denial but because he valued human life and its richer possibilities. "One's life, the enterprise he is here upon," he said, "should certainly be a grand fact to consider, not a mean or insignificant one. A man should not live without a purpose, and that purpose must surely be a grand one. But is this fact of 'our life' commonly a puff of air, a flash in the pan, a smoke, a nothing?" [38] It is true, of course, that much of "Economy" told how he had gone without, and that he made the most of the bravery of his renunciations; but what was really central was that he had experimented to find out just how important the commodities of life were. Simplifying was not so much doing without as seeing what was essential, that is, whether or not things served the grand ends of human life, if possessions helped one possess life; and that was why, in order to make his point, his strategy was so reductive. He had learned from the economy of nature that "the grand necessary of life for the brute creation is food; next, perhaps, shelter, *i.e.* a suitable climate; thirdly, perhaps, security from foes." [39] These were the essentials on the commodity level of life, necessary to any higher life, and he did not deny them. But in the business metaphors that ruled the chapter he wanted to see how far one needed to be *mortgaged* to them. His conclusion (actually the belief he used "Economy" to prove) was that they were not so important as society—materialistic society—assumed, that they were, as they seemed on the level of brute creation, the means, not the ends of life. Like Emerson in "Commodity" he indicated the mediate uses of nature: ". . . this mercenary benefit," Emerson said, "is one which has respect to a farther good. A man is fed, not that he may be fed, but that he may work"—or, as Thoreau put it when he returned to the subject in "Conclusion," "Were preserved meats invented to preserve meat

---

[37] J, I, 436. One is reminded of Carlyle's remark: "The Fraction of Life can be increased in value not so much by increasing your Numerator as by lessening your Denominator."

[38] J, IV, 430.

[39] J, III, 459.

merely?" [40] Nature, in all her bounty, could be cruel, if man made commodities, the goods of life, his final good: she could put a house and barn on one's back, and make anxiety out of one's necessities.

Thoreau did not consider simplicity a palliative, as the way to make the best of an abhorrent condition. Indeed, his own example showed that he had adopted it to be rid of the condition, to seek his freedom from society, to clear away inessentials, the "trifles," to use Emerson's word, that frittered away one's life. "To the rarest genius it is most expensive," he wrote in the *Week*, "to succumb and conform to the ways of the world." [41] Simplicity was but the first requirement of perceiving the "grand fact," of preserving the "vital heat" without being "cooked *à la mode*"; [42] to simplify was to make significant, to discover principles, and in his own economy it served this end. He had always lived a simple life, partly because he was not an economic man, but also because he had accepted Emerson's view that "the poet's habit of living should be set on a key so low that common influences should delight him," and because, in his role of social critic, he found that one could only speak truly (absolutely) from the vantage of "voluntary poverty." [43] In terms of his own immediate desire for renewal, however, simplification (and "Economy") became a representative anecdote of *Walden*, for he went to the Pond to recover the reality he had lost, to find it again by reducing the problem of perception to its simplest terms—man and nature. Simplification, in this sense, was his ascetic, the severe discipline by which he hoped to concentrate his forces and purify the channels of perception; and because of this he often substituted "poverty" for "simplicity," thereby hal-

[40] C, I, 14; W, II, 353.

[41] W, I, 362.

[42] W, II, 14-15.

[43] C, III, 29; W, II, 16. See Shepard, ed., *The Journals of Bronson Alcott*, p. 261: "Emerson said fine things last night [January 5, 1852] about 'Wealth,' but there are finer things far to be said in praise of Poverty, which it takes a person superior to Emerson even to say worthily. Thoreau is the better man, perhaps, to celebrate that estate, about which he knows much, and which he wears as an ornament about himself. . . ." Van Wyck Brooks pointed out in "The Literary Life in America" (1921) that in America there was no alternative—no aristocratic tradition and no tradition of voluntary poverty—to the bourgeois life (*Three Essays on America*, New York, 1934, p. 203). Both Alcott and Thoreau might be used in the creation of a tradition of voluntary poverty.

lowing the process with religious associations of renunciation and higher dedication. In 1857, bringing to the surface the submerged imagery of *Walden*, he wrote,

By poverty, *i.e.* simplicity of life and fewness of incidents, I am solidified and crystallized, as a vapor or liquid by cold. It is a singular concentration of strength and energy and flavor. Chastity is perceptual acquaintance with the All. My diffuse and vaporous life becomes as the frost leaves and spiculae radiant as gems on the weeds and stubble in a winter morning. You think that I am impoverishing myself by withdrawing from men, but in my solitude I have woven for myself a silken web or *chrysalis*, and nymph-like, shall ere long burst forth a more perfect creature, fitted for a higher society. By simplicity, commonly called poverty, my life is concentrated and so becomes organized, or a Κόσμος, which before was inorganic and lumpish.[44]

Society as Thoreau found it, however, was the cause of his diffuse and vaporous life—that "false society of men," in the lines he quoted from Chapman, that "for earthly greatness/All heavenly comforts rarefies to air." [45] Society and its economy were but the symbol of his own external or empirical self. Society was not only the grubbing of a John Field but the grublike condition, as he implied in "Higher Laws," when he compared the gross-feeding man to the larva, and said that "there are whole nations in that condition . . . whose vast abdomens betray them." [46] The kind of simplicity he had in mind, accordingly, could hardly be practiced *in* society, for, as the above passage indicated, simplicity was a simplification *from* society, a withdrawal from its larval state to nature, where the transformation he sought could take place. And that transformation would be a purification because Thoreau heaped on society all the associations of his lapse: the slimy, bestial, torpid, reptilian life; coarseness, sloth, and sensuality; rot and stench. Nature, therefore, became the crucial term, the place of spiritual alchemy, and, as the dramatic action of *Walden* suggested, the symbol of his rejection of society. But it was also only the middle term in the progression from a lower to a higher society: nature was not Thoreau's final goal, but rather the place of renewal, and out of it, as his own utopian descriptions of ideal human relations and communities revealed, he hoped would come a higher, a spiritually or inwardly formed—that is, an organic—

---

[44] J, IX, 246-47.

[45] W, II, 37.

[46] W, II, 238.

society.[47] He did not propose nature as a permanent mode of life, any more than Emerson did in his treatise; he proposed it rather as a re-creative process of spiritualization, whereby one sharpened his sight and discovered again, in an organic world so unlike society, the possibilities and the principles of a new life. One went to nature to lose society, to die out of the old world, to find oneself and the foundations of a new world.

He went to the woods, therefore, to try this experiment, with no intention of abandoning society or of going primitive. Instead, by beginning from scratch, he would relive all human life and history and test the achievement of civilization by what he found, hoping, of course, to demonstrate that choice was still possible and to re-orient society by showing what had been lost on the way.[48] What he had done for himself he wanted above all to do for society: to join the primitive virtues—whether of the American Indian or the Homeric Greek—to the genuine virtues of civilization; to join country and city, nature and society, sense and thought; to make the organic communion and harmony and joy of the one the foundation of the other. "It is surprising," he remarked, as if discovering it anew, "how much room there is in nature. . . . I enjoy the retirement and solitude of an early settler." But he went on to say: "and yet there may be a lyceum in the evening, and there is a book-shop and library in the village, and five times a day I can be whirled to Boston within an hour." [49] It is too easy to forget in Thoreau's description of the ecstasy of the wild that he would have missed the advantages of civilization, that his problem of doing without society would have been simple if his problem had not been doing with it. After all, he read Homer and wrote a book in the woods, and, except for his retired situation, he lived a remarkably civilized and social life. Indeed, this had been part of his satisfaction: he had gone to nature because, among other reasons, it permitted an

---

[47] In "Literary Ethics" (C, I, 175) Emerson wrote: "The reason why an ingenious soul shuns society, is to the end of finding society."

[48] In a narrower sense Thoreau also relived the history of Concord. His aim was well described in 1856 when he wrote: "Human life may be transitory and full of trouble, but the perennial mind, whose survey extends from that spring to this, from Columella to Hosmer [a Concord farmer and friend of Thoreau], is superior to change. I will identify myself with that which did not die with Columella, and will not die with Hosmer" (J, VIII, 245).

[49] J, IV, 478-79.

uncluttered and simple life, giving him time to be truly civilized.[50] And one of the paradoxes he exploited in making this point was that society did not civilize men, but barbarized them; reduced them, in fact, to a level of want below that of the savage. It was the simple self-sufficiency and adjustment to environment of the Indians (and of the woodchopper, too) that appealed to him, not their elementary demands on life, and had he gone to Typee he would have been as impatient to leave as Melville had been. Primitivism, he learned with some disenchantment on his trips to the forests of Maine, was at best only tonic. And in his *Journal* he wrote that "the savage lives simply through ignorance and idleness or laziness, but the philosopher lives simply through wisdom. In the case of the savage, the accompaniment of simplicity is idleness with its attendant vices, but in the case of the philosopher, it is the highest employment and development. The fact for the savage, and for the mass of mankind, is that it is better to plant, weave, and build than do nothing or worse; but the fact for the philosopher, or a nation loving wisdom, is that it is most important to cultivate the highest faculties and spend as little time as possible in planting, weaving, building, etc." In developing this thought, he came to the conclusion that his own stance as philosopher in *Walden* should have made clear: "There are two kinds of simplicity,—one that is akin to foolishness, the other to wisdom. The philosopher's style of living is only outwardly simple, but inwardly complex. The savage's style is both outwardly and inwardly simple." What he disapproved of was "their limited view, not in respect to *style*, but to the *object* of living," pointing out that the "view" was everything, that "a man who has equally limited views with respect to the end of living will not be helped by the most complex and refined style. . . ."[51] It was the primitive style, therefore, that attracted him, not the "barren simplicity of the savage," and this is what he meant when he said that "the civilized man is a more experienced and wiser savage."[52]

[50] Undoubtedly he had been influenced by Pythagoras and by the Hindu scriptures. In 1841 he had written of the latter: "The simple life herein described confers on us a degree of freedom even in the perusal. . . . Wants so easily and gracefully satisfied that they seem more like a refined pleasure and repleteness" (J, I, 277-78).

[51] J, V, 410-12.

[52] J, VI, 336; W, II, 44.

He simplified not to economize time but to spend it, to shed the burdens of planting, weaving, and building; and after the novelty of his account of his life wore off and the sense of freedom it created faded away, his audience still measured him by the limited view, and considered him, as his neighbors always had, a spendthrift. He was aware of this, of course, for it was the atmosphere in which he lived his life.[53] That was reason enough for trying to meet his audience with "Economy," rather than with a truer title such as "The Art of Life"—and that was why he employed humor rather than contempt, which would have been so easy for him. "Economy" had a serious, weighty, utilitarian significance for his audience; they may have wondered what the village saunterer could say on so grave a subject; but it was also a word of many meanings which Thoreau could exploit to reverse the judgment of his neighbors on his own perverse way of living. Their interest had been caught, of course, by the curiosity they had for his unusual life in the woods, but he kept it by speaking of what he had done in the current coin: in dollars, cents, and half cents. He calculated his life for them, reducing it to a pittance; but the irony, of course, was that on so little he had got so much *life*, that he did not carry a house on his back (though in the case of the Hollowell farm he was tempted), or possess a corner of the world, but had all the landscape for his own, time (which Franklin said was money) to read, to sit idle all day, to walk, boat, fish, to saunter at his ease and enjoy those bounties of nature that society had not yet, nor ever would, package and sell. "Give me the poverty," he exclaimed triumphantly when cursing Flint, "that enjoys true wealth." [54] He had a self, too, that he could hug, one that was not at the beck and call of others, twisted and thwarted by innumerable demands and responsibilities which were customary but not essential. Though he figured everything closely and knew the value of means, he was hardly a good bourgeois, neither a Robinson Crusoe nor a Benjamin Franklin. He was, of course, a plebeian himself, who, schooled in economies, kept strict accounts and paid his debts, and where he could tried to get the best price for his wares, but he abjured getting and spending. His economy was spiritual: to get and spend one's life. Thus, though *Walden* was as autobio-

[53] He was the idler who had once set fire to the woods. In the opening remarks of the manuscript of *Walden* (HM 924) he joked about the owl and the cock lecturing on astronomy when they should have been asleep.

[54] W, II, 218.

graphical as Franklin's story of his youth and middle years and in its ·way a model for success (Thoreau told Blake, however, that he had "no designs on men at all"),[55] it undermined the Franklinian virtues and the goal of comfort they served. Bookkeeping left off with the means of life; there was no schedule for spending a day— how different Thoreau's day in "Sounds," where even the train provided a contrast to his own timekeeping—and no instrumental method of earning virtue. There were none of Franklin's social virtues and only scorn for his do-goodism. And the way to wealth, Thoreau might have said (for behind his remarks he was poking fun at the patron saint of State Street and Main Street), was not the way to health. When he wrote Blake, who was trying to use *Walden* for his guide, he gave the spirit of his economy: "It is surprising how contented one can be with nothing definite,—only a sense of existence. . . . O how I laugh when I think of my vague, indefinite riches. No run on my bank can drain it, for my wealth is not possession but enjoyment." [56]

Indeed, the way to wealth was the way to lives of quiet desperation. That was what he wanted to tell his neighbors, and that their mean and sneaking lives were not of the nature of things—that, as he had discovered in his own case, meanness robbed one of his birthright. Had he not learned from his own experience that economy was only the first chapter of life (as it was of his book)? And had he not learned that the cure, like the anxiety if not the disease, was individual? That self-reliance was the only remedy? He spoke in the first person, then, not only because he felt that it was more honest, but in order to emphasize the individual, to show that "life" is an individual affair with unlimited possibilities of choice, and that however much one lived in society, the balance, the experience, was finally reckoned in the soul. Having already wit-

[55] W, VI, 259. In this letter Thoreau also wrote: "To what end do I lead a simple life at all, pray? That I may teach others to simplify their lives?— and so all our lives be *simplified* merely, like an algebraic formula? Or not, rather, that I may make use of the ground I have cleared, to live more worthily and profitably? I would fain lay the most stress on that which is the most important,—imports the most to me. . . . As a preacher, I should be prompted to tell men, not so much how to get their wheat bread cheaper, as of the bread of life compared with which *that* is bran. Let a man only taste these loaves, and he becomes a skillful economist at once." That is why Thoreau said that he would tempt men with "the fruit, not with the manure."
The letters to Blake and Ricketson, which forced Thoreau to explain himself to his disciples, are an excellent gloss on *Walden*.
[56] W, VI, 294.

nessed the fate of Fruitlands and Brook Farm, he entered on his own experiment alone, knowing, as he said in his review of Etzler's book, that "we must first succeed alone, that we may enjoy our success together." [57] In his equation for life, the self, as much as nature, was a permanent factor; and, like Whitman, he wanted to proclaim the "simple separate person." But although he used the "I," like Whitman, he spoke representatively. "If I seem to boast more than is becoming," he said in *Walden*, "my excuse is that I brag for humanity rather than for myself. . . ." [58] He omitted to say, however, that "I can well afford the tone of braggart there is so much truth in what I say." [59]

Before he bragged, however, he analyzed the "outward condition or circumstances" [60] of men, building up the contrast with his own life, with his inner condition, his freedom and joy. He worked from the outside and surface of life to its center: the book turned inward, going deeper and deeper, exploring the folds of nature and being. And what was true for the entire book was true of the chapter on "Economy," producing a similar perspective by incongruity. From this perspective (it was the result of the double universe of Transcendentalism, with its prudential and spiritual levels, levels which made possible a comic treatment),[61] men seemed everywhere to be "doing penance," working, as the Protestant ethic instructed them, in order to expiate their guilt. "There are some," Thoreau said in the list of those to whom he directed his book, "who complain most energetically and inconsolably of any, because they are, as they say, doing their duty." [62] But even here, he suggested, they had misread the "old book" [the Bible], had sold their souls for a mess of pottage, forgetting the injunction against "laying up treasures which moth and rust will corrupt. . . ." [63] From this insinuated religious perspective it was a "misfortune . . . to have inherited farms, houses, barns, cattle, and farming tools," for these

---

[57] W, IV, 299.

[58] W, II, 55.

[59] HM 924.

[60] W, II, 4.

[61] It was comic, however, only when one viewed the prudential from the spiritual level. When these levels, as we shall see, were translated into the empirical and real selves, and the spiritual was viewed from the prudential, it was tragic.

[62] W, II, 4, 18.

[63] W, II, 6.

were "inherited encumbrances," a convenient example of enslavement to the past, to tradition—obstacles which prevented a man
from following his own calling, binding him with "the factitious
cares and superfluously coarse labors of life," stealing his leisure
(he would have said that an empty bag can stand straight),
robbing him of his own "bloom" and disabling him for the "finer
fruits" of life. The end product, of course, was not a man but a
"machine," a man who would never grow, as Thoreau had, "like
corn in the night. . . ." [64]

Having himself, he admitted, led a mean and sneaking life, he
gave a bill of particulars that is still convincing and downright
shameful:

I have no doubt that some of you who read this book are unable to
pay for all the dinners you have actually eaten, or for the coats and
shoes which are fast wearing out or are already worn out, and have
come to this page to spend borrowed or stolen time, robbing your cred-
itors of an hour. It is evident what mean and sneaking lives many of
you live, for my sight has been whetted by experience; always on the
limits, trying to get into business and trying to get out of debt, a very
ancient slough, called by the Latins aes alienum, another's brass, for
some of their coins were made of brass; still living, and dying, and buried
by this other's brass; always promising to pay, promising to pay, to-
morrow, and dying to-day, insolvent; seeking to curry favor, to get
custom, by how many modes, only not state-prison offences; lying, flat-
tering, voting, contracting yourself into a nutshell of civility, or dilating
into an atmosphere of thin and vaporous generosity, that you may
persuade your neighbor to let you make his shoes, or his hat, or his coat,
or his carriage, or import his groceries for him; making yourself sick, that
you may lay up something against a sick day, something to be tucked
away in an old chest, or in a stocking behind the plastering, or, more
safely, in a brick bank; no matter where, no matter how much or how
little.[65]

He compared this servitude to Negro slavery, finding this northern variety even worse, and the servitude of opinion that made it
possible, that made a man the slave driver of himself, still worse.
Society, of course, gave this servitude a form and rationale and
made it appear to be necessary; and it was for this reason that
Thoreau began the defense of his own life by preaching self-
emancipation, by asking men, if only in the pages of his book, to
see how differently things might be from the vantage of self-

[64] W, II, 5-7, 124.
[65] W, II, 7-8.

reliance. For self-reliance, as Emerson had shown in his *Essays* (*First Series*), was the first condition of entering on the new life: with man at the center, instead of at the circumference, perspectives altered radically; all things served him, old fetters snapped, blindness fell away, and he discovered a new world where he was able to form his relations anew. Nothing less than this abrupt shift seemed the sufficient cure, nothing less would take one out of the machine of society into the organic world, or transform the inorganic and lumpish into a cosmos.

Walden dramatized this shift: unlike the *Week*, it put society fully on record and forced Thoreau to recover all the positions of his life, to enact the doctrine of self-reliance by withdrawing from his old relations (appropriately on Independence Day) and forming the new. Inevitably this self-reliance, with its repudiation of society, brought—as it also had in the case of Emerson and Whitman—the charge of egotism. But one need only consider the conditions of desperation, of waste, hurry, and restlessness that Thoreau had relentlessly described, to see that self-reliance (and the pride in self that goes with it) might even be a virtue. Observing the American of Emerson's manhood and Thoreau's youth, de Tocqueville, for example, distinguished between the pride that "cannot endure subordination" and that led the individual to take up "with low desires without daring to embark on lofty enterprises, of which he scarcely dreams," and the pride born of genuine self-assurance. "Thus," he said, "far from thinking that humility ought to be preached to our contemporaries, I would have endeavors made to give them a more enlarged idea of themselves and of their kind. Humility is unwholesome to them; what they want most is, in my opinion, pride." [66] An enlarged idea of man and lofty enterprises —these were the essence of the pride that Thoreau also preached. "To devote your life to the discovery of the divinity in nature—or to the eating of oysters! Would they not," he wrote, "be attended with very different results!" [67]

Desperation and conformity were the keynote of his social analysis; joy and freedom the alternatives he proposed. He built his chapter on "Economy" on a series of juxtapositions, all of which were based on the difference between the outer and the inner life:

[66] *Democracy in America*, ed. by Phillips Bradley, New York, 1945, II, 248.
[67] Houghton. MS AM 278.5.

social servitude *vs.* self-reliance; fashions in clothing, shelter, furniture, education, and reform *vs.* his own experiments in these matters; and the old life *vs.* his aspirations for the new. On one side there were circumstances, the past, tradition and routine—his "scurvy" self,[68] his social or empirical self—and on the other, hopes for the real self, for that inner expansion that would cast the old skin and prepare the conditions for creating a new organic world (a cosmos) in terms of his inner necessities. The change he desired was not so much a rejection of all that was represented by society as it was a transformation out of it, an organic change; for between the levels of prudence and spirit, society and nature, he recognized organic continuities. *Walden* may have seemed a rejection because of the radical withdrawal it dramatized, but its natural images suggested gradual transformation through growth, withdrawal being only the symbolic equivalent of the purification that was necessary when the old life had become fixed beyond growth. He did not deny those necessities represented by society; but he wanted them to be used to liberate rather than to enslave man. "The soil, it appears, is suited to the seed," he wrote, "for it has sent its radical downward, and it may now [once the necessities had been secured] send its shoot upward also with confidence. Why has man rooted himself thus firmly in the earth, but that he may rise in the same proportion into the heavens above?—for the nobler plants are valued for the fruit they bear at last in the air and light, far from the ground, and are not treated like the humbler esculents, which, though they may be biennials, are cultivated only till they have perfected their root, and often cut down at top for this purpose, so that most would not know them in their flowering season." [69] To the ends of flower and fruit, he preached economy and tried his experiment.

Originally he had used the passage beginning with "the mass of men lead lives of quiet desperation" to introduce and organize the opening pages; now he used it to summarize and for transition to fundamental questions about "the chief end of man" and "the true necessaries and means of life." [70] Such questions implied a choice, but he pointed out that the common mode of life was actually accepted without making any. The value of nature, how-

---

[68] W, II, 37.

[69] W, II, 17.

[70] W, II, 9.

ever, which he now introduced for the first time as a symbol of change in the images of sun and morning, was that it renewed the opportunity for choice and offered the occasion of the eternal now, the present, living experience by which the past could always be tested. With Whitman, Thoreau believed that

> There was never any more inception than there is now,
> Nor any more youth or age than there is now,[71]

and one of the major articles of his faith in organicism, accordingly, was that everything is possible, that the past is a kind of death, forms out of which life had passed.

He was not so unmindful of history as one might assume from his views of the past. For the issue was not, as has often been supposed, a repudiation of all history, but rather a refusal to serve the authority of the past. Thoreau appropriated the wisdom of the past, even corroborated his own experience by that of history, and tried his experiment with book in hand—in "Reading" he extolled the spiritual uses of the past. He rejected only the prudential failures of history, what Parker had called the "transient," those institutional compromises and expediencies that were used by the passing generation to limit the enterprises of the new, that, as he himself had known, were forced on the young by the position and power of the old, and which had stood in the way of his calling. In fact, Thoreau's argument for the open future was expressed in the language of the psychology of experience and was very much like that used later by Randolph Bourne in his battle with the elders: that age is a hardening, a loss of "life," a living on past experiences (as Thoreau himself knew only too well); that youth, facing the world anew, in its fresh experience, is more sensitive to the needs of present "life"; that youth, therefore, is better qualified to give advice, or rather that the advice of the elders is not fitting; and that "life" is always novel, an untried experiment which the elders try to contain in an old morality, when what is needed is a morality formed by actual choice, a morality of experience. The common notion that "the whole ground of human life" [72] has been gone over —here was the cynicism of age and the seduction of history, a notion born of weariness and faithlessness that did not speak, as Thoreau believed nature did, to the inexhaustible possibilities of joy.

---

[71] Section 3, "Song of Myself."

[72] W, II, 10.

He was reacting, therefore, not so much against history as against the decay and lapse of which devotion to history was the outward sign. History itself was a record of lapse, at least if one read it as Emerson taught his generation to, psychologically, as the exponent of states of mind. This was also the way in which he suggested that nature be read; but where history was linear and could be read in terms of the stages of man, from youth to age, from unconscious, sensuous joy to self-consciousness, from the springtime of Greece (which Thoreau wanted to restore) to the autumn of New England, nature could be read cyclically, as a forever renewing spirit, as the force of life itself, the eternal harbinger of spring and youth. History was but the record of one impulse of nature; whenever one returned to the living foundations, history itself had a new birth. From this point of view, history was the crust of human experience; like society and the empirical self, it was the fixed form of past experience; beneath this surface, however, in nature and the real self, there was a living force, older than history but eternally young, always there to break through and to bestow an unformed future.

The possibility of choice, therefore, was as close as nature and the real self. Outer necessity could be replaced with inner freedom by self-reliance, by establishing, as "Song of Myself" also demonstrated, a primary relation with the cosmos. And as Whitman would show, only less emphatically, the means was simplification or the lessening of one's dependence on society, which for both was the outward or empirical self. "I will go to the bank by the wood and become undisguised and naked"—these are Whitman's words, but Thoreau in "Economy" was enacting a similar withdrawal and divestment. Judged by such primary relationships, the essential function of economy, of food, shelter, and clothing, was to preserve the "vital heat"—the heat of life and spirit; luxuries and comforts were "positive hindrances." [73] When he anatomized them in long sections of the chapter, they became the source of a considerable Veblenesque humor, except that for Thoreau life itself was being conspicuously consumed.

One must always take Thoreau's argument for minimums in the context of the point he is making: that we waste our lives securing more than we need, that we overdo fundamentals and reserve nothing for the true ends of life. One must remember, too, that

[73] W, II, 15.

Thoreau had a Spartan (or Puritan?) contempt for luxury, that he believed that "it does not cost much for . . . heroes to live; they do not want much furniture. . . ." [74] For, if taken literally, his Spartanism would diminish most of the beauty of life, would reduce all economy to physiological necessity on the material level and would leave beauty on the spiritual level. In his reductiveness it might even seem that he had forgotten that culture and civilization are themselves the result of a symbolizing process in which essentials acquire more than their minimum value—that they serve the ends of life by satisfying intangible wants and by expressing the personality. His critics had felt this even though they had never articulated it. But what they had failed to see in his treatment of clothing and shelter and furniture, indeed in the entire experiment at Walden Pond, was that he was not only testing civilization in terms of necessities but creating a life organically—by extension, a culture, a society, and a civilization—that he was divesting himself only to the end of clothing himself anew in garments better fitted to his inner needs. There was, in fact, no other reason for preaching self-reliance—his individualism and functionalism went together; and he wisely chose clothing and shelter for his examples because they were outward forms that intimately touched the individual and that the individual believed he could alter.

His remarks on clothing had their origin, perhaps, in the fact that he had gone to Harvard College in an unfashionable green coat and that his own rugged and still unfashionable garments, which he described with evident pride, were those of Irish laborers. His perceptions concerning their social use, however, were as sharp as Lear's, and his working-class dress as much the sign of his equalitarian sympathies as Whitman's. Clothing, he pointed out with reference to the organic fitness of the bark of a tree, did not fit the wearer like his skin, nor fit his character, nor did it even, in many cases, serve its true utility of keeping the vital heat. Instead, it disguised the self, "cloaked" it, as he wrote Blake, in the seeming of novelty, fashion, and opinion, adding a cover of respectability and pretension that denied human equality. Prompted by the occasion of getting a new coat, he told Blake that "our garments are typical of our conformity to the ways of the world. . . ." [75] When he first canvassed this subject in a passage on the costume

---

[74] W, I, 367.

[75] W, VI, 226. The entire letter develops this theme.

of Swiss singers, he said that fashionable dress was *"exos*trious, building without." [76] And in his humorous account of being fitted for a coat he wrote a parable on the difficulty of retaining one's individuality in society. All this was to be expected, fashion being open game to any critic; but the meaning of this clothes philosophy suddenly emerged in a series of images of discovery and retirement and internal growth, images of inward rather than outward change radiant with Thoreau's purpose of shedding the old by radical inner transformation: "Perhaps we should never procure a new suit . . . until we have so conducted, so enterprised or sailed in some way, that we feel like new men in the old. . . . Our moulting season, like that of the fowls, must be a crisis in our lives. The loon retires to solitary ponds to spend it. Thus also the snake casts its slough, and the caterpillar its wormy coat, by an internal industry and expansion. . . ." [77]

Houses, too, were *exos*trious (a pun on *indus*trious), a kind of outward garment, more costly, more encumbering, and more confining. These unwieldy clothes—he told the myth of Momus in the original version—took most men half their lives to purchase outright, destroyed their leisure to loaf and invite their souls, made property owners of them and tied them to institutions, and, in the end, only enclosed them in a narrow space. It was when Thoreau considered all this, especially the fact that houses kept one out of the open air, that he praised the convenient shelter of the Indians and said that the unencumbered life was a divine gift. For here again he conceived of life as a journey jeopardized by fixity: the primitive man, at least, was a "sojourner in nature," who had not yet undergone the civilizing process that made men "the tools of their tools," that turned the wayfaring man into a farmer, the tent into a house, and the house into the "tomb" of the next generation. "We now no longer camp as for a night," he said, "but have settled down on earth and forgotten heaven." [78] And even fine houses, as in the case of fashionable clothes, were generally an outward show rather than the expression or function of the indweller—houses whose foundations he distrusted because they had no basis in "beautiful housekeeping and beautiful living," houses which had

---

[76] J, I, 199.

[77] W, II, 26.

[78] W, II, 41. He said later (p. 53) that "'carpenter' is but another name for 'coffin-maker.'"

not been, like those of the Puritans, built from the foundations up.[79] "Let our houses first be lined with beauty," he advised, using an image of organic functionalism, "where they come in contact with our lives, like the tenement of the shellfish, and not overlaid with it." [80]

This advice was addressed specifically to the problem of architectural ornament, and, after a brief section on building his own house, Thoreau returned to it with considerable vehemence because he had misunderstood Horatio Greenough's theory of functionalism. He had learned of Greenough's ideas from a letter that Greenough had sent to Emerson, and though his own belief—"It would be worth the while to build still more deliberately than I did, considering, for instance, what foundation a door, a window, a cellar, a garret, have in the nature of man, and perchance never raising any superstructure until we found a better reason for it than our temporal necessities even" [81]—was everything Greenough desired, it seems that Thoreau had to call Greenough's theory "dilettantism" because Emerson approved of it. "Greenough's idea," he said, "was to make architectural ornaments have a core of truth, a necessity, and hence a beauty." [82] He objected because he thought that Greenough had begun "at the cornice, not at the foundation," that he had only "put a core of truth within the ornaments," instead of beginning with the "indweller" and the human problem of building truly "within and without." [83] He was probably misled because architecture was a fine art ("They can do without *architecture* who have no olives nor wines in the cellar") [84] whose styles were as offensive to him as the styles of literature, offensive because they were lacking in sincerity. "What of architectural beauty I now see," he said, "I know has gradually grown from within outward, out of the necessities and character of the indweller, who is the only builder,—out of some unconscious

---

[79] W, II, 42-43.

[80] W, II, 44. See also pp. 51-52 for Thoreau's use of the shell image.

[81] W, II, 50.

[82] J, III, 181 (January 11, 1852). Emerson received Greenough's letter on January 5, 1852. See Rusk, ed., *The Letters of Ralph Waldo Emerson,* IV, 271-72.

[83] W, II, 51.

[84] W, II, 52. He approved of the humble dwellings of the poor. And he was angered by the luxuries that were purchased at the expense of the poor, especially the Irish who were degraded by labor. See W, II, 38.

truthfulness, and nobleness, without even a thought for the appearance ["mere ornament" in the original]; and whatever additional beauty of this kind is destined to be produced will be preceded by a like unconscious beauty of life." [85] The house was the man as the style was the man: so he built his hut and his book. "Grow your own house, I say," he wrote in the *Journal*. "Build it after an Orphean fashion. When R.W.E. and Greenough have got a few blocks finished and advertized, I will look at them. When they have got my ornaments ready I will wear them." [86]

He acknowledged that "I built too heedlessly to build well," [87] but when he described his ideal house in "House-Warming" he had grown a house, at least in his imagination, that expressed the man. His description, like that of the house in "The Landlord," was set in the context of friendship and society; he was more concerned with using the house to symbolize human qualities than with architecture proper; and yet nowhere else did he show what he meant when he demanded that a door, a window, a cellar, etc. have their foundation in the nature of man.

I sometimes dream of a larger and more populous house, standing in a golden age ["not a gilded one"], of enduring materials, and without gingerbreadwork, which shall still consist of only one room, a vast, rude, substantial, primitive hall, without ceiling or plastering, with bare rafters and purlins supporting a sort of lower heaven over one's head . . . where the king and queen posts stand out to receive your homage . . . a cavernous house, wherein you must reach up a torch upon a pole to see the roof . . . a house which you have got into when you have opened the outside door, and the ceremony is over . . . containing all the essentials of a house, and nothing for house-keeping, where you can see all the treasures of the house at one view, and everything hangs upon its peg that a man should use; at once kitchen, pantry, parlor, chamber, store-house, and garret; where you can see so necessary a thing as a barrel or a ladder, so convenient a thing as a cupboard, and hear the pot boil ["instead of a tinkling piano"] and pay your respects to the fire that cooks your dinner and the oven that bakes your bread ["bread, I say, not biscuit"], and the necessary furniture and utensils are the chief ornaments. . . .[88]

Here indeed the house was all inside and architecture had become the indweller. "This frame, so slightly clad," he said when he had

[85] W, II, 52; HM 924.
[86] J, III, 183.
[87] HM 924.
[88] W, II, 268-70; HM 924.

his hut under way, "was a sort of crystallization around me, and reacted on the builder." [89]

If clothing and shelter were a kind of skin, furniture was "our *exuviae*" [90]—the cast skins of others and of ourselves. Furniture, of course, was a fine symbol of the burden of tradition, and Thoreau exploited nationalist sentiment to make his point—and imagery, too, that recalled a line of thought beginning with Crèvecoeur: "I look upon England to-day," Thoreau wrote, "as an old gentleman who is travelling with a great deal of baggage, trumpery which has accumulated from long housekeeping. . . . When I have met an immigrant tottering under a bundle . . . I have pitied him, not because that was his all, but because he had all *that* he could carry." Furniture was baggage and a trap, however, because Thoreau was working from the assumption of freedom to move and change— "My gay butterfly," he said, "is entangled in a spider's web then." [91] His image of the trap turned the problem into one of life and death, and he advised the remedy of burning or "purifying destruction." [92] The remedy was drastic, but once more it was not so much a simple rejection of tradition as a transformation out of it—an impulse in the affirmative spirit of Emerson's remark, "Digest and correct past experience; and blend it with the new and divine life." [93] The emphasis was on purification (inner change) rather than destruction (outer change), for the "busk" or ritual burning practiced by the Mucclasse Indians, which Thoreau cited, was only one part of a vegetation ritual, a dying out of the old into the new that also required fasting, abstinence, and purification. The busk was properly sacramental, the symbol of inner purity, of the desire for renewal from within. Rejection itself was not the guarantee of such a change, indeed belied the organic possibilities of growth. To move out of one condition into another, to cast one's slough, to stir into wakefulness—these, like the mystery of life-from-death behind the feast of the new corn, were transformations, the kind of change *Walden* so effectively dramatized because its natural symbols recaptured the deepest mysteries of vegetation myth.

---

[89] W, II, 95.

[90] W, II, 73.

[91] W, II, 73-74.

[92] W, II, 75.

[93] C, I, 175.

In the intervals between his account of society, Thoreau placed a record of his hopes and of the initial stages of his experiment. Thus he made explicit the contrast between low and high views of life and between restlessness and purposive self-reliance. He hinted at how he desired to live and what enterprises he cherished, providing a prospectus, somewhat like Whitman's "Inscriptions," of what was to follow.[94] He began with his desire to live in the eternal present, and "Where I Lived, and What I Lived For" and the concluding fable of the artist of the city of Kouroo described his success. Then in the celebrated passage of the hound, bay horse, and turtledove, he represented, as he explained to an inquisitive correspondent, his "losses"—though even in his reply he was evasive, saying that the "hound and horse may *perhaps* be the symbols of some of them," and indicating that he had lost "a far finer and more ethereal treasure, which commonly no loss of . . . will symbolize." [95] Many have tried to determine what his losses were and the source of his symbols; even Emerson suggested that the hound was the book he would have liked to have written, the bay horse his desire for property, and the turtledove the wife of his dream.[96] But Emerson never recognized that Thoreau had lost reality, and he seems to have forgotten that Thoreau had selected for *The Dial* this passage from Mencius: "If a man lose his fowls or his dogs, he knows how to seek them. There are those who lose their hearts and know not how to seek them. The duty of the student is no other than to seek his lost heart." [97] Next—and this was not a part of his original *Journal* entry, but an addition that expressed the enterprise of his years of decay—"To anticipate, not the sunrise and the dawn merely, but, if possible, Nature herself!" —to pierce to the heart of things, to discover the laws of the

---

[94] W, II, 18ff.

[95] W, VI, 301-2.

[96] Cited by Vivian C. Hopkins, *Spires of Form: A Study of Emerson's Aesthetic Theory*, Cambridge, 1951, p. 243n.

[97] *The Dial*, IV (Oct., 1843), 206. The other selections define superiority in terms especially applicable to Thoreau, and are a gloss perhaps on what Thoreau meant when he told of the man who had lost his hound, and in seeking it had found a man—Thoreau himself (W, II, 306). By "heart" Mencius meant man's innate goodness, which was lost by his contact with the world. See especially Mencius' allegory of the Bull Mountain, which was once covered with trees but was despoiled by woodchoppers—perhaps Thoreau's lament for the shores of Walden Pond, similarly despoiled and conveying the same kind of loss, is an echo of this famous story.

seasons and of inspiration, growth, and maturity, and, as he had
set down as an afterthought in the *Journal*, "To find the bottom of
Walden Pond. . . ." [98] His entire experiment was dedicated to the
former, and achieved in "Spring"; and in "The Pond in Winter" he
succeeded in the latter. Finally, he tried "to hear what was in the
wind . . . and carry it express"—to express the spirit—a vocation
as unrewarded and unrecognized (never "audited," he punned) by
his neighbors as his "self-appointed" superintendence of nature and
the wild.

One of his losses, apparently, was his failure to fulfill his desire
for social influence, to turn his private good to public account. In
the thinly veiled anecdote of the Indian basket weaver, who
thought that he had only to make his baskets in order to sell them,
he told of the failure of the *Week*. "I too had woven a kind of
basket of a delicate texture," he confessed, "but I had not made
it worthy any one's while to buy them." He had learned, however,
to make it worth some one's while to buy them by the time he
wrote *Walden:* "Economy" was his come-on. And yet he put most of
the blame for his failure to win social acceptance in his calling on
society itself. He said that he studied how "to avoid the necessity
of selling them"; he asserted that "the life which men praise and
regard as successful is but one kind"; and he explained that, un-
successful in this venture, "I turned my face more exclusively than
ever to the woods"—all of which was as true of his present intentions as of those of the Walden period. Whether society bought his
wares or not, he said that he would continue to make them, like
Hawthorne's artist of the beautiful and his own artist of the city
of Kouroo, finding the value of his work in the work itself: in the
spiritual transformation of the artist. *Walden,* then, was a defense
of his vocation and of any independent undertaking, and in the
framework of "Economy," a defense of intrinsic rather than ex-
trinsic reward. For Thoreau was not unaware of the costs of the
self-reliance he was preaching. He knew it required a determined
heroism, what David Riesman calls "the nerve of failure"—the
strength "to defend an independent view of the self and of what
life holds," the courage "to face aloneness and the possibility of
defeat in one's personal life or one's work without being morally
destroyed. . . . simply the nerve to be oneself when that self is not
approved of by the dominant ethic of a society." [99]

[98] J, I, 435.
[99] *Individualism Reconsidered*, pp. 66, 48.

With these losses for his background, he described for the first time his purpose in going to Walden in a passage that brilliantly fused the imagery of self-reliance and spiritual discovery with that of commerce:

If your trade is with the Celestial Empire [the contemporary China trade and his own commerce with the heavens, with reality], then some small counting house on the coast [his hut at Walden Pond] in some Salem harbor, will be fixture enough. You will export such articles as the country affords, purely native products, much ice and pine timber and a little granite, always in native bottoms [his theory of native, organic literature]. These will be good ventures. To oversee all the details yourself in person; to be at once pilot and captain, and owner and underwriter [self-reliance; firsthand experience]; to buy and sell and keep accounts; to read every letter received, and write or read every letter sent; to superintend the discharge of imports night and day; to be upon many parts of the coast almost at the same time . . . to be your own telegraph, unweariedly sweeping the horizon, speaking all passing vessels bound coastwise; to keep up a steady despatch of commodities, for the supply of such a distant and exhorbitant market; to keep yourself informed of the state of markets, prospects of war and peace everywhere, and anticipate the tendencies of trade and civilization [the seer], —taking advantage of the results of all exploring expeditions, using new passages and all improvements in navigation;—charts to be studied, the position of reefs and new lights and buoys to be ascertained, and ever, and ever, the logarithmic tables to be corrected, for by the error of some calculator the vessel often splits upon a rock [the use and revision of history] . . . universal science to be kept pace with, studying the lives of all great discoverers and navigators, great adventurers and merchants, from Hanno and the Phoenicians down to our day; in fine, account of stock to be taken from time to time, to know how you stand. It is a labor to task the faculties of a man,—such problems of profit and loss, of interest, of tare and tret, and gauging of all kinds in it, as demand a universal knowledge.

And Walden, he said, forcing the reader to grasp his meaning or to anticipate it, was "a good place for business," "a good post and a good foundation." [100]

III

He began his trade with the Celestial Empire in March, 1845— in spring, in the season of renewal itself—by withdrawing himself from society, by casting his skin. Like the "torpid" earth and the "torpid" snake he had responded to the influence of the spring sun, had felt "the influence of the spring of springs," and had been

[100] W, II, 22-23.

aroused to seek "a higher and more ethereal life." [101] In effect, he had been reborn, as Emerson had said in *Nature:* "In the woods . . . a man casts off his skin, as a snake his slough, and at what period soever of life is always a child." [102] The first spring made it possible for Thoreau to recapitulate the entire history of his life from youth to maturity and made the second and dramatic rebirth of the chapter on "Spring," which was here prefigured in the same symbols of the melting pond, the returning birds, and the stray goose, the earned reward of his conscious endeavor and faith, a more eternal one because he had penetrated to the spring of springs itself. The change that had taken place in entering on his new life was now reflected in the easy and open exposition—direct prose that gave the feeling of relaxed leisureliness and yet of crisp, purposeful work that had acquainted him with his materials and that had stirred his sympathies and his senses. And the change was rhapsodized in "Where I Lived, and What I Lived For" in the ecstasy of discovering a new world, in the imperatives, ringing with his own success, on wakefulness and the morning life and on deliberate living. He had found a world that was agreeable to his imagination. "Both place and time were changed," he said, "and I dwelt nearer to those parts of the universe and to those eras in history which had most attracted me ["lived," he had said in the manuscript, "in a more primitive and absolute time"]." [103] When he described his situation at the Pond and the hut he had recently framed, he established their values in terms of the mountain imagery that had always signified for him the dewy, pure, and auroral life. His hut was "clean" and "airy," reminding him of a hut he had seen on his trip to the mountains in 1844; a house, he said, that was fit for the gods, where one might hear celestial music. Here, he wrote, "the morning wind forever blows, the poem of creation is uninterrupted. . . ." [104] Here, indeed, was Olympus; and the pond reminded him of a mountain tarn, whose calm surface, "full of light and reflections," like the pond in "Spring," was "a lower heaven." [105] He explained these impressions in the original version by saying that "my thoughts were so leavened with expectation

---

[101] W, II, 45-46.

[102] C, I, 9.

[103] W, II, 97; HM 924. See also W, II, 144.

[104] W, II, 94.

[105] W, II, 96.

that the whole region where I lived seemed more elevated than it actually was"; and he admitted that "when there was no elevation in my spirits the pond did not seem elevated like a mountain tarn, but a low pool, a silent muddy water and place for fishermen."[106] In this way he acknowledged the old problem of the two selves, the task he had set himself when he wrote, "Every man is tasked to make his life, even in its details, worthy of the contemplation of his most elevated and critical hour."[107] And yet, in his attempt to renew the real self, his description of a "new and unprophaned" universe was accurate. He was, as he wrote in the quatrain on the shepherd, striving to live high, to pluck the life everlasting, the edelweiss that Emerson said signified noble purity. In the manuscript of this passage he gave the key to his mountain and morning imagery: "On the tops of mountains, as everywhere to hopeful souls, it is always morning."[108]

He did not find himself in this auroral and olympian world as he had in his youth, for he now "wished to live deliberately," to find a *point d'appui* beneath the "illusory foundations" of habit and routine.[109] Now he had to maintain his elevation by discipline, by consciously reworking the materials of his life. Thus, when he built his hut, the container of his vital heat, he did not reject the old—did not forgo the materials, tools, or wisdom of the past, or of his old self—but dismantled it, purified it, and rebuilt it anew, and with different purposes in mind. He purchased his boards from James Collins, an Irish laborer on the Fitchburg railroad, whose "dark, clammy, and aguish" shanty could well represent the lives of quiet desperation he was leaving behind and with which he wanted to contrast his own life. The essential frame of his house came directly from nature, as did the stones and sand of his chimney. The boards were a kind of skin or clothing (like the plaster he later applied, but which he disliked), and these were purified—bleached and warped back by the sun.[110] When he occupied his house in July, therefore, it was "merely a defence against the rain, without plastering or chimney, the walls being of rough weather-stained boards, with wide chinks, which made it cool at

---

[106] HM 924.
[107] W, II, 100.
[108] HM 924.
[109] W, II, 100, 106, 108-9.
[110] W, II, 47-48.

night." He had a clean and airy dwelling, open to all the influences of nature. "I did not need to go out doors to take the air," he said, "for the atmosphere within had lost none of its freshness." [111]

Thoreau did not build his hut outright, any more than one builds the self; he built his hut as he needed it, to meet the developing seasons of man, and he used it as a symbol of the growth of consciousness. If in times of ecstasy he used the cycle of day and night as the symbol of the ebb and flow of inspiration ("Sounds" is such a day), he had now learned to extend the analogy to the year. "The day is an epitome of the year," he wrote. "The night is winter, the morning and evening are the spring and fall, and the noon is the summer." [112] These seasons also followed the development of consciousness as Emerson had read them in history: "The Greek was the age of observation; the Middle Age, that of fact and thought; ours, that of reflection and ideas." [113] This explains, perhaps, why the first springtime period of *Walden* was so full of allusions to Greece ("Morning brings back the heroic ages"—"It [the hum of a mosquito] was Homer's requiem; itself an Iliad and Odyssey in the air . . ."—"Olympus is but the outside of the Earth everywhere"—"With unrelaxed nerves, with morning vigor, sail by it [the whirlpool of dinner], looking another way, tied to the mast like Ulysses"); why "Reading" turned back to the classics of antiquity; why the second spring ushers in the Golden Age—why Miss Ethel Seybold, who has studied Thoreau's use of the classics, called *Walden* "the Homeric experiment." [114]

Thoreau's development in *Walden* began in the summer, a kind of extended spring, for, as he said, "There is more day to dawn"; [115] it was characterized by nooning or contemplation, by the rapt reverie of "Sounds," in which he sat in his "sunny doorway from sunrise till noon . . . amidst the pines and hickories and sumachs, in undisturbed solitude and stillness, while the birds sang around or flitted noiseless through the house, until by the sun falling in at [his] west window . . . [he] was reminded of the lapse of

[111] W, II, 94-95.

[112] W, II, 332.

[113] Emerson, J, IV, 110. See also C, I, 109.

[114] "Where I Lived, and What I Lived For"; Seybold, *Thoreau: The Quest and The Classics,* Chap. III. The allusions to Greece, however, were balanced by allusions to Oriental scripture: he could only regain his Greece by purification.

[115] W, II, 367.

time." [116] Summer, therefore, was the season in which his senses
were all alive, the season of external and outdoor life, when there
were no barriers to communion, when he enjoyed "the bloom of
the present moment." [117] It was that period of his life which he
commemorated in "Solitude," where, in trying to explain to his
neighbors why he was not lonely, he glorified "the friendship
of the seasons," the "sweet and beneficent society in Nature,"
the sympathy and kindredness of things—the "infinite and unaccountable friendliness . . . like an atmosphere sustaining
me. . . ." [118] He said, much as Emerson had in *Nature*, that "there
can be no very black melancholy to him who lives in the midst of
Nature and has his senses still," that to a "healthy and innocent
ear" even the storm was "Aeolian music"; and his senses, as he
demonstrated in these chapters, "were as acute as Indians. . . ." [119]
He redefined solitude in terms of nearness, just as he had redefined
economy in terms of essentials; he was not alone because he was
closer to the circulations of being, because, like Whitman realizing
himself in nature, he found that "God is my father & friend, men
are my brothers, and nature is my mother and my sister." [120] "Solitude," therefore, like the first chapter of *Nature*, was praise to
sympathy, to the conditions of the ecstasy that underlay the transcendentalist's faith: "This is a delicious evening, when the whole
body is one sense, and imbibes delight through every pore. I go
and come with a strange liberty in Nature, a part of herself. . . .
Sympathy with the fluttering alder and poplar leaves almost takes
my breath away. . . ." Beginning "Solitude" with these lines, Thoreau used the more effective present tense; but, in fact, as his
allusion to Hebe indicated, he was advising a cure for himself as
well as his neighbors. Open all your pores to nature, live in all
the seasons—these had been the injunctions of his years of decay.

---

[116] W, II, 123-24.

[117] W, II, 123.

[118] W, II, 145-46. Thoreau was describing that "greatest delight" of which
Emerson spoke in referring to the "occult relation between man and the
vegetable" (C, I, 10). "Shall I not have intelligence with the earth? Am I not
partly leaves and vegetable mould myself?" Thoreau echoed at the close of
"Solitude." The whole chapter, in fact, amplifies Emerson's single line: "I am
not alone and unacknowledged."

[119] W, II, 145; HM 924.

[120] HM 924. Thoreau was trying to make clear that the physical isolation
which Lane and many others protested was not the equivalent of spiritual
isolation.

He invoked the goddess Hebe because she had "the power of restoring gods and men to the vigor of youth," because "wherever she came it was spring." [121] His hut, open to nature, almost one with nature like the woodman's hut in "A Winter Walk," he now used as the symbol of his attempt to renew this sympathy.

As long as possible he preferred to remain outdoors and to be warmed by the sun. But toward the end of summer he began to build his chimney and fireplace—"the most vital part ["the nucleus and heart"] of the house." [122] Again he used secondhand materials, this time striking the bricks clean with a trowel. He had already laid the foundation in the spring, and now slowly, a course of bricks at a time, he deliberately built his chimney—the symbol of the self. He said that he "proceeded slowly" because his chimney "was calculated to indure for a long time"; and he made the symbol explicit by saying that "the chimney is to some extent an independent structure, standing on the ground and rising through the house to the heavens; even after the house is burned it still stands sometimes, and its importance and independence are apparent." [123] The chimney, appropriately, was finished by November, and when "the north wind had already begun to cool the pond," he began to have a fire. "I now first began to inhabit my house," he said, "when I began to use it for warmth as well as shelter." [124] Finally, before winter, he shingled and plastered, completely closing himself off from the elements—internalizing his life. "I withdrew yet farther into my shell," he wrote, "and endeavored to keep a bright fire both within my house and within my breast." [125]

As this process makes clear, selfhood was the final fruit of maturity. But the process also brought a change from outer to inner, from unconsciousness to consciousness; and though consciousness was undoubtedly a gain, the imagery of winter and self-containment suggests that it also was a loss, the reason for Thoreau's sense of otherness. He spoke of the change as a kind of hibernation; indeed the hut was a kind of cocoon. Though he did other things, at least in "House-Warming," which covered the transition from autumn to winter and whose theme was keeping the vital heat, he said that gathering wood for his fire was his chief

[121] W, II, 154.

[122] W, II, 266-67; HM 924.

[123] W, II, 267.

[124] W, II, 267-68.

[125] W, II, 275.

employment. There is an emphasis on keeping alive, on maintaining "a kind of summer in the midst of winter";[126] he speaks of lamps used to prolong the "day." There is a thickening of his outer garments, an apparently necessary coarsening and hardening. Even certain functions, like cooking, now take place indoors. Nature does not sustain him now as it did in the earlier chapters; there is no identity between the Me and Not-me. Instead, exposed to the weather, he said that "my whole body began to grow torpid" and that he recovered his faculties and prolonged his life only when he reached "the genial atmosphere of my house. . . ." For there he had left "a cheerful housekeeper," the fire, his own "clear flame"; [127] and the fire was a captive spirit, somewhat like the air bubbles in the first ice on the pond, which, he explained, eventually created the breakup and booming of spring by acting as a lens, focusing the heat of the sun and melting the ice.

The hut was perhaps the most obvious symbol of building his life, but his occupations in the woods also followed the cycle of the seasons, the growth of consciousness, and the increasing need to penetrate to the spring of springs. The first major symbol of this was the beanfield. After the earlier chapters on "Sounds" and "Solitude" (and the companion chapter on "Visitors," originally called "Society"), chapters of leisure, he turned to work, to what Emerson called discipline in *Nature*. Originally, Thoreau had introduced his own example of labor with a passage on the nobility of the common workingman, but he probably omitted it because, as in every example from building his hut to gathering wood, he wanted to affirm that the value of work was the work itself. He had worked in the beanfield, moreover, not so much for the sake of beans (reviewers made much of this diet, though Thoreau, following Pythagoras, did not eat beans) as for the sake of participating in the natural processes, for intimacy with nature, because he believed that farming was a natural and unspecialized vocation, a primitive and universal one, that men were cultivators, as Varro said, before they were citizens.[128] "They attached me to the earth," he said of his beans, "and so I got strength ["and health"] like Anteus." [129] Undoubtedly this chapter was a part of his modern epic on farm-

[126] W, II, 280.
[127] W, II, 279-80.
[128] J, VI, 107.
[129] W, II, 171; HM 924.

ing, for he was instructing his neighbors, as he had in his remarks on forests in "House-Warming," on the uses of the wild; his field, he pointed out, "was, as it were, the connecting link between wild and cultivated fields. . . ." [130]

The beanfield, however, served other purposes still more significant. In this chapter he was able to raise up the imagery of seeds that he had already planted—"The soil, it appears, is suited to the seed . . ."—". . . we will not forget that some Egyptian wheat was handed down to us by a mummy"—"Leaven, which some deem the soul of bread, the *spiritus* which fills its cellular tissue . . . first brought over in the Mayflower, did the business for America . . . this seed I regularly and faithfully procured . . ."—"All that I could say, then, with respect to farming on a large scale [apropos the Hollowell farm] . . . was that I had my seeds ready." [131] He was able to prepare for the imagery of fruit and ripening—the woodchopper's thoughts "rarely ripened"; Flint's fields bore no crops, his meadows no flowers, his trees no fruit, only dollars; "the ambrosial and essential part of the fruit is lost with the bloom which is rubbed off in the market cart . . ."; "In October I went a-graping. . . ." [132] And finally, he could prepare for the chapter on "Spring," where he referred to "the divine seed" of man and the " 'germs of virtue,' " by the explicit analogy of the seeds of virtue. [133]

For what he was planting were the seeds of "sincerity, truth, simplicity, faith, innocence, and the like," and his harvest, he hoped, would be "a new generation of men." [134] The soil unfortunately was "lean and effete," exhausted by the Indians who had grown beans centuries before, but by drawing "fresher soil" around his plants, which he preferred to manure and whose freshness Evelyn said had a power of attracting "virtue," he was able to get a crop. [135] The entire process dramatized the idea of renewal, and the constant vigilance and weeding the necessity of discipline, a discipline he made heroic by translating into military terms. On the social level he was farming "the dust of my ancestors . . . to

---

[130] W, II, 174.
[131] W, II, 17, 28, 69, 93.
[132] W, II, 166, 218, 192, 263.
[133] W, II, 346-47.
[134] W, II, 181.
[135] W, II, 171, 175, 179.

redeem the meadows they have become," [136] or, as he said in the *Week*, planting the seeds of institutions. "He who eats the fruit, should at least plant the seed," he said; "aye, if possible a better seed than that whose fruit he has enjoyed. . . . Defray thy debt to the world; eat not the seed of institutions, as the luxurious do, but plant it rather . . . that so, perchance, one variety may at last be found worthy of preservation." [137] "The Beanfield" was an example of Thoreau's idea of organic social reform, of the reform that returned to the economy of nature rather than to economy, and whose seeds, therefore—as he indicated in his philological pun on "spica" and "spe" and "gerendo"—were hope-bearing.[138]

This labor, of course, was also an example of self-reform; and the fact that it was now his summer and early-morning work makes it especially interesting. Had he followed the seasons faithfully, summer would not have been devoted to such laborious discipline, and he did try to suggest in the earlier chapters that it was a period of leisure and communion. He had, in fact, raised beans during the summer at the pond—primarily for economic reasons; now, however, he used this work as a symbol of his own need in these later years to make contact with nature. It might have stood for the arduous scientific discipline he had imposed on himself (he said that he was determined to know beans), although, at the same time, it stood for the more casual (or Emerson's "genial") participation in nature that helped him see nature out of the side of his eye. His work also became an example of the kind of labor Emerson required of the American scholar, labor, as Thoreau had said in "Raleigh," that removes the palaver from one's style; and it was an example of the value of staying at home, of working one's native soil. Planting and hoeing beans, indeed any organic process, could easily represent the creative process of the romantic artist; and anticipating the Artist of the railroad cut in "Spring," Thoreau said that he dabbled "like a plastic artist in the dewy and crumbling sand. . . ." [139] He was working to the end of expression, and his "instant and immeasurable crop" was inspiration and "tropes and expression" [140]—not only the correspondence

---

[136] J, III, 334.

[137] W, I, 129-30.

[138] W, II, 184.

[139] W, II, 173.

[140] W, II, 175, 179.

of hawk-wave-thought, but the parable of the chapter itself. Here was an example of reasoning from one's hand to one's head. "It was a singular experience," he wrote in the original version, "that long acquaintance of cultivator with beans. . . ." [141]

What made it so unique? Certainly any other activity would have yielded similar truths. But in the only passage which seems to break the continuity (both the narrative sequence and sense of the present) of the chapter, Thoreau recalled his first visit to the pond, blending his memory of past satisfactions with those of the present and turning nostalgia into hope, when he wrote in the last of several versions:

When I was four years old, as I well remember, I was brought from Boston ["the city"] to this my native town, through these very woods and this field, to the pond. It is one of the oldest scenes stamped on my memory. ["The country then was the world—the city only the gate to it."] And now to-night my flute has waked the echoes over that very water. The pines still stand here older than I; or, if some have fallen, I have cooked my supper with their stumps, and a new growth is rising all around, preparing another aspect ["a wilder and worthier"] for new infant eyes. Almost the same johnswort springs from the same perennial root in this pasture, and even I have at length helped to clothe that fabulous landscape of my infant ["youthful"] dreams ["imagination"], and one of the results of my presence and influence is seen in these bean leaves, corn blades, and potato vines. [142]

Permanence and change, and a sense that at last the change is consonant with his childhood dreams—this is the meaning the passage conveys. In "The Ponds," where he returned again to his youth, he told of his former ecstasy, how he had floated over the surface as the zephyrs willed, "dreaming awake"; but he went on to say that "since I left those shores the woodchoppers have still further laid them waste" and to add that "my Muse may be excused if she is silent henceforth. How can you expect the birds to sing when their groves are cut down?" [143] But he discovered that in spite of all the ravages of woodchoppers and railroads and ice cutters the pond was itself unchanged, "the same water which my youthful eyes fell on," and that, as he confessed, "all the change

---

[141] HM 924.

[142] W, II, 172; HM 924. For another and fuller version see J, I, 380-81. In HM 924 he said that the pond was his "proper nursery." In J, I, 158 he wrote: "Do not thoughts and men's lives enrich the earth and change the aspect of things as much as a new growth of wood?"

[143] W, II, 213.

is in me."[144] He had discovered his own pristine eternal self, and by cultivating beans, by discipline, he was changing the aspect of the pond, that is, the shore, making it—his life—more agreeable to his imagination. "Why, here is Walden," he wrote, "the same woodland lake that I discovered so many years ago; where a forest was cut down last winter another is springing up by its shore as lustily as ever; the same thought is welling up to its surface that was then; it is the same liquid joy and happiness to itself and its Maker, ay, and it *may* be to me."[145]

That the pond was the real self and the shore the empirical self was made clear in the chapter on "The Ponds." Indeed, Thoreau dramatized in brief what the entire book dramatized in the sequence of chapters on "The Beanfield," "The Village," and "The Ponds." For he turned from his private discipline in the field to the village, where everything he had said in "Economy" was given actuality, and then to the pond. The chapter on the village ran over into that on the ponds, the significant link being these lines: ". . . not till we have lost the world, do we begin to find ourselves, and realize where we are and the infinite extent of our relations."[146] Just as he had left the city and had come to the pond in his recollection, so now he had left the village, and in both instances he had found his real self. As for his empirical self, the self he wanted to purify, it was symbolized by the stony shore:

> It is no dream of mine,
> To ornament a line;
> I cannot come nearer to God and Heaven
> Than I live to Walden even.
> I am its stony shore,
> And the breeze that passes o'er;
> In the hollow of my hand
> Are its water and its sand,
> And its deepest resort
> Lies highest in my thought.[147]

And in a variant of the poem:

> It is a part of me which I have not prophaned
> I live by the shore of me detained.
> Laden with my dregs

---

[144] W, II, 214. On p. 361 he wrote: "Things do not change; we change."
[145] W, II, 214.
[146] W, II, 190.
[147] W, II, 215.

> I stand on my legs,
> While all my pure wine
> I to nature consign.[148]

He even punned on its name: "*Walled-in* Pond." [149]

Thoreau used the pond, of course, as a symbol; it was not simply the well or fountain, say, of Hawthorne. Instead it became a symbol of all his cherished values—of eternity, of the past, of spring and morning, of the Indian, of the Golden Age, of purity, and of the ecstasies he had known. "I thank God," he wrote in the *Journal*, "that he made this pond deep and pure for a symbol." [150] The most remarkable characteristics of the pond were its purity, depth, and transparency, its coolness and constancy, and its lack of inlet or outlet. "Walden plainly can never be spoiled by the woodchopper," he remarked in the *Journal*, "for, do what you will to the shore, there will still remain this crystal well." [151] Thoreau described it patiently, lovingly, and at great length. Speaking of the colors it reflected, he transformed it into the soul: "Lying between the earth and the heavens, it partakes of the color of both." [152] Sometimes it was "more cerulean than the sky itself"; he called it "Sky water," identifying it with the heavens because of its nature and color, and because he found depth and height symbolic equivalents.[153] "Water, which is more fluid and like the sky in its nature," he noted, "is still more like it in color." [154] He spoke of the color of its "iris," of the earth as a face and the pond as the "earth's eye; looking into which the beholder measures the depth of his own nature"—the very window of the soul.[155] It was the "distiller of celestial dews," and its surface betrayed the "spirit" in the air: "It is continually receiving new life and motion from above"—its ripples were the equivalents of the vibrating wire, and the pond

---

[148] HM 924. See Bode, ed., *Collected Poems of Henry Thoreau*, p. 288.

[149] W, II, 203.

[150] J, III, 232; W, II, 316. The pond was obviously the center, the focal point of the book; in this respect he had good reason to drop the subtitle.

[151] J, III, 35.

[152] W, II, 196.

[153] W, II, 196, 209. In HM 924 he added: ". . . our imaginations require a depth in the earth beneath corresponding to the visible height of the heavens above."

[154] J, IV, 134. See W, II, 210-11, where he described floating on the pond in terms of floating in the air, and where the fish reminded him of birds.

[155] W, II, 196, 206.

was the harp.[156] Though some thought it bottomless, it was not, and its bottom was "pure sand," with only a little sediment (the accumulation of fallen leaves, that is, of Thoreau's seasons) in the deeper parts, but no mud, and even in winter "a bright green weed" could be found growing there.[157] Its surface, moreover, was "a perfect forest mirror," reflecting all phenomena perfectly as the untarnished mind should, indeed blindingly reflecting light.[158] Even its fish ("Ideas,—are they not the fishes of thought?") were "cleaner, handsomer, and firmer" because of the coldness and purity of the water—he called them "ascetic fish"; the frogs, so humorously treated in "Sounds," were "clean"; and there were no suckers.[159]

Having already prepared for this symbolic use of the pond, he even gave a mythical account of its origin; how a hill, "which rose as high into the heavens as the pond now sinks deep into the earth," shook and suddenly sank—a version (or an inversion) of the Fall. And then he returned to his own fable of the old settler, which he had used to explain why he was not lonely at the pond and which he referred to again in "Former Inhabitants; And Winter Visitors" to explain his notion of society: ". . . that ancient settler [God] . . . came here with his divining-rod [pun], saw a thin vapor rising from the sward, and the hazel pointed steadily downward, and he concluded to dig a well here." [160] He called the

---

[156] W, II, 199, 209. In J, II, 57-58, the source of this line, Thoreau wrote another version of the poem cited above.

[157] W, II, 198-99. In W, I, 250 Thoreau wrote: "Methinks my soul must be a bright invisible green."

[158] W, II, 209, 207.

[159] J, III, 232; W, II, 204-5, 197, 206. See also J, XI, 351. On November 14, 1836, Thoreau entered the following in his first notebook: " 'From the primitive word Ver, signifying water . . . is derived the word verité; for as water, by reason of its transparency and limpidness, is the mirror of bodies— of physiscal êtres, so also is truth equally the mirror of ideas—of intellectual êtres, representing them in a manner as faithful and and [sic] clear, as the water does a physical body.' Gebelin.—Monde Primitif.—Dictionnaire Etymol. Francoise" (MA 594).

[160] W, II, 202-3. For the divining rod see also W, II, 109, 312. Thoreau prepared for this chapter by speaking of fishing in "the Walden Pond of their own natures" (p. 145), of "an old settler and original proprietor, who is reported to have dug Walden Pond, and stoned it, and fringed it with pine woods; who tells me stories of old time and of new eternity" (p. 152), of the woodchopper who was an example of genius in the lower grades of life, "who are as bottomless even as Walden Pond was thought to be, though they may be dark and muddy" (p. 166). The darkness and muddiness were the signs

pond "'God's Drop.'" [161] And later, in "Former Inhabitants," he explained the failure of those who had been before him by saying that they had not used their water privilege—"Ay, the deep Walden Pond and cool Brister's Spring —privilege to drink long and healthy draughts at these, all unimproved by these men but to dilute their glass." And even now he was disturbed by the villagers who forgot the sacred purposes of bathing and drinking, and thought "to bring its water, which should be as sacred as the Ganges at least, to the village in a pipe, to wash their dishes with! —to earn their Walden by the turning of a cock or drawing of a plug!" [162]

He also used the pond as a symbol of his own spiritual history. In "Higher Laws" he defended hunting and fishing because they were "the young man's introduction to the forest, and the most original part of himself." He said that "he goes thither at first as a hunter and fisher, until at last, if he has the seeds of a better life in him, he distinguishes his proper objects, as a poet or naturalist it may be. . . ." [163] In "The Ponds" Thoreau described these summer or youthful pursuits; it was only in "The Pond in Winter" that he had found his proper object, had gone beneath the surface of the pond and angled "for the pond itself. . . ." [164] He told how in his youth he had fished the pond, how he had floated passively on its surface, how at that time he was rich "in sunny hours and summer days, and spent them lavishly. . . ." [165] Now, however, he had made his "home by the shore" [166] and his purposes were deepening, and though he placed the chapter in the summer period of the book, he could not help seeing it in the light of his mature experience. Thus his description of midnight fishing, one of the most brilliant passages in the book, perfectly conveyed the sense of communion (as did the passage on floating) as well as a sense of the mystery of the depths: [167]

---

of physicality—of torpidity and sleep. Thoreau acknowledged: "My nature may be as still as this water, but it is not so pure, and its reflections are not so distinct" (J, III, 404).

[161] W, II, 215.

[162] W, II, 291, 213.

[163] W, II, 235.

[164] W, II, 236. In HM 924 he remarked: "I angled for Walden two years and upward and had a glorious [?]."

[165] W, II, 213.

[166] W, II, 194.

[167] He also used the unknown nests (W, II, 205-6) to suggest mystery and prepare for his discoveries in "The Pond in Winter."

These experiences were very memorable and valuable to me,—anchored in forty feet of water, and twenty or thirty rods from the shore, surrounded sometimes by thousands of small perch and shiners, dimpling the surface with their tails in the moonlight, and communicating by a long flaxen line with mysterious nocturnal fishes which had their dwelling forty feet below, or sometimes dragging sixty feet of line about the pond as I drifted in the gentle night breeze, now and then feeling a slight vibration along it, indicative of some life prowling about its extremity, of dull uncertain blundering purpose there, and slow to make up its mind. At length you slowly raise, pulling hand over hand, some horned pout squeaking and squirming to the upper air. It was very queer, especially in dark nights, when your thoughts had wandered to vast and cosmogonal themes in other spheres, to feel this faint jerk, which came to interrupt your dreams and link you to Nature again. It seemed as if I might next cast my line upward into the air, as well as downward into this element which was scarcely more dense. Thus I caught two fishes as it were with one hook.[168]

This passage bears comparison with Melville's "The Mast-Head" and with the fishing in Hemingway's "Big Two-Hearted River," and although Thoreau never suggested that his later fishing for the pond might be "tragic," what had made that fishing necessary was.

Besides its seasonal change, its freezing and breaking up, and the fact that it was "commonly higher in the winter and lower in the summer," the pond fluctuated over the years in response to "the deep springs." [169] These "tides," as Thoreau called the rise and fall of the pond, represented the over-all movement of his life, those unaccountable rhythms and pulses of inspiration.[170] Although he reported that the pond was five feet higher than when he had lived there and as high as it had been thirty years before—measurements that did not correspond to the facts of his life—his remark that "I have observed one rise and a part of two falls, and I expect that a dozen or fifteen years hence the water will again be as low as I have ever known it" did seem to fit his experience.[171] The significant facts, however, were that these changes required many years and that the rising waters, killing the shrubs and trees at the edge of the pond, left "an unobstructed shore." [172] Like the rising waters at the end of the book, these were purificatory, one

[168] W, II, 194-95.
[169] W, II, 200-201.
[170] HM 924.
[171] W, II, 201. See J, VI, 226-27 (April 27, 1854).
[172] W, II, 201.

more example of the renewal of the natural processes already symbolized in the pond which the sun dusted and in which "all impurity presented to it sinks. . . ." [173]

If Thoreau had not memorialized Walden and so made its name imperishable, it should, by rights, have been called "Thoreau's Pond." For as he said of Flint's Pond, "let it be named from . . . [some] child the thread of whose history is interwoven with its own. . . ." [174] It was clearly his own self-image: "Many men have been likened to it, but few deserve that honor," he wrote. "It is the work of a brave man, surely, in whom there was no guile!" He compared it to himself, "living thus reserved and austere, like a hermit in the woods"—acquiring purity. [175] And like his own life, which was "too pure to have a market value," he "rounded this water with his hand, deepened and clarified it in his thought, and in his will bequeathed it to Concord." [176] He wanted it to serve society as he believed the reformer should, by the example of his "greater steadfastness," like the sun in its orbit, and he said that "this vision of serenity and purity . . . seen but once . . . helps to wash out State Street and the engine's soot." [177] And he wanted it to remind his readers of the permanent springs beneath their lives. In a passage prefiguring his own rebirth in "Spring" he wrote: "Perhaps on that spring morning when Adam and Eve were driven out of Eden Walden Pond was already in existence, and even then breaking up in a gentle spring rain accompanied with mist and a southerly wind, and covered with myriads of ducks and geese, which had not heard of the fall, when still such pure lakes sufficed them. Even then it had commenced to rise and fall, and had clarified its waters, and colored them of the hue they now wear, and obtained a patent of heaven to be the only Walden Pond in the world. . . . Who knows in how many unremembered nations' literatures this has been the Castalian Fountain? or what nymphs presided over it in the Golden Age?" [178]

Having established the pond as the soul, Thoreau also made it, in the closing paragraphs on Flint's, Goose, and White ponds, a

---

[173] W, II, 209.
[174] W, II, 217-18.
[175] W, II, 214-15.
[176] W, II, 221, 214-15.
[177] W, II, 81, 215.
[178] W, II, 199.

symbol of retired and forever pure nature. And in turning to "Baker Farm," where he worked hard to make the transition, he set the chapter on "The Ponds" in the context of his summer ramblings in nature. With "Baker Farm," the next two chapters, "Higher Laws" and "Brute Neighbors," belonged to his summer experience, all bound together, superficially at least, by the common theme of fishing. Setting out to go fishing "to eke out my scanty fare of vegetables" (a hint of the problem of "Higher Laws"), he came to Baker Farm and John Field; and contrasting his leisure with Field's bogging—he told Field that although he "looked like a loafer" he was actually getting his living in the woods—he used the chapter to express his faith in the uncommitted life.[179] In the manuscript version he wrote, "Lead such a life as the children that chase butterflies in a meadow. . . . live free and persevere as you were planted. Grow wild according to thy nature. . . ." [180] But coming home with his string of fish, he made the transition to "Higher Laws," where the crucial issue was this hunger for the wild and his mature concern with ascetic discipline.[181]

We have already seen why this chapter was the confession of his resolution for purity in his later years and why the beanfield had become his discipline in summer. In it, as in "The Ponds," however, he told the history of his life in nature, a history of growing self-consciousness and coarsening, but also a history of finding his proper objects. He could no longer live like the child, for his instinct toward the wild had been replaced by "an instinct toward a higher, or . . . spiritual life. . . ." [182] He added in the manuscript that "some would say that the one impulse was directly from God, the other through nature" [183]—a remark he wisely omitted because it revealed the actual disharmony he now experienced in nature. This chapter, nevertheless, told that story, and because of its unusual tone and theme, Thoreau followed it in "Brute Neighbors"

[179] W, II, 225, 227.

[180] HM 924.

[181] His problem now was posed by the question, "How shall a man continue his culture after manhood?" "All wisdom," he answered, echoing Oriental scripture, "is the reward of discipline conscious or unconscious" (Houghton. MS AM 278.5). In HM 924 there was an epigraph from Saadi on the title page on the need for obedience to law.

[182] W, II, 232. This problem emerged again in "Walking," a defense of the wild in which the key metaphor was religious—"*Sainte-Terrer*." By means of this metaphor the actual wild was subtly spiritualized. See J, XI, 450 for a similar transformation of the wild.

[183] HM 924.

with his humorous dialogue between the Poet (the younger Channing) and the Hermit (himself). The dialogue did the work of
the transitional sentence he omitted: "But practically I was only
half converted to my own arguments, for I still found myself fishing
at rare intervals." [184] And the humor was self-protective: though
the dialogue helped him make the point of "Economy" once more,
it was a mock pastoral in which poet and hermit alike were playing
at their serious vocations, and in which the obvious breach in
discipline destroyed the hermit's "budding ecstasy." [185] But having
treated his most important concerns sportively and thus having
brought his narrative back to its summer level—and this seems the
only excuse for the dialogue—Thoreau returned, in the remainder
of "Brute Neighbors," to the higher uses of nature for which he
was purifying himself, to the correspondences or spiritual meanings it had for him.

"Why," he asked, "do precisely these objects which we behold
make a world?" And he answered that "they are all beasts of
burden . . . made to carry some portion of our thoughts." [186] Mouse,
phoebe, robin, partridge, otter, raccoon, woodcock, ant, stray dog
or cat, loon and duck—all bore a meaning, from that of the simple
friendliness of the mouse to that of the serenity and wisdom in the
eye of the infant partridge with which he identified himself.[187]
The ant war he described made it possible for him to show the
strife in nature and in civilization, and to trace war from Homer's
time through Concord Fight and Bunker Hill to Austerlitz and
Dresden and the Mexican war ("red republicans" vs. "black im-
perialists")—even, perhaps, in its internecine character and incon-
clusiveness, to suggest his premonition of the Civil War.[188] And
the loon, whose autumn return he described, not only helped him
make the transition to autumn, as did the ducks, but enabled him
to enact the play of inspiration itself. Indeed, chasing the loon—
a bird he compared to a fish and said visited the deepest part of
the pond—became the symbol of his search for inspiration. Con-

[184] HM 924.

[185] W, II, 249.

[186] W, II, 249.

[187] W, II, 251. "Such an eye," he said, "is coeval with the sky it reflects.
The woods do not yield another such gem. The traveller does not often look
into such a limpid well." He also spoke of the pond as an eye and as a jewel.

[188] In "My Books I'd Fain Cast-Off, I Cannot Read" (1842), he had already
mentioned the ant war.

sciously trying to pursue it ("While he was thinking one thing in his brain, I was endeavoring to divine his thought in mine"), he was balked; and he found that passivity was necessary, that "it was as well for me to rest on my oars and wait his reappearing as to endeavor to calculate where he would rise. . . ." That he did not succeed even then, that the loon always raised his "demoniac" laugh "in derision of my efforts," and, finally, that an east wind came "and filled the whole air with misty rain, and I was impressed as if it were the prayer of the loon answered, and his god was angry with me"—these were signs, like the "tumultuous surface" of the pond, that the serene communion of summer was gone.[189]

If the pond was the soul, then what Thoreau did there was also the record of his inner life. In "House-Warming," where he gathered the autumn fruits and built his chimney and winter finally set in, his life began to turn inward. To keep his vital heat—his faith— was now his problem. Winter, as he depicted it in "Former In- habitants; And Winter Visitors," was the period of his greatest solitude, when visitors were fewest, when his life was reduced to routine, when even though "the master of the house was at home," the "Visitor" never came—at least not from the town.[190] It was the time of thought and memory, of his communion with the former inhabitants of the pond whose lives introduced the possibility of failure. It was a sleepy time, reminding him of "that winter that I labored with a lethargy," falling asleep over *Gondibert*, a time when he lulled himself to sleep with reminiscences, when, like the owl, he awaited "the dawning of his day." [191] And it was the proper time for considering friendship as a spiritual necessity— not those friendships of his youth, those companions of his external life, but those companions of his thoughts whose discourse sum- moned "the old settler" and "expanded and racked my little house. . . ." [192]

This and the succeeding chapters recapitulated the spring and summer chapters, taking up solitude, the resources of the natural scene, sounds, and the pond, only in a different mood. In "Winter Animals" the catalog of sounds and animals conveyed a sense of

---

[189] W, II, 259-62. Thoreau copied from *The Harivansa:* "Thought tor- mented by desires, is like the sea agitated by the wind" (J, II, 190).

[190] W, II, 292, 298.

[191] W, II, 285-86, 291, 293-94.

[192] W, II, 297.

impoverishment—the wilder animals hunted in former times were gone; of spiritual restlessness—the whooping pond turned in its sleep, the fox sought "expression" and struggled for "light," the bustle of squirrels and mice wakened him; and of bravery under duress—there were still the hardy jays and chickadees, the lean but vigorous and elastic hares, and the "brave bird," the partridge, "not to be scared by winter," which, like Thoreau, was "Nature's own bird," living "on buds and diet drink." [193] "Every winter," Thoreau said in "The Pond in Winter," "the liquid and trembling surface of the pond, which was so sensitive to every breath, and reflected every light and shadow, becomes solid to the depth of a foot or a foot and a half. . . . it closes its eyelids and becomes dormant for three months or more. . . . After a cold and snowy night it needed a divining rod to find it." [194]

In "The Pond in Winter," however, Thoreau did not fully develop, as one might expect, the theme of loss. He did indeed suggest his discontent and spiritual uneasiness: "After a still winter night I awoke with the impression that some question had been put to me, which I had been endeavoring in vain to answer in my sleep, as what—how—when—where?" Of course he could not answer this question in his sleep, for it was the question of life itself which only waking would answer. And therefore he went on: "But there was dawning Nature, in whom all creatures live, looking in at my broad windows with serene and satisfied face, and no question on *her* lips. I awoke to an answered question, to Nature and daylight." [195] This awakening was the beginning of his rebirth, a process that began in the conscious endeavor to find the bottom of the pond, that reached a crescendo in "Spring," and that served as the living testimony of his conclusion—"Only that day dawns to which we are awake. There is more day to dawn. The sun is but a morning star." [196] "Moral reform," he said when he first fixed the meanings of morning and awakening, "is the effort to throw off sleep. . . . To be awake is to be alive." [197]

He began "The Pond in Winter," therefore, with his morning work or ritual, going in search of water. Like the winter fishermen,

[193] W, II, 301, 305.
[194] W, II, 312-13.
[195] W, II, 312.
[196] W, II, 367.
[197] W, II, 100.

who were wise in natural lore, men of "real faith" (he punned)
who knew where summer had retreated and whose life was passed
"deeper in Nature than the studies of the naturalist penetrate,"
Thoreau also cut his hole in the ice; and if he was no longer a fisherman himself, he could still glory in the fabulous pickerel of Walden,
and find what was more important to him, that "its bright sanded
floor [was] the same as in summer." [198] He was now penetrating
the deeps to find his faith, fathoming "unceasingly," as he wrote
in his youth, "for a bottom that will hold an anchor, that it may
not drag." [199] He said he "was desirous to recover the long-lost
bottom of Walden Pond," and he made it clear, by his verbal play
on "bottom" and "foundation," that he was seeking his foundation.[200]
The foundation of his faith, as his survey of the pond indicated, was
the doctrine of correspondence; and what he needed to prove
again was the law that guaranteed that the actual corresponded
to the unseen reality. He discovered the "general regularity" of
the bottom and, what was more surprising to him, "its conformity
to the shores," a conformity "so perfect that a distant promontory
betrayed itself in the soundings quite across the pond, and its
direction could be determined by observing the opposite shore." [201]
He also found to his surprise that "the line of greatest length
intersected the line of greatest breadth *exactly* at the point of
greatest depth. . . ." This, he wrote in the manuscript version,
pointed "to a general law"; it applied to oceans (the exploration
of the Over-Soul) as well as ponds, to mountains and valleys, to
capes and bars—"This rule . . . is universal." [202] Thus he discovered
law and harmony in nature, at the same time that he realized anew

---

[198] HM 924; W, II, 313-14.

[199] J, I, 54.

[200] W, II, 315. Waking and sleeping merge with foundation and surface in
this chapter.

[201] W, II, 318.

[202] HM 924. The transcendentalists, of course, made much of correspondences
and analogies. But they went further than most who read the symbolism of
nature, attempting, in fact, to create a science of correspondence. Analogy for
them was not a game in which one sought for resemblances, but a study of
real relationships, a way of expressing law. Here Thoreau *verified* that law;
here one sees that he had gone beyond the literary correspondences of
"Sounds"—correspondences expressing chiefly the subjective play of his
mind—to correspondences founded on the nature of fact. His whole life moved
in this direction, and he was true to it in *Walden* by speaking of his early
ecstasy in terms of sound and his later ecstasy in terms of sight. For sight, as
Emerson wrote, was the condition of self-consciousness (C, I, 109).

that truth was perspectival. "If we knew all the laws of Nature," he wrote, "we should need only one fact . . . to infer all the particular results at that point." But because "we know only a few laws ["the particular laws are as our points of view"] . . . our result is vitiated, not, of course, by any confusion or irregularity in Nature, but by our ignorance of essential elements in the calculation. Our notions of law and harmony are commonly confined to those instances which we detect; but the harmony which results from a far greater number of seemingly conflicting, but really concurring, laws, which we have not detected, is still more wonderful." [203]

This law also applied to man, for "as there is no exclusively physical nor exclusively moral law, this is as true in ethics as in physics. . . ." [204] "Draw lines through the length and breadth of the aggregate of a man's particular daily behaviors and waves of life into his coves and inlets," he suggested, "and where they intersect will be the height or depth of his character. Perhaps we need only to know how his shores trend and his adjacent country or circumstances, to infer his depth and concealed bottom." [205] This was the kind of character analysis Thoreau wanted applied to himself, a kind of superb topographical phrenology, which he carried out in terms of low, smooth, and Achillean shores, and projecting brows. Applied to himself, of course, it would have revealed "a corresponding depth in him" [206]—the hero whose center would have been Walden Pond itself. And once the pond was the soul, coves, inlets, and shores, the sea and navigation, provided the imagery for a conceit that seemed irresistible:

. . . there is a bar across the entrance of our every cove, or particular inclination; each is our harbor for a season, in which we are detained and partially land-locked. These inclinations are not whimsical usually, but their form, size, and direction are determined by the promontories of the shore, the ancient axes of elevation. When this bar is gradually increased by storms, tides, or currents, or there is a subsidence of the waters, so that it reaches to the surface, that which was at first but an inclination in the shore in which a thought was harbored becomes an individual lake, cut off from the ocean, wherein the thought secures its own conditions, changes, perhaps, from salt to fresh, becomes a sweet sea, dead sea, or a marsh. At the advent of each individual into this life

[203] W, II, 320.
[204] HM 924.
[205] W, II, 321.
[206] W, II, 321.

[he made the moral clear], may we not suppose that such a bar has risen to the surface somewhere? It is true, we are such poor navigators that our thoughts, for the most part, stand off and on upon some harborless coast, are conversant only with the bights of the bays of poesy, or steer for the public ports of entry, and go into the dry docks of science, where they merely refit for this world, and no natural currents concur to individualize them.

Walden Pond, obviously, was such an individual lake, a sweet sea, that "private sea" of thought, the self that Thoreau in "Conclusion" advised his contemporaries to explore.[207]

Exploring the pond, finally, was a contemplative labor to be contrasted with the utilitarian skimming of the pond by the ice cutters, and a conscious endeavor to be contrasted with the ecstasies of his youth. Plumbing the depths he found "a bright green weed," the symbol of organic life and soul, which, he said, "was very agreeable to behold in mid-winter"; [208] and while surveying the pond he discovered the manifestation of the same organic law in the undulation of its apparently rigid surface. And the ice, which others were harvesting, was now for him the sign of his own purity rather than dormant state, the sign of that "new austerity" he spoke of in "Higher Laws" which permitted the "mind [to] descend into his body and redeem it. . . ." [209] In reading *The Harivansa* he had noted that "'the heart filled with strange affections is to be here below purified by wisdom,'" and that "'the operation which conducts the pious and penitent Brahman to the knowledge of the truth, is all interior, intellectual, mental. They are not ordinary practices which can bring light into the soul.'" [210] The pure Walden water mingled with the sacred waters of the Ganges, in the famous conclusion of this chapter, because Thoreau had translated the ice, a commodity exported to all parts of the world, into "solidified azure," a symbol of purity and spirit.[211] So also, "Higher Laws" and "The Pond in Winter" were joined together by the ascetic disciplines of Oriental philosophy—by that morning philosophy which he was now performing.

Rebirth came with spring. It was anticipated toward the end of

[207] W, II, 321-22, 354.
[208] HM 924.
[209] W, II, 246.
[210] J, II, 190-91.
[211] W, II, 324.

"The Pond in Winter" when Thoreau wrote that "in thirty days more, probably, I shall look from the same window on the pure sea-green Walden water there, reflecting the clouds and the trees, and sending up its evaporations in solitude, and no traces will appear that a man has ever stood there." [212] And it was announced at the beginning of "Spring," in a passage Thoreau apparently added on the booming and breaking up of the pond in obedience to the "absolute progress of the season"—"its law to which it thunders obedience . . . as surely as the buds expand in the spring." [213] The booming, moreover, was due to "the influence of the sun's rays," a morning phenomenon chiefly, when the pond "stretched itself and yawned like a waking man. . . ." [214] "Who shall resist the thaw?" he wrote in the winter of 1852. "Let all things give way to the impulse of expression. It is the bud unfolding, the perennial spring. As well stay the spring." [215]

Gradually the weather grew warmer, the snow and ice began to melt, the "circulations" began in the rills and rivulets, purging "the blood of winter," and Thoreau no longer needed to gather wood for his fire, assured now that nature would keep his vital heat.[216] In the thawing clay of the railroad cut he saw "the Artist who made the world and me" give way to the impulse of expression.[217] Indeed, his description of the thaw, one of the most brilliant and best sustained analogies in transcendental writing, was a myth of creation *as expression,* an elaborate metaphor of the organic process of art and nature and self-reform, of the creative and shaping power of Idea, and the renewal that proceeds from the inside out. And it was more than that: a metaphor of birth, and a metaphor of purification.

The thaw was first of all a flowing, a "bursting out" of the "insides of the earth," the unfolding of "the piled-up history" of geology.[218] The thawing obeyed the law of currents and the law of vegetation, a stream that took the form of leaves and vegetation. Thoreau called it a "grotesque or mythological vegetation," and it

---

[212] W, II, 328.

[213] W, II, 330, 333.

[214] W, II, 332.

[215] J, III, 232.

[216] W, II, 336.

[217] W, II, 338.

[218] HM 924; J, IV, 383.

reminded him not only of foliage, but of "brains or lungs or bowels, and excrements of all kinds." "I feel," he wrote, "as if I were nearer to the vitals of the globe. . . ." [219] This excremental character suggested "that Nature has some bowels, and . . . is mother of humanity. . . ." For the frost coming out of the ground was Spring, a newly-delivered child, "Earth . . . in her swaddling clothes" stretching forth "baby fingers on every side." In an image of life-from-decay that would have pleased Whitman, he wrote: "Fresh curls spring from the baldest brow." [220] He saw in the thaw not only the birth but the development of man: in the streams of clay the formation of blood vessels, in sand the bony matter, in finer soil the flesh —in fact, the process by which rivers were formed and valleys created served as an analogy for the creation of the human face. "What is man," he wrote, "but a mass of thawing clay? . . . Who knows what the human body would expand and flow out to under a more genial heaven?" For "more heat or other genial influences," he hinted, "would have caused it to flow yet farther." [221] Melting was self-transcendence.

In the *Week* he had written that "Nature is a greater and more perfect art, the art of God" and that "man's art has wisely imitated those forms into which all matter is most inclined to run, as foliage and fruit." [222] Now he elaborated this idea. Watching the sudden creation of the sand foliage, he said that "I am affected as if in a

[219] HM 924; W, II, 337-38.

[220] W, II, 340.

[221] W, II, 339-40. In HM 924 he indicated what he meant by adding the following: ". . . stretched on a bank in paradise. Have we not unsatisfied instincts?"
It is interesting to compare Thoreau's conscious use of the imagery of the sand bank with his personal responses. When he saw "the naked flesh of New England" in the sands of Lake Cochituate, he wrote: ". . . this is my home, my native soil; and I am a New-Englander. Of thee, O Earth, are my bone and sinew made. . . . To this dust my body will gladly return as to its origin. Here have I my habitat. I am of Thee" (J, III, 95; see also J, III, 97). These passages and his personal response to the genial influence of the thaw (J, V, 34-35) add one more meaning perhaps to his intention of redeeming the dust of his ancestors.

[222] W, I, 339-40. See also W, I, 167. In HM 956 he wrote: "The leaf is her [nature's] constant cypher [sic]." In a draft of "Autumnal Tints" he wrote: "I remember one who proposed to write an epic poem to be called The Leaf. This would be a sufficiently broad and fertile theme, considering the origin and end of the leaf, and that botanists regard all the parts of a plant as modified leaves merely. . . . A leaf might be taken for [the] emblem of Nature" (Houghton. MS AM 278.5).

peculiar sense I stood in the laboratory of the Artist . . . had come to where he was still at work, sporting on this bank, and with excess of energy strewing his fresh designs about." He saw the earth laboring with "the idea inwardly" and expressing itself "outwardly in leaves. . . ." [223] At first he explained this process philologically, suggesting in the radical meanings of lobe, leaf, and globe not only the uniformity of law in rivers, ice, trees, and the globe itself, but the stages of evolutionary growth and purification. Having shown the leaflike character of liver and lungs and feathers and wings, he concluded: "You pass from the lumpish grub in the earth to the airy and fluttering butterfly. The very globe continually transcends and translates itself, and becomes winged in its orbit." [224] Then he wrote that "this one hill side illustrated the principle of all the operations of Nature. The Maker of this earth but patented a leaf." He had read Goethe seriously, and having tried to illustrate the principle himself, he omitted, as he so often did on revision, the explicit statement of his intention: "Show me how to make a leaf: and I will make you a world, and beings like you to inhabit it." [225]

The moral Thoreau drew from the process of the thaw was the central law of his life: "There is nothing inorganic." He now affirmed: "The earth is not a mere fragment of dead history, stratum upon stratum like the leaves of a book, to be studied by geologists and antiquaries chiefly, but living poetry like the leaves of a tree, which precede flowers and fruit,—not a fossil earth ["The earth is not a graveyard full of skeletons," he said in the manuscript, "but a granary full of seeds"], but a living earth; compared with whose central life all animal and vegetable life is merely parasitic. Its throes will heave our exuviae from their graves." And this law applied to man and the higher society he needed: ". . . the institutions upon it," he wrote, "are plastic like clay in the hands of the potter." [226] Hoeing beans, he had himself been a plastic artist making the soil express itself in leaves; and in "Former Inhabitants" he had identified himself with Wyman the potter, who lived deepest in the woods and who did not pay his taxes. "I had read of the potter's clay and the wheel in Scripture," he remarked, stating his theme in brief, "but it had never occurred to me that the pots we

---

[223] W, II, 337-38.

[224] W, II, 338.

[225] W, II, 340; HM 924.

[226] W, II, 340-41.

use were not such as had come down unbroken from those days
. . . and I was pleased to hear that so fictile an art was even practised in my neighborhood." [227] It had not occurred to his neighbors
either that at Walden he had been practicing this fictile art, that
he was a re-former who likened his work to that of the thaw with
its "gentle persuasion" and who did not break but melted things;
whose work was an example of the symbolic imagination, of conforming his life to the idea in his mind, and who, as Emerson wrote
in *Nature*, having started "in his slumber," awakes to find that
"Nature is not fixed but fluid. Spirit alters, moulds, makes it." [228]
At Walden he was creating such an organic life for himself, and
ultimately for society. "Again, perhaps, Nature will try," he wrote,
"with me for a first settler. . . ." He was the "Champollion" de-
ciphering the hieroglyphic [the leaf] of nature, "that we may turn
over a new leaf at last." [229]

In Thoreau's experience the thawing at the railroad cut was
always associated with the ecstasy of the resounding telegraph
wire, an ecstasy comparable to the thawing only in its suddenness.
The harp analogy, however, did not afford the possibilities of
symbolic richness, nor would it have so grandly pulled together the
themes of *Walden*. But in omitting it Thoreau tried to make the
many *Journal* observations of the later years that composed the
passage the vehicle for ecstasy, and he succeeded in conveying
something more and something less than the harp conveyed. The
ecstasy was not spontaneous or unconscious, but intellectual; it
followed from his mature study of nature and his perception of
law, an ecstatic praise of this guarantee in nature but not the
former ecstasy he was seeking. It was an example of his belief that
"the intellect is a cleaver; it discerns and rifts its way into the
secret of things." [230] But as an example of his conscious endeavor in
nature it represented the intellectual basis from which the more

---

[227] W, II, 288.

[228] W, II, 341; C, I, 72, 76.

[229] W, II, 291, 340. Apropos of wells, he also socialized his own experience:
"I trust that in this new country many wells are yet to be dug" (HM 924).
He socialized his life in the spirit of a remark by Charles Emerson, whose
"Notes from the Journal of a Scholar" he admired: "If to need least, is nighest
to God, so also is it to impart most. There is no soundness in any philosophy
short of that unlimited debt" (*The Dial*, IV [July, 1843], 91).

[230] W, II, 109. This remark was made in the context of Thoreau's desire to
work through the surface to reality.

successful symbols of ecstasy—the melting pond and the soaring hawk—were struck.

Thoreau began to build toward ecstasy by mentioning the irrepressible joy of the squirrels, the "carols and glees" of the brooks, the first sparrows and bluebirds, with their songs of "younger hope than ever," and the green grass, "the symbol of perpetual youth," which like "human life but dies down to its root, and still puts forth its green blade to eternity." "What at such a time," he asked, "are histories, chronologies, traditions, and all written revelations?" [231] For Walden, too, had begun to melt and sparkle in the sun, its "bare face . . . full of glee and youth, as if it spoke the joy of the fishes within it, and of the sands on its shore. . . ." "Such is the contrast," he wrote, "between winter and spring. Walden was dead and is alive again." [232] The change he had sought by the discipline of purity had come with "the change from storm and winter to serene and mild weather, from dark and sluggish hours to bright and elastic ones"; and like the dawning of inspiration this "memorable crisis" was "seemingly instantaneous at last." "Suddenly," he wrote, sharpening the contrasts of the original passage—

Suddenly an influx of light filled my house, though the evening was at hand, and the clouds of winter still overhung it, and the eaves were dripping with sleety rain. I looked out of the window, and lo! where yesterday was cold gray ice there lay the transparent pond already calm and full of hope as in a summer evening, reflecting a summer evening sky in its bosom, though none was visible overhead, as if it had intelligence with some remote horizon. I heard a robin in the distance, the first I had heard for many a thousand years . . . the same sweet and powerful song as of yore . . . the pitch-pines and shrub-oaks about my house, which had so long drooped, suddenly resumed their several characters, looked brighter, greener, and more erect and alive, as if effectually cleansed and restored by the rain ["and fitted once more to express immortal beauty and make a part of this world which is called Κόσμος or beauty"]. . . . As it grew darker, I was startled by the *honking* of geese. . . . Standing at my door, I could hear the rush of their wings. . . . So I came in, and shut the door, and passed my first spring night in the woods.[233]

---

[231] W, II, 342-43.

[232] W, II, 344.

[233] W, II, 344-45; HM 924. The original passage of March 26, 1846 (J, I, 400-401), was reordered and heightened. The most significant phenomenon was the pond reflecting a summer sky. Thoreau knew from Humboldt that water is sometimes blue when the sky is overcast—that water is self-reflective

With the coming of his spring had come "the creation of Cosmos out of Chaos and the realization of the Golden Age." And with creation, which he supported with citations from Ovid's *Metamorphoses*, a host of images of new birth, infancy, and innocence; a sense of new freedom, release, hope, and pardon. The world into which he had been reborn was the eternal present, that golden age, before the fall of man, when man " 'cherished fidelity and rectitude' " and was sufficient in his virtue, a time when " 'Punishment and fear were not,' " the trees had not been felled, and " 'mortals knew no shores but their own.' " [234] And for Thoreau, finally, the symbol of this transformation was not the butterfly which the logic of his metaphors demanded, but the hawk, which sported alone in the morning air with "proud reliance"—the bird he associated with falconry, nobleness, and poetry, and with his own lonely heroism; the bird, he wrote, "that soars so loftily and circles so steadily and apparently without effort [because it] has earned this power by faithfully creeping on the ground as a reptile in a former state of existence." [235] The hawk symbolized his ultimate liberation from the senses, the final emancipation of Oriental discipline. At last, as he noted in *The Harivansa*, he was " 'free in this world, as birds in the air, disengaged from every kind of chain.' " [236]

Thoreau, of course, closed his book with the fable of the beautiful bug that had come out of the dry leaf of an old table of apple-tree wood. In fact, he made this fable recapitulate his themes: "Who knows what beautiful and winged life, whose egg has been buried for ages under many concentric layers of woodenness in the dead dry life of society, deposited at the first in the alburnum of the green and living tree, which has been gradually converted into the semblance of its well-seasoned tomb . . . may unexpectedly come forth from amidst society's most trivial and handselled furni-

---

(J, V, 121). Thoreau spoke of the pond as "a lower heaven" (W, II, 96) and said that the sky underlay the earth (J, III, 100). Reflection also indicated the intimacy of heaven and earth (J, II, 438) and was the first promise of summer (J, IV, 147). The passage might be compared with Rousseau's first night at the Hermitage.

[234] W, II, 348.

[235] W, II, 349; J, III, 108. In HM 924 he crossed out the fact that "it had no mate in the world." The hawk symbolized soaring thought (J, III, 143), and it was compared with the poet—"A hawk's ragged wing will grow whole again, but so will not a poet's" (J, IV, 103).

[236] J, II, 191. See J, XI, 305, 450-51.

ture, to enjoy its perfect summer life at last!" [237] In the manuscript of "Spring," where he proposed the tonic of wildness, he had written that "he [God] is a very *present* help in trouble, but the chief trouble is that we live in the past and in tradition, where he is not." [238] The contrast was implicit in "Spring," but Thoreau made it explicit in "Conclusion," by returning to the issues of economy and society, self-reform and discovery. And there his biting and forceful remarks on restlessness and desperation, and his injunctions to find a foundation to live in the truth and to make one's relations, were crystallized in a parable of his own life and vocation. For in order to affirm the open prospects of the eternal present, he had fashioned *Walden,* as he himself had lived, after the example of the artist of the city of Kouroo.

There was an artist in the city of Kouroo who was disposed to strive after perfection. One day it came into his mind to make a staff. Having considered that in an imperfect work time is an ingredient, but into a perfect work time does not enter, he said to himself, It shall be perfect in all respects, though I should do nothing else in my life. He proceeded instantly to the forest for wood, being resolved that it should not be made of unsuitable material; and as he searched for and rejected stick after stick, his friends gradually deserted him, for they grew old in their works and died, but he grew not older by a moment. His singleness of purpose and resolution, and his elevated piety, endowed him, without his knowledge, with perennial youth. As he made no compromise with Time, Time kept out of his way, and only sighed at a distance because he could not overcome him. Before he had found a stock in all respects suitable the city of Kouroo was a hoary ruin, and he sat on one of its mounds to peel the stick. Before he had given it the proper shape the dynasty of the Candahars was at an end, and with the point of the stick he wrote the name of the last of that race in the sand, and then resumed his work. By the time he had smoothed and polished the staff Kalpa was no longer the pole-star; and ere he had put on the ferule and the head adorned with precious stones, Brahma had awoke and slumbered many times. But why do I stay to mention these things? When the finishing stroke was put to his work, it suddenly expanded before the eyes of the astonished artist into the fairest of all the creations of Brahma. He had made a new system in making a staff, a world with full and fair proportions; in which, though the old cities and dynasties had passed away, fairer and more glorious ones had taken their places. And now he saw by the heap of shavings still fresh at his feet, that, for him and his work, the former lapse of time had been an illusion, and that no more time had elapsed than is required for a single scintillation from the brain of

---

[237] W, II, 366-67.

[238] HM 924.

Brahma to fall on and inflame the tinder of a mortal brain. The material
was pure, and his art was pure; how could the result be other than
wonderful? [239]

---

[239] W, II, 359-60. Thoreau frequently used a parable to end a chapter, as
in "Economy" and "Higher Laws." The parable of the artist was obviously his
own work, full of revisions, with his characteristic pun ["lapse" and "elapsed"],
with transparent personal allusions such as the desertion of his friends. Nor
did he, always scrupulous in the matter of borrowing, use quotation marks.
Though he spelled it in his own way, Kouroo was clearly Kuru, Kooroo, or
Curu, the nation that fought the Pandoos in the *Mahabharata,* the sacred land
that Arjuna was assigned to protect in the *Bhagavad-Gita.* Thoreau may have
first come across it in the *Laws of Menu,* where it is referred to as the country
of Brahmanical sages (see *The Dial,* III [Jan., 1843], 332). These Brahmins
also carried staves. In writing this passage Thoreau may also have recalled
Menu's saying that "from a Brâhmana, born in that country, let all men on
earth learn their several usages." In *The Dial* (III, 332) he cited Menu's "The
hand of an artist employed in his art is always pure." The section on time and
inspiration recalls stanza 11 of his poem on "Inspiration" and a passage in
J, III, 279; his remarks on redemption through art recall passages on the
art of the American Indians (J, V, 526) and the morality of art (J, III, 30-31).
The lesson of the *Bhagavad-Gita*—not the lesson of passivity, but of dis-
interested work and contemplation—was already a part of his thought. In a
letter to Blake he cited: " 'Free in this world as the birds in the air, disengaged from every kind of chains, those who have practiced the *yoga* gather
in Brahma the certain fruit of their works. . . . The yogi, absorbed in contemplation, contributes in his degree to creation. . . . Divine forms traverse
him . . . and, united to the nature which is proper to him, he goes, he acts
as animating original matter.' " In another, he advised work as a higher discipline, "the means by which we are translated." Again he told Blake, "How
admirably the artist is made to accomplish his self-culture by devotion to his
art!" And finally, in a letter in which Brahmanical abstraction and work were
joined, he advised Blake, "Make your failure tragical by the earnestness and
steadfastness of your endeavor, and then it will not differ from success (W, VI,
175, 222, 235). See also J, XII, 344.

Chapter VIII

KNIGHT OF THE UMBRELLA AND BUNDLE

> If America was found and lost again once, as most of us believe, then why not twice?
>
> —Thoreau, *Cape Cod*

> A book should contain pure discoveries, glimpses of *terra firma*, though by shipwrecked mariners, and not the art of navigation by those who have never been out of sight of land. *They* must not yield wheat and potatoes, but must themselves be the unconstrained and natural harvest of their author's lives.
>
> —Thoreau, *A Week on the Concord and Merrimack Rivers*

I

Two major projects occupied Thoreau in the last decade or so of his life: the history of the discovery and exploration of America and his "Kalendar" of the natural phenomena of Concord. Both interests, which were more consuming than the meager published results suggest, were joined by Thoreau's desire to restore the aboriginal and permanent America to America, to give America, by rediscovering it and repossessing it, that natural environment in which he himself had found a spiritual home. While his contemporaries were moving west, acting out the last chapter of the epic of discovery, he stayed at home, driving his roots into and taking his strength from his native soil, giving his life and imagination to a place that it might at last become meaningful; and when he traveled to Maine, Canada, Cape Cod, even to Minnesota, he traveled back into the past, retraced the paths of exploration, to find again those shores and rivers and mountains and Indians that first greeted the discoverers of the New World.

He traveled much in the years following the Walden experiment, not only, as he admitted, to give his intellect an airing and to gather experience for a winter's harvest of lectures, but to advance his nature study and extend his private researches. The travel books he wrote, like the lectures and articles from which they were later composed, were his attempt to find an audience; they were popular because travel books were then the rage—and Thoreau knew his audience and the tradition well enough to call one of his books *A Yankee in Canada*. His travel books, however, though they helped to establish his fame after his death (they were published in 1864, 1865, and 1866), have since been overshadowed by *Walden* and his political and social essays, and, minor works though they are, have been read at a discount because of his own disclaimers on travel and the generally easy and humorous manner in which he wrote them. The humor of travel, on which he often capitalized, was the humor of inexperience: to begin *A Yankee in Canada* with "I fear I have not got much to say about Canada, not having seen much; what I got by going to Canada was a cold [which of course you do not wish me to communicate to you]"[1] was to insure its reception but not its lasting claim on our attention. And though the humor, especially of *Cape Cod* and *A Yankee in Canada*, has a serious undermeaning and also adds much to one's impression of the warmth of Thoreau's character, it has apparently turned away readers in search of Thoreau's recognizable major themes.

If his treatment of travel was humorous, travel for Thoreau was still anything but recreation. In *A Yankee in Canada*, where he made a point of his difference from other tourists, he said that "the genuine traveller is going out to work hard, and fare harder"—and, since "honest travelling is about as dirty work as you can do," he wore his old clothes.[2] His travel books, of course, conveyed his sense of the value of leisure and his hunger for the uncommitted life of adventure; and with his umbrella and bundle he signalized

[1] W, V, 3; HM 949.

[2] W, V, 32.

his readiness for whatever the road offered; a traveler mistaken for peddler and thief, who took the less-traveled roads, not as Irving did out of a nostalgia for changeless retreats, but in order to meet with the essential experience of a place: to know the way of life there and how the people had mastered their environment. For Thoreau travel was hard work because besides his umbrella and bundle he carried all the facts he had gathered in preparation for the time when he would *see*, when the accuracy of previous accounts would be tested by his own encounter with the thing. He traveled with guidebook and chart in hand, and with expectations sharpened by long reading in the history, climate, and natural lore of the place; and every trip, casual as it might seem to the reader, was planned to the end of corroboration. In the midst of his Walden experiment, he went to the Maine woods to see the forest and the howling wilderness, and later, as his studies of the Indian deepened, to see the Indian in his native environment. He went to Canada, enticed by his early studies in discovery and colonial history, studies that afterward became laborious and thorough, that ranged from the Norse sagas to the Jesuit Relations, almost all of which he read in the original, to local histories and the most recent and popular works, such as Samuel Hammond's *Hunting Adventures in the Northern Wilds* and Captain Mayne Reid's *The Young Voyageurs, Forest Evils, The Hunter's Feast* and *Boy Hunters*.[3] If he went to Cape Cod for the first time to know the sea, he returned again and again because, as the printed record of his first three excursions showed, it had become important to him as a landmark in the discovery of the New World. And when he went to Minnesota in search of health, he was undoubtedly drawn once more by his interest in the Indian and by all that he had read of the French discoverers whose explorations of the interior of the continent, as well as whose coastal surveys, made them for him the true discoverers of America.

II

Of all of Thoreau's travel books, *The Maine Woods* best reveals his development, simply because each excursion was complete in

[3] See Cameron, *Emerson The Essayist*, II, 195-98, for the books Thoreau borrowed from the Harvard College Library, 1850-60; Thoreau's *Fact-Book on Nature* (Widener Collection), part of which was reprinted by Arthur Christy in *Colophon*, no. 16, 1934; Willson, *The Influence of Early North American History and Legend on the Writings of Henry David Thoreau*.

itself. Like *Cape Cod,* it covered three trips extending over a period
of years. Though the development is also apparent in *Cape Cod,*
especially in the last chapter on the discovery of America, the later
excursions were worked into the narrative of the first, and *Cape
Cod,* therefore, was a more unified work. In all of his travel writing,
however, Thoreau followed his actual itinerary, and thus the material of the narrative itself determined his treatment. Although all
of his trips to Maine were confined to the same area—that extending
north of Bangor to Eagle Lake and the headwaters of Canadian
rivers, with Moosehead Lake to the west and the east branch of
the Penobscot and the Penobscot to the east, and with Ktaadn
roughly in the center—each had a different itinerary; and since his
trips to Maine were farther apart in time, having been taken in
1846, 1853, and 1857, each had a different goal and a different
quality.

The first trip, for example, was taken during the Walden years,
when he was in good health and eager to compare his "sylvan" experiment with an experience of the primitive wilderness. This trip
was perhaps his greatest adventure, the equivalent in his career
of Mark Twain's *Roughing It* or perhaps of Parkman's trip in the
same year along the Oregon Trail; nothing he ever wrote was so
irrepressibly adventurous, so full of delight in frontier hardship
and skill and masculinity, so full of Thoreau's sense of release and
expectancy. The second trip does not convey this excitement because Thoreau had become more of an observer than participant,
a poet-naturalist who was unwilling to hunt the moose and a more
seasoned traveler for whom the wilderness was a less ecstatic experience. One recognizes a change in style: it has less of the
direct matter-of-fact seriousness of the first, is more jocose and
satirical because he is not so completely one, as he formerly was,
with what he sees. The last trip cannot be judged so readily by its
style because the narrative had not been prepared for the reader,
having been taken from the *Journal.* Nevertheless, Thoreau shares
his enjoyment here and is more relaxed; his learning is lighter and
his humor is easier—all perhaps because at last he had found an
Indian (as he did not on the second trip) who was worthy of
study. Over a period of eleven years, then, his interest in the
wilderness, upon which he staked so much, did not diminish but
took instead a less absolute place in his thought; he began to
place it in the context of civilization much in the same way that his

comparative botanizing helped him place Concord; his private experience became less important to him than what he saw, and he became an observer who extended his range to the study of men—not only to the Indian whose life in the woods brought him close to the aboriginal condition the first explorers saw, but to the hunter, logger, and pioneer who, in the mid-nineteenth century, were re-enacting all the stages in the founding and settlement of America.

"Ktaadn" was the first of Thoreau's travel articles—that is, if we make the distinction which should be made between his travels and his more poetically rendered excursions such as "A Walk to Wachusett." It was probably solicited by Horace Greeley, a busy editor who took the trouble to act as Thoreau's literary agent and who sold it to *The Union Magazine*. In this way he did as much to further Thoreau's career as Emerson did; for if Emerson helped Thoreau by suggesting the field of nature writing, Greeley, with his check for fifty dollars, opened the door to the kind of writing that would pay and for which Thoreau had equally substantial gifts. Thereafter, for the next ten years in fact, Thoreau published his travels in *Putnam's Monthly Magazine* and *The Atlantic Monthly* until the editorial mishandling of his manuscripts aroused his anger and forced him to close the door. When Greeley received "Ktaadn" he had told Thoreau that his article "on Maine scenery" was "too fine for the million," [4] yet nothing that Thoreau wrote was better suited to a popular audience; and while he was arduously gathering the materials for his Kalendar, the only fruits of which were "Autumnal Tints" and "Wild Apples," his travel writings kept him before the public. There was indeed something too fine for the million—a never fully developed but deep and abiding concern for the renewal of America—but there was always the immediate appeal of the scenery: there were always the rivers, lakes, and primitive forests, the sea and the desert, or the Great River of Canada, as if Thoreau had gone in search of the elemental facts of nature; and certainly, one of his gifts was his ability to restore these facts by means of his own historically sharpened sensibility to their original grandeur. Maine and Cape Cod, even eastern Canada, moreover, were out-of-the-way places whose appeal, if not to the extent of Typee or Tahiti, lay in the possibility of strange and exotic adventure.

---

[4] W, III, ix.

Now "Ktaadn" was an adventure up the Penobscot into the wilderness above Nicketow, an adventure culminating in the ascent of Mt. Ktaadn, a mountain first ascended by white men in 1804, and again only as recently as 1836, 1837, and 1845. For Thoreau, who took the stance of a civilized man (which indeed he was), it was his first experience with "the grim, untrodden wilderness" [5] where the river was the only highway and where, as in the days of the Canadian *voyageurs,* one still had to travel by batteau. The batteau, in fact, had a prominent place in his narrative comparable to the canoe in the later excursions—and as he shot the rapids he was more exhilarated than he had ever been before while boating. This dangerous mode of traveling gave "new emphasis" to the Canadian boat song that he had known from his youth, for, as he remarked, it described "precisely our own adventure and was inspired by the experience of a similar kind of life. . . ." [6] His aim on all his travels was always to come into the conditions that would provide the experience of a similar kind of life; and as he went from the civilization of Bangor, the port through which the white pine forest passed into lumber, to Oldtown, where the once-powerful Penobscots reminded him of rum and the fur trade and the history of their extinction, to the burning clearings of settlers and to the loggers' camps still deeper in the woods, he retraced in reverse order the process of civilization until he came at last to unhandseled nature, to the naked, inviolable rocks of Ktaadn.

The wilderness and Ktaadn were what he had come to see, but as he passed in rapid review of civilization and saw the beginnings of trade and the divestment of the forest, he was distressed by the waste and the inevitable doom of the wilderness—first made aware perhaps of the need to preserve the wild, a theme which, with increasing insistence, he developed in his later years. Although he admired the sturdy self-reliance and worldliness of settlers like George McCauslin and Tom Fowler, who served as his guides, and was so much involved in his own Walden experiment that he advised the poverty-stricken and the emigrant to "begin life as Adam

---

[5] W, III, 12. Fannie Hardy Eckstorm makes much of the fact that Thoreau was not a woodsman in "Thoreau's 'Maine Woods,'" *The Atlantic Monthly,* CII (August, 1908), 242-50. This essay is the best introduction to *The Maine Woods* and one of the finest general appraisals of Thoreau ever written. Mrs. Eckstorm's "Notes on Thoreau's 'Maine Woods'" has been printed in *The Thoreau Society Bulletin,* LI (Spring, 1955), 1, 3.

[6] W, III, 42.

did" [7] in the woods; although he approved of the utilitarian functionalism of the loggers' camp and the skill and heroism of loggers
and drivers, he did not see in these signs, as he did later, the warrant of progress but rather of destruction. His heart was set on the
wilderness, on a pure nature uninhabited by man, where the moose
and the Indian had "never been dispossessed, nor nature dis-
forested." [8] On his other trips to Maine he was always aware of the
presence of man, but when he ascended Ktaadn the wilderness of
his dream was realized, and he was reminded that, even though
America had leaped to the Pacific, there were "many a lesser Oregon
and California unexplored behind us," that civilization had only a
slight tenure in America, that within a day or two from Concord
"there still waves the virgin forest of the New World." [9]

The nature he discovered in the wilderness, however, was not
entirely what he had expected. The uninterrupted forest was "even
more grim and wild" than he had anticipated, "a damp and intricate
wilderness, in the spring everywhere wet and miry," and its aspect
was "universally stern and savage" save for the lakes, which he
felt were "mild and civilizing in a degree." [10] Here, he found, "one
could no longer accuse institutions and society, but must front the
true source of evil." [11] For here, as he made his way to Ktaadn, he
found the primordial world of "gray, silent rocks," a dreary and
desolate scenery with ancient trees as "old as the flood," and path-
less places that reminded him of Satan's difficulties through Chaos.[12]
He had ascended mountains before, and in his last years was to
return to them as if compelled to try once more their inspirational
powers; but the ascent of Ktaadn did not work that miracle, no
more than did the sea at Cape Cod, because he was overcome by a
vast, titanic, and inhuman nature. He was reminded, he said, "of
Atlas, Vulcan, the Cyclops, and Prometheus. Such was Caucasus
and the rock where Prometheus was bound. Aeschylus had no doubt
visited such scenery as this. It was vast, Titanic, and such as man
never inhabits." Describing his own impressions, he said that

some part of the beholder, even some vital part, seems to escape through
the loose grating of his ribs as he ascends. He is more lone than you can

[7] W, III, 16.
[8] W, III, 89.
[9] W, III, 91.
[10] W, III, 88.
[11] W, III, 18.
[12] W, III, 67-68.

KNIGHT OF THE UMBRELLA AND BUNDLE 361

imagine. There is less of substantial thought and fair understanding in him than in the plains where men inhabit. His reason is dispersed and shadowy, more thin and subtile, like the air. Vast, Titanic, inhuman Nature has got him at disadvantage, caught him alone, and pilfers him of some of his divine faculty. She does not smile on him as in the plains. She seems to say sternly, Why came ye here before your time. This ground is not prepared for you. Is it not enough that I smile in the valleys? . . . I cannot pity nor fondle thee here, but forever relentlessly drive thee hence to where I *am* kind.[13]

One wonders how much this experience, coming earlier in Thoreau's development, would have altered his conception of nature; if, say like Melville, he had known the sea in his youth instead of the pastoral nature of Concord. For now he realized as never before "the presence of a force not bound to be kind to man," an otherness which was not conditional—a phase of his inspirational process—but absolute. On Ktaadn he had a presentiment of the alien, cold, indifferent nature of naturalism: here was "*Nature*," "primeval, untamed, and forever untamable," a savage and awful Earth "made out of Chaos and Old Night" with which man was not to be associated. Instead of "Mother Earth" here was "Matter"—"the home, this, of Necessity and Fate." Here, he found, "was no man's garden, but the unhandseled globe. . . . a specimen of what God saw fit to make this world. . . . some star's surface, some hard matter in its home!"[14] The Creator of Ktaadn was obviously not the Artist of the railroad cut; for matter here was not fluid and obedient to idea, and even his body, Thoreau felt, had become matter which was strange to him. Overcome and unmoored by this experience, he wrote the most frenzied passage he was ever to write, a passage that could not be passed off as extravagance: "What is this Titan that has possession of me? Talk of mysteries! Think of our life in nature,—daily to be shown matter, to come in contact with it,—rocks, trees, wind on our cheeks! the *solid* earth! the *actual* world! the *common sense! Contact! Contact! Who* are we? *where* are we?"[15] This passage is difficult and perhaps ambiguous, for in one sense Thoreau felt the sublimity of this otherness, the elemental purity and awful grandeur of it. But "contact" was a word he never used when describing his sympathy with nature, not even

---

[13] W, III, 70-71.

[14] W, III, 77-78.

[15] W, III, 79. See W, VI, 319-20, where, in a letter to Blake, he recalled this experience and wrote: "You must ascend a mountain to learn your relation to matter, and so to your own body, for *it* is at home there, though *you* are not."

in *Walden* where he spoke of his desire to reach "hard bottom and rocks in place," [16] and here it seems to suggest the recognition of otherness rather than the overcoming of it. To be reminded by *contact* of this otherness would indeed have changed his life in nature, would, as the "*Who* are we? *where* are we?" indicates, have destroyed the possibility of communion.

When he looked back on this first excursion, therefore, he resolved his difficulties by moralizing his experience in terms of the forest rather than the mountain, and thus the newness of the New World lost some of its terrors. The wilderness of the Indian was primitive enough, and he could even contemplate his Walden life there—"a flute to play at evening here, while his strains echo to the stars, amid the howling of wolves; [to] live, as it were, in the primitive age of the world, a primitive man." [17] The life of the Indian (who, incidentally, did not pry into the secrets of the gods, who respected the sacred and mysterious mountaintop) was as far back into history as he wanted to go. And though the life of the Indian reminded him that "America is still unsettled and unexplored," [18] and made it possible for him to maintain his belief in the virtue of the wild, when he went to the Maine woods thereafter, visions of a more genial and humanized nature invaded his mind.

If "Ktaadn" introduced Thoreau to the primitive life, like Melville's *Typee*, it also took him as far back into time as he could go, to rocks as primordial as those of the ancient religious structures Melville mused over, and, if not to savage physicality, to matter equally unredeemed by mind. "It was a place," Thoreau wrote, "for heathenism and superstitious rites,—to be inhabited by men nearer of kin to the rocks and to wild animals than we." [19] Undoubtedly this experience was reflected in the chastened primitivism of *Walden*, as it was in his second trip in 1853 which dramatized the conflict between the hunter and the poet-naturalist and the unresolved problem of "Ktaadn"—if primitive nature and civilization are contemporary in America, how should one use nature? Were it not for these problems, "Chesuncook," with its account of the hunting of the moose, would have an attraction comparable to that of

[16] W, II, 108.

[17] W, III, 87.

[18] W, III, 90.

[19] W, III, 78.

The Green Hills of Africa. But even though Thoreau did his best to make the hunt exciting—measuring the moose, as Melville did the whale, to suggest its great size, citing "the quaint John Josselyn" on the moose's " *'transcendentia,'* " and retelling Governor Neptune's Indian fable in which the moose was once a whale left stranded when the sea withdrew—he no longer had the "strange thrill of savage delight" he spoke of in *Walden,* he no longer had the temptation to devour a woodchuck raw. In "Higher Laws," where this conflict was thoroughly explained, he said that he was only hungry for that "wildness which he [the woodchuck] represented." [20] Such was his hunger for the moose in "Chesuncook," and by creating a mythical beast as much a symbol of the wilderness as Faulkner's bear he was incapable of sharing in the abandon of the hunt. "I had not come a-hunting," he said, "and felt some compunctions about accompanying the hunters, [but] I wished to see a moose near at hand, and was not sorry to learn how the Indian managed to kill one. I went as reporter or chaplain to the hunters. . . ." [21] His compunctions, not his inability to hunt, stood between him and his narrative, and the excitement of the hunt was dissipated by the judgment he passed on it: in the death of the moose he saw the doom of the wilderness.

Reflecting on the killing of the moose, he said that "the afternoon's tragedy, and my share in it, as it affected the innocence, destroyed the pleasure of my adventure." [22] Though he preferred to live like a philosopher on the fruits he had raised, he thought that he might with satisfaction spend a year in the woods hunting and fishing, not for sport, but merely for subsistence. For what appalled him, as it had Natty Bumppo, was the wanton waste, the base and coarse motives of the "hirelings" and even the Indians who did not come to the forest out of love for the wild but "to slay as many moose and other wild animals as possible." [23] And what was true of the moose was also true of the white pine which was almost as scarce. While his companions continued the hunt, therefore, Thoreau went naturalizing, enacting that love of nature which distinguished the poet from the hunter and the lumberman, and which provided the framework for his remarks, made famous by

---

[20] W, III, 125-28, 163-64; W, II, 232.

[21] W, III, 109-10.

[22] W, III, 132.

[23] W, III, 133.

Lowell's deletion, on the immortality of the pine. The lumberman, he said, was not the lover of the pine, but the poet—"It is the living spirit of the tree, not its spirit of turpentine with which I sympathize, and which heals my cuts. It is as immortal as I am, and perchance will go to as high a heaven, there to tower above me still." [24]

Even if the poet made a higher use of the wilderness, it was ultimately in the interest of poetry, in the humanization of nature, that the poet should turn to a nature something less than wild. As a "resource and a background, the raw material of our civilization," the wilderness, however, continued to be necessary for Thoreau. For strength and beauty, for inspiration and true recreation, "the poet," he wrote, "must, from time to time, travel the logger's path and the Indian's trail, to drink at some new and more bracing fountain of the Muses, far in the recesses of the wilderness." [25] This was the reason why, in these later years, he became a champion of natural preserves and advised his neighbors to keep their woods and fields for a "common"—why he glorified the Boxboro woods and the Easterbrooks country, places still as wild and shaggy and swampy as the Maine woods.[26] Here, at least, one would not have "to gnaw the very crust of the earth for nutriment." [27] And yet for "a permanent residence" he felt that "our smooth, but still varied landscape" was better. Where he had once believed that the revitalization of poetry required the wild and had belittled the English nature poets, he now returned to that tradition: "The partially cultivated country it is which chiefly has inspired, and will continue to inspire, the strains of poets. . . ." For he now realized that the poet's path was not the logger's but the woodman's, that the "logger and pioneer have preceded him . . . banished decaying

---

[24] W, III, 134-35. Lowell solicited "Chesuncook" in 1858, although the trip was made in 1853, just a month after Lowell himself had been in the Moosehead Lake region. Lowell is said to have objected to Thoreau's pantheism, but he may well have been discomfited by the obvious superiority of Thoreau's account. Lowell admitted in his "A Moosehead Journal" that there was nothing of Moosehead Lake in it; indeed, reading it today one cannot see the woods for the words.

Thoreau introduced this theme again in a long attack on the lumbermen in the third part (see W, III, 253-54).

[25] W, III, 172, 173.

[26] W, III, 172; J, XIV, 224-31, 241-49; J, V, 239-40; J, X, 112. Thoreau, of course, has been recognized as a conservationist, but this label hides the fact that what he wanted to conserve most was man: the recreative aspects of nature. He is really closer to the planners who advocate "green belts."

[27] W, III, 170.

wood and the spongy mosses which feed on it, and built hearths and humanized Nature for him." [28] In the dreamy state from which the call of the moose aroused him, he had seemed to be "floating through ornamental grounds," he had seen "an endless succession of porticoes and columns, cornices and facades, verandas and churches," and he had lost himself in the thought of "that architecture and the nobility that dwelt behind and might issue from it." [29] In the midst of the wilderness had he been dreaming of Concord? Of the higher society?

Perhaps it was Thoreau's growing awareness of his inability to master the wild that turned him from his youthful exaltation of the Indian to those exacting studies of Indian life of his last years. This interest, of course, increased along with his researches in the discovery of America; for like the poets of American "epics" who had gone before him, he saw in the Indian the first chapter of American history. This chapter, however, was almost always forgotten, though the "antiquities" of "our predecessors" could be easily found, as Thoreau often found arrowheads, by turning the soil. "Why, then," he asked, "make so great ado about the Roman and the Greek, and neglect the Indian?" He studied the Indian because, as he said, "New earths, new themes expect us. Celebrate not the Garden of Eden, but your own" [30]—he was stirred by the heady national consciousness that had awakened a sense of the need for an American past. But he also studied the Indian because he was "the indigenous man of America" who had mastered the aboriginal environment of America. "If wild men, so much more like ourselves than they are unlike, have inhabited these shores before us," he wrote, "we wish to know particularly what manner of men they were, how they lived here, their relation to nature, their arts and their customs, their fancies and superstitions. They paddled over these waters, they wandered in these woods, and they had their fancies and beliefs connected with the sea and the forest, which concern us quite as much as the fables of Oriental nations do." [31]

To this end Thoreau hired Indian guides on his last two trips to

---

[28] W, III, 171-73. His description of the proper balance of wild and civilized —a place where one did not need to quarrel about huckleberries, and the wild did not prevail over the pastoral—answers to the Concord he had known before the "evil days" of fences.

[29] W, III, 131.

[30] J, X, 118.

[31] J, XI, 437-38.

Maine. Joe Aitteon accompanied him in "Chesuncook," but in spite
of his skill, with his popular airs (he whistled "O Susanna") and
his confession that he could not live in the woods as his ancestors
had, he was not enough of an Indian to kindle Thoreau's imagination. The Indian did not have the prominent part in "Chesuncook"
that he did in "The Allegash and East Branch"; and only the
episode at the Indian camp was given over to him in "Chesuncook."
There, sharing the Indians' dwelling (though the dirt bothered
him), amidst the moose hides stretched and curing on poles and
the carcasses left on the ground, Thoreau, who knew their history
better than the Indians did, was "carried back at once three hundred
years." The method of smoking moose meat reminded him of
what he had seen in de Bry's *Collectio Peregrinationum* (1588)
and his experience of the campfire recalled the sufferings of the
Jesuit missionaries. What he had learned of the Abenaki language
in Father Rasles' *Dictionary* was confirmed, and listening to their
talk, he felt that he "stood, or rather lay, as near to the primitive
man of America . . . as any of its discoverers ever did." "These
Abenakis gossiped, laughed, and jested, in the language in which
Eliot's Indian Bible is written," he said, "the language which has
been spoken in New England who shall say how long? These were
the sounds that issued from the wigwams of this country before
Columbus was born; they have not yet died away. . . ." [32]

When Thoreau went to Maine for the last time he was fortunate
to find a guide whose forest ways as well as the sounds of whose
language had not yet died away. Although he had represented his
tribe at Augusta and Washington, had felt the attraction of great
cities like New York, had called on Webster; although he had a
neat frame house at Oldtown, was worth six thousand dollars, sent
his boy to school with the whites, and kept the Sabbath even in
the wilderness, Joe Polis, unlike most Indians, had made good use
of civilization without losing any of his woodcraft. Not only could
he handle the canoe expertly, he could build one; he knew how to
make spruce thread, skillfully splitting roots with his knife while
he used his teeth as "a third hand," and he could make pitch (the
secret of which he kept from Thoreau) in order to repair his canoe
on the spot.[33] He was completely at home in the wilderness, having
those finer senses, the "Indian wisdom," that Thoreau praised in

[32] W, III, 148-58.
[33] W, III, 225-26.

the "Natural History." His familiarity with nature had sharpened
and educated his senses and had made him self-reliant. "His Indian
instinct," Thoreau wrote, "may tell him still as much as the most
confident white man knows. He does not carry things in his head,
nor remember the route exactly like a white man, but relies on
himself at the moment." [34] He could call a muskrat, make a new
kind of herb tea every night or a lily-bulb soup, tell the medicinal
use of every plant, and find his way through the woods so easily
that it seemed uncanny even to Thoreau. Indeed, he had good
reason to lament, as Thoreau recorded, "that the present generation
of Indians 'had lost a great deal.' " [35] He taught Thoreau his language, as he had agreed to—a language always specific and so full
of the geography of the place that Thoreau was reminded that
he was not one of the earlier discoverers of the Maine woods, that
"it was thus well known and suitably named by Indian hunters
perhaps a thousand years ago." [36] His religious chant, finally,
carried Thoreau back "to the period of the discovery of America,
to San Salvador and the Incas, when Europeans first encountered
the simple faith of the Indian." [37]

Carried back beyond the dispossession and degeneration of the
Indian, Thoreau realized anew their natural faith: "There was,
indeed, a beautiful simplicity about it; nothing of the dark and
savage, only the mild and infantile. The sentiments of humility and
reverence chiefly were expressed." [38] And when almost immediately
afterward he discovered phosphorescent wood—his great find on
this excursion—the wild lost some of its terror for him. "I little
thought," he wrote, making a symbol of this discovery, "that there
was such a light shining in the darkness of the wilderness for me."
Unable to humanize the wilderness sufficiently, he now strengthened
his faith in nature by recognizing that the Indians had found spirit
there: "Nature must have made a thousand revelations to them
which are still secrets to us." "I exulted," he wrote, "like 'a pagan
suckled in a creed' that had never been worn at all, but was bran
new. . . . I let science slide. . . . I believed that the woods were not
tenantless, but chokeful of honest spirits as good as myself any

[34] W, III, 205.
[35] W, III, 259.
[36] W, III, 298.
[37] W, III, 198.
[38] W, III, 198.

day. . . ." His humor here guarded a faith that had been worn and that was only partially restored; for it was no longer the confident Thoreau of the *Week* who wrote, "I have much to learn of the Indian, nothing of the missionary." [39]

Indeed, in spite of all that Joe Polis taught him of the possibility of a sympathetic communion with the wild, and in spite of his feeling that "here was travelling of the old heroic kind over the unaltered face of nature," [40] the wilderness still had its terrors. The swamp at Mud Pond carry, where he took the wrong path, was the genuine wilderness "ready to echo the growl of a bear, the howl of a wolf, or the scream of a panther," and only in retrospect could he treat it humorously: "a howling wilderness does not howl: it is the imagination of the traveller that does the howling." [41] The "denseness of the forest, the fallen trees and rocks, the windings of the river, the streams emptying in, and the frequent swamps to be crossed" made him "shudder." [42] When his companion was lost in a desolation of burnt-over trees, jutting rocks, rapids and falls— a landscape that in the telling at least Thoreau transformed into a Gothic setting worthy of Brockden Brown—he was overcome not only by anxiety for his hapless friend but by the sudden awareness of his own impotence in the wilderness.[43] And once the initial feeling of release wore off, even the impenetrable forests that enclosed and darkened the rivers depressed him, until he looked forward to the "liberating and civilizing" expanse of the lakes.[44] The lakes were openings in the sky, they let in light, and the "influx of light merely," Thoreau said, making light and dark carry spiritual meaning, "is civilizing." [45] Lakes, he wrote, "give ample scope and range to our thought." [46] He sympathized, therefore, with the settlers who clustered around lakes for the sake of neighborhood and who, he thought, were establishing "great centres of light." [47] And cleared land now excited him: "Such, seen far or near, you know at once to be man's work, for Nature never does it. In order

[39] W, III, 200-201.
[40] W, III, 260.
[41] W, III, 342.
[42] W, III, 307.
[43] W, III, 286, 288.
[44] W, III, 219.
[45] W, III, 233, 265.
[46] W, III, 219.
[47] W, III, 219.

to let in the light to the earth as on a lake, he clears off the forest on the hillsides and plains, and sprinkles fine grass-seed, like an enchanter, and so carpets the earth with a firm sward." [48] The advance of civilization to Nicketow, an outpost eleven years before, did not elicit the jeremiad of his first excursion. Instead in one image he condensed the entire course of civilization: "not long since, similar beds [of fir twigs] were spread along the Connecticut, the Hudson, and the Delaware, and longer still ago, by the Thames and Seine, and they now help to make the soil where private and public gardens, mansions and palaces are." [49] Rivers were the paths of discovery and the highways of civilization; the wilderness was the soil of civilization. If he disapproved of the misuse of nature they inevitably introduced, he no longer wholeheartedly despaired, for having known the darkness of the wilderness, he knew the value of light.

In a letter to Blake, who did not like what he had read of Thoreau's "Canada story" in *Putnam's Monthly Magazine,* and in his own introductory remarks, Thoreau belittled his excursion to Canada.[50] And yet from the time he had read Colonel Hall's *Travels* and copied out the *voyageur's* song during his college years, his interest in Canada had grown.[51] In fact, after his visit in 1850 he went to work in earnest, searching through the Harvard College Library for everything pertaining to Canada, making out those extensive lists of books which were always the warrant of his seriousness.[52] Perhaps he belittled *A Yankee in Canada* because he could not make sufficient use of what he had read, believing as he did, and demonstrating it in *Cape Cod* (which benefited from these studies), that "decayed literature makes the richest of all soils." [53] Except for the Great River, the falls, and the forests beyond the farms that beckoned to him, his actual trip did not bring him so close as he desired to the Canada of the early explorers, the Jesuits, the Indians, and the fur traders. Unexpectedly, with something of

[48] W, III, 258.

[49] W, III, 317.

[50] W, VI, 215.

[51] Cameron, *Emerson The Essayist,* II, 192, 202;   MA 594.

[52] MA 595, Extracts Relating to Canada. Thoreau's bibliography, extracts, and comments cover 38 pages. He also read the Geological Surveys of Canada for 1853, 1854, 1855, 1856. See Thoreau MS, Berg Collection.

[53] J, III, 353.

a shock, it brought him instead to a foreign country where French rather than Indian was spoken, where the spires of Notre Dame rather than the pine filled the sky, where the fortifications of Quebec dominated the scene, where Montreal reminded him of Paris and Edinburgh instead of the Indian village of Hochelaga and Quebec made him think of the ports of Boulogne, Dieppe, Rouen, and Havre de Grace, where the farming seigniories of eastern Canada did not remind him so much of settlers in a new world as of Norman peasants still working in the shadow of the feudal institutions from which America might have freed them. "I rubbed my eyes," he wrote of Quebec, "to be sure that I was in the nineteenth century. . . . I thought it would be a good place to read Froissart's Chronicles. It was such a reminiscence of the Middle Ages as Scott's novels." [54] And when he walked to Ste. Anne, one of the most unchanged parts of Canada, he confessed that

to a traveller from the Old World, Canada East may appear like a new country, and its inhabitants like colonists, but to me, coming from New England and being a very green traveller withal . . . it appeared as old as Normandy itself, and realized much that I had heard of Europe and the Middle Ages. Even the names of humble Canadian villages affected me as if they had been those of the renowned cities of antiquity. To be told by a habitan, when I asked the name of a village in sight, that it is *St. Feréol* or *St. Anne,* the *Guardian Angel* or the *Holy Joseph's;* or of a mountain, that it was *Bélange* or *St. Hyacinthe!* As soon as you leave the States, these saintly names begin. . . . I began to dream of Provence and the Troubadours. . . . They veiled the Indian and the primitive forest, and the woods toward Hudson's Bay were only as the forests of France and Germany.[55]

As the title suggests, *A Yankee in Canada* belongs to the tradition of American travel books whose aim was to repay in kind the European travelers' ridicule of America. If it was not quite *The Innocents Abroad,* Thoreau's trip to Canada was still the equivalent, for one who made much of little, of a tour to Europe. It shows us what he might have done in Europe, how much he could have done in that rich field of observation, especially if he had been willing to use his exceptional gift for setting the present fact in the context of the past human experience with which it had been allied. In any case, it had a twofold success: it did for Canada in a less systematic way what Emerson did for English institutions and

---

[54] W, V, 23.

[55] W, V, 56-57.

character in *English Traits;* and more dramatically than *English Traits,* it supported Thoreau's contention, made in a college theme, that a writer's "nationality may be even more striking in treating of a foreign than a domestic subject," that the traveler himself "will be the most conspicuous object." [56]

Indeed, Thoreau's conspicuous Yankee character is one of the charms of the book. A social critic at home, and occasionally in this book, Thoreau was nowhere else so unguarded and unqualified about his faith in America. As Twain had done in *The Innocents Abroad,* he made sport of the crude—that detached yet superior— curiosity of his compatriots. Uncharacteristically, he had taken the train to Montreal and had found himself among tourists—tourists who were bid for on the quays by voluble caleche drivers (he himself used one in his haste to see everything), who went in parties and dutifully ran down the sights in order, and who, with Yankee irreverence, at Notre Dame "bet that the candles were not wax, but tin." [57] Thoreau, of course, remained apart, always one step ahead of them, but the same curiosity and freedom characterized him; and he, too, took in the sights and searched out others less accessible, like the ruins of Chateau Richer, or never meant for careful study, like the fortifications of Quebec. His attitude was theirs: "Well . . . here I am in a foreign country; let me have my eyes about me, and take it all in." [58] He did his share of gaping as a proper innocent should, catching the novel surface of things, and remembering the dogcarts, markets, restaurants, domestic arrangements, and shrines. Though Notre Dame evoked more serious thoughts for him than for the others, he did not respond so much to its art as to its size (he always carried a measure or improvised one), and the novelty of nuns and priests elicited from him a kind of anti-Catholic sentiment that would have stirred in the memories of his readers the *Awful Disclosures* of Maria Monk. The clergy seemed effeminate to him, and he described one curé he met as "a sleek friar-like personage" with "no work to do"; the nuns, he felt, could have used "a smart switching," and he described them waiting "demurely . . . while a truck laden with raisins ["were they for some jolly fat friar to nibble? or to flavor his porridge?"] was driven

[56] "National and Individual Genius," Sanborn, *Life,* p. 107. In *Putnam's Monthly Magazine,* where portions of it appeared in 1853, it was simply called "An Excursion to Canada."

[57] W, V, 14.

[58] W, V, 31.

in at the seminary of St. Sulpice, never once lifting their eyes from the ground." [59] When he visited the fortress at Quebec for a second time he joined the tourists, and "seeing that nobody walked with the red-coated commandant," he said that "I attached myself to him, and though I was not what is called well-dressed [his palm-leaf hat and his "unspeakably cheap" brown linen duster were "a thoroughly Yankee costume"], he did not know whether to repel me or not, for I talked like one who was not aware of any deficiency in that respect." [60] The military was the constant butt of his humor: of a sentinel he remarked, "We stood close by without fear and looked at him," and the bare-kneed Highlanders drew his ridicule every time he saw them, until he concluded that they went bare-legged to increase the attraction and that "if you wish to study the muscles of the leg about the knee, repair to Quebec. This universal exhibition in Canada of the tools and sinews of war reminded me of the keeper of a menagerie showing his animals' claws." [61] Much of the humor that distinguishes this book from the others was the result of the irreverence bred of his feeling of American superiority. From the start he preferred his "thin and nervous countrymen" to the "solid, red-faced, burly-looking Englishman" or the oxlike Canadians; he preferred the libertarianism of the American to the formality of the Englishman; even the custom of tipping the hat and saying good day in eastern Canada seemed servile to him—"a Yankee," he added, "has not leisure for it." [62] "The Yankee," he claimed, "though undisciplined, had this advantage at least, that he especially is a man who, everywhere and under all circumstances, is fully resolved to better his condition . . . while the virtue of the Irishman, and to a great extent the Englishman [had he been in eastern Canada at the time of this comparison he would have included the habitan], consists in merely maintaining his ground or condition." [63] Such was the measure of all he saw, and with it he judged the institutions that had shaped the Canadian character— the Church, the Military, and the Feudal Land System.

Perhaps the most interesting thing about Thoreau's attitude

<hr />

[59] W, V, 46, 47, 15, 16; HM 949.

[60] W, V, 28, 31.

[61] W, V, 25, 79. This seems an odd response for Thoreau, who elsewhere speaks approvingly of nakedness. So, too, his remark on the leisure of the clergy—unless it was directed at the busy-ness of the clergy at home.

[62] W, V, 9, 47.

[63] W, V, 10.

toward the Church, which always aroused in his contemporaries who went to Europe an unwilling but deep response, was how much he granted to it. The first thing he saw in Montreal was Notre Dame, the largest church in North America, a symbol of Catholic power, around which, accordingly, he gathered his thoughts. Every village, of course, was dominated by its often splendid church, and he was impressed, especially in eastern Canada, by the fact that he was in "a thoroughly Catholic country" where "there was no trace of any other religion." [64] The simple reverence of the people always stirred his sympathy, for reverence, he believed, was a sentiment that was all but dead in the Yankee character; but, as one expects, he was skeptical of miraculous cures and Catholic education. The latter, he said (and was to remember in his description of Alek Therien, the wood-chopper in *Walden*), was a process "not of enlightening, but of obfuscating the mind . . . and the pupils received only so much light as could penetrate the shadow of the Catholic Church." [65] After seeing so many wayside shrines, he "could not look at an honest weathercock . . . without mistrusting that there was some covert reference in it to St. Peter." But if he felt that the Catholics had "fallen behind the significance of their symbols," he still believed that the "Catholic are the only churches . . . which are not wholly profane." [66] What impressed him most in Notre Dame was "the quiet religious atmosphere of the place," open every day and not only on Sundays, suitable "to serious and profitable thought." The pictures, statues, and candles blurred into an impression of a great cave with sparkling stalactites, into a natural shrine, a thinking place of value to philosophy and poetry as well as religion. He was led by this course of thought to the remark that Curtis omitted in *Putnam's*, that "I am sure but this Catholic religion would be an admirable one if the priests were quite omitted." But the image of the cave led as inevitably to Thoreau's equally pointed remark: "In Concord, to be sure, we do not need such [churches]. Our forests ["Walden Wood"] are such a church, far grander, and more sacred." [67]

---

[64] W, V, 52.

[65] W, V, 46. In HM 949 he added: "All they learn is to make the sign of the cross."

[66] W, V, 46, 13, 12.

[67] W, V, 13-14; HM 949.

To the Military he granted nothing, having the ingrained hostility of most Americans toward such establishments as well as that of the patriot toward the redcoats. Their presence everywhere and their constant drills were signs of "England's hands holding the Canadas," and he judged "by the redness of her knuckles [that] she would soon have to let go." [68] Though the cause of much amusement to him, the "guarding, regarding, and disregarding [of] all kinds of law," the futility of discipline and precision marching, disturbed him deeply. It led him to some of his sharpest social criticism, as when, for example, he wrote of their drill: "The problem appeared to be how to smooth down all individual protuberances or idiosyncrasies, and make a thousand men move as one man, animated by one central will; and there was some approach to success. . . . They made on me the impression, not of many individuals, but of one vast centipede of a man, good for all sorts of pulling down; and why not then for some kinds of building up?" As in his review of Etzler's book, he was not opposed to the social harmony and cooperation he saw in the drill, but to the unworthy aim, to the merely physical association unprompted by the heart; for association itself, "such a co-operation and harmony" animated by love, was now for Thoreau "the very end and success for which government now exists in vain. . . ." [69] The reason it could not come to pass, whether in redcoats or American citizens, was that "all true manhood was in the process of being drilled out of them," destroying their "originality and independence." "It is impossible," Thoreau remarked, "to give the soldier a good education, without making him a deserter. His natural foe is the government that drills him." He advised the philanthropist, therefore, "not [to] drill a few, but educate all," to teach men "so to respect themselves, that they could not be hired for this work. . . ." [70]

Though he wrote humorously of the walls of Quebec, he also made them the basis of one of his finest essays on institutions and government. The fortifications of Quebec, like Notre Dame in Montreal, were conspicuous if only because of the money that had been poured into them; the wall was the "main thing" in Quebec, the "only remarkable walls we have in North America. . . ." Out of curiosity and "patriotism" he studied them inside and out, until he

---

[68] W, V, 16.

[69] W, V, 16-17.

[70] W, V, 27.

feared that he might become "wall-eyed." [71] He committed the gates to memory, against the day his country might need this intelligence, though he hardly thought that fortifications would avail in an age when the static was giving way to the mobility of mind. "If seven champions were enough against the latter [the gates of Thebes]," he said, "one would be enough against Quebec, though he bore for all armor and device only an umbrella and a bundle." [72] For fortifications, which reminded him of the Middle Ages, were clumsy, useless instruments like the baggage of tradition his neighbors carried; they were not the real "work of the age." [73] If he had once been fired by the heroism of the Middle Ages, nothing shows better how much his conception of the hero had been transformed since the days of *The Service*. Walls, he wrote, "do not consist with the development of the intellect. Huge stone structures of all kinds, both in their erection and by their influence when erected, rather oppress than liberate the mind. They are tombs for the souls of men, as frequently for their bodies also. The sentinel with his musket beside a man with his umbrella is spectral." [74] The military ardor, of course, remained, but the hero now fought with the weapons of his age, the schoolhouse and the printing press, which, he said, "occupied a position which commands such a fort as this." [75]

When he used the huge structures of stone to draw together his final appraisal of Canadian institutions in "The Walls of Quebec," he had in mind as well the churches which were also, according to law, built of stone, and he had already discussed the feudal laws of land tenure that kept the population of Montmorenci County backward and stationary. He had already seen men, in a country abounding in water power, sawing logs to pave the streets, and he had been pained by the cheapness of men; and if the women laboring in the fields did not pain him, it was only because their outdoor work was preferable to that of the girls in New England mills. It is significant that he did not comment on the misuse of water power in the mills—significant because in comparing Canada and New England he was something of a partisan of progress, like

[71] W, V, 74, 76.
[72] W, V, 74.
[73] W, V, 77.
[74] W, V, 78.
[75] W, V, 79.

Whitman, translating the old and the new, which were his major terms, into servitude and freedom. "Every New England house," he wrote, "has a front and principal door opening to the great world, though it may be on the cold side [that is, facing north], for it stands on the highway of nations, and the road which runs by it comes from the Old World and goes to the far West; but the Canadian's door opens into his backyard and farm alone, and the road which runs behind his house leads only from the church of one saint to that of another." [76] This difference between an open and closed society, rather than soil and climate, accounted for the physical and intellectual inferiority of the habitan. "In some respects," Thoreau said, "they were incredibly filthy. It is evident that they have not advanced since the settlement of the country, that they were quite behind the age. . . . Even in respect to the common arts of life, they are not so far advanced as a frontier town in the West three years old. . . . They are very far from a revolution; have no quarrel with Church or State, but their vice and their virtue is content." [77]

This willingness to rest in the old institutions, moreover, explained why Canada, though wild and unsettled, impressed Thoreau "as an older country than the States. . . ." "Those who first built this fort," he wrote, "coming from Old France with the memory and tradition of feudal days and customs weighing on them, were unquestionably behind their age; and those who now inhabit and repair it are behind their ancestors or predecessors. ["It is a specimen of the old world in the new."] Those old chevaliers thought that they could transplant the feudal system to America. It has been set out, but it has not thriven." [78] For instead of taking up the land as the American did, "'without reference to, or acknowledgement of, any other man,'" the habitan, like the Normans centuries before, lived in villages for the sake of neighborhood and paid his tithes, mill rents, and mutation fines. Thus, Thoreau concluded, "the French have occupied Canada, not *udally,* or by noble right, but *feudally,* or by ignoble right. They are a nation of peasants" [79]—a people who had not grown because they had forfeited their manhood and individuality, the springs of

---

[76] W, V, 59.

[77] W, V, 64.

[78] W, V, 80-81; HM 949.

[79] W, V, 82. Thoreau, however, was attracted by the stability of the habitans, by their self-sufficient agrarianism, and by their social virtues. See W, V, 68.

change, and because they willingly served those institutions which should have served them.

Canada taught the exponent of civil disobedience that the private man was worth more in the United States, that "if your wealth . . . consists in manliness, in originality, and independence, you had better stay here." [80] In America there was still so little government that the American could put it out of mind; it did not parade itself daily before his eyes. "An American," Thoreau exulted, "cares, comparatively, little about such things, and is advantageously nearer to the primitive and the ultimate condition of man. . . . Give me a country where it is the most natural thing in the world for a government that does not understand you to let you alone." [81] The sentiment here still echoes with the fervor of "Civil Disobedience," but one should remember that he approved of governmental interference for the general welfare,[82] that he was not objecting to government but to what we now call the State. In Canada he learned how governments become States, how the servant became master, how by displaying the symbols of its power it forced the tributary glance of its citizens.

In the closing chapter on the St. Lawrence River, which was not printed in *Putnam's*, Thoreau turned from "what I saw," as he told Blake,[83] to what most deeply engaged his imagination. "I wished to go a little way behind that word *Canadense*," [84] he said; and he did so by retracing his travels, returning from Ste. Anne to Quebec, and by steamer to Montreal, following the Great River that the explorers had taken into the interior of the continent. As he looked out from the citadel at Quebec, he now saw "beyond the frontiers of civilization." He was now reminded of Indian hunters and the unknown wilderness to the north, and "all historical associations [the fort, the church] were swept away again by an influence from the wilds and from Nature. . . ." [85] The Great River itself, whose size and navigability made it for him the greatest river in the world and whose history he related, brought him again into the undiscovered New World and recalled the expectancy of the Old World in this new-found land—old maps like that in Ortelius'

[80] W, V, 82.
[81] W, V, 83.
[82] See W, III, 97; W, IV, 169-70, 171.
[83] W, VI, 215.
[84] W, V, 101.
[85] W, V, 89.

Theatrum Orbis Terrarum (1570) having already caught up with Cartier's discovery in 1535. In one night by steamer, but in many pages of history, he traveled the river that Cartier, Jean Alphonse, Roberval, Champlain, and Charlevoix had known and explored, passed the places where adventurous soldiers and missionaries had undergone the trials of planting a civilization. And since the French were for Thoreau *the* discoverers of America, having, unlike the English, a "spirit of adventure" that took them beyond the shores into the interior, he was deeply stirred by "what would have been the history of this continent if . . . this river had emptied into the sea where New York stands!" [86]

When he got to Montreal, however, and climbed Mt. Royal, he found that, although all that Cartier had said of it was true, the prospect had changed. "Instead of an Indian town far in the interior of a new world," he wrote, "we found a splendid and stone-built city of white men, and only a few squalid Indians offered to sell us baskets at the Lachine Railroad Depot, and Hochelaga is, perchance, but the fancy name of an engine company or an eating-house." [87] The forces that had ultimately dispossessed the Indian in Canada had, of course, also dispossessed them in America, but America, unlike Canada, had grown because her early settlers had come not "to hunt, and fish, and convert," but "to live in earnest and with freedom." [88] If, with Parkman, he was personally attracted by the heroism of the French explorers, he saw nevertheless that the war for the continent had been one of institutions. He heartily approved of the French treatment of the Indians and the assimilation of their ways by the habitans—that is to say, he found their relation to the wilderness superior to that of the English. He did not, however, approve of their relation to the Old World, and in striking the balance between his major symbols—Europe (feudalism), the Wilderness, and America—he chose America, because the freedom there was the largest gain and because the values of the wilderness, which were also the values of freedom, might still be preserved.

Thoreau went to Maine to see the wilderness, to Canada to see the Great River, and to Cape Cod to see the ocean—as Thomas Wentworth Higginson said, "the domain of external Nature . . . was

[86] W, V, 67, 95.
[87] W, V, 99.
[88] W, V, 67.

his peculiar province. . . ." [89] On each excursion, however, he had fronted those natural facts that had first been seen by the discoverers and that had made the planting of America so difficult and heroic; and in each excursion he added a chapter to what might have been, had he lived long enough, a history of the founding and settlement of America. He put the natural facts on record —one expects no less from him: he even studied the great western rivers before he went to Minnesota in 1861. But natural facts were not his goal, for, as he said in introducing *Cape Cod,* "I did not see why I might not make a book on Cape Cod, as well as my neighbor [Alcott] on 'Human Culture.' It is but another name for the same thing. . . ." [90] What concerned him most was how the natural facts of the New World had taken up the imagination and energy of men, the impress they had left on human culture—and these excursions, more than anything else he wrote, were full of history, of men and the details of their lives. By fronting these natural facts anew, centuries later, he was also trying, as he had in *Walden,* to awaken in his generation a faith in discovery—in spiritual discovery. For if he related the history of the discovery of the shores of America, it was only to show that the same ardor and heroism were still necessary for the discovery of the interior. "It is natural that we should be enterprising," he wrote in the *Journal,* "for we are descended from the enterprising, who sought to better their fortunes in the New World." [91] Like "economy," however, "enterprise" and "interior" were words that he had to redefine for his generation, in this case not by his own experiment in the woods but by those of past generations whose grandeur was often more imposing when contrasted with those of the present.

When he went to Cape Cod he did not find the green breast of a new world, but a sandy, wave-beaten cape that, like an arm extended into the sea, had welcomed to America mariners from Thorwald to John Smith and emigrants from the Pilgrims to the Irish of the *St. John.*[92] This drama of sea, sand, and ship revived in his

[89] "Cape Cod," *The Atlantic Monthly,* XV (March, 1865), 381.

[90] W, IV, 3.

[91] J, III, 270.

[92] Thoreau playfully connected himself genealogically with the first discoverers, the Vikings: "But whether Thor-finn saw the mirage here or not, Thor-eau, one of the same family, did; and perchance it was because Leif the Lucky had, in a previous voyage, taken Thor-er and his people off the rock in the middle of the sea, that Thor-eau was born to see it" (W, IV, 192). See also J, III, 304-5; Bronson Alcott, *Concord Days,* Boston, 1872, pp. 18-19; A. and W. Ricketson, eds., *Daniel Ricketson and His Friends,* pp. 57, 78.

mind with every glance over the illimitable ocean, with every step on the barren waste, with the sight of passing ships and the debris of shipwreck. This was the perspective he had in mind when he said in closing, "A man may stand there and put all America behind him." "From Boston to Provincetown is twice as far as from England to France," he wrote, using distance, as he had on all of his excursions, in contrast to time, "yet step into the cars, and in six hours you may stand on those four planks, and see the Cape which Gosnold is said to have discovered. . . ." [93] He had himself made his way on foot along the great outer beach from Nauset Light to Race Point, and had worked his way in his narrative through history to where he might have begun: to Provincetown and the discovery of America.[94] Indeed, facing eastward, his imagination embraced Europe and those ports from which the enterprising had once departed—embraced the entire myth of discovery to which in turn he gave new life:

The nearest beach . . . on the other side . . . was on the coast of Galicia, in Spain, whose capital is Santiago, though by old poets' reckoning it should have been Atlantis or the Hesperides; but heaven is found to be farther west now. At first we were abreast of that part of Portugal *entre Doure e Miño,* and then Galicia and the port of Pontevedra opened to us. . . . The bold headland of Cape Finisterre, a little north of east, jutted toward us next, with its vain brag, for we flung back,—"Here is Cape Cod,—Cape Land's-Beginning." A little indentation toward the north . . . we knew was the Bay of Biscay. . . . A little south of east was Palos, where Columbus weighed anchor, and farther yet the pillars which Hercules set up; concerning which when we inquired at the top of our voices what was written on them . . . the inhabitants shouted *Ne plus ultra* (no more beyond), but the wind bore to us the truth only, *plus ultra* (more beyond), and over the Bay westward was echoed *ultra* (beyond). We spoke to them through the surf about the Far West, the true Hesperia, ἕως πέρας or end of the day, the This Side Sundown, where the sun was extinguished in the *Pacific,* and we advised them to pull up stakes and plant those pillars of theirs on the shore of California, whither all our folks were gone,—the only *ne* plus ultra now.[95]

The vistas of discovery were the framework of his narrative. He

---

[93] W, IV, 273, 269.

[94] Throughout Thoreau used history for digression, contrast, and humor; and somewhat in the manner of the *Week* he used history to get over the barren places of his excursion. Yet he managed to tell of how the Pilgrims got here and how they got the Cape from the Indians, to relate the history of the fisheries, crops, clams and oysters, the history of religion, and some events of the revolutionary period.

[95] W, IV, 177-79.

began with Cape Cod itself, with the name which for him always stood for a thing—with Cape, which with his typical philological skill he followed through the French *cap* and the Latin *caput* and *capere* to the meaning he had in mind: "the part by which we take hold of a thing"; and with Cod, which derived from the codfish Bartholomew Gosnold caught there in 1602, but the significance of which (as of discoveries) Thoreau established by means of the Saxon *codde,* "'a case in which seeds are lodged. . . .'"[96] Cape Cod was the spit of sand by which the discoverers took hold of America, and it was from this seed that America had her start. So too, the sea, upon which Thoreau believed we were still embarked on the voyage of life, was the "'laboratory of continents'"—the origin of all things and the seat of life, as naturalists now recognized, from which life advanced to dry land. "The dry land itself," he said, "came through and out of the water in its way to the heavens. . . ."[97] And one of the fruits of the sea, found by the discoverers, was America.

The sea, of course, was the most important natural fact, comparable as a symbol of nature and the element of discovery in *Cape Cod* to the forest wilderness of Maine. It is interesting, therefore, to find it linked not only with discovery but with shipwreck and death. For shipwreck, too, provided a framework and motif for his narrative: the shipwreck of the *St. John* was his introduction to the Cape, and the shipwreck of a lumbering schooner his farewell. On the beach he found the washed-up cargo of the *Franklin;* and wreckers, charity houses, the history of Highland Light, tombstones, and the custom of dating events from memorable shipwrecks only added to the dirge he heard in "the pure and unqualified strain of eternal melody"[98] coming from the sea. He was fully aware of the human suffering, that "the ancients" would have represented "this voracious beach" as "a sea-monster with open jaws, more terrible than Scylla and Charybdis."[99] He listened eagerly to the Wellfleet oysterman who told of the wrecks of the *Franklin* and the *Cambria,* a Chromis or a Mnasylos listening to

---

[96] W, IV, 3-4. See also pp. 166-67, where Thoreau tells of the seeds washed ashore from the *Franklin.* His moral here was that "shipwrecks may . . . contribute a new vegetable to a continent's stock."

[97] W, IV, 127-28.

[98] W, IV, 71.

[99] W, IV, 163. His allusions to Homer, especially for the sound and color of the sea, are especially numerous.

Silenus' tale of whirlpool and shipwreck.[100] He recalled the shipwreck at Fire Island in which Margaret Fuller had been lost, having
himself been sent to recover her remains.[101] He was ready to
believe his companion, Channing, who told him that the stormy sea
was more *"tumultuous"* than the rapids of Niagara.[102] And he
would have agreed with Ishmael, whose first awareness at New
Bedford of the hazards of going to sea taught him that "there is
death in this business of whaling. . . ." [103]

For, as it had for Whitman, the sea "whisper'd" death to him—
perhaps even deliciously. Compassionate though he was, and never
forgetful of the toll the sea had taken at Cape Cod, Thoreau accepted death, as the inhabitants of the Cape did, with a certain
matter-of-fact inevitability, as a part of the economy of daily life
and nature. It was true, of course, that the women of the Cape,
both past and present, had had their " 'hysteric fits,' " and that their
grief had contributed to the "unhealthful development of the religious sentiment here. . . ." But like a Puritan of old, bred in a
faith that faced the grim realities, Thoreau did not respect the
"snivelling sympathies" that had made religion in his day "a singular
combination of a prayer-meeting and a picnic." [104] He did not have
a shred of sentimentality, and though he was a transcendentalist
dedicated to the heart, he did not share in the soft religion and
sentimentalism that, in its waning, had replaced a tougher faith.
When he wrote out the history of American religion in the bio-
graphical anecdotes of the leading ministers of the Cape, he approved of the Rev. Samuel Treat who was "a Calvinist of the
strictest kind, not one of those who, by giving up or explaining
away, became like a porcupine disarmed of its quills. . . ." [105]

One's attitude toward death is perhaps as much a test of one's
religious faith as it is (according to Whitman, who transformed the
sentimentalism of his time) of one's poetry. With the decline of
Calvinism and the rise of Deism, death became a major theme of

---

[100] W, IV, 92-94. Thoreau quotes Virgil's *Eclogues,* VI, 74-77.

[101] W, IV, 107-8.

[102] W, IV, 210.

[103] "The Chapel," *Moby-Dick.*

[104] W, IV, 46-47, 108, 48.

[105] W, IV, 49. One wonders if Thoreau was parodying Cotton Mather's
ecclesiastical history of Puritan worthies. In any case, Thoreau found some
parallels between Treat's life and his own, and identified especially with the
Rev. Benjamin Webb.

Freneau and later of Bryant; then Irving opened the door to sentimentalism. The transcendentalists, however, to judge by the in-
frequency of this theme in their works, did not follow their age.
Death, nevertheless, was also a test of their faith, all but shattering
it for Emerson in the death of his son and for Thoreau in the death
of his brother John. If nature did not console them to the extent
that it did Bryant or Whitman, still they were able to rebuild their
faith; but death had chilled them, and it seems that they were only
able to maintain their faith by closing off forever the channels of
grief. Thus Thoreau wrote that "a man can attend but one funeral
in the course of his life, can behold but one corpse." [106] Sentimentalism, moreover, was a danger, like waters that, once admitted
through the dike he had reared, might overwhelm him. He was
not entirely the stoic Emerson thought him, for when the occasion
was life—the life of a moose or even a pine—he could loose his
emotions almost to the verge of sentimentality.

"The Shipwreck," with which he introduced his readers to the
Cape, was therefore a test for a writer seeking popularity in an
age of sentimentalism. His difficulty, as he confessed in the manuscript, was that "I could not make this shipwreck seem like what I
thought it ought to be." [107] Undoubtedly the title he had chosen
recalled for him, as it did for the reader, Irving's account of the
shipwreck in *The Sketch Book:* here was an approved theme for
sentimentalism. But Thoreau handled the theme with a brilliant
and affecting objectivity, with a reportorial skill worthy of Hemingway.

Some were rapidly nailing down the lids, and others were lifting the
lids, which were yet loose, and peeping under the cloths. . . . I saw
many marble feet and matted heads as the cloths were raised, and one
livid, swollen, and mangled body of a drowned girl,—who probably had
intended to go out to service in some American family,—to which some
rags still adhered, with a string, half concealed by the flesh, about its
swollen neck; the coiled-up wreck of a human hulk, gashed by the rocks
or fishes, so that the bone and muscle were exposed, but quite blood-
less,—merely red and white,—with wide-open and staring eyes, yet
lustreless, dead-lights; or like the cabin windows of a stranded vessel,
filled with sand. Sometimes there were two or more children, or a parent
and child, in the same box, and on the lid would perhaps be written with
red chalk, "Bridget such-a-one, and sister's child." . . . I have since heard
. . . that a woman who had come over before, but had left her infant

[106] W, IV, 11-12.
[107] HM 13206.

behind for her sister to bring, came and looked into these boxes, and saw in one,—probably the same whose superscription I have quoted,—her child in her sister's arms, as if the sister had meant to be found thus; and within three days after, the mother died from the effect of that sight.[108]

The sympathy in this account is obvious, but it is controlled by the carefully observed facts, which do more perhaps than a gushing heart could. And lest it be thought absent, Thoreau's "humane interest" was implicitly contrasted with the indifference of the sea-weed pickers, who benefited by the storm, and with other spec-tators, who, having witnessed the wreckage or having settled a fact upon which they might have had a bet, went their way un-moved.[109]

Thoreau's own impressions followed his description and might have disturbed his readers more, for he sympathized with the waves and the wind, and with the shore whose beauty had been trans-formed into the sublime by the presence of death. For death itself, however, he had no sympathy: "If this was the law of Nature, why waste any time in awe or pity? . . . Why care for these dead bodies? They really have no friends but the worms or fishes." [110] He was moved instead, in the presence of death, as he was in the presence of the stormy sea, by the sublime; and he closed his account by describing a later excursion to this very beach, when he had gone swimming and the "ocean did not look . . . as if any were ever shipwrecked in it; it was not grand and sublime, but beautiful as a lake." [111] This contrast placed death and shipwreck in the total economy of nature, but it also dramatized those powers which he had gone to the Cape to see.[112] The first excursion, which was the

[108] W, IV, 6-7. The account in HM 13206 is more detailed. The power of Thoreau's images is perhaps attested to by Robert Lowell's use of them in "The Quaker Graveyard in Nantucket."

[109] His humanity was apparent elsewhere in his description of the Humane House built for shipwrecked sailors. Channing, he reported, told Thoreau that he "had not a particle of sentiment. . . . " Thoreau replied that he "did not intend this for a sentimental journey" (W, IV, 78).

[110] W, IV, 11-12. In *Walden* (W, II, 350) he was cheered by the death of natural things, by the evidence of nature's sacrifice to the end of life itself.

[111] W, IV, 18.

[112] See W, IV, 27. The organization of the book was such that the reader was periodically reintroduced to the sea out of a lull. Two chapters of human interest, for example, come between the shipwreck and Thoreau's first walk on the beach; a chapter on the Wellfleet oysterman prepared for the next major description of the sea, as did the chapter on Highland Light for the last.

basis of his narrative, had been made in the stormy October of 1849—and he advised his readers to visit the Cape at such a time. For then the vast and savage ocean had made its deepest impression on him, and he had realized, as he had on Ktaadn, that chaos still reigned. "There is naked Nature," he wrote, "inhumanly sincere, wasting no thought on man. . . ." Here, he realized, was a wilderness that would never be subdued, where whales were cast ashore and sharks advanced to the wharves of civilization, where every venture promised the experience of Noah.[113] Here, as Stephen Crane had found with the same shock, were gulls at home in the storm; and here was a species of kelp fifteen hundred feet long that symbolized for Thoreau "those grotesque and fabulous thoughts which have not yet got into the sheltered coves of literature"—that symbolized as well his own inability to fathom the sea of ultimate meanings.[114]

A later generation might have found in Thoreau's response to the sea—and also in his response to the dreary waste of the Cape—the authentic note of naturalism. The forces that they would have interpreted naturalistically, however, he interpreted in terms of the sublime. And rather than narrowing his conception of nature, these forces reminded him of the "Mystery, Power, Silence" at the heart of things and of the reverence and worship which he was powerless to withhold in the presence of the Creator.[115] He recognized that this "placid ocean . . . will ruthlessly heave these vessels to and fro, break them in pieces in its sandy or stony jaws, and deliver their crews to sea-monsters. It will play with them like sea-weed, distend them like dead frogs, and carry them about, now high, now low, to show to the fishes, giving them the nibble. This gentle ocean will toss and tear the rag of a man's body like the father of mad bulls, and his relatives may be seen seeking the remnants for weeks along the strand." [116] In its rages and calms the sea was but another analogue of the rough and the smooth that figured in his dream of life and whose alternations he could never predict.[117] And yet, as in his other dream of the dark wood and the sunny pasture, he believed that the perilous way would lead to pleasant

[113] W, IV, 186-89.

[114] W, IV, 70.

[115] See "The Sublimity of Death," Sanborn, *Life*, pp. 142-48.

[116] W, IV, 125.

[117] J, IX, 210-11.

prospects. He knew that the power that destroyed also nurtured, that the sea was also the home of fragile sea jellies, that the restlessness of the sea was the sign of its life. Even the succorless sand —those "barren swells" where the walker "must soon eat his heart" —succored the poverty grass.[118] Thus the sea and the desert, the constant images of this experience, did not strike him as a hostile environment, but reminded him rather of the elemental world of Ossian and of the heroic.[119] The Wellfleet oysterman (John Newcomb), in spite of the humor of his situation, had the reverential attitude Thoreau admired—he had "a sense of his own nothingness" and was willing to live " 'just as God sees fit and disposes.' "[120] But he was also heroic, having lived the dangerous life of the Cape, having wrested his living from the sea. He represented for Thoreau the daily bravery and endurance that he saw everywhere on the Cape, that hardiness strengthened by the elements that Crèvecoeur had also praised in his account of Nantucket. Men were not subdued on the Cape; they had persevered in the face of the encroaching sea and the shifting sands. Every day they put to sea, and "the history of one of their ordinary trips," Thoreau said, "would cast the Argonautic expedition into the shade."[121] And others before them had tried the sea with even greater faith and expectation that they might make their lives here, and that others still, like the emigrants of the *St. John,* might find these shores.

That they did not find these shores, however, was not a cause for grief, for like the discoverers they had found other shores than they expected. The shipwreck of the *St. John* was only a footnote in the annals of discovery, in which Columbus, for one, as Thoreau pointed out, had braved an unknown sea and accepted the peril of shipwreck, and instead of the Garden of Eden, which he thought he had found, had found a new world. "Even the expeditions for the discovery of El Dorado, and of the Fountain of Youth," Thoreau wrote, "led to real, if not compensatory discoveries."[122] In the spiritual sense of discovery opened by Thoreau's view of the sublime, moreover, the emigrants of the *St. John* had made an ideal and compensatory discovery:

[118] W, IV, 136-37.
[119] W, IV, 91.
[120] W, IV, 82; HM 13206.
[121] W, IV, 140-41.
[122] W, IV, 121.

[They] were coming to the New World, as Columbus and the Pilgrims did,—they were within a mile of its shores; but before they could reach it, they emigrated to a newer world than ever Columbus dreamed of, yet one of whose existence we believe that there is far more universal and convincing evidence—though it has not yet been discovered by science —than Columbus had of this; not merely mariners' tales and some paltry drift-wood and sea-weed, but a continual drift and instinct to all our shores. I saw their empty hulks that came to land; but they themselves, meanwhile, were cast upon some shore yet further west, toward which we are all tending, and which we shall reach at last, it may be through storm and darkness, as they did. . . . No, no! If the St. John did not make her port here, she has been telegraphed there. The strongest wind cannot stagger a Spirit; it is a Spirit's breath. A just man's purpose cannot be split on any Grampus or material rock, but itself will split rocks till it succeeds.[123]

There was a *plus ultra,* a yet farther west, a " 'far wild,' " a westering as spiritual for Thoreau as it was for Whitman, and its vistas were as welcome even though the portals were death.

That is why, when he reviewed the history of the discovery of New England in the chapter on Provincetown, his final words were in praise of the Pilgrims. He had only scorn for the English as explorers: they were traders and sailors, not discoverers; they touched the shores but did not explore the interior; and they did not even leave valuable maps of the coast as the French had. His disparagement of the English was due in part to his attempt to correct the historical errors of Bancroft, Hildreth, and other New England historians who were unaware of or minimized what Thoreau called "the Ante-Pilgrim history of New England. . . ." [124] But it was probably due in greater part to his personal identification with men of imagination and the spirit of adventure. Much of what he had read of the history of New France for *A Yankee in Canada,* all of the names, if not the tracings he had made, of old maps, were now used to glorify the French.[125] And yet, just as individual freedom was a more important achievement of English settlement than the feudal institutions of Canada were of the settlement of the French, so the enterprise of the Pilgrims was superior in kind to that of the adventurers. "It must be confessed," Thoreau wrote, "that the

---

[123] W, IV, 12-13.

[124] W, IV, 228.

[125] One of the most important books he read was Richard Biddle, *A Memoir of Sebastian Cabot; with A Review of the History of Maritime Discovery,* Philadelphia, 1831. See MA 595.

Pilgrims possessed but few of the qualities of the modern pioneer. They were not the ancestors of the American backwoodsmen. . . . Nevertheless, the Pilgrims were pioneers, and the ancestors of pioneers, in a far grander enterprise." [126]

It would be unfair to leave these travel books with their themes exposed without saying something of what they reveal of Thoreau's "southerly side." Mrs. Fannie Hardy Eckstorm, who first used this admirable epithet, was also the first to point out that in *The Maine Woods* one is most of all introduced to Thoreau himself, and that here "he appears to better advantage than when he skied among the lesser gods of Concord." What she said of *The Maine Woods* applies as well to the other travel excursions: "It is sometimes the advantage of a second-rate book that it endears the writer to us." The Thoreau of the travel books "smiles at us." [127] He is not on the defensive, as he was from first to last at Concord, because his stakes were less and he had nothing to prove; in the intervals his travels commemorate he was free from the judgment and expectations of his transcendental worthies, neighbors, and disciples, and also free from the terrible burdens he imposed on himself because Concord was his place of work (as he severely reminded Ricketson) and his time was running out. We find him, instead, outside of his familiar fields, manfully owning up to his own inexperience, being tested merely as a man; and in the regard of Indian, habitan, or oysterman, he proved to be other than the Thoreau who, we are told, chilled "the social affections." [128] In the travels one finds the same Thoreau who sang "Tom Bowling" and who danced and stepped on Alcott's toes: the Thoreau who spent a night in an Indian camp and who raced Joe Polis over the carry, who spent the night with habitans conversing by means of chalk on the oiled tablecloth, and who passed an evening in spirited talk with the oysterman—even though he took sick from an oyster he had eaten experimentally on the beach. No more than he retailed unimportant information or displayed superior learning, as one critic believes, was Thoreau intellectually arrogant, egotistical, or incapable of sympathizing with "humble, low nobility." [129]

[126] W, IV, 256-57.
[127] "Thoreau's 'Maine Woods,'" pp. 243-44.
[128] C, X, 456.
[129] Edward B. Hinckley, "Thoreau and Beston: Two Observers of Cape Cod," *The New England Quarterly*, IV (April, 1931), 217-19.

III

"No," Thoreau wrote Ricketson, "I have a real genius for staying at home."[130] Unfortunately, in his need for a spiritual guide and for "dear poetic friends," the genial Ricketson did not take this first of many hints. Within a week of the publication of *Walden*, the Quaker of "Brooklawn" in New Bedford, a man of leisure with polite interests in literature and nature and a shanty on his own estate, had written Thoreau a long confessional letter establishing a friendship which, in spite of the exchange of visits and the greatest solicitude, was one-sided, and in which "Dear Walden" ("My Dear Gabriel," "Respected Friend," "my kind Mentor," he later called him) first realized the importunities of fame. Though his admirers and disciples increased after the publication of *Walden* and he was well served by Blake and Theodore Brown of Worcester, Marston Watson of Plymouth, and Thomas Cholmondeley of Shropshire, England (who sent him a magnificent gift of Oriental books),[131] it was equals he needed and not disciples. He might have been thinking of himself when he told Ricketson that the most one could do for Channing was to appreciate his genius, for he had not set himself up as a "physician" for men who spoke too easily of the vernal influences of nature. Those influences, in fact, were no longer vernal; and besides, nature was not his background, but his place and work, and Concord, he said, was "home,—home,—home." So he told Ricketson: "I am so wedded to my way of spending a day,—require such broad margins of leisure, and such a complete wardrobe of old clothes, that I am ill-fitted for going abroad. . . . The old coat that I wear is Concord; it is my morning-robe and my study-gown, my working dress and suit of ceremony, and my night-gown after all. . . . *Cars* sound like *cares* to me."[132]

Ricketson's needs, however, were so great that he would not be put off, neither by such well-turned suggestions nor by abrupt departures and long silences. "I must appeal to you as a brother man," he wrote imploringly. "I am in need of help. I want a physician, and I send for you as the one I have most confidence in." "Give

<hr />

[130] W, VI, 248. These letters as well as Ricketson's can be found in A. and W. Ricketson, eds., *Daniel Ricketson and His Friends*. Those quotations not noted are from pp. 23-131 of this book.

[131] Thoreau's letters to Cholmondeley on receiving these books show that he was not incapable of gratitude. See Berg Collection.

[132] W, VI, 262.

me your hand, Gabriel, and lead the way," he asked another time, admonishing and warning, "I am quite humbled at your halting—the cords of love do not draw you, and I have none stronger to bring into requisition, but I shall not release you without a struggle." And again, later: "May I not also claim as a birthright to rank in your fraternity [he had Blake and Brown in mind], as a disciple, at least? Please not reject me. Failing in you I shall be bankrupt, indeed. Shall echo respond to my complaint, 'Is there none for me in the wide world,—no kindred spirit?' 'None'?" But having by this time been chastened by Thoreau's replies, he added, "Don't be alarmed, 'Amicus Mihi,' you shall be as free as air for aught me."

One might think that Thoreau, who needed friendship all his life, would have responded sympathetically. But the friendship with Ricketson was hardly what he meant by friendship; it did not satisfy Thoreau's necessities, and although he accepted the relation for what it offered of recreation (and as a convenient opportunity to study the local history and Indians of New Bedford), it was not a substitute for uncomplaining nature, the only sustainer of these years. As he told Ricketson, *Such are my engagements to myself, that I dare not promise to wend your way. . . . When my vacation comes, then look out.*" [133] Indeed, it was Thoreau himself who needed a physician, for as early as the spring of 1855 the signs of his fatal illness had appeared: seasons, especially in spring and summer, of unaccountable weakness, followed by partial recoveries in the fall and winter. His legs began to give out—"I believe," he wrote Ricketson, "that God *does* delight in the strength of a man's legs" [134]—and more and more he had to use a wagon in his daily excursions. In 1857 he told Ricketson of his "two-year-old invalidity," [135] and by that time the major obstacle to his work had become his physical health. In December, 1860, he caught cold and was confined until March, 1861, and in May he made a last attempt to regain his health by going to Minnesota. But throughout these years he was never in good health, and the autumn not only reminded him of the ripening year but "to make haste and finish our work before the night comes." [136] Sickness had made him postpone

[133] W, VI, 271.
[134] W, VI, 267.
[135] W, VI, 306.
[136] J, XI, 273.

too much; after "these long months of inefficiency and idleness," after these enforced vacations, he could not spare any time from his harvest. Thus, though Ricketson chided him—"I thought that you were a man of leisure. . . . You appear to be hugging your chains. . . . [I] cannot see the desperate need of your penance"—he replied, "I remember that, among other things, I wished to break it to you, that, owing to engagements, I should not be able to show you so much attention as I could wish, or as you had shown me." With each invitation over the years the reply was the same: "The truth is, I have my enterprises now as ever, at which I tug with ridiculous feebleness, but admirable perseverance. . . ." Or "I have an immense appetite for solitude. . . ." And finally, after a terrible silence, Thoreau explained to Ricketson that he could be more attentive to courtesies because he had "fewer or less exacting private pursuits." "But life is short," he wrote, speaking for himself, "and there are other things also to be done." [137]

And what remained to be done could only be done in Concord. "I am engaged to Concord and my own private pursuits by 10,000 ties," he explained to Ricketson who once suggested his teaching elsewhere, "and it would be suicide to rend them." [138] It was true, of course, that Thoreau traveled more in these years than he had ever done, compelled in part by a profound desire to revisit the scenes of former experiences and in part by the need for health, but most of all by the need to extend his studies of the aboriginal environment of America. These studies were of a comparative nature closely associated with similar investigations in Concord, and they helped him determine the extent of her wilderness character and deepened his sense of her historic past. His interest in Concord, however, was not parochial. "Thank Heaven," he said in *Walden,* "here is not all the world." [139] Concord was merely that piece of ground he had traveled most, had delved deepest into, had enriched with years of sympathetic association—he had, as he wrote Blake, found in "oceans and wildernesses far away, the material of a million Concords. . . ." [140] But if he had followed the discoverers on his excursions to Maine, Cape Cod, and Canada, he

[137] W, VI, 270, 275, 313.

[138] W, VI, 285. One wonders if the "10,000 ties" referred to the Chinese way of speaking of the sum of all the things in the universe.

[139] W, II, 352.

[140] W, VI, 187.

was *the* discoverer in Concord, exploring to another end, that of finding for their discoveries a place in the spirit of man. "It is easier to discover another such a new world as Columbus did," he had written in the *Week*, "than to go within one fold of this which we appear to know so well. . . ." [141] From that time he had been laying back the folds of nature, searching for her laws, and by a sympathetic experience trying to find in all her phenomena the corresponding values for man. Within his small township, which he knew he would never fully know, he was demonstrating—by exploring in behavior and method—how men might yet possess a new world.[142] Walking in Concord was one thing, but the value of travel itself he impugned because he had learned that from short acquaintance with a fact—that is, without a rich outlay of "experience"—one could not hope to gather its significance. "Live at home like a traveler," he therefore advised Blake. "It should not be in vain that these things are shown us from day to day. . . . What a fool he must be who thinks that his El Dorado is anywhere but where he lives!" [143] Travel and discovery, as he had shown in *Walden*, were but the metaphor for a way of life. "Where is the 'unexplored land' but in our own untried enterprises?" he reminded Blake. "To an adventurous spirit any place—London, New York, Worcester, or his own back yard—is 'unexplored land'. . . . These are the regions of the Known and of the Unknown. . . . You must make tracks into the Unknown." [144] And commenting on his own life in the *Journal*, he said that "if you have ever done any work with . . . the imagination and fancy and reason . . . you have to that extent cleared the wilderness." [145]

He had spent almost his entire life clearing the wilderness of Concord. Here had been his seedtime, and with the expectation of harvesting his crop, his sense of rootedness deepened until he felt a "terrene" sympathy for the earth with which he had mixed so much of his life. "For thirty years," he remarked, "I have annually observed . . . the freshly erected winter lodges of the musquash along the riverside. . . . This may not be an annual phenomenon to you. It may not be in the Greenwich almanac . . . but it has an im-

---

[141] W, I, 409.

[142] Speaking of staying at home he remarked: "They were bold navigators once who merely sighted these shores. We were born and bred further in the land than Captain John Smith got" (J, XII, 397).

[143] W, VI, 347.

[144] W, VI, 362-63.

[145] J, IX, 350.

portant place in my Kalendar. So surely as the sun appears to be in Libra or Scorpio, I see the conical winter lodges of the musquash rising above the withered pontederia and flags." [146] The kind of sympathy and preparation that had made him such a perceptive traveler, so capable (to the amazement of Mrs. Eckstorm) of seizing essential matters in a short time, he had tirelessly given to Concord, and he knew that it would be futile to look elsewhere for the fruit of the seeds he had sown. The best book, he reminded himself, for he now hoped to "conquer fate by thought," "is not the book of him who has travelled the farthest over the surface of the globe, but of him who has lived deepest and been the most at home. . . . We require that the reporter be very permanently planted before the facts which he observes, not a mere passer-by. . . . A man is worth most to himself and to others, whether as an observer, or poet, or neighbor, or friend, where he is most himself, most contented and at home. . . . Familiar and surrounding objects are the best symbols and illustrations of his life. . . . The poet has made the best roots in his native soil of any man, and is the hardest to transplant." Then, applying the moral to himself he remarked: "Here I have been these forty years learning the language of these fields that I may the better express myself. If I should travel to the prairies, I should much less understand them, and my past life would serve me but ill to describe them. Many a weed here stands for more of life to me than the big trees of California would if I should go there." [147] His past life was his root, much more important to him, as he confessed, now that his ecstasy was scant, and now that he felt that his senses were worn out, his spirit evaporated, and his wonder becoming extinct. "Our past experience," he wrote, "is a never-failing capital which can never be alienated, of which each kindred future event reminds us." [148] And again, in the language of possessions, he wrote: "Our stock in life, our real estate, is that amount of thought which we have had, which we have thought out. The ground we have thus created is forever pasturage for our thoughts. I fall back on to visions which I have had." [149] In the season of ebbing power he knew that memory alone would make him "a competent witness." [150]

---

[146] J, XII, 389.

[147] J, X, 405, 190-91.

[148] J, IX, 364.

[149] J, IX, 350.

[150] J, IX, 365.

This need for the past, for the environment that was the visible expression of his life, accounted for his commitment to the same way of life and his resistance to change. Against the forces of illness, Admetus, friends, and success he fought a holding battle, fully aware of the sacrifices he asked of himself and others. Even the prospect of lectures that followed *Walden* disturbed him, for they jeopardized his leisure and destroyed the "incomparably great . . . advantages of obscurity and poverty. . . ." And when he had failed as a lecturer he was glad, having again "a longer and more liberal lease of life. . . ." [151] At least surveying, which he continued to do as late as 1860, had the advantage of keeping him at home in his fields, and contributed to his researches into the history of Concord. For he was now as deeply concerned with Concord's past as with his own, and he extended the range of his associations with her phenomena, which he was at last preparing for his Kalendar, to those of early chroniclers, historians, and elder inhabitants, which he might have used someday in a more collective history of the town. What that history would have been, one can only guess from the materials he so assiduously collected: certainly it would have included the primordial wilderness of shaggy trees and swamps and the unalterable hills, streams, and ponds, and the wild animals long since exterminated; the Indian as he lived then and the later history of his wars and of his dispossession; the discovery of New England and the founding of Concord, with the best of Bradford and Josselyn and William Wood and Cotton Mather extracted; the old ways as his imagination made them out in the old Hunt house and in Minott's place; and the stories of Minott, the Concord Herodotus, and the lives not only of Concord's saints but of her "characters"—Melvin, Rice, and Goodwin. The *Week* and *Cape Cod* suggest both the flavor and the method of such a history, and one can be sure that it would have been not only the history of discovery, settlement, and civilization, but primarily a history of the reaction of many generations to the natural environment. For unlike the great elm whose history covered more than half of that of Concord and whose unnecessary fall went unnoticed and unmourned except by him, both his Kalendar and his history, he hoped, would be left as stays against time, the proofs, the "specimens of what the township was," so that

[151] J, VII, 46; J, IX, 214.

later generations might find in his faithful testimony, as he had in that of others, the communion of perception.[152] What he had seen "face to face," as Whitman had written in "Crossing Brooklyn Ferry," "Others will see. . . . Fifty years hence. . . . A hundred years hence, or ever so many hundred years hence." This was Thoreau's favorite among Whitman's poems, and for good reason: his devotion to the past and to the present was really the measure of his faith in the future and of his faith in the inalienable permanence, the organic continuance, of nature and man. And that that life might continue, he fought for the full use of his shortening time, that in the writing he had still to do he might "give back life for life." [153]

He continued in his old ways, then, because he already had a master plan and needed only to fill in the details. He had already discovered the correspondence of the seasons of nature and the seasons of man, which was the foundation of his Kalendar, and now a fuller month-by-month record remained to be made. The recurrence of the seasons, of course, was still a condition of his mature ecstasy, but although the thaws of spring and the ripening of autumn still moved him, he was not so concerned with the changing seasonal weather as he once had been. Originally he had noted the phenomena of the changing year in order to anticipate their reappearance and prompt his ecstasy; now ("See and hear chewinks,—all their strains; the same date with last year . . .")— now this had become more routine.[154] After *Walden,* which expressed his enduring faith in the seasons, his *Journals* became increasingly a repository of scientific facts. He became an inspector of phenomena, relying more and more on manuals and guides, using a telescope, a thermometer and other measuring instruments; an experimenter who made sugar from maple and birch sap; indeed a scientist who examined the droppings of crows and foxes, noted with care the markings of birds, and even killed a mouse. Where once he had told how the summer felt to him, he now merely recorded the temperatures, and instead of his former rhapsodies over the cricket he merely noted in the *Journal,* in a kind of shorthand, the barest fact: "Have heard the alder *cricket* some days. The

---

[152] J, VIII, 130-32; J, XI, 299-300.

[153] J, XI, 457.

[154] J, VII, 334.

turning-point is reached." [155] In the winter of 1855-56 he no longer looked for signs of spring but measured the snow, and in each season he studied a particular phenomenon: nests in the winter of 1856, foliage in the autumn of 1857 (when he also went wooding and nutting), swamps in the winter of 1857-58, rivers in the summer of 1859 and the spring of 1860, and forests from 1859 through 1860.

Every critic has recognized this change in Thoreau and has seen in it the sign of his lapse and failure.[156] And yet the last eight *Journals* which bear this testimony also bear the testimony of Thoreau's steadfast rejection of science. It is true, of course, that he was less disturbed by his objectivity, and even proud of his uncanny knowledge: "I knew that a crow had that day plucked the cedar berries and barberries by Flint's Pond and then flapped silently through the trackless air to Walden, where it dined on fisherman's bait, though there was no living creature to tell me." [157] His science, however, was merely a discipline to the end of greater familiarity, and his use of scientific nomenclature the means to a "distincter recognition and knowledge of the thing." He explained that "with the knowledge of the name . . . that shore is now more describable, and poetic even. . . . My knowledge now becomes communicable and grows by communication. I can now learn what others know about the same thing." [158] Instead of signifying his failure, his reliance on science signified a greater maturity and success: to be scientific for Thoreau was not to abandon the ultimate poetic use of the fact but to be public and objective. He was driven by his studies to know the entire natural environment, and in this great labor science was an economy; and now, before he offered his poetic reading of the fact, he wanted to know what the fact itself was and what others as well as himself had found it to be. His science, his insistence on accuracy, was also an act of social faith; he was a "natural historian" because he used science in the way he did history.

In the considerable barrenness of these *Journals*, it is easy, of course, to mistake his intermediate use of science for a terminal

---

[155] J, VIII, 444.

[156] For Thoreau's comment on this change see J, IX, 156-58.

[157] J, VIII, 135. See J, VII, 418, 421, where in his familiarity with the environment he is to his companion Channing as Natty Bumppo to the various representatives of the clearings.

[158] J, XI, 137.

one. But he was not the tool of his tools. Besides his many protestations against systems and "prying instruments" and his praise for the old poetic naturalists, like Konrad Gesner, there is sufficient evidence to show that, given time, he would have transformed these facts into tropes.[159] At the time that he was carrying out his maple-sugar experiment, for example, he wrote Blake:

I see by the newspapers that the season for making sugar is at hand. Now is the time, whether you be rock, or white maple, or hickory. I trust that you have prepared a store of sap-tubs and sumach spouts, and invested largely in kettles. Early the first frosty morning, tap your maples,—the sap will not run in summer, you know. It matters not how little juice you get, if you get all you can, and boil it down. I made just one crystal of sugar once, one twentieth of an inch cube, out of a pumpkin, and it sufficed. Though the yield be no greater than that, this is not less the season for it, and it will be not the less sweet, nay, it will be infinitely the sweeter.

Shall, then, the maple yield sugar, and not man? Shall the farmer be thus active, and surely have so much sugar to show for it, before this very March is gone,—while I read the newspaper? While he works in his sugar-camp let me work in mine,—for sweetness is in me, and to sugar it shall come,—it shall not all go to leaves and wood. Am I not a *sugar maple* man, then? Boil down the sweet sap which the spring causes to flow within you. Stop not at syrup,—go on to sugar, though you present the world with but a single crystal,—a crystal not made from trees in your yard, but from the new life that stirs in your pores. Cheerfully skim your kettle, and watch it set and crystallize, making a holiday of it if you will. Heaven will be propitious to you as to him.

Say to the farmer: There is your crop; here is mine. Mine is sugar to sweeten sugar with. If you will listen to me, I will sweeten your whole load,—your whole life.

Then will the callers ask, Where is Blake? He is in his sugar-camp on the mountainside. Let the world await him. Then will the little boys bless you, and the great boys too, for such sugar is the origin of many condiments,—Blakians in the shops of Worcester, of new form, with their mottoes wrapped up in them. Shall men taste only the sweetness of the maple and the cane the coming year? [160]

He had lost nothing by his science; he had gained. He could still reason from his hands to his head, and granted the occasion, which Blake frequently provided, he could preach as eloquently as the Puritans, whose plain style he admired. He could make a common process a metaphor of poetic inspiration itself, a metaphor of his vocation and its rewards, and he could demonstrate in this

[159] J, XII, 171; J, XIII, 149ff.

[160] W, VI, 278-79.

crystal of sugar how life should be sweetened. And if facts were sugar, he was still able to distill the sugar of sugar.

To a different but equally rich purpose he could use the kind of facts represented by his measurement of the snow; for while he was about this measuring he was also reading in various historical collections about the heavy snows of colonial times, especially the Great Snow of 1717 (he copied out Cotton Mather's account), and through his experience recapturing the past.[161] Similarly, when John Quincy Adams of Carlisle killed a Canada lynx in 1860, Thoreau carefully measured the stuffed skin and noted its markings, comparing what he observed with the descriptions of Emmons and Audubon; but what really excited him, causing him to return again for another look, was the fact that even now a former inhabitant of Concord was still abroad. He refused to accept the opinion of others, that it was a Canada or a Siberian lynx; he knew colonial history too well; it was *his* lynx, "it belongs here,—I call it the Concord lynx." [162] And again, when he visited the Inches wood, his eyes opened to both the phenomena and history: "This wood is said to have been a great resort for pigeons. We saw one large pigeon-place on the top of the hill where we first entered it. Now used. Seeing this, I can realize how this country appeared when it was discovered. Such was the oak woods which the Indian threaded hereabouts." [163] Many of the observations of the *Journals* were the result of his attempt to know the whole of nature, that is to say, its past; for when he saw the lynx or the great oaks he was reminded that he lived in "a tamed, and, as it were, emasculated country," that primitive nature, which interested him most, was gone. "I take infinite pains to know all the phenomena," he wrote, "thinking that I have here the entire poem, and then, to my chagrin, I hear that it is but an imperfect copy that I possess and have read, that my ancestors have torn out many of the first leaves and grandest passages, and mutilated it in many places." [164] In his own back yard as well as in his travels, therefore, he purposely looked for the perfect copy, and by extensive reading he tried to find the original leaves of the mutilated poem. And as these studies in field and book took him back to the past, so also they renewed his hunger for the wild, stirred his interest in forest preserves and

---

[161] J, VIII, 163-65.

[162] J, XIV, 78-81, 142.

[163] J, XIV, 230.

[164] J, VIII, 220-21.

conservation, and awakened in his mind, only now in the widest social sense, the vision of America that this primitive heritage once, perhaps still, promised.

The final justification of Thoreau's gargantuan researches—(that he had any energy left is amazing: the *Journals* were only one record book; there were notebooks of extracts on natural history and the Indian, carefully made charts of the phenomena he had observed over the years, résumés of the phenomena of a single month, and indexes)—the final justification would have been his Kalendar. What the Kalendar would have been is not hard to imagine, for "Autumnal Tints" was planned for it, and his résumés, as well as proposed chapters, like "November Lights," suggest its scope; and Blake's editing of the *Journals* by seasons (*Early Spring in Massachusetts, Summer, Winter, Autumn*) was undoubtedly an attempt to be true to its spirit. It is harder, however, to realize that the Kalendar would have been not only an account of the seasons' phenomena, enriched by the patient observation of many years, which Thoreau believed necessary to a truthful report, but the capstone of all his endeavors. It would have been a study of the entire economy of nature ("I wish to know an entire heaven and an entire earth") and of her laws, a *Walden* writ large, with the focus of the individual widened to include the insights of all mankind, of an Aristotle, Theophrastus, Pliny, Darwin, or Agassiz.[165]

Thus, he tapped his maple trees not only because this was an immemorial occupation of early spring which he might have used in a chapter on March, but because the essential phenomenon was the *flowing* of sap. And it was not idle scientific curiosity that led him to study the droppings of a crow or of a fox. He might, of course, learn in this way the habits of an unseen crow or the recent feeding of a fox—"Observed in the droppings of a fox the other day, with fur, some quarter-shaped (or triangular segments) seeds, and roughish, which may have been seeds of rose hips." [166] But again the essential phenomenon was seeds. As early as 1850, in fact, he had begun an essay on the dispersion of seeds. In the manuscript he spoke of his "purpose in this chapter," but the chapter was never written.[167] His studies of seeds and their dispersal, however, were more extensive than one would expect from what he did with them;

---

[165] J, VIII, 221. See his notebook of extracts on natural history, Berg Collection.

[166] J, XIV, 232.

[167] Berg Collection.

his address on "The Succession of Forest Trees" was merely an installment, though there are suggestions in it of the unifying themes of his Kalendar. "When we experiment in planting forests," he said, "we find ourselves at last doing as Nature does. Would it not be well to consult Nature in the outset? for she is the most extensive and experienced planter of us all. . . ." [168] His Kalendar would have been a record of growth, a record of the *process* of the total economy of nature, his final tribute to the alchemy of nature, to which he alluded at the close of his address, the "perfect" alchemist "who can transmute substances without end. . . ." [169] And naturally he would have begun with seeds and would have transmuted with his own alchemy ("she is the most extensive and experienced planter of *us* all") every phenomenon and the entire Kalendar into a calendar of human aspiration, growth, and harvest. "Though I do not believe a plant will spring up where no seed has been," he told the farmers of the Middlesex Agricultural Society, "I have great faith in a seed—a, to me, equally mysterious origin for it. Convince me that you have a seed there, and I am prepared to expect wonders. I shall even believe that the millennium is at hand, and that the reign of justice is about to commence, when the Patent Office, or Government, begins to distribute, and the people to plant the seeds of these things." [170] The work he had planned was nothing less than turning all science, all nature, into a poem for man; it was a staggering, perhaps grandiose, undertaking; but the stores he had accumulated to this end were a greater testimony of the energy and purpose that he brought to this work than of any lapse into science.

Seed. Flower. Fruit. He did not live to write out the entire process, only the faith in the eternity that this process inspired in him: "The eternity which I detect in Nature I predicate of myself also. . . . I am encouraged, for I recognize this steady persistency and recovery of Nature as a quality of myself." [171] Perhaps because he felt that his own year was ripening he turned to autumn first, sketching a lecture on the huckleberry and completing another on the autumn foliage. Throughout the 1850's he had collected notes

[168] W, V, 197-98.
[169] W, V, 204.
[170] W, V, 203.
[171] J, VIII, 222-23.

KNIGHT OF THE UMBRELLA AND BUNDLE 401

on fruits (mostly wild), some 575 pages on raspberries, blueberries, huckleberries, plums, grapes, apples, nuts, acorns, pine cones, etc. —an intimate history of fruits and nuts as refreshing as Virgil's *Georgics.* Indeed, he began a lecture on fruits in which he defined the uses of maturity: "The value of these wild fruits is not in the mere possession or eating of them, but in the sight & enjoyment of them. The very derivation of the word Fruit would suggest this. It is from the Latin *Fructus,* meaning that which is *used* or *enjoyed.* If it were not so then going a-berrying & going to market would be nearly synonymous experiences. . . ." [172]

He had gone a-berrying so much that it had become the symbol of his vocation—Emerson, in fact, had made this his major criticism —and when he wrote out his notes on the huckleberry he made them, as he made all his autumnal pieces, the justification of his vocation, the fruit of his life. The profusion of berries, of course, was the sign of nature's beneficence, the sign of the ease with which one might still get his living by going to nature, and inevitably this reminded Thoreau of the Indians who "made a much greater account of wild fruits than we do. . . ." [173] Citing observers from Champlain (1615) to Owen (in *The Geological Survey of Wisconsin* . . . , 1852), he supported his claim that the Indians had taught us how to dry berries and what to taste, and that they had found the huckleberry to be among the most important. Thus the huckleberry came to stand for the American environment and for the common fields, now fenced, that he had ranged in his youth. And they represented as well the subsequent loss: "I well remember with what a sense of freedom & spirit of adventure I used to take my way across the fields with my pail . . . toward some distant hill or swamp, when dismissed for all day, and I would not now exchange such an expansion of all my faculties, or call it if you please such a point of view merely, for all the learning in the world. Liberation & enlargement such is the fruit which all culture aims to secure." [174] Toward such liberation and enlargement, and for

[172] See J, XIV, 273-74. The materials for this lecture are in the Berg Collection. He made a similar distinction in the manuscript draft of "Love" and "Chastity and Sensuality." The end of marriage, he wrote, was not the propagation of the species but its maturation; "the ultimate fruit of a tree is not the seed, but much more a flower or rather a flourishing tree" (HM 13196).

[173] Berg Collection.

[174] Berg Collection. In choosing the huckleberry Thoreau was true to his youthful ideals. With Emerson, he found that first and third thoughts correspond. See W, VI, 242, 332.

the education of the senses, he also proposed the preservation
of forests and village commons; but the native fruits also suggested
another education, equally important: "They educate us & fit us
to live in New England." [175] This had been the goal of his own
work, and he was able to give it the importance he believed it
deserved by employing once more the associations of discovery
and commerce. "Most of us are still related to our native fields,"
he wrote, "as the navigator to undiscovered islands in the sea.
We can any afternoon discover a new fruit there. . . ." To go
a-berrying was to explore a new world; this was preferable to
voyaging for pineapples, for the native fruits were more important
than the imported ones. "No, it is not those far-fetched fruits
which the speculator imports that concern us chiefly," he wrote
with undaunted faith in a native literature, "but rather those that
you have fetched yourself in the hold of a basket, from some far
hill or swamp, journeying all the long afternoon, the first of the
season, consigned for your friends at home." [176] But literary nation-
alism aside, the importance of berrying was not the berries but
the experience, the real or finer fruit that could never be brought
to market—"the amount of development we get out of it," the flavor
of life itself.[177] The end of life was not to gather fruit but like it
to become ripe oneself. "There is no ripeness," he said, "which is
not something ultimate in itself, & not merely a perfected means
to a higher end. In order to be ripe it must serve a transcendent
use. The ripeness of a leaf being perfected (for ought we know) it
leaves the tree at that point & never returns to it. It has nothing to
do with any other fruit which the tree may bear, and only genius
[as he demonstrated in "Autumnal Tints" and "Wild Apples"] can
pluck it. The fruit of a tree is neither in the seed, nor the timber—
nor is it the full grown tree itself—but it is simply the highest
use to which it can be put." [178] He was not troubled, therefore,
that his neighbors looked with compassion on him, thinking a
"mean and unfortunate destiny" made him walk the fields and
woods alone.[179] For huckleberrying was the symbol of his first
and last joys and of that ripeness that communicated nothing less
than its own beauty and fragrance. He would engineer for America

[175] Berg Collection; J, XIV, 274.
[176] Berg Collection; J, XIV, 273-74.
[177] Berg Collection.
[178] Berg Collection; J, XII, 24.
[179] J, IX, 121.

by huckleberrying, for by "going a-huckleberrying in the fields of thought" he could "enrich all the world with his visions and his joys." [180]

Somewhere in his lecture on fruits he had planned to point out the difference between "big" and "little" things, or rather, by what he said of little things like berries, to reverse the common sense. "Whatever they [his compassionate neighbors] know & care but *little* about," he had intended to begin one version of his lecture, "is a little thing, & accordingly almost every thing good or great is little in their sense, & is very slow to grow any bigger." Even "to obey the higher law," he added, unable to restrain the bitterness of long misunderstanding, "is generally considered the last manifestation of littleness." [181] Definition, philological pun, humor—these were some of the means he used in his lifelong attempt to turn common into transcendental sense; and the same necessity to shock his neighbors into *seeing* inevitably drove him to dramatize, against the foil his neighbors presented him, his own way of life. The dramatic principle, of course, was given birth by his conception of the hero and the polarity of transcendental thought; and it was either explicitly, as in the *Week* and *Walden,* or implicitly, as in "A Winter Walk," in the structure of much of his work. It was there by implication in his treatment of huckleberrying, and even in his determination to use homely and little things like seeds, berries, foliage, and wild apples to carry the burden of his greatest themes. Many readers, unfortunately, have dismissed Thoreau's final essays because their nominal subject appears too slight for the author of *Walden;* and the judgment implied in their critical neglect, it seems, is that they are works wisely overlooked because they were the result of diminished powers. But nowhere else was Thoreau so successful in making nature herself speak for him: these essays were indeed the ripened fruit of the artist, who by a lifetime of seeing had seen so well and so much that natural things had become the transparent images of his thought.[182]

---

[180] J, XII, 400.

[181] Berg Collection.

[182] "He would be a poet," he wrote in "Walking," "who could impress the winds and streams into his service, to speak for him; who nailed words to their primitive senses . . . transplanted them to his page with earth adhering to their roots; whose words were so true and fresh and natural that they would appear to expand like buds at the approach of spring . . . ay, to bloom and bear fruit . . . annually, for the faithful reader, in sympathy with surrounding Nature" (W, V, 232).

He was proud that he had seen, and was now preparing to bring what he had seen to market. "Autumnal Tints," admittedly incomplete, was his first lecture, one that displayed his unfailing sensibility and that dramatized his uncommon perceptions and long apprenticeship to "little" things. "Why," he exclaimed at the end, "it takes a sharp-shooter to bring down even such trivial game as snipes and woodcocks; he must take very particular aim, and know what he is aiming at." [183] In the more congenial image of the sportsman he told how he had trained himself, watched unweariedly, prayed and sacrificed for, and anticipated, his game, how "after due and long preparation, schooling his eye and hand, dreaming awake and asleep," he had got the quarry "his townsmen never saw nor dreamed of. . . ." [184] Armed by anticipation, he had seen the resplendent autumn foliage that his unseeing neighbors had always assumed was brown and sere, and armed with the faith that he had earned by this seeing, he believed that "if he [the hunter] lives, and his game-spirit increases, heaven and earth shall fail him sooner than game; and when he dies, he will go to more extensive, and, perchance, happier hunting-grounds." [185] Like Emerson in the parable of the seven men who viewed the same field, Thoreau was aware of the fact that "a man sees only what concerns him," that the scientist, or better yet the New England selectman with churches and taxable land in his eye, would not see what the poet saw. "Nature," he said, "does not cast pearls before swine." [186] One must remember, however, that this lusty brag was for mankind, that he was using himself as a stock personality, and that the intended use of "Autumnal Tints," indeed of the entire Kalendar and of his own seeing, was to prepare others, by giving them the idea or the image—by putting the scarlet oak in their eye—to anticipate and to see.[187]

One reason that they had not seen was that American poets had not yet sufficiently used their native fields for poetry, and that English poetry, in the absence of such brilliant foliage, had not prepared them for it. Another was the concern with trifles, that preoccupation with their own gardens that kept them from elevating

---

[183] W, V, 287.

[184] W, V, 287-88.

[185] W, V, 288.

[186] W, V, 286, 285.

[187] J, X, 115, 131.

their view "to see the whole forest as a garden." [188] And still an-other, perhaps the most telling, was the ingrained hostility to beauty, the suspicion that treachery lurked in color and form, the incapacity for joy. "One wonders," Thoreau remarked, "that the tithing-men and fathers of the town are not out to see what the trees mean by their high colors and exuberance of spirits, fearing that some mischief is brewing. I do not see what the Puritans did at this season, when the Maples blaze out in scarlet. They certainly could not have worshipped in groves then. Perhaps that is what they built meeting-houses and fenced them round with horse-sheds for." [189] Against this enmity to joy and this starvation of the senses, he deliberately emphasized his exhilaration and joy in colors, parading the scarlet almost for its own sake in page after page, comparing the trees to living liberty poles and the whole splendid show of October to an annual fair to be properly enjoyed by gypsies, "a race capable of wild delight," or even by "the fabled fauns, satyrs, and wood-nymphs. . . ." [190] Though autumn had for him the usual associations of harvest and death, the leaves that taught him how to die did not preach in the Puritan strain; for unlike the church, a tree, he said, was a *perfectly living* institu-tion," just what the "starved and bigoted religionists" needed to dispel "the most barren and forlorn doctrine. . . ." [191] He thought the sugar maples in the common worth even the death of the selectman who had helped to plant them because they had "filled the open eyes of children with their rich color unstintedly so many Octobers." [192] And he thought that they would teach the young, as they had taught him, that "man's spirits should rise as high as Nature's,—should hang out their flag, and the routine of his life be interrupted by an analogous expression of joy and hilarity." [193]

They taught him, moreover, a different attitude toward death. The leaves fell because of the frost and rain and unusual heat of Indian summer, and their fall was the great harvest of the year. Their brilliant reds were duplicated in the evening and the year

---

[188] W, V, 284.

[189] W, V, 262-63.

[190] W, V, 274-75. There are echoes here of Hawthorne's "The May-Pole of Merry Mount."

[191] W, V, 277.

[192] W, V, 272.

[193] W, V, 275.

—in the October sunsets. Even the globe itself was a ripened fruit on its stem, and the fallen leaves floating in the river reminded him of "Charon's boat." [194] The dry leaves were "clean, crisp substances," and the leaves of the scarlet oak, "lifted higher and higher, and sublimated more and more, putting off some earthiness and cultivating more intimacy with the light each year," were a symbol of transcendence.[195] But just as often, the red leaves and grasses reminded him of regimental banners, of soldiers grounding their arms, of Indians in file or encamped—even of Raleigh offering his cloak to Elizabeth. For red was his "color of colors," the color of blood and earth and wine, the hue of virtue, bravery, and the strength of maturity, the color of ripeness, mellowness, and perfection, rather than of decay.[196] He was celebrating ripening, not death, and though he spoke of death, of ripening as the preparation for the fall of the leaf, he set his reflections on death in the context of the joyous and brave life that made it possible for him to accept it so gently. The scarlet oak, the "late and unexpected glory" of the year, braving out November, seemed to say, "We Scarlet ones . . . have not given up the fight." [197] They were still full of sap, and because of this the last color of the year, which they represented, was the most intense and "vivacious," even surpassing "all that spring or summer could do." [198] "Color stands for all ripeness and success," he wrote in the *Journal* of 1858 when he was preparing his lecture. "We have dreamed that the hero should carry his color aloft, as a symbol of the ripeness of his virtue." [199] In ripeness itself the soldier of *The Service* had found his standard, in the autumn of his life another golden age.[200]

As for death, his faith in the seasons, and his exultation over the

[194] W, V, 267.

[195] W, V, 266, 278.

[196] W, V, 254.

[197] W, V, 281.

[198] W, V, 283-84.

[199] J, XI, 243.

[200] J, XIV, 259. Thoreau's treatment of the leaf and its seasons can be suggestively compared with that of Horatio Greenough ("An Artist's Creed," *A Memorial of Horatio Greenough*, ed. by Henry T. Tuckerman, New York, 1853, pp. 192-98) where the leaf becomes the symbol of organic fulfillment—of Greenough's organic creed:

> Beauty is the promise of function.
> Action is the presence of function.
> Character is the record of function.

victory of having passed through all seasons to completion, robbed it of its terrors.[201] The falling leaves were but "repaying the earth with interest what they had taken from it." [202] They, too, were giving life for life, and though Thoreau never quite equated leaves and poems, he thought of his sentences as fruit and of his work in these last years as the crop he was bringing to harvest.[203] He knew that "we are all the richer for their [leaves'] decay," and that, like his work, they deepened and enriched the soil: "It prepares the virgin mould for future cornfields and forests, on which the earth fattens." Decay, moreover, was not death, for the leaves still lived "in the soil, whose fertility and bulk they increase, and in the forests that spring from it." Indeed, they stooped to rise, "to mount higher in coming years, by subtle chemistry, climbing the sap in the trees. . . ." As if assured of this never-failing metamorphosis, "How beautifully," he wrote, "they go to their graves! how gently lay themselves down and turn to mould! . . . They that soared so loftily, how contentedly they return to the dust again, and are laid low, resigned to lie and decay at the foot of the tree, and afford nourishment to new generations of their kind. . . ." Men, he said when he made the analogy explicit, for all their "boasted faith in immortality," did not shed their bodies "with such an Indian-summer serenity," nor did they muse as he did, when autumn had turned the whole earth into a pleasant cemetery, on the time when "the loosestrife shall bloom and the huckleberry-bird sing over your bones," and "the woodman and hunter shall be your sextons, and the children shall tread upon the borders as much as they will." [204] But such was the way in which the leaves had taught him how to die. And it was thus that, with his scythe and with "horse-raking thoughts," he had gathered the meaning of things that had stood so long in vain.[205]

He had also gathered from the meaning of the seasons the assurance that his life had not been in vain, that everything has

---

[201] It was not an easy victory: winter still presented a horrible barrenness. See J, XI, 298, 320-21, 445. But like the steadfast trees, the "Poor knights" of his poem on "The Fall of the Leaf," he waited bravely "The charge of Winter's cavalry." See Bode, ed., *Collected Poems of Henry Thoreau*, p. 238.

[202] W, V, 268-69.

[203] J, XIII, 238; W, VI, 231.

[204] W, V, 269-70.

[205] W, V, 256-57.

its season and bears its fruit, and that it was best to cultivate the
tree that one had found would bear fruit in his soil. In his first
Journal he had written that "the season will mature and fructify
what the understanding has cultivated," and now that his youth
was past he was no longer so interested in morning and spring
as in the harvest of thought of his "seed-time of character." [206]
Autumn was preferable to spring and summer, for the autumnal
man was ripe throughout and bore his fruits—those palatable
fruits, whether of music, poetry, love, or character, that would communicate his flavor.[207] This ripening had been achieved by staying
at home, by guarding against the "premature hardening" of
European travel, and by time: by a slow growth to maturity.[208]
Commenting on the American character, Emerson had remarked
that "though an admirable fruit, you shall not find one good, sound,
well-developed apple on the tree"; and Thoreau, as fully aware of
the hurried nurture and greenness of American genius, wrote of the
poets who matured early that "their fruits have a delicious flavor
like strawberries, but do not keep till fall or winter." "Others," he
said, thinking of himself, "are slower in coming to their growth.
Their fruits may be less delicious, but are a more lasting food and
are so hardened by the sun of summer and the coolness of autumn
that they keep sound over winter." [209]

In explaining his own nurture and the quality of his fruit, Thoreau chose for his symbol the wild apple tree, though there were
other plants or trees which had personal correspondences for him,
like the cinquefoil, pokeweed, lichen, barberry, pine, shadbush,
shrub oak, red maple, and scarlet oak, that he might have employed. Useless plants, in any case, appealed to him for his coat of
arms, and he chose the wild apple not only because, like the scarlet
oak, it ripened late, but because, like the shrub oak, it was "lowly,"
and like the beard grass, it was despised by farmers and lived on
wild and neglected soil.[210] With the wild apple, of course, he
could contrast the cultivated apple, and relate his attempt to redeem the wild for New England to the history of the longest
cultivated and most humanized fruit. But as a private symbol, he

[206] J, I, 18; J, VI, 426.
[207] J, V, 501-2, 364.
[208] J, V, 344.
[209] Emerson, J, VII, 294; J, VI, 190.
[210] J, X, 198.

had other reasons for choosing this indigenous fruit. He may not have known that Emerson in the early days had written his brother William that "Thoreau is a scholar & a poet & as full of buds of promise as a young apple tree"—though in these last years, when his friendship with Emerson was beyond repair, he must have recalled how much Emerson had expected of him, how he had cultivated him, and how disappointed he was that he had chosen to grow wild, so unlike his teacher and his disciples.[211] In a passage he omitted from "Wild Apples," he had compared the "sleek nursery boy" to the sour and crabbed and impeded apple, how "at length, thanks to his rude culture, he attains to his full stature, and every vestige of the thorny hedge which clung to his youth disappears, and the adverse events that once kept him under now harmlessly rub against his firm trunk, and he bears golden crops, whose fame will spread through all the nations for generations to come, while that thrifty nursery boy, who was his competitor [was he thinking of Stearns Wheeler?], will perchance have long since ceased to bear his engrafted fruit, and have decayed." [212] He had chosen not to bear engrafted fruit; he knew that he had not been, as Lowell made out after his death, one of "the pistillate plants kindled to fruitage by the Emersonian pollen. . . ." [213] If he was the most remarkable in Lowell's last estimate, it was because he had really heeded Lowell's advice in *A Fable For Critics*—

> Fie, for shame, brother bard! With good fruit of your own
> Can't you let neighbor Emerson's orchards alone?

—long before Lowell had given it. Nothing disturbed him more, when he thought of fame in these autumn years, than that his claim to remembrance might only be his connection with Emerson. Indeed, "Wild Apples" was his attempt to state his unique claim to fame. Though he only alluded in it to the pear, making his distinction there the broader one of cultivated and saunterer's apples, of tame and wild, in his *Journal* he pointed out, knowing full well that Emerson raised pears, the difference between the "aristocratic fruit" and the apple fit for "republican" tastes.[214] In this passage Emerson, of course, was the proprietor who personally tended his

---

[211] Rusk, ed., *The Letters of Ralph Waldo Emerson*, II, 402.

[212] Houghton. MS AM 278.5. See also W, V, 307, where the wild apple is a "prince in disguise" and its fruit the choicest sought by "foreign potentates."

[213] "Thoreau," *My Study Windows*, Boston and New York, 1871, p. 199.

[214] J, XIV, 113-14.

pears while the hired man barreled the apples; but if Thoreau could still remember his first residence as handy man at the Emersons'—and the occasional curt notes still requesting his services should have reminded him—he could also take pleasure in knowing that the apple was more beautiful, fragrant, and excellent in flavor than the pear. And that was one reason why he wrote:

> I sing the wild apple, theme enough for me,
> I love the racy fruit and I reverence the tree.[215]

He reverenced the tree because it was a "natural growth like the pines and oaks," because, like the independent and enterprising man, it had migrated to the New World and made its way among the aboriginal trees; because, scorned and "browsed on by fate," it had endured and borne "its harvest, sincere, though small."[216] And though he associated the apple with the history of man's use of nature, showing in the range of his allusions how he would have humanized the natural facts of his Kalendar—though he saw its universal connection with peaceful agricultural life and tied it to the westering impulse of mankind, he loved the fabulous wild apple most, the apple with the racy and wild American flavor, unplanted and uncared-for by man, late-bearing, and never brought to market. There was, of course, an aboriginal crab apple unmodified by cultivation, but Thoreau had only found this "long-sought" apple on his last excursion to Minnesota, and the apple he celebrated instead was that which, like himself, had strayed from the cultivated stock.[217] For though the wild apple was a patent symbol of his life—as scrubby, stout, and thorny as Thoreau himself, who was fully aware that his own crabbedness had been the protective crust of his interior growth—in a more general sense it was a symbol of the virtue of the wild, of the "spirited fruit" of his life in nature.[218] That was why he called it the saunterer's apple, the apple with the "wild flavors of the Muse, vivacious and inspiriting," and why he insisted that its "pleasant bitter tang" could only be savored out of doors.[219] "It takes a savage or wild taste," he said, "to appreciate a wild fruit." And generalizing further he exclaimed:

[215] J, X, 138.

[216] J, X, 137-38; W, V, 300-301.

[217] W, V, 302.

[218] In its thorniness, he said, "there is no malice, only some malic acid" (W, V, 304).

[219] W, V, 308, 312.

"What a healthy out-of-door appetite it takes to relish the apple of life, the apple of the world. . . ." [220] These apples that had absorbed the seasons, moreover, had to be eaten in season, with one's senses healthily invigorated by walking; and in telling how their beauty, fragrance, and flavor were to be appreciated, how these "unspeakably fair . . . apples not of Discord, but of Concord," varicolored by the experience of life and consigned to all men, were to be used, he was pointing out how his fruit, his Kalendar, was to be used. "I would have my thoughts," he said, "like wild apples, to be food for walkers, and will not warrant them to be palatable, if tasted in the house." [221]

That men might not "sit in chambers, seemingly safe and sound, and yet despair, and turn out at last only hollowness and dust within, like a Dead Sea apple," he offered them the wild that had nurtured his life and sustained his joy.[222] He invited them to taste the "Wood-Apple" and the apples of the dells, pastures, and meadows; the Concord, the Assabet, and the "Wine of New England"; the "Truant's Apple" and the "Apple whose Fruit we tasted in our Youth"; the "Beauty of the Air"; and the "Saunterer's Apple" ("you must lose yourself before you can find your way to that"); instead of Iduna's apples, which restored the aging gods, he offered the equally restorative wild.[223] But he knew that he was speaking from memory, that even in the Easterbrooks country the wild apple trees were almost gone, that the *urbaniores* or civilized apple trees were replacing the *sylvestres*. "The era of the Wild Apple," he lamented, "will soon be past. It is a fruit which will probably become extinct in New England." Fences and orchards and grafted trees would efface the wild, and "he who walks over these fields a century hence," he said, "will not know the pleasure of knocking off wild apples"—and many other pleasures besides.[224] And having begun with the solaces of the apple sung in the Bible, he now ended with the prophecy of Joel: " 'The vine is dried up, the fig tree languisheth; the pomegranate tree, the palm tree also, and the apple tree, even all the trees of the field, are withered: because joy is withered away from the sons of men.' " [225]

---

[220] W, V, 313.

[221] W, V, 314.

[222] W, VI, 356.

[223] W, V, 316-17.

[224] W, V, 321.

[225] W, V, 322.

As he reviewed his life in "Autumnal Tints" and "Wild Apples," Thoreau renewed his faith in the virtues of the wild. Even though the Maine woods had taught him that the wilderness was not entirely fitted for man, he found it necessary to use the "wild" in speaking of the kind of culture that had made it possible for him to bear such fruit. For what he had discovered in living out his faith in nature was the special value of the nurture of the New World, that liberation and enlargement, the conditions of a free and unique individual growth. The wild, of course, had been a commitment of his whole life, associated primarily with "Nature"; but because he fully shared the national mythology of his day in which the nature of America was set against the civilization of Europe, the wild was also associated with the frontier, with the West. By means of these associations he put absolute freedom and wilderness together—though in reading Richard C. Trench's *On The Study of Words* (1852), he found a philological warrant for the connection that especially pleased him: "*Wild*—past participle of *to will*, self-willed." [226] The West, then, was not only nature, the place of primeval vigor, but also the place of freedom and self-determination, and from his youth it had stirred his imagination as much as the heroic ages of mythology and the crusades of a later time.

In spite of these potent associations, however, he did not intend to go West himself—no more than he intended by walking merely to take exercise. He refused to go West not because the enterprise and adventure it suggested to him had lost their attraction, but because to most Americans it meant minding the main chance— the rapacity that ended in fences—the go-ahead kind of success that he had forsworn. The restlessness of his century did not appeal to him, and even in "Walking," where the embers of his heroic ideal in *The Service* still glowed, he managed to convey by his tone and the leisureliness of his prose, as he also had in his other autumnal pieces, the Oriental contemplativeness he hoped would root the American character. Indeed, much in the same way that he defined walking to rid it of the rootlessness and superficiality he identified with travel, so he defined the West, using the very national mythology to his own ends.

---

[226] *Fact-Book*, Widener Collection. In *The Maine Woods* Thoreau equated the idea of liberty with one's attitude toward the wild (W, III, 170); in *A Yankee in Canada* he said that the lack of government in America brought men "nearer to the primitive and the ultimate condition of man . . ." (W, V, 83).

Walking, of course, was the fundamental metaphor of his art of life, his mode of discovery, and in explaining it he was once more defending himself against the charge of idleness. But in recounting the necessities of "leisure, freedom, and independence" it required, in setting the saunterer against the *villain* or degenerate villager, in speaking of his need for the tonic of walking in the Concord vicinity and his presentiment of the "evil days" when the landscape would be fenced in, he was arguing from the small to the large, from Concord to America.[227] If he glorified sauntering by deriving its meaning from *à la Sainte Terre*, going to the Holy Land, and by making his walks a spiritual crusade, he also gave the West this ideal meaning; and the crusade he had been fighting all his life became a crusade to reconquer this holy land from the infidels—as he said, to "keep the New World *new*," to "preserve all the advantages of living in the country." [228]

Moreover, when he turned from his reflections on the art of walking to the direction of his walks, he was able to establish his spiritual associations with the West by identifying the "subtile magnetism in Nature" that compelled him to the West and Southwest with the westering tendency of mankind.[229] With Whitman, whose open road and conception of American personality had their counterparts in "Walking," Thoreau saw the westward movement of history as a progressive march toward freedom, as an attempt to repossess the vigor and the unshackled condition that had been forfeited by too much civilization. "We go eastward," he said, "to realize history and study the works of art and literature, retracing the steps of the race; we go westward as into the future, with a spirit of enterprise and adventure." [230] He said that he went eastward only by force, but that westward he went free, that "the earth seems more unexhausted and richer on that side"; and by linking his own desire to leave the city with the "prevailing tendency" of his countrymen toward Oregon and with the westward course of empire, the saunterer of Concord became the representative of the general movement of mankind.[231]

As the meaning of his own sauntering and his hunger for the wild played against this national myth, it became clear, however, that

[227] W, V, 207, 213, 216.

[228] J, XII, 387.

[229] W, V, 216.

[230] W, V, 218.

[231] W, V, 217-18.

he had evoked it to the ends of spiritual rather than manifest destiny. For the West was ultimately the locus of his dreams. The Indians, he knew, believed that heaven lay to the southwest, and in that direction they looked, as he had done when his inspiration waned, for the harbingers of summer. There stood the mountains of his dreams and the Hesperides, visited only by the setting sun. In fact, instead of calling his essay "Walking" he should have called it "Stepping Westward," taking his title from the anecdote about Wordsworth with which he began the original lecture: "Wordsworth on a pedestrian tour through Scotland, was one evening, just as the sun was setting with unusual splendor, greeted by a woman of the country with the words, 'What, are you stepping westward?' and he says that such was the originality of the salutation, combined with the associations of the hour & place that 'Stepping westward seemed to be a kind of *heavenly* destiny.' " [232] He did not use this in his final version, but transferred its spirit to his closing paragraphs, where the setting sun of November and of his own year flooded the west side of the woods, and in that golden light all "gleamed like the boundary of Elysium, and the sun on our backs seemed like a gentle herdsman driving us home at evening." [233] In the last days of his illness, as he pieced out the lecture of 1851 with fragments of his faith and confessions of his lost ecstasy, sunset inevitably heightened the morning philosophy he still preached. The prospect of death made "Walking" his last testament, but as he sauntered into the sunset he still believed—and beautifully expressed it in his last sentence—that "an adventurous spirit turns the evening into morning." [234] He was still seeking the "Beautiful" rather than the "Useful" knowledge, a "Sympathy with Intelligence"; and all of his walks from first to last had but symbolized his desire "to travel in the interior and ideal world. . . ." [235] The West he ultimately spoke for was the portal of spirit, the way to being.

To preserve these spiritual possibilities became the work of his last years, all the more pressing because as a surveyor he was disturbed by the parceling of the land. "Man's improvements," he said, "simply deform the landscape, and make it more tame and cheap. . . . the Prince of Darkness was his surveyor." [236] When he

[232] Houghton. MS AM 278.5. See also J, II, 46-47.

[233] W, V, 247.

[234] J, II, 94. This was omitted in the final version. In "Night and Moonlight" he also turned dark to light.

[235] W, V, 239-40, 217.

[236] W, V, 212.

went huckleberrying he realized, as he had in rediscovering the wild in Beck Stow's swamp and in the Easterbrooks country, that the whole country was becoming "a town or beaten common" and that men were not grateful enough that they had lived part of their lives "before these evil days came." [237] "In old countries, as England," he wrote in 1861, "going across lots is out of the question. You must walk in some beaten path. . . . We are tending to the same state of things here. . . ." [238] Undoubtedly his own invalidism intensified his awareness of this loss; indeed, throughout his last years he had a great desire for the wild life he had known at Walden, a desire to "go off to some wilderness where I can have a better opportunity to play life . . ."—comparing the panoramas of the Rhine and the Mississippi in "Walking," he said that the present was still the heroic age and, in the imagery of *Walden,* that "the foundations of castles were yet to be laid. . . ." [239] And deeply concerned with the loss of his spiritual vigor, with the failure of friendship and society, he turned, as he had before, to nature, and even more to the promise of nature in the West. Writing Cholmondeley of his illness, his disagreement with his friends and neighbors, and the gathering storm of sectional conflict, he said: "I am still immersed in nature, have much of the time a living sense of the breadth of the field on whose verge I dwell. The *great west* and *northwest* stretching on infinitely far and grand and wild, qualifying all our thoughts. That is the only America I know. I prize this western reserve chiefly for its intellectual value. That is the road to new life and freedom. . . . That great northwest where several of our shrubs, fruitless here, retain and mature their fruits properly." [240]

The previous discoveries of mankind, Thoreau believed, had been prompted by this same hunger for the nourishment and vigor and freedom of the wild. That was why he claimed that "in Wilderness is the preservation of the World" and that "life consists with wildness." [241] All nations, he said, had survived as long as the soil was not exhausted; Romulus and Remus suckled by a wolf was not a meaningless fable, for the strength of nations, and their poetry, mythology, and philosophy, came from their contact with the wild. He reminded his generation—a generation that had read Bryant

---

[237] J, XI, 78-79.
[238] J, XIV, 306.
[239] J, VII, 519; W, V, 224.
[240] October 20, 1856. Berg Collection.
[241] W, V, 224, 226.

and Cooper and had seen the paintings of Thomas Cole—of the course of empire, that when the primitive basis of civilization is gone, when the groves are cut down, not only do poets cease to sing, but civilization (he cited Greece, Rome, and England) decays and perishes. And man, too, weaned from nature by culture, nurtured solely in cities and society, became so inbred and tamed that he lost his wild or real self, and deserved only the name of the herd to which he belonged. No more than in *Walden,* however, did Thoreau relinquish civilization or expect men to go wild: he wanted to preserve the forest and to preserve the wild in man only to keep civilization open on one side and to leave portions of man uncultivated. In the wild he saw the possibility of a higher cultivation; here the real self would not have to go to market, but could express itself—its wildness and joy and desire for the liberty to live free from all laws except those of its Maker. Here a man might yet give his genius play and find the nurture he needed to mature *his* fruit.

The complete cultivation of man was, of course, the very thing affirmed for America by its mythology. Hadn't Whitman, who accepted this mythology as the program for his poetry, celebrated the completion of man in himself? And hadn't Emerson made the test of our civilization the men it produced? Having accepted the idea inherited from the eighteenth century that "climate" shapes man, they had placed the unique possibilities of the American in the amplitude of nature. With Margaret Fuller—and so many more —they believed that America, "with ample field and verge enough to range in and leave every impulse free, and abundant opportunity to develop a genius wide and full as our rivers, flowery, luxuriant, and impassioned as our prairies, rooted in strength as the rocks on which the Puritan fathers landed," would inevitably produce a new man.[242] With Thoreau they repudiated Buffon's disparagement of the American environment, preferring instead the "encouraging testimonies" of Michaux and Humboldt, and Guyot's belief that " 'America is made for the man of the Old World.' " [243] Indeed, in "Walking" Thoreau was the most eloquent spokesman of this faith:

If the moon looks larger here than in Europe, probably the sun looks larger also. If the heavens of America appear infinitely higher, and the stars brighter, I trust that these facts are symbolical of the height to

[242] Wade, ed., *The Writings of Margaret Fuller,* p. 359.
[243] W, V, 220-22.

which the philosophy and poetry and religion of her inhabitants may one day soar. At length, perchance, the immaterial heaven will appear as much higher to the American mind, and the intimations that star it as much brighter. For I believe that climate does thus react on man,—as there is something in the mountain-air that feeds the spirit and inspires. Will not man grow to greater perfection intellectually as well as physically under these influences? Or is it unimportant how many foggy days there are in his life? I trust that we shall be more imaginative, that our thoughts will be clearer, fresher, and more ethereal, as our sky,—our understanding more comprehensive and broader, like our plains,—our intellect generally on a grander scale, like our thunder and lightning, our rivers and mountains and forests,—and our hearts shall even correspond in breadth and depth and grandeur to our inland seas. Perchance there will appear to the traveller something, he knows not what, of *laeta* and *glabra,* of joyous and serene, in our very faces.[244]

But there were other testimonies less encouraging; and by asking "else to what end does the world go on, and why was America discovered?" [245] Thoreau challenged the easy acceptance of this faith. Against the hollowness of national sentiment and against the time when "American liberty," as he wrote in "Walking," might "become a fiction of the past," he put the testimony of his own life and work, his mythology of man in American nature.[246] Long before "Walking" he had written that

> All things invite this earth's inhabitants
> To rear their lives to an unheard-of height,
> And meet the expectation of the land. . . .[247]

With sincerity he could now evoke this mythology because he had contributed to it, because he had given his life to it and had demonstrated better than anyone in his generation its substantial truth: the ripest fruits of his sauntering were his discovery of the interior beyond the shores of America and his heroic example of how to meet the expectation of the land.[248]

[244] W, V, 222-23.

[245] W, V, 223.

[246] W, V, 233.

[247] Bode, ed., *Collected Poems of Henry Thoreau,* p. 135.

[248] The continuing force of Thoreau's vision of man and nature can be seen in one of the earliest American philosophies of regional planning—a book by Benton MacKaye, appropriately called *The New Exploration* (New York, 1928). For Thoreau's influence see Lewis Mumford, "The Renewal of the Landscape," *The Brown Decades,* New York, 1931. And for the growing appreciation of Thoreau's scientific achievements in the study of environment, see Philip and Kathryn Whitford, "Thoreau: Pioneer Ecologist and Conservationist," *Scientific Monthly,* LXXIII (Nov., 1951), 291-96.

INDEX

Reason, the, 5, 33
Reform, 349; example in *Walden*,
331; Thoreau on, 151-57, 246;
Thoreau's lecture on, 248-55;
Transcendentalists' hope for, 10-
13
Reid, Mayne: *Boy Hunters*, 356;
Forest Evils, 356; *The Hunter's
Feast*, 356; *The Young Voy-
ageurs*, 356
Religio Medici (Browne), 57, 68
Representative Men (Emerson),
36
"Resolution and Independence"
(Wordsworth), 194
Richter, Jean Paul, 65
Ricketson, Daniel, 45n, 75n, 260,
388; relations with Thoreau,
389-91
Riesman, David: on the "nerve of
failure," 322
Ripley, Rev. Ezra, 35
Ripley, George, 1, 4, 12, 19, 194;
on *A Week*, 219n
Roberval, Sieur de, 378
Ross, Alexander: *Mystagogus
Poeticus*, 189-90
Roughing It (Twain), 357
Rousseau, Jean Jacques, 20, 177
Rowlandson, Mary White, 165

Saadi, 339n. *The Gulistan*, 69
Sanborn, Franklin B., 28, 30, 34;
on *The Service*, 82
Santayana, George, 106
Sartor Resartus (Carlyle), 1, 16,
204n
Schiller, Friedrich von, 208, 294
Schlegel, Friedrich von, 124-25.
*Lectures on the History of Lit-
erature, Ancient and Modern*,
43-44
Science, 46, 113-14; Thoreau on,
105, 107-8, 274-78, 396-400
Scott, Sir Walter, 36n
Scottish Common-Sense philoso-
phy, 27, 30, 32

"Self-Reliance" (Emerson), 82
Sentimentalism, 383
Seven Arts, The, 76
Sewall, Ellen, 60
Seybold, Ethel, 326
Shakespeare, William, 22, 39, 40,
127, 132, 150
Sidney, Sir Philip, 128, 132, 135
Sigourney, Mrs. Lydia: *Traits of
the Aborigines of America. A
Poem*, 111
Silence: Confucius on, 70. *See also*
Sound
Simplicity, 269, 302-7
*Six Months' Residence and Travels
in Mexico* (Bullock), 111
Sketch Book, The (Irving), 42n,
383
Sketches of a Tour to the Lakes
(McKenney), 111
Slavery, 270
Society, 83-84, 91, 103, 125-26,
177, 305-6, 311-12; friendship
as, 251; Thoreau on, 76; and
Thoreau's decay, 268-70
Socrates, 22, 253
Solitude, 20-21, 74, 181; Emerson
on, 180; Lane on, 179; Thoreau
on, 40-41
"Song of Myself" (Whitman), 8,
53, 65, 203, 248, 297, 301, 315
"Soul's Errand, The" (Raleigh),
131, 135, 136
Sound, 114-15, 116, 121-22;
Browne on, 64-65; Fuller on,
67n-68n; Herbert on, 67n-68n;
in *The Service*, 87-88; and si-
lence, 70, 135-36; of the tele-
graph harp, 265-67; Thoreau
on, 65-67
Southey, Robert: *The Curse of
Kehama*, 70n
Spenser, Edmund, 132
"Sphinx, The" (Emerson), 71
Standish, Miles, 165
Staten Island: Thoreau's stay at,
101, 139-47, 173-74

1123 EP